SOCIAL AND ECONOMIC CHANGE IN THE PAMIRS (GORNO-BADAKHSHAN, TAJIKISTAN)

This is the first book to deal comprehensively with the history, anthropology and recent social and economic development of the Pamiri people in Gorno-Badakhshan, Eastern Tajikistan since Olufsen and Schultz published their monographs on the Pamirs in 1904 and 1914. After the collapse of the Soviet Union, such high mountain areas were more or less forgotten and people would have suffered severely from their isolation if an Aga Khan Foundation project of 1993–4 had not afforded broader support. A picture of an almost surrealistic world: Pamiri income and living conditions after 1991 dropped to the level of a poor Sahelian country, former scientists, university professors and engineers found themselves using ox-ploughs to plant potatoes and wheat for survival. On the other hand, a literacy rate of 100 per cent and excellent skills have proved to be an enormous human capital resource for economic recovery, resulting in an increase in agricultural production which during Soviet times had never occurred.

Frank Bliss is Professor for Development Anthropology at Hamburg University and partner of Bliss & Gaesing – Associated Consultants, planning and evaluation participatory development programmes.

SOCIAL AND ECONOMIC CHANGE IN THE PAMIRS (GORNO-BADAKHSHAN, TAJIKISTAN)

Frank Bliss

Translated from German by Nicola Pacult and Sonia Guss
with the support of Tim Sharp

Routledge
Taylor & Francis Group
LONDON AND NEW YORK

First published 2006
by Routledge
2 Park Square, Milton Park, Abingdon, Oxon OX14 4RN

Simultaneously published in the USA and Canada
by Routledge
270 Madison Ave, New York, NY 10016

Routledge is an imprint of the Taylor & Francis Group

Typeset in Times New Roman by
Keystroke, Jacaranda Lodge, Wolverhampton
Printed and bound in Great Britain by
MPG Books Ltd, Bodmin

British Library Cataloguing in Publication Data
A catalogue record for this book is available from the British Library

Library of Congress Cataloging in Publication Data
Bliss, Frank.
Social and economic change in the Pamirs : (Gorno-Badakhshan, Tajikistan) / Frank Bliss ; translated from the German language by Nicola Pacult and Sonia Guss with support of Tim Sharp.– 1st ed.
p. cm.
Simultaneously published in the USA and Canada by Routledge.
Includes bibliographical references and index.
1. Kåuçhistonåi Badakhshon (Tajikistan)–Economic conditions. 2. Kåuçhistonåi Badakhshon (Tajikistan)–Social conditions. 3. Ethnology–Pamir Region. I. Title.
HC421.3.Z7K843 2005
958.6–dc22 2005001405

ISBN10: 0–415–30806–2
ISBN13: 9–78–0–415–30806–9

CONTENTS

ILLUSTRATIONS

Plates

Figures

Tables

PREFACE

The idea for this book was born one summer evening in 1997 in the small village of Roshorve in the upper Bartang valley. I had, together with several colleagues, driven up to the 3,000 m line at which the village lay in the course of a monitoring mission for the Pamir Relief and Development Programme (PRDP), sponsored by the Aga Khan Foundation (AKF) and the Deutsche Gesellschaft für Technische Zusammenarbeit (GTZ). After a ten-hour journey, we had managed to reach the most remote community of Tajikistan, perhaps even of all former Soviet central Asia. Immediately after our arrival, a sheep was slaughtered for us, which was later served together with bread, potatoes and other regional products on a large carpet. We barely had time to eat before several musicians came to the house of our host, playing the *rabôb* (a type of violin) and several tambourines, and singing old songs from the Pamirs. Even though it was late, women, men and children joined us from all around and we danced until midnight. Exhausted, we finally fell into the steppe rug beds prepared for us.

Before falling asleep, I turned the day's events over in my mind. The bumpy drive through the gorges of the Bartang, precarious bridges, being stuck in a side stream with the Russian jeep, being pulled out of the icy water by friendly farmers, finally arriving in Roshorve with the sunset, where we were greeted by a group of young girls with bread and salt as well as by music. Then the unforgettable evening with more music and the joy of dancing and the prospect of many more exciting days at the foot of the Peak of the Revolution (Pic Revolutija) with its altitude of 6,794 m, in a region practically cut off from the rest of the world. What occupation could be more interesting than that of an ethnologist? By the next morning, when we were able to begin the day with freshly baked bread with butter and tea, it was clear to me that someone ought to write about the people in the Pamirs, their eventful past and their enormous present problems after the collapse of the Soviet Union and the independence of Tajikistan.

My monitoring duties for the PRDP (renamed in the interval, due to an extension of area of operation, MSDSP, Mountain Society Development and Support Programme) did not end until 1998. They were followed by missions to the Kyrgyz Republic and other countries which left me no time to pursue my idea, even though I had already taken around 2,500 pictures specifically for the planned publication.

But in 2001 I could finally take up the idea again. The first enquiry to the Curzon publishing company and its editor-in-chief Jonathan Price was immediately accepted. The idea for a book about a mostly forgotten region of central Asia, which, because of the events in Afghanistan, found itself once more in the public spotlight, immediately found approval and after another trip to the Pamirs in 2003, my seventh to Tajikistan in all, the project could finally be realised.

Without the support of many participants, the logistics of travel and data collection from 1995 to 1998 and in 2003 would certainly not have been possible. I found much support, especially for the latest trip, in His Excellency Hakim Ferasta, ambassador of His Highness the Aga Khan in Tajikistan, with whom the project team was already able to discuss important questions about the development of the region in earlier years. The difficulties of our various stays in Gorno-Badakhshan were overcome through the skills and hard work of the project manager of the PRDP/MSDSP Yogdor Faizov and the national programme director Mohammed-Amin. Physically taxed, certainly, by long drives in the jeep over many thousand of kilometres on stony mountain trails and foot marches in the thin air of the mountain settlements, was my translator Nazira. When other members of the group could rest after the drive, Nazira would accompany me to the interviews, helping me with the notes as well after returning from the tours. The same devotion was shown by my colleague Mamadsaid Saidamidovitsh, who tirelessly did his own research, prepared sketches of the villages we visited, and later prepared the interviews. Part-time members of the party, as interviewers, were Shoista Nazarbekovna, Ruqiya Mastibekovna, and Aziza Jumakhonova. Finally, the committed linguistics student Ruhafzo helped me in my interviews. My special thanks go to all those persons named above.

Mamadsaid also helped in taking the numerous pictures in the villages we studied. We also received further pictorial material from the ethnography museum in Khorog as well as from the city library, along with part of the Russian literature on the Pamirs. It should also be emphasised that we received further documents from the village bookstore in Tusyan. It would probably not have been possible in any other country of the so-called ‘Third World’ for a village with 343 households to have its own bookstore, and even, as in this case, have a sense of its own history. Some of the pictures printed in this publication are taken from the travel literature of the nineteenth century or early twentieth. The author owes the Linden-Museum in Stuttgart a debt of gratitude for providing some figures for Chapter 4. The same is true for Markus Hauser who granted the author the right to use two recently drawn maps of Gorno-Badakhshan. Unless otherwise labelled, the remaining pictures were taken by the author himself. These are dated (from 1995 to 2003) accordingly.

No ethnographical research can occur without its key informants. As a representative for the many men and women who patiently talked with us, Abû Bakîr from Murghâb Town is mentioned here. He also repeatedly invited us to visit his yurt camp, where he presented us with small sections from the life of the transhumance livestock herdsmen. The teacher Mubarakshov and his wife Bibishon from Tusyan also took us into their house, presented us to many other families in the small village or accompanied us to the fields – for the potato harvest, for example. Mubarakshov of all people was forced to experience what it means to live in such an extreme environment as the Pamirs when a landslide in 1996 destroyed part of his house.

The cooperation of the *khalifa* of Roshorve (Bartang) cannot remain unmentioned. He instructed us for hours on the traditions of the Pamiri, their agriculture, their methods of animal husbandry and their private life. But more than that, the old man turned his guests' every wish into reality: whether it was a spontaneous music and song evening in his house, the organisation of another song and dance evening with different groups in the old cinema of Roshorve, or the presentation of different crafts by the persons concerned. *Khalifa* Zurbek Nashkirjev also brooked no opposition to his accompanying us to the canal construction works in the upper Bartang valley and, after a long day, reaching for the *rabôb* himself. It is to him (Plate 0.1), a man who was born at the time of Stalin, who spent his youth during the worst period of forced acculturation and who, fully cognizant of the risks, salvaged the holy books of the Ismailis as well as the knowledge of his father and grandfather for the present, that this book is dedicated.

Note on the transliteration

The search for a functional, uniform transliteration method for terms from the Pamiri, Tajik, Arabic and Russian languages remains an insoluble problem. Even the most commonplace or regional names such as Khorog or Shugnân diverge greatly in spelling according to the different transliterations used by English, German, French or Russian authors. In the end, a unified system of transliteration was abandoned for the present volume, as well as the use of diacritical signs as they are set down in the *Encyclopaedia of Islam*. Place names and local designations are therefore written in such a way as to make their pronunciation as clear as possible to English readers. However, when warranted, signs are used to show the lengthening of vowels, so as to come as close as possible to the actual pronunciation (Roshân, Shugnân). Clearly identified place names in quotations from the works of other authors are adapted to this system.

Frank Bliss

Plate 0.1 The *khalifa* of Roshorve reads one of the holy books of the Ismailis that his father hid during Stalin's religious persecutions after 1936/7 (1997).

ABBREVIATIONS

ACTED	Agency for Technical Cooperation and Development (French NGO)
AKDN	Aga Khan Development Network
AKF	Aga Khan Foundation
AKFED	Aga Khan Fund for Economic Development
Arab.	Arabic
ARF	Agricultural Reform Programme
BMZ	Bundesministerium für wirtschaftliche Zusammenarbeit und Entwicklung (Federal Ministry for Economic Cooperation and Development)
Chin.	Chinese
CIDA	Canadian International Development Agency
CIS	Confederation of Independent States
CP	Communist Party
CPSU	Communist Party of the Soviet Union
CSS	Committee for State Security (former KGB)
EC	European Commission
ECHO	European Community Humanitarian Assistance Office
Enc. Islam	*Encyclopaedia of Islam*
ESF	Enterprise Support Facilities (of AKDN)
EU	European Union
FAO	Food and Agriculture Organisation of the United Nations
FRG	Federal Republic of Germany
GBAO	Autonomous Oblast of Gorno-Badakhshan (Gorno-Badakhshanskaja Avtonomnaja Oblast)
GDP	gross domestic product
GDR	German Democratic Republic (East Germany until 1991)
GNP	gross national product
Gr	Greek, Greece
GTZ	Deutsche Gesellschaft für Technische Zusammenarbeit (German Technical Cooperation)
H	Year of Hiğra (Islamic calendar)

HAP	Humanitarian Assistance Programme
HDI	Human Development Index
IDA	International Development Association (part of the World Bank group)
IFC	International Finance Corporation (part of the World Bank group)
IFRC	International Federation of Red Cross and Red Crescent Societies
IMF	International Monetary Fund
inh.	inhabitant/s
IRP	Islamic Renaissance Party
KGB	Soviet (Internal) Secret Service
M&E	Monitoring and Evaluation
MSDSP	Mountain Societies Development and Support Programme (enlarged PRDP since 1997/98)
MSF	Médecins Sans Frontières
NGO	non-governmental organisation
NOVIB	Nederlandse Organisatie Voor Internationale Ontwikkelingssamenwerking (Netherlands Organisation for International Development Cooperation)
p.a.	per annum
p.d.	per day
p.h.	per head
PRDP	Pamir Relief and Development Programme (see MSDSP)
PSF	Pharmaciens sans frontière
RR	Russian Republic
RRb	Russian rouble
st	sotikh (Russian unit of square measure of 100 square metres)
SU	Soviet Union
TASIF	Tajikistan Social Investment Fund (World Bank)
TJR	Tajik rouble 1US$ = 290 TJR (September 1996) 1US$ = 750 TJR (September 1997) 1US$ = 880 TJR (October 1998) 1US$ = 1,650 TJR (mid-1999) 1US$ = 2,200 TJR (mid-2000)
TJS	Tajik Somonî, since 30 October 2000 (1US$ = 3.15 TJS in winter of 2003/4)
UNHCR	United Nations High Commissioner for Refugees
US-AID	US Agency for International Development
USSR	Union of the Socialist Soviet Republics
VO	Village Organisations
WB	World Bank
WFP	World Food Programme

1

INTRODUCTION

The basic situation

The central Asiatic Pamir region was, until well into the last decades of the nineteenth century, one of the least explored areas of the world. Apparently poor in resources and at first strategically unimportant, the high mountain country had remained, until the beginning of the 'Great Game' around 1870, at the periphery of historical events. The defence capabilities of its inhabitants may have contributed to the fact that neither the Chinese, the Hellenic Bactria, the Islamic expansion forces, the Mongols under Ghengis Khan and his successors, nor even the Moghul rulers, could (or would) bring the Pamir under their direct control. Even when in the eighteenth and nineteenth centuries the Emirate of Bukhara and the Afghani kingdom took possession of parts of the Pamir, it hardly constituted an annexation as such but rather a nominal rule, more or less confirmed by the tribute delivered by the otherwise independent local lords.

The first concrete reports on the Pamir available in Europe were probably from Marco Polo, who at least crossed the highlands on his voyage to the Great Khan of the Mongols from 1273 to 1274 (Lentz 1933b: 1–31). After the Venetian, no European returned to the region until Father Benedict Goez in 1603, who, however, failed to leave a detailed description and therefore added nothing to our previous knowledge (see p. 86). Thereafter, for almost two and a half centuries, the Pamir remained of no interest at all to Europeans until Lieutenant Wood of the Indian Navy delivered the first detailed report of this area in 1841. *A Journey to the Source of the River Oxus* is about a ride in the eastern Pamir in 1838 in order to search for the source of the Pyandsh (also to be found in the literature as Pjansh, Pandsh, etc.) that is also the Oxus of Antiquity (Wood 1872). Despite a few treatises in geographical circles, the journey initially had few consequences, and the Pamir and its population remained unnoticed for some decades more.

This situation changed dramatically when, in the late 1860s, indications of Russian expansion into central Asia became apparent to British India. At the same time a weak point on their northern border in the Hindu Kush was diagnosed and, after some preliminary research, the British realised with some surprise that the Pamir region represented, in terms of global politics, a no-man's land between

China, Russia and British India. In consequence, the following years witnessed increasing competition between the British and the Russians, at first in the exploration of the so-far geographically practically unknown Pamir region. This was followed by 25 years of fighting over spheres of influence and borders whose value was perceived according to imaginary or actual security interests: the so-called 'Great Game' had begun and would occupy British Indian and Russian politicians for almost three decades. Ironically at the end of 1895, and after considerable trouble, almost exactly the same borders were established as had already been suggested in 1873. However, exploration of the region contributed greatly to filling out the 'white stain on the map'.

Thanks to the 'Pamir Convention' of 1895, the border between British India and Tsarist Russia was definitively set along the artificial partition line of Wakhân (see Chapter 3). The result was that, after a few years in which old frictions between Afghanistan and the Russian protectorate of Bukhara over parts of the Pamir slowly subsided, political and scientific interest in the Pamir declined. The Great Game was over and the emergence of the Soviet Union in 1917 turned an apparently uninteresting area into a practically unreachable one. Thus, although small-scale studies in and about the Pamir were still conducted, the region remained – barring a few Russian, German and one or two French expeditions – once more outside any sphere of interest, specialist circles excepted (Figure 1.1).

This situation changed once more when the first signs of a second Great Game appeared. By 1979 the Pamir had already been turned by Soviet forces into a secondary deployment point for the occupation of Afghanistan. But it would be another decade or more before the Pamir, or rather the former Soviet and present Tajik Gorno-Badakhshan, made it once again onto the front pages of the international press. With the fall of the Soviet Union, Tajikistan declared its independence on 9 September 1991. Over the following years, frictions emerged between individual political or rather regional power- and interest-based factions in the country that ultimately resulted in a devastating civil war. This really only ended in 1997.

Already brought to the edge of economic collapse by national independence, the impact of the war on Tajikistan was to cause a complete implosion of the economy and a humanitarian catastrophe of far greater proportions than in any of the other former Soviet republics. The fact that the 'opposition', which after losing the fight for the capital Dushanbe continued the war partly from Afghanistan and partly out of Gharm and Gorno-Badakhshan, was controlled by Islamic forces immediately attracted Western attention. In fact, from the end of 2001 Tajikistan became a deployment point for the US in its fight against international terrorism in its Afghan guise of the Taliban and al-Qaîda. This war is in reality nothing other than the continuation of the fight for the oil reserves of Central Asia, which had already been introduced at the beginning of the 1990s when the US still expected support from the Taliban (see Rashid 2002).

The humanitarian catastrophe that had already begun to develop in Tajikistan in 1992 undoubtedly reached its regional peak in the Pamir region of the Autonomous

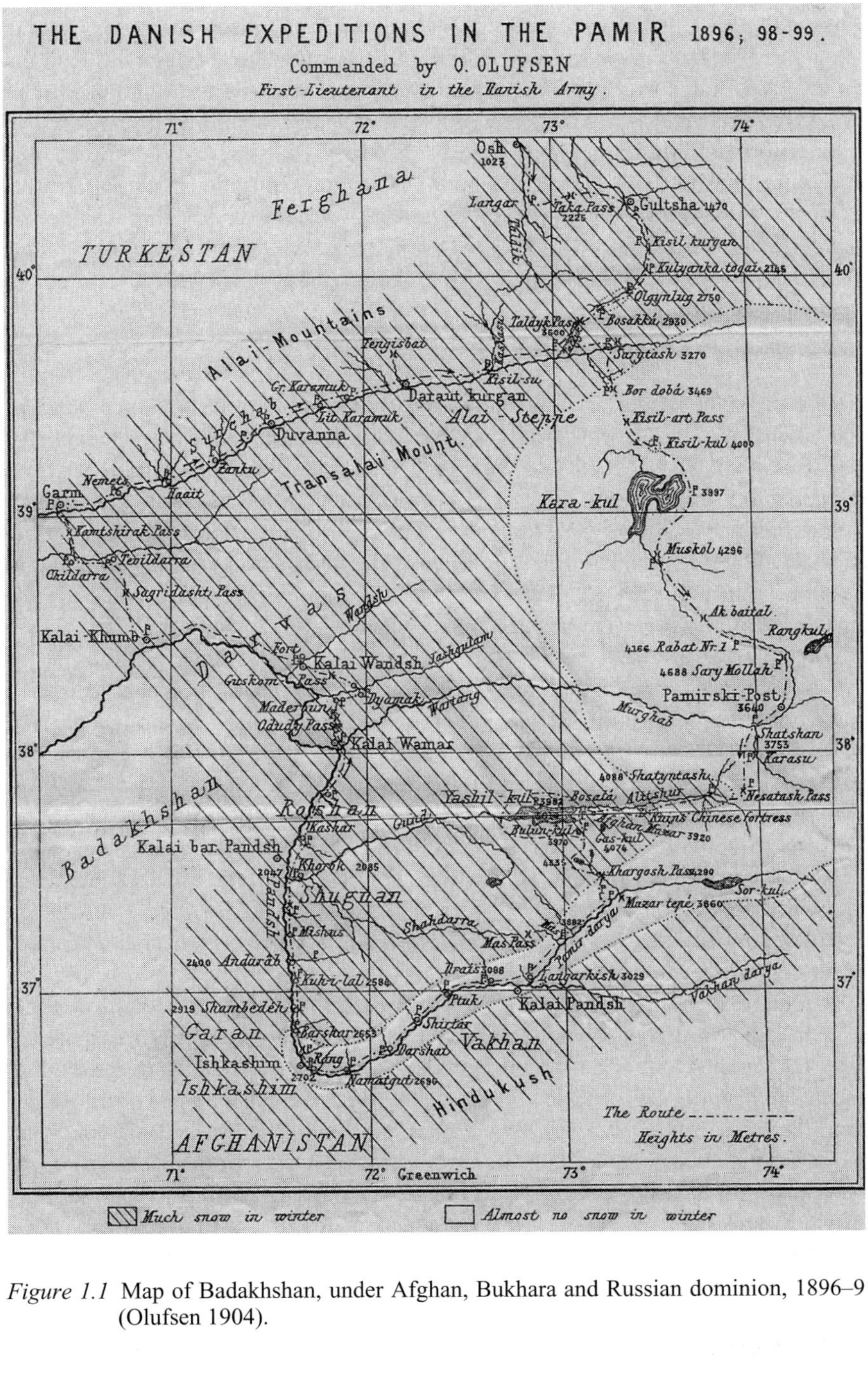

Figure 1.1 Map of Badakhshan, under Afghan, Bukhara and Russian dominion, 1896–9 (Olufsen 1904).

Oblast of Gorno-Badakhshan (Gorno-Badakhshanskaja Avtonomnaja Oblast = GBAO)[1] from 1993 onwards. In order to appreciate the scale of the catastrophe, some brief background is required. The high valleys of the Pamir and the deep-cut valleys of the Pyandsh and its inflows have supported a small Indo-European (Indo-Aryan) mountain folk for at least 3,000 years. These people, after centuries of oppression and internal fighting, had by 1990 finally achieved a minimal state of wealth, first through integration into the Tsarist empire but more particularly through Soviet improvements after the Second World War. Yet this wealth was not entirely due to their own diligence, but included substantial transfer payments from the Soviet central government as well. Consequently, in 1993 only 10–20 per cent of Gorno-Badakhshan's food needs were still produced locally.

Moreover, the 180,000 or so mountain people, as well as several tens of thousands of refugees from the civil war, were effectively cut off from the rest of Tajikistan in the winter of 1992–3. The only direct route from Dushanbe through the Tavildara (Gharm) valley and over the passes of the Darwâs range to Khorog, the capital of GBAO, had been bombed in several places so that, apart from beaten tracks, every sort of direct connection to the Pamir region was cut. A third-class road through Kulyab along the Afghan border to Darwâs was equally unusable due to a landslide and military blockades. Thus until 1998 the only feasible route led through Uzbekistan and Kyrgyzstan (Ferghâna valley, Osh) and then the Murghâb (Pamir highlands) to Khorog, in a detour of 1,400 km (see Figure 1.2).

An open road would definitely have made the provision of humanitarian help more feasible, yet in 1993 direct support from the central government would hardly have been possible. Apart from the fact that Gorno-Badakhshan had found itself on the wrong side in the war, the economic plight in the rest of Tajikistan was anyway very severe. For example, it was supposedly not rare for 11- to 12-year-old girls to be sold for a sack of wheat (see Bruker 1997: 3). Consequently only nine – according to other sources seven – per cent of the previous supply of food reached Gorno-Badakhshan from the rest of Tajikistan. Gorno-Badakhshan therefore found itself in a situation similar to that of a 'lost world' in an unreachable region of the planet.

A glance at the people's pre-existing situation may provide a better understanding of the gulf that now confronted them. Between 1950 and 1990, a backward region of central Asia had been brought, for various reasons[2] and with substantial effort and at enormous cost, to a level of material wealth at least five times greater than that of neighbouring Pakistan, China and Afghanistan. Even though there existed substantial differences in income between a sovkhoz director and a simple worker in Gorno-Badakhshan, the average standard of living of most families was substantial. Every third household owned a car and almost all families had a TV set. Our interview partners (teachers for example) talked about learning holidays they had taken in the 1970s and 1980s in far-off areas of the Soviet Union and even in Eastern Europe. Each larger town had its own high school and hospital. For a rural region, the proportion of academics to the general population was

Figure 1.2 Area map of Tajikistan, Gorno-Badakhshan and neighbouring countries, 2003. Reprinted with permission of the author. Copyright Markus Hauser, the Pamir Archive.

exceptional. Even in the smallest villages, German (at least) was taught as a second language, while cinemas were already to be found in middle-sized villages. Plays by Schiller and Goethe were performed alongside those of Soviet poets such as Gorki – not only in the capital, Khorog, but on tour in provincial towns as well.

Agriculture was mechanised as much as possible under local conditions (slopes, small scattered fields) and the most important workers in the sovkhozes and kolkhozes were fully trained agronomists as well as mechanical and agricultural engineers. In contrast, only 100 m away on the Afghan side of the Pyandsh, Stone Age tools were still in use. Almost all the houses had electricity, many of them running water as well. In the space of one generation, heating and cooking went from relying on wood to using electricity or coal. In Khorog there were cheap rental apartments with bathrooms and central heating. In other words, even though the population had no civil freedoms in the Western sense, people enjoyed, even according to modern standards, relatively happy and materially secure lives, especially after certain religious as well as other social freedoms were accorded in the 1980s.

The civil war destroyed everything, even though national independence and the end of subventions from Moscow had already sowed the seeds for material collapse. Although in 1992 and 1993 some food products, a little clothing and a few spare parts and fuel still arrived from central Tajikistan, by 1994 these flows had ebbed to an irrelevant trickle so that by 1995, when I arrived in Khorog to evaluate German participation in the humanitarian actions of the Aga Khan Foundation, regional and individual reserves had been exhausted. In the area of agricultural production and in the upkeep of the infrastructure, this meant that for want of spare parts and fuel hardly any tractors could still run, and thus practically all the industries in Khorog had come to a standstill. Neither the factories nor governmental institutions paid wages and, indeed, until the introduction of the Tajik rouble (TJR), there wasn't even a currency. Bundles of Russian roubles were worthless, not just because of inflation but also because there simply was nothing left in the markets to buy.

City children who had previously been clothed and cared for in the secondary schools had to go in rags, whereas village people who were used to working with books began to sew primitive boots out of untanned leather. In one village we met a young widow with four children who, in the autumn, owned no more than two blankets. The winter, with its temperatures of –25°C was already approaching. Everything in the house had already been used up or exchanged against food. A few potatoes had come from supportive neighbours who barely had anything themselves. The concrete paving around the city blocks and in the squares of Khorog had been wrenched up to plant potatoes. In the parks of the capital and in backyards, barley was sown or herb beds planted. The fact that young men drifted in search of work and asked their elders for help in building an ox plough only showed how much the economy had collapsed. It also indicates that people had begun to see their situation clearly and no longer regarded it as a temporary lull.

The 'Agricultural Reform' programme that, starting in 1996/7, was supposed to lead to privatisation of agriculture and a production revolution, at least confirms this view. This was in strong contrast to the views of individual former high government and Communist Party functionaries who on the one hand lived on humanitarian help while on the other still believed in 1998 that the whole catastrophe was really only a temporary lull. In all seriousness, they insisted to us that help from Russia would be coming soon and that the socialist production system therefore need not be changed in any way. Without outside humanitarian help, practically none of those living in GBAO could have survived after 1993. Naturally, emigration out of Pamir would have been possible, but where would the people, who in part had just escaped the civil war in Tajikistan, have gone to?

Tajikistan seemed to have been forgotten by the international community. Apart from a few million dollars from the European Union and a few other donors, practically no support was provided by the rich countries of the West. It was truly fortunate for the inhabitants of GBAO that the Aga Khan, as head of the Ismaili religious community, intervened with an extensive assistance programme. Traditionally, the Pamiri in the eastern districts of Roshân, Shugnân, Ishkashim and Wakhân are Shiites, belonging to the subdivision of the 'Seven Imâm-Shia' (see Chapter 6). Although their relations with their religious leader in Bombay, India had been violently cut off under Stalin, perestroika during the 1980s had allowed a cautious rapprochement to take place. In 1993, the *imâm*, as the Ismailis call their leader, took equal responsibility for the Shiites and Sunnites of Pamir and introduced emergency measures through the Aga Khan Foundation in Geneva. These measures were later built up into a development programme.

The first task was to transport basic food products over 700 km via Kyrgyzstan and through the Murghâb into the side valleys of the Pyandsh, for which an enormous flotilla of trucks was rented. Further measures included providing agricultural inputs and cultivation counselling, as well as developing new agricultural land by building irrigation canals and privatising land ownership as the basis for increasing productivity. Since providing for over 230,000 people was too expensive even for the Aga Khan Foundation, a call for help was sent out to the international community. Among other agencies, the German Federal Ministry for Economic Cooperation and Development (BMZ) announced it was ready to finance part of the humanitarian action. The Deutsche Gesellschaft für Technische Zusammenarbeit (German Technical Cooperation, or GTZ) was, as executing agency, charged to evaluate the humanitarian measures.

Study methods

Together with a staff member of the GTZ, I was able to travel to Pamir for such an evaluation for the first time in May 1995. The trip itself was already time-consuming. The flight landed in Tashkent (Uzbekistan). From there we travelled in cars, the truly uncomfortable Russian jeeps, to the Ferghâna valley on the other side of Osh in Kyrgyzstan, arriving after a 14-hour ride (Plate 1.1). The next morning, at 4.0 a.m., we continued over the Alai and Trans-Alai passes, past Lake Kara-kul and over the Ak-baîtal pass (4,655 m) through the – even in May – icy highlands of the Murghâb. After a stop in Murghâb town, not to mention passing through to date at least ten controls by various border guards, the police of three different countries, and Russian border guards as well (see Chapter 10), we embarked on the last 320 km of a 1,400-km-long tour through three countries to Khorog.

Later on, once the logistics had been arranged, the trip became more comfortable as we could take the plane to Osh and had to drive 'only' the 700 km or so through Alai and Murghâb. The overland link between Dushanbe and Gorno-Badakhshan was only reopened towards the end of 1998, shortly after my mission had been completed. The main access road in the Murghâb and to Khorog, a mixture of bad asphalt and rather good dirt road, basically came to an end in the capital. From Khorog, a narrow fortified road led to Ishkashim and Roshân, and to the Darwâs district. There were also within the valleys (Shakhdara, Wandsh and Yasgulem) various sections of tarred road, but for want of repairs, and taking into account the numerous landslides in GBAO, they were in pretty bad shape, so that transportation really required an all-terrain vehicle. Access to the more remote villages was generally via dirt roads, which were, like the main 'road' in the Bartang valley, rather adventurous (see pp. 184–188). If one had to cross a tributary of the Bartang in the summer months, then it was only possible in the mornings when the snow

Plate 1.1 The author with some village elders in a village near the Chinese border. In a Kyrgyz village it is the custom that only the elders (*aksaqal*) welcome male visitors. Meetings with women have to be organised separately (1998).

had not yet started to melt too much. Where the vehicle could not go, we had to travel on foot. More than once, strong arms helped us cross a stream on a rickety, narrow wood plank-and-rope construction (Plates 1.2, 1.3).

Thanks to the strong support of the Aga Khan Foundation and strong local commitment (for many other development projects unimaginable), our first evaluation mission was carried out successfully. Despite the transportation problems, we managed to visit all the districts of GBAO and speak to hundreds of men and women. Although we were there because of the general privation in the land, none of the village communities allowed us to waive their right to offer us hospitality and shelter for the night. The support from the project and the population continued until the end of my time in GBAO, and allowed us to visit practically the whole region with all of its side valleys and to include it in the result observation system.

This system works as follows: first, the economic, socio-political and social situation is reviewed. For that, the different sources of income and their situation were documented, as well as the details of diet, social infrastructure (e.g. schools, health providers) and the communal development situation. The level of popular consciousness was also investigated: how did people evaluate their situation, where did their priorities lie for the solution of their biggest problems and what was their stand on development alternatives (see Chapters 9 and 10)? The goal was

Plate 1.2 The team repairing access to a bridge in order to allow the car to cross a river (1998).

Plate 1.3 Team members cross a 'bridge' over the rapids of the Bartang river. This is the only access to the village of Shadûd (1995).

also to see how the old Soviet system was evaluated and how, for example, land privatisation might be accepted as an alternative.

All those concerned were included in the survey. Thus, in each village, not only were private households interviewed, but also the village leaders, the former representatives of the Soviet system such as kolkhoz and sovkhoz directors, and religious leaders. At the district level, the available statistics were collected and interviews were conducted to determine the favoured development options, current potential, and the most severe constraints. This work was relatively easy, for despite some difficult circumstances yet to be described (e.g. unpaid salaries, absolutely no operating resources), all the various functionaries still continued to work. Thus, important basic data that is often unavailable even in countries with ten times the income of Tajikistan continued to be collected.

In order to be able to demonstrate the achievement of the changes planned under the Pamir Relief and Development Programme (PRDP), it was necessary to choose representative villages so as to be able to follow developments there. Given the available resources, complete documentation was unthinkable. Thus, two villages in each district were chosen as samples, for which more detailed data was collected. Apart from a history of the village, which served to better understand the changes since the collapse of the Soviet Union, the data concerned mostly agricultural production, available food (per household), the development of irrigation and thus of usable land, energy provision, employment, living conditions, clothing etc. These villages were chosen according to certain criteria that included average climatic conditions, available land or grazing grounds and number of animals, general infrastructure and, not least, the interest of the population in taking part in the monitoring. Because the monitoring entailed many rounds of discussion as well as the collection of personal data, sample status had to be voluntary. But our requests were never refused. On the contrary: later on invitations piled up to include other villages in the monitoring.

As a start, individual households in the sample villages were studied and tested. During the house visits, we experienced an open-heartedness that we had not expected in a situation of such extreme deprivation. The people showed us their small stores and told us about every possible way to earn an income, no matter how small. Some felt almost ashamed at not being able to tell us exactly how many buckets their last potato harvest had yielded. The high rate of general education was naturally an advantage, for almost all the men and women in GBAO could write and count. 'Leave your questionnaire here and we will gather all the details', was the answer in several cases. These offers led us, in 1998, to leave the household questioning and the general communal data collection completely in the hands of contact persons in the reference villages.

An important and often-used method of data collection was group discussion, carried out as focus group discussions and as general village or village section gatherings. The focus group discussions worked well from the beginning and brought good results – for example on the state of the canal construction work, the past and future questions of maintenance or the evaluation of individual cultivated products. Not so with the village discussions. Especially at the beginning of 1996, discussions only ensued with difficulty due to the Soviet tradition of acclamation democracy. Many of those present simply didn't dare to tell us their opinion. This led us to reduce the size of the discussion groups and to prepare them better. If a question was explained and even introduced by taking the position of a devil's advocate, then the opinions came more directly. By 1998, no one hesitated any more in presenting a personal opinion in any of the villages.

Younger farmers and women took part in the discussions to different degrees. Their participation at the village level was extremely variable. (Plates 1.4, 1.5). The women's situation in the GBAO is certainly in no way comparable to that in the neighbouring Islamic states (see pp. 153–155, 267–270), yet formal equality of rights in the working world and before the law did not always provide sufficient support, even in the Communist socio-political system. The same general remark also applies to young people. Within socialism, to attain one's majority at 18 still didn't mean that one was equally entitled to voice one's opinion. Therefore, in order to grasp the ever-important opinions of the younger generation and of the women, two different tracks were taken: one was to hold gatherings on the condition that an equal number of men and women or older and younger villagers be invited; the other was to hold discussions only with women or only with younger men. Talks with young girls took place mostly on an individual basis, or else they took part in the mixed discussions with their mothers.

Plate 1.4 The team is received in one of the most isolated villages of the upper Bartang near Lake Sares. Men constitute the welcoming committee, but women and girls participate in the meeting (1997).

Plate 1.5 Traditional reception in the village of Nisûr (upper Bartang valley). At the village entrance virgins offer bread and salt to the visitors (1997).

In parallel to the interviews, observation (including participatory observation), as well as photographic documentation, was used. The pictures were to serve a double purpose: first, we wanted to document the situation in the villages in photographic form so as to be able to establish optically the changes over the course of the PRDP. Thus we could document that people in many villages already felt motivated by the small progress achieved between 1995 and 1998 in the way they improved the exteriors of their homes, rehabilitated public buildings or rebuilt canals. Second, the pictures taken during the first visit and quickly developed in Khorog were used to show our thanks to our participants. We shared them out generously between the households taking part in the project, which led during the next visit to a much quicker and more open beginning to the talks. In the course of our work, a third reason was added – namely, a photographic documentation of Gorno-Badakhshan for this publication.

Meanwhile, the observation already mentioned was systematically applied. Thus every village study began with a walk through the settlement and its agricultural areas. On these occasions the different types of land use (field, orchard, pasture), the quality of the soil (slope, stones, irrigation facilities) or the state of the irrigation facilities were investigated. In the same way the social infrastructure, (e.g. kindergartens, schools, health facilities), the communications links (e.g. bridges, roads) and in some cases the presence of markets were compiled through observation – and naturally also through accompanying interviews. A plan was drawn of each village, usually with the help of seasoned farmers, on which such things as changes in the evaluation of used land could be laid out later on.

Participatory methods of data collection were not limited to drawing this sort of plan. Every village appraisal – as well as the yearly appraisals later on during the course of project monitoring – was, for example, accompanied by a problem and priority census. These censuses gathered and prioritised the village's most urgent problems as seen by groups of ten men and ten women who had been invited from various backgrounds. The same approach was used to establish solution priorities and, in individual cases, to identify possible solutions. Thus whereas in 1996 poor food supply was without exception the most serious problem for all groups, later on other things were added thereby documenting at the same time deficiencies and progress. So that when in 1998 the unsatisfactory state of the schools became the most serious problem in Tusyan, it meant that on the one hand the food situation had improved, but on the other that the high school could barely be used any more for lack of even minimal heating supplies.

The monitoring system as presented here was abandoned after 1999 because it was seen as requiring too much effort and by some even as being too academic. Yet the results were very much in demand as initial humanitarian assistance was slowly transformed into broad support for endogenous development processes. The methods introduced to the villages by the monitoring process proved to be especially useful in setting development strategies and priorities by those concerned. Moreover, the results of the project monitoring process between 1996 and 1998 are the basis for this book. Although new progress was documented during a more recent field visit in 2003, it would not have been possible for a single researcher to collect within a reasonable time-frame the mass of data that was collected by the village-supported studies.

On the subject of the book

It is now necessary to consider the area studied and delimit it both geographically and conceptually. In the title, we speak of the 'Pamirs', and doubtless the subject is the inhabitants of the Pamir range. But what are 'the Pamirs'? A similar word first appears in the writings of the seventh-century Chinese Buddhist pilgrim Hiouen-Thsang (Hiouen-Thsang 1857; see also pp. 82–83, this volume), who mentions a *Pomilo*, which comes very close to the Kyrgyz word for the mountainous land, *Pamil*. The term can also be found in the Chinese Tang history as *Pomi* (around AD 750). With the term *Pamier* in the work of Marco Polo, the attribution becomes free of doubt. The later word *Pamir* (locally *Pomir*) probably dates from the sixteenth century (see Curzon 1896: 14–15).

Linguistically, the word 'Pamir' probably describes a specific form of mountain and valley. Kreutzmann, basing his thesis on several other authors, gives the translation as *pâ* = mountain and *mira* = 'broad area' (1996: 50–51). This description is based on the plateaux (= broad areas) in a high mountain range, which accurately describes the character of the Murghâb and its side valleys and is also characteristic of the neighbouring parts of Pamir in the Afghan Wakhân. Another interpretation of this term, just as plausible, by Satulowski includes the elements *mir* and *pan* or *pai*, the first to be translated as 'mountain' and the second as 'foot', which would make 'Pamir' the 'mountain foot' or 'mountain socle' (1964: 21).

Other origins, especially from popular etymology, are possible but not very probable. Thus Mursajew offers several alternatives (1956: 252–254): (1) the derivation from the Sanskrit word *mir* meaning 'lake' – though there are many lakes in Pamir, they are not truly characteristic of the landscape; (2) *Pa-i-michr*, which in Uzbek (?) means 'socle of the sun' – in Afghanistan, in his times, this expression was also used to mean 'the socle of the sun' (that is, the 'socle of Mithra', the sun-god of the ancient Iranians).

In many reports one also finds *Bamyar*, a Persian compilation of *pay-I-mehr*, which makes the Pamir into the 'roof of the world' (see Dor and Naumann 1978: 24–25). Some authors point to the fact that the Kyrgyz do speak of Pamir as the Roof of the World, using the expression *Bam-I-duniah* (see Von Hellwald [1875] 1880: 238). *Pa-mir*, 'Property of the Mir' is another variation, which is, however, somewhat too banal for a regional name so often used (ibid.).[3]

However, the word *Pamir* in the translation we prefer (according to Kreuzmann), cannot strictly speaking be applied to as wide an area as that of the seven or eight Pamirs as they are presented in geographical introductions. The Kyrgyz themselves do not know any one region with the name of Pamir, but understand under Pamir's landscapes the common denominators that we have seen in the above-mentioned *pâ mir*. Therefore, it is better to call the area we are studying not *Pamir*, but *the Pamirs* (see pp. 18–20). Here, too, Satulowski gives a somewhat different interpretation. For him, *pamir* does not designate a particular type of landscape but a specific valley, thus called by the Kyrgyz at the end of the nineteenth century that valley through which flows the source of the Pyandsh, coming from Lake Sari-kul (former Lake Victoria) (1964: 20).

A further refinement is that the subject of this book is not the Pamirs in general, but those high mountain valleys belonging to Tajikistan and thus to Gorno-Badakhshan. There exists a profusion of literature about 'the Pamirs', or individual regions having nothing to do with the former Soviet area. Whoever searches the academic literature under the key word 'Pamir' will be rather surprised. De Grancy and Kostka speak, for example, in the most extensive scientific work ever to be published on the Pamir region (1978), about the 'Great Pamir' in Wakhân without ever having set foot in GBAO. Yet they had, indeed, studied Badakhshan, and even the Wakhân region and the Wakhî population of Badakhshan – but only on the Afghan side. Here one must once more give an explanation.

Often, Pamir or the Pamirs are described as a part of Badakhshan. The word 'Badakhshan' (Gorno-Badakhshan means nothing more than 'mountainous Badakhshan') is used for a region encompassing northern Afghanistan with its capital Faizabad, continuing along the Wakhân band (see Figure 1.1) and the current oblast of Gorno-Badakhshan. The claim that Badakhshan formally designates only the Afghan area on the left of the Pyandsh (Pandsh) therefore cannot be upheld as the individual parts of Badakhshan show continuity, both politically and culturally (for example, linguistically), on both the left and right sides of the Pyandsh. Thus in the middle of the nineteenth century most of the regions of Shugnân to the right of the Pyandsh lay in what is currently GBAO, 80–90 per cent of Roshân was to be found on the current Tajik side, and at least one-third of Wakhân was in the same situation. Only Darwâs, today a district of Gorno-Badakhshan, was formally not part of Badakhshan at all, although one-third of it lay in what is now Afghanistan. In fact, the entire region on both sides of the Pyandsh belonged to the Emirate of Bukhara and was only divided in 1895 according to the Pamir Convention. Since then, a part of Darwâs now belongs to Afghan Badakhshân while another part became the Darwâs rayon (district) of GBAO.

In the light of this historical situation, every scientific study of 'Pamir' encounters the difficulty that each piece of information on 'the Pamirs', 'Badakhshan' and even the individual regions or socio-political units such as 'Wakhân', 'Shugnân' or, indeed, 'Darwâs', must be carefully examined to ascertain whether the former Soviet or the Afghan part is meant. In practice, however, the problem is less acute as until 1895, and indeed in some cases even until the closure of the borders in the 1930s, the people to the right and left of the Pyandsh not only spoke the same language but also belonged to the same socio-political unit, intermarried and practised economic exchange.

Many authors, lamenting the sad state of sources for the late nineteenth century and the early twentieth, also openly admit that they have mostly relied on documents concerning the area on the right side of the Pyandsh. Not only have statistics for that region been collected since the Russian occupation, but Russian and later Soviet researchers carried out many studies that are almost non-existent for the neglected Afghan area. On the other hand, I have also based this book on information about the area officially belonging to Afghanistan since 1895, as good recent (since the 1960s) social studies about Gorno-Badakhshan are rare whereas ethnological study of the Afghan Wakhân has made great progress.

Of the seven Pamirs cited by Dor and Naumann (1978: 25), four lie within Tajikistan. These are (1) the Khargushî Pamir ('Rabbit-Pamir'), which is none other than the basin around Lake Kara-kul on the southern edge of the Trans-Alai Mountains (Figure 1.3); (2) the Rang-kul Pamir ('Pamir of the Colourful Lake') around the lake of the same name in the far east of Gorno-Badakhshan not far from the Chinese border; (3) the Sariz Pamir ('Pamir of the Yellow Track'), the heart of the Murghâb around Murghâb town (the former Russian military station Pamirskij Post); and (4) the Alitshur Pamir, consisting of the valley of the river of the same name. The other Pamirs are the Tshong or Great Pamir, the Kitshik or Small Pamir, both lying in the Afghan Wakhân, and the Taghdin-bash Pamir ('Pamir of the Mountain Top') in Chinese territory.

Since all the Pamir zones in GBAO lie above 3,000 m, some parts even above 4,000 m, agriculture is barely possible. The climate of the Pamir region (see pp. 26–27) – that is to say, apart from the cold, and also the dryness of a high mountain steppe – limits vegetation to no small degree, which also limits the resources

Figure 1.3 Map of Gorno-Badakhshan and the Afghan Wakhân Corridor, 2003. Reprinted with permission of the author. Copyright: Markus Hauser, the Pamir Archive.

for animal husbandry. Accordingly, settlement in GBAO occurs mainly in the lower and more protected valleys of the river system of the Pyandsh, Gund (Gunt) and Bartang where about 90 per cent of the current Pamiris in Badakhshan have always lived. The Gharm valley to the west of Trans-Alai and the mountain of Peter the First do not belong to Gorno-Badakhshan, although the higher part of the area is often associated with the Pamir region in the literature under the name of Karategîn. Where relevant the bibliographies of the histories of the few villages on the upper course of the Wakhsh (Gharm) river, or its source river the Muk-Sû, will be included in the comments.

A last remark to readers who are contemplating a trip to the region: the road to Khorog from Kyrgyzstan (Osh) can theoretically be used all year round, but the direct route from Dushanbe to Darwâs may be closed during some of the winter months (usually November/December to May). A more southerly track along the Afghan border to Darwâs is extremely difficult. Travelling in Pamir is dangerous, even in May, especially in the pass areas between Murghâb and Kyrgyzstan. On 25 May 1995 we were almost snowed in with our all-terrain vehicle at the Kisil-Art (Kisil-Yart) pass, at a height of over 4,000 m. The following year, a vehicle of the Aga Khan Foundation was caught for three days in the middle of Murghâb in a –20°C snowstorm. Even without considering such constraints as access permissions for foreigners, the presence of Russian border patrols that are much more nervous and trigger-happy at night, and the bad infrastructure, make GBAO a difficult and dangerous travel area. (In late 2004, most Russian border posts in the Pamirs were handed over to the Tajik army.)

2

GENERAL FEATURES OF GORNO-BADAKHSHAN

Physical geography

The geographical importance of the Pamir region varies greatly according to the different perspectives of the various scientific publications. If the enormous highland plateau of China is taken into consideration, together with the Tarim Basin and the Takla Makhân desert, the Pamir quickly shrinks to occupy a rather marginal position on the western rim of the mountainous massif as a whole. However, in relation to actual mountain ranges, the Pamir occupies a central position. A glance at the maps – for example in Capus (1890a: 3) and Reclus (1881: pl. 1) – shows that the most important mountain chains of central Asia begin or at least meet there. To the north over the Alai, the mountains form a continuous chain over thousands of kilometres as the Tien-Shan, the Alai-Taû and finally the Altai. In the south, counting its secondary mountains, the Hindu Kush also extends to the south-west into Pakistan and Afghanistan. To the south-east, the impressive mass of the Himalaya and the Tibetan highlands extends over more than 20 degrees of latitude. Only in the west does the Pamir descend steeply with the streams that drain the Alai into the Tajikistani heartlands.

The Pamir region is usually defined as a square of some 300 km on each side. This equates to a surface area of about 62,000 sq. km, of which the oblast of Gorno-Badakhshan alone makes up 47,000 sq. km. The Trans-Alai range, with the peak of Lenin (7,134 m) and that of Korshenewskaja (7,105 m), may be considered as marking the northern border with Kyrgyzstan. The Kashgar-Kandar range, that includes the highest peaks of the region, the Kungur II (7,719 m) and the Mustag-Ata (7,546 m), marks the Pamir's eastern border with China. The Pyandsh forms a natural border for the Pamir to the south and south-west (see Figures 1.1, 1.2; Plates 2.1, 2.2).

The Tajikistani Pamir region can be divided into two parts that are differentiated by their landscape and vegetation: the Western and Eastern Pamir. The Eastern Pamir is a high-altitude plateau that is cut and bordered by mountain ranges of up to 5,800 m whose deepest valleys already lie at 4,000 m. In the centre of the region lies the actual plateau, or great Pamir, in a transitional landscape of alternating Pamir-hollows and steep V-formation alpine valleys (see Rickmers 1930: 54). The

Plate 2.1 Near Roshân city the Pyandsh loses its force and flows gently through a series of serene lakes (1995).

Plate 2.2 A typical view of the Pyandsh river in the southern Darwâs area. On the left Afghan side is a typical isolated settlement with a few acres of fields on alluvial land deposited by a small conflux (1995).

four Pamirs that also carry the same name on the Tajik side (see p. 15 and pp. 41–42) represent especially grand Pamir landscapes. Each side-valley in the Eastern Pamir region in fact forms a smaller Pamir of its own.

The boundary regions of each Pamir often present desert landscapes bordered by crumbling mountains. Large areas are covered with rubble, boulders and moraine deposits, the tracks of immense glaciers of the past (see Satulowski 1964: 15–16). Despite the high altitude and the enormous mass of the mountains, one does not feel as though one were in a high mountain range due to the small difference in altitude between the Pamir valleys and the mountains (Plates 2.3, 2.4).[1] The 5,700-m-high Koksukurbashi was thus described by Rickmers, perhaps with some truth, as a 'Riesenhügel' (giant mound) (1930: 50). More rugged valleys in the Pamir are often the remnants of ancient surfaces carved out by water and ice (ibid.: 62 fig.).

The appearance of the outer mountains of both the Eastern and Western Pamirs is influenced by their relative altitudes, for the valley bottoms are often very deep. The variations range from around 1,200 m in Darwâs and 2,200 m in Ishkashim (Rickmers 1930: 280). Coupled with mountain altitudes of over 6,000 m, such as Karl Marx peak between the Pyandsh and the Shakhdara valley, there is a huge difference in height. This already lends a ragged and wild appearance to the land. If the amount of rubble in the area of the Pamir high plateaux has already been remarked upon by many travellers, the slopes of the side-valleys of the Pyandsh are even more littered with rubble fields of at least 1,000 m relative height. This

Plate 2.3 Track on a typical Pamir plain with marginal vegetation leading to a Kyrgyz summer camp at about 4,200 metres (1996).

Plate 2.4 Landscape in a typical small Pamir with the upper Aksu river some kilometres below the village of Shaîmak (1998).

makes both road and canal building all the more difficult (Plates 2.5, 2.6). Whether the sandy surfaces in the upper Pyandsh valley represent a further stage of mountain weathering is not yet clear. In any case, true Barkhan dunes with their characteristic horseshoe shapes can be found there as the two upper source rivers of the Pyandsh, the Pamir-Darya and Wakhân-Darya respectively, meet near the village of Langar.

The characteristics of high alpine mountains are also present in the Western Pamir, especially in the area of the Peter the First range and the Academy range up to the Trans-Alai. In the middle of the mountain massif, Communism peak (recently renamed into peak Ismaîl Somonî) stands out. At 7,495 m it is the highest mountain of the former Soviet Union.[2] Geologically, the massifs of the Rush chain and the Shakhdara chain in the south and south-west also belong to this mountain type, even if their heights are 'only' a paltry 6,726 m (Karl Marx peak) and 6,510 m (Friedrich Engels peak) (Plate 2.7). Characteristic of the Western Pamir, and especially of the southern ranges, are the deep, narrow gorges with rapids at their bottoms (Plate 2.8).[3] At the other extreme are the massive glaciers that often snake across the landscape for many kilometres. At almost 72 km, the Fedshenko glacier is one of the longest in the world. The Amu-Darya, or Pyandsh, owes its existence to this glacial zone – as does Lake Aral, now irreparably damaged through overuse of water for cotton irrigation.

Surrounded by rugged mountain ranges, the Pamir, especially in the older literature, is represented as a zone of relatively easy passage. This is why the region has, despite its sterility, served as a place of transit for thousands of years. This

Plate 2.5 An enormous scree slope along the track to the upper Bartang valley (1997).

image is, however, only partly correct. Because of the bisecting mountain ranges described above, and the ruggedness of the border zones and of the Eastern Pamir, year-round passage through the area is only possible along a very few routes (see pp. 49–51).

For example, passage through GBAO from west to east was not possible at all in winter until the road from Darwâs to Khorog and then to Ishkashim was built. Even in summer, travelling that route – particularly through certain river valleys – was extremely difficult. Until late into the Soviet period there were generally only narrow footpaths, or donkey trails, through the region at the very most. Rickety constructions of planks, stones and wickerwork clung precariously to the cliffs over the raging rapids below, 'one often knows not how' (Lentz, in Rickmers 1930: 222). But these structures are still used today on the Afghan side (see Plate 4.41; also pp. 184–188, this volume). The 'easy' passes of Ak-baîtal in the Murghâb (4,655 m) and Kizil-art in the Trans-Alai (4,200 m) as well as the easterly routes from the Indian Chitral via Ishkashim (Afghanistan)[4] to Tashkurgân or Kashgar in China, on the other hand, pose few problems in the summer. However, they are only open in winter under the best weather conditions. Consequently the Pamir did not represent a good through-route at all. It simply represented the only possible passage through the central Asiatic mountains.

The numerous high mountain lakes of Pamir ensure that, apart from two exceptions, the area enjoys ample drainage. The first exception is the Khargushî or Kara-kul Pamir, which drains into the lake of the same name. The second is the Rang-kul Pamir not far from the Chinese border, whose rainfall flows into Lake

Plate 2.6 A typical inflow to the Pyandsh river. The consequent alluvial deposits are the basis for agriculture and housing (1997).

Plate 2.7 The beginning of the Shakhdara valley with the 'pyramids' of Karl Marx peak (6,726 m) and Friedrich Engels peak (6,510 m) in the background (1997).

Plate 2.8 In the middle Bartang valley rocks reach down to the river leaving almost no space for the road (1995).

Rang-kul. Other lakes like the Yashi-kul or the Sari-kul (formerly Lake Victoria) accumulate water for the larger rivers that drain them. Otherwise such lakes are simply crossed by a large river, as the Yashi-kul is by the Gund. The rest of the Pamir valleys, as well as the boundary mountain ranges, provide the source waters for the Pyandsh or Amu-Darya (the Oxus of Antiquity).[5]

For a long time the actual source of the Pyandsh river was a subject of contention among geographers. The supposition that the Pyandsh basically originates in the Wakhân-Darya was in the 1870s one of the bases for disagreement between Russia and British India. In any case the Russian side accepted this supposition, because this would have included parts of the Afghani Wakhân as part of the Khanate of Kokand and would thus have given the latter to Russia after the invasion of 1875. The British, on the other hand, considered that the current Bartang (called Murghâb in its upper course) was the true source, and on this basis in 1873 accepted somewhat hastily, being ignorant of the Russian view on the subject, a border 'along the Pyandsh'. Only later on, in the course of explorations carried out in the context of the 'Great Game', was the true state of things understood – namely, that the Pamir-Darya, and thus a river between the other two, was most probably the source.

If we assume that the Pyandsh does indeed spring from the Pamir-Darya, then Wood was indeed partly correct when he considered the Sari-kul lake, which he was the first European to view in February 1838, as the 'source of the river Oxus' (1872). There is a purely academic discussion which throws doubt on this assumption. It sees the Bartang, with a seasonally greater flow and probably greater in length, as the actual main source of the Amu-Darya. However, it must be conceded that the Sari-kul is not, in fact, the 'source' of the Oxus but rather a sort of reservoir fed by several brooks which themselves cross small pools. Strictly speaking one should consider the longest of these brooks as the source stream.

From the lower source lake, Sari-kul, the Pamir-Darya shoots down through narrow gorges. In the 100 km to Langar, where the confluence with the Wakhân-Darya from Afghanistan occurs and the actual Pamir is formed, the river descends an impressive 1,116 m. In the next approximately 200 km to Khorog there is a descent of another 1,029 m (see Olufsen 1904: 8). Together with other tributaries above Langar, the Pyandsh has a total of five source rivers, thus giving it its name ('five'). As it flows through extremely steep gorges, 1,000 to 2,000 m deep, between the Hindu Kush and Pamir, the roaring mass of water and certainly the inaccessibility of the riverbanks definitely make the Pyandsh valley between Sari-kul and Darwâs one of the most impressive natural sights of western central Asia.

Up to the mouth of the Gund near Khorog there are only unimportant, though occasionally voluminous, tributaries. The Gund, however, its own flow almost doubled before it reaches Khorog thanks to the Shakhdara tributary, swells the flow in the Pyandsh by almost 80 per cent. After this, the most important tributary in GBAO is without doubt the Bartang, which for a long time ran through the most inaccessible gorges. Above Lake Sares, created by an earthquake (see pp. 28–30), the part up to Murghâb town is called the Murghâb (Murghâb = 'water near which birds nest'). In the rest of the upper course, the now tiny river is called Aksu (Ak-su).[6] Its source lies not far to the east of the Sari-kul, so that both main arms of the Pyandsh – although more than 900 km long – spring from the same mountain massif (cf. map in Rickmers 1930, scale 1:1,000,000 and official map Tadshikskaja SSR 1974, scale 1:1,000,000).

Below the mouth of the Bartang, the Pyandsh gathers two more tributaries worth mentioning in GBAO, the Yasgulem and the Wandsh (Vanj). These spring from the glaciers around the Ismaîl Somonî peak in Western Pamir.

The waterways of the Wandsh system are especially tumultuous and their water levels can change within a few hours due to diurnal snow melt. Summer after-noons can thus bring a flood that is equally perilous to man and beast. In a less acute way this pattern can also be seen in the tributaries of the Bartang and Shakhdara.[7] In addition to these daily changes in flow, especially in the summer, there are also great seasonal differences. Thus whereas in summer areas that are not prone to flooding quickly dry out, lower-lying areas are at risk from rising water levels as snow and glaciers continue to melt. In the Bartang valley or by the Wandsh one can observe how during this time the water 'nibbles' at the cultivated river banks and frequently tears away pieces of fertile land, some of them containing fruit trees. As there are no areas in reserve in the river valleys, in some places the available cultivatable soil is in this wise being slowly but inexorably reduced.

Living conditions, especially in the Eastern Pamir, are extreme. Luknizki (1954: 213) characterises the climate as 'härter als in der Arktis' ('stuffier than in the Arctic'), for the air there is not as thin as in the Pamir with its average altitude of over 4,000 m. In 1934, temperatures of –51.2°C were measured at the Bash-Gumbes pass. Until then, the lowest measured and officially confirmed temperature had been –46.7°C in Murghâb (see Rickmers 1930: 271). In the winter of 1995/6, temperatures of under –54°C were reliably measured once more,[8] with the consequence that even some of the yaks didn't survive. The average temperature is decisive: in Murghâb town, at 3,640 m, an average air temperature of –1°C was measured in 1929, ranging from –17.8°C in January and 13°C in July. Diurnal temperature peaks of up to 40°C contribute to the fact that the snowline is extremely high, at 4,800 to 5,500 m. The Pamir biological station not far from Murghâb town measured a temperature of 33°C at 1.0 p.m. and one of –6.4°C at 4.0 p.m on 9 July 1934. As a consequence of such swings, stones burst and cliffs crumble (see Luknizki 1954).

Such enormous daily variations in temperature are also important for people. Intense sunshine in summer, combined with very dry air, compels even the Kyrgyz, who are adapted to the climate, to take protective measures. Mursajew reports that they rub their faces and hands with mutton suet (1956: 261). The shepherds of the Pamir also use appropriate protective measures. Although for a while one could buy sunscreen everywhere in GBAO (as one could anywhere else in the Soviet Union), since the economic crises after the civil war only the traditional methods remain available.

In most of the high plateaux of Eastern Pamir, yearly precipitation totals around 70 mm, and in Murghâb 58.6 mm (Rickmers 1930). About half of this falls as summer rain from July to August. Consequently, not the rain but ice and snow melt from the boundary mountains is the source of the Pamir rivers and thus of all human life in Eastern Pamir. The rain, or the snow, in the high valleys helps support the growth of a meagre fodder base for the animals, but droughts may last for several years.

The Pamir winter lasts from October to April and sometimes into May. Even at the end of May there can be snowstorms for which the shepherds must at every moment be prepared. The amount of snow can vary greatly from valley to valley. Whereas some valleys near Murghâb remain almost snow-free throughout the year, a few kilometres further to the west 20, 30 or even 50 cm snowfalls cover the ground. Because of the constantly varying climatic conditions, the snow comes in the dozens of different states chronicled by the Kyrgyz (Rickmers 1930: 51). Decisive for the people is whether the yaks can find fodder under the snow. For this reason, snow that has thawed and refrozen the same day represents the worst possible situation.

The seasons can vary greatly everywhere in GBAO; that is to say, the spring with its period of growth may be as many as 14 days late (see Rickmers 1930: 38). This can have an extreme impact on the harvests in the valleys of the Western Pamir.

In the Western Pamir, however, winter temperatures are distinctly more 'moderate' than in the Murghâb, with an inter-year average of around 8°C. The average temperatures are about –8°C in December, but quickly rise to –3°C in January. The growing season begins in March or the beginning of April at the latest. In Khorog the monthly average temperature in summer is (at an altitude of 2,160 m) 19.2°C in June to 22.5°C in August. Although the winters are relatively mild, enough snow may already have fallen by November so that the traffic between the valleys comes to a halt until April or May. In West Pamir (Shugnân, Roshân and Darwâs rayon), annual precipitation is about 250 mm, and in wet years up to 300 mm.

Rickmers errs when he sets the limit of barley cultivation, and thus of agriculture in general, at only 2,000 m (1930: 284). At least currently, barley and even wheat still ripen at 3,000 m and often even provide a yield at 3,300 m and occasionally at 3,650 m (e.g. in Javshangoz, upper Shakhdara valley).

Despite the arid climate, the area referred throughout this book is rich in water. However, most of the high mountain lakes are salty and of no use to man or beast. The brooks and streams that are fed by the glaciers represent an impressive average water yield. The average flow of the Pyandsh around Khorog is estimated at 500 to 800 cubic metres a second. However, droughts may still occur in the upper regions. In the winter, glacial discharge is minimal whereas in the summer in the middle altitudes the entire water supply, bound in the form of snow and ice, can melt. Thus, depending on the area, the brooks may dry out, starting July/August. This means that irrigation-based agriculture, on which the people of Pamir are forced by the climate to depend, suffers in many places from water shortage.

On his voyage to the source of the Oxus, John Wood already encountered a typical phenomenon of the central Asian mountains: the earthquakes. In his case, the earthquake was followed by strong aftershocks.[9] Near his campsite 12 of the 25 villagers died, with one house burying all its inhabitants completely. Overall, several hundred people died from that earthquake (1872: 184–185). Olufsen speaks of recurring earthquakes during his expedition, which he attributed at first to 'collapses within the mountains' (1900: 147). The collapse of the old castle in Darwâs around that time was the result of an earthquake (Olufsen 1904: 46). The Wandsh district of the Pamirs is particularly plagued by earthquakes that often destroy the villages (Olufsen 1911: 33).[10]

Apart from earthquakes, though perhaps caused by them, 'snow and stone slides and avalanches are of every day occurrence, and falling fragments of rock often destroy the villages and cultivated fields, on which occasions also many human beings are killed' (Olufsen 1911: 26). A violent landslide in 1995/6 destroyed a whole village with over 20 houses in the Wandsh valley. In another case in 1996, three houses were destroyed in Khorog itself and two people died. An especially impressive cliff which had collapsed during an earthquake and come to a stop only metres away from the Khorog market hall can still be viewed today.

Screes can also be caused by prolonged rainfall. In another example in Tusyan, during which three homes were destroyed, a leaking canal had been the cause. The plateau, soaked through for months, suddenly slid. A viscous mass flowed down, pushed several walls over and then solidified in the buildings, so that all the household goods were destroyed. When larger overhangs slide into narrow valleys, they sometimes pull the side-walls along with them and thus gain impressive mass. If this is then temporarily held up it can lead to an even greater subsequent slide in which whole villages, together with their cultivated land, vanish within seconds under the boulder-strewn mud. In the last three decades about half a dozen such incidents have been reported. All caused extensive damage, but, due to forewarning, not all were lethal. In the Bukhara period, and again after the collapse of the Soviet Union, a landslide, even if there were no deaths, had the potential to wipe out an entire village.

Definitely the most spectacular landslide, described many times in the literature, happened on 19 February 1911 near Ussoi in the upper Bartang valley, and thus along the upper course of the Murghâb river. The overhang of an impressive mountain, looming about 3,000 m above the Murghâb, started sliding and collapsed with unimaginable violence into the valley. The earth was said to have trembled throughout the entire Pamir region all the way to Afghanistan. A good description of the events on that day can be found in Luknizki (1957: 243–250). According to the author, had a whole city stood at the scene it would have vanished without a trace. Yet it so happened there was only a small village (*kishlak*) in the vicinity with about a hundred people (200 according to other estimates), plus their livestock and of course a few hectares of fields and orchards. Over two billion cubic metres of massive stone and mud bore down on the village, where a thousand cubic metres would have been enough to flatten it. Six billion tons, according to

Luknizki, was the weight of the 700 to 800-metre-high and 8-kilometre-wide collapsed cliff. The event caused earthquakes to shake surrounding villages, and houses collapsed and buried people and animals. There seem to have been only three survivors in Ussoi, who provided the only eyewitness account:

> Im Februar 1911 war ich mit Freunden nach Sares gegangen, das zwanzig Kilometer flussaufwärts lag, um dort an einem Fest teilzunehmen. An einem dieser Festtage wurde die Gegend von einem Erdbeben erschüttert . . . Die gesamte Bevölkerung von Sares kam eiligst aus ihren Hütten herausgekrochen, die dann beim zweiten Erdbeben einstürzten. Menschen kamen dabei in Sares aber nicht ums Leben. Zu diesem Zeitpunkt brachen im Bereich der Siedlung Ussoi Felsen herab, im Nu stieg eine dichte Staubwolke auf und entzog das Gebiet unseren Blicken. Und diese Staubwolke stand einige Tage über ihm, erst drei Tage später war es möglich, zu der Stelle vorzudringen, an der Ussoi einmal gestanden hatte. Von dem Kishlak war auch nicht die geringste Spur mehr übriggeblieben; alle Bewohner, die sich zum Zeitpunkt des Bergsturzes in der Siedlung aufgehalten hatten, waren tod . . .
>
> (Luknizki 1957: 244)

One outcome of this event was that a mass of rubble about 800 m high formed in the Murghâb river valley. Depending on various estimates it was from 5 to more than 8 kilometres wide. It began to dam the river, so that by October 1911 this natural dam had already caused the formation of a reservoir some 20 km long, reaching all the way to the village of Sares and forcing its inhabitants to flee. In the autumn of 1913, the lake was measured for the first time by Russian scientists from Pamirskij Post (now Murghâb town). It had by this time grown to 28 km in length and an average of 1.5 km in width. Its greatest depth was 279 m. The water level rose by 36 cm each day. Information about this lake was only made public – and thus only then aroused scientific interest – in 1914. However, it was becoming more and more difficult to reach the lake, as the rising waters covered all but the steepest mountain slopes.

However, it was noted that, starting in April 1914, water had begun to seep through the dam and form small rivulets. In 1925 the rivulets had become a breach, with a flow of 70–78 cubic metres per second.[11] One of the problems this posed was the possibility of the dam bursting one day and causing an enormous flood crest. This would not only destroy all life in Bartang but would also cause great damage in the Pyandsh all the way to southern Tajikistan. Further studies revealed this scenario to be unlikely because of the enormous width of the dam. In 1934 it was also observed that the lake had increased to a length of 60 km and a depth of 500 m. Since then, water flows into and out of the dam have achieved a balance and the lake has ceased growing (see Mursajew 1956: 250–251).

It is, however, astonishing that in subsequent reports about the landslide of 1911 it was overlooked that in the following years the Murghâb, and with it the Bartang, that had previously been the river in the Pamir region with the highest flow (seasonally at least), almost completely dried up. This must have had important consequences for local water supplies, especially for the intricate water collection system for irrigation in the cotton areas of Tajikistan.

Natural resources

As with the climate, there are very great differences between the flora and fauna of the high valleys of Eastern Pamir and that of the deep-cut river valleys in Western Pamir. There are extensive Russian studies on the flora, some of which go back to Ivanov (Iwanow) and Fedshenko (Fedschenko, Fedtshenko) (1903–7; see Schultz 1916). According to these studies, the flora of Eastern Pamir is relatively poor and restricted to about 300 species. Weed and grass steppes predominate, becoming sparse prairie near the rivers. These provide nearby grazing grounds, some of which can even be used year-round (for example in the village of Konakurgan near Murghâb town; see Plate 2.9). In some areas, high moors with strong turf genesis are created (Plate 2.10). This is dug up with spades by the inhabitants of the upper Shakhdara and Gund valleys, dried, and then used in the villages as peat fuel, sometimes after being transported a long way.

Among the herbs, the most common species are types of Artemesium and Astralagus, and especially, at least in the past, wild lavender, which the Kyrgyz

Plate 2.9 A rich pasture for yaks and cattle near the village of Javshangoz (3,250 m) in the upper Shakhdara valley (1998).

Plate 2.10 A high mountain stream at about 4,200 m with live peat soil. The peat is dried and burned when no other fuel is available (1998).

call *tereske* (von Schulz 1916: 208) or 'tergsen'. Since the plant is so closely bound up with Kyrgyz culture, it is also called 'Kyrgyz lozenge'. The *tereske* that is sometimes dried and used as fuel, the only one available apart from cattle dung especially for the Pamiri in the high valleys, could in fact be part of a group of similar plants, as other authors talk of different species (of lavender). Agachanjanz translates 'tereske', for example, as 'Hornmelde' (German term; Latin: *Eurotia/ Krascheninnikovia ceratoides*) (1980: 26). We had the impression that a kind of wild rosemary and other, non-aromatic plants were also occasionally tagged by the Pamiris with the Kirgisi term '*tereske*'. More will be said of this plant in Chapter 4 (see pp. 176–178), where the threat of ecological catastrophe through overuse of plants for fuel is discussed.

The grasses of the Pamir are very nutritious but, due to the low rainfall, grow so sparsely that grazing animals can never 'get a mouthful' (original: 'nie mit vollem Mund fressen können') (von Schulz 1916). Other plants that grow on the flat marshes around lakes and in river basins with poor drainage seem to be edible, at least to yaks. Geiger also mentions wild leek or spring onion as being an important plant, from which the Pamir is supposed to have got its Chinese name of Thsung-ling or 'Onion Mountain' (1887: 54). Another important plant, because like *tereske* it can be used for fuel, is *Acantolimum diapensioides*, which grows in cushion-like formations.

Juniper (*juniperus pseudosabina*) used to be found everywhere in the Pamir region, even up to 3,820 m in the Langar area. At the higher altitudes it grows only in dwarf form, but reaches true tree height at around 3,200 m, as in the upper Bartang valley. Its local name is *artsha*. It provides an excellent wood both for building and for fuel. Posts made out of *artsha* last for centuries, which is why this tree is now almost completely extinct in the region.

Agachanjanz reports that the wood of the *artsha* tree was also used for burials. Graves needed to be covered with rafters from this wood so the deceased would have a roof over their heads for eternity (1980: 54–55). A few lone trees, possibly several thousand years old, have probably survived only because they enjoy an almost religious significance or else designate a holy place. Plate 2.11 shows the last individual tree, protected by the local people, in a great radius around Roshorve. Situated as it is at the foot of Pic Revolutija (Revolution peak), it represents a special sort of natural monument and even has religious significance. However, during our last visit in June 2003 we had to accept that even this magnificent tree has been severely damaged by the local people.

The vegetation in the populated river valleys is much richer than in the Pamir high valleys. Alpine meadows and shrubbery may already be found at the base of the mountains. At a height of 3,910 m one can still observe Salix sp. and *Myriacaria germanica*. Somewhat lower can be found honeysuckle and wild blackcurrant. Rickmers also adds dog-rose, Ephedra and holly (1930: 63). Ivanow cites creepers, reeds, roe, willow, dwarf birch, mountain poplar, bramble, liquorice root, the above-mentioned honeysuckle, spurge, and also blackcurrant as main species

Plate 2.11 The most impressive *artsha* tree in the Roshorve area at an altitude of 3,100 m. The tree is probably several hundred years old and grows at the base of Pic Revolutija (6,667 m) (1997).

(quoted in Curzon 1896: 18). Among the wild plants along the river banks, wild roses and a whole gallery of buckthorns can be found (see Rickmers 1930: 97, pic. visa).

At altitudes below 3,000 m, the only 'forests' of Pamir can be found. However, only in a few places, as in the valley of the middle Shakhdara or the Gharm-Tshashma Darya, do we find rather large trees of the juniper variety and more extensive woods of tall willows on riverine islands (Plate 2.12). Near Langarkish, Zunk (Zank), and on some islands in the Pyandsh river near Ishkashim, etc., one can find extensive copses of willow, poplar, birch and *hippophae*, intertwined with hawthorn, clematis, honeysuckle and wild rose (see Olufsen 1904: 113). Naturally, due to the fuel shortage that has existed since 1992, wood reserves near villages have practically disappeared wherever it has not been possible to restrict cutting to branches of trees instead of the whole tree. The bush forest in the upper altitudes of Western Pamir from around 3,200 m downwards is strongly characterised by willows and poplars. The latter have been planted in great numbers for use as building material, as well as in more recent times for fuel (see von Schulz 1916: 210). The undergrowth is thicker here and dominated by clematis. Different sorts of grasses can be found everywhere. From 2,700 m downwards, groves of birches and *populus suaveolens* are found (see Schultz 1916). Lower still (that is, just above the altitude of Khorog at around 2,200 m), aspen, mountain ash and maple – as well as wild fruit trees – grow. These latter include apricot, apple, pear, walnut and pistachio. In the undergrowth one finds raspberry and gooseberry in the company

Plate 2.12 One of the last forests in the Pamirs, this one in the upper Shakhdara valley between Sejd and Javshangoz at about 2,900 m (1997).

of those bushes already named (cf. Geiger 1887: 56). The almond is obviously also native to the area. Below this level, mulberry trees appear in great numbers and seem have their widest range in Roshân.

The existence of fruit trees has almost always been underestimated in the literature. Small apples, apricots and plums can still be harvested up to almost 3,000 m in the Gund, Shakhdara and Pyandsh valleys. In Sejd, in the upper Roshtkala valley at 2,850 m, fruit represents an important source of vitamins even though at this altitude the harvest varies greatly from year to year. Good quality wine can be made from fruit grown below 2,000 m. The theme of fruit trees will be touched on again in the discussions on agriculture in Chapter 4 (see pp. 116–118), as without its rich fruit reserves the years of famine in GBAO after the civil war would have been even more severe.

Similarly, the many wild herbs that are still used in home remedies today are mentioned only as footnotes in the literature. Unfortunately, most of them could not be identified as our informants only knew the local names for them. However, we think we have definitely identified wild camomile, mint, sage and balm-mint, as well as oregano and balm.

The Pamir sheep (*Ovis polii*), probably closely related to the Tibetan sheep (*Ovis Ammon*), is without doubt the most famous animal of the Pamir and also its symbol. It was first identified by Marco Polo, as its name indicates, and was rediscovered by Prschewalkij (Prshevalsskij, Przewalski) in central Asia. The *kutshkar*, as the animal is called by the Kyrgyz, was formerly much more widely distributed than at present. It is now endangered by too intensive hunting, especially by the Kyrgyz. The horns of the large sheep were and remain a favourite house decoration and play an important role in a religious context. In the literature, animals with a body length of almost 2 metres and a height of almost 1.2 metres are described. It can weigh up to 295 kg. The horns were measured in one case at 1.45 metres (see Geiger 1887: 58).

Ibexes (*Capra ibex sibirica*) can still be observed in large numbers today, both in the high plateaux of Eastern Pamir and along the edges of the river valleys. Its pelt is used for the upper part of Pamiri boots whose soles are made from stouter yak leather. Especially common in some valleys are the wild goats that, apart from the marmots, were the animals we could always see fleeing from us. The *kijik*, as the Kyrgyz call them, are even shyer than the Marco Polo sheep and commensurately more difficult to hunt.

The yak, which produces a fatty milk that is drunk raw or made into yoghurt, cheese, butter and sweet or sour cream, only feels at home at altitudes above 3,000 m. More will be said about this animal in connection with the Kyrgyz economy on pp. 197–201. There have not been any wild yaks in the Pamir for the last 150 years at least.

To at least the turn of the twentieth century, other sorts of wild sheep (*Ovis karelini*), ibexes, numerous foxes, hares, marmots and other small rodents, together with wolves, perhaps a bear or two, as well the lone tiger, lived in the Pamir.[12] Grey or silver foxes, hares and especially marmots can still be found in large numbers, the latter, however, only to be found in masses at the higher altitudes of Eastern Pamir. The red marmot (*Arctomys flavinum*) even founds large colonies near roads. It is not eaten and therefore not hunted.

Bears have become rarer, but can still be encountered. In 1998 a case from the same year was reported in which a bear had stolen or destroyed a farmer's seed supply, as well as his fertiliser, and was killed. These bears are either the larger *Ursus isabellinus*, also indigenous to the Himalayas, or the smaller Indian bear (*Mellivora indica*). The most dangerous animal of the Pamir, apart from the tiger, is or was the snow leopard (*Leopardus uncia*). There are also reports of attacks by the mountain leopard (*Felis irbis*), which in earlier times used to break into barns. To keep at least one's sheep and goats in the house was thus not so much a sign of poverty as a necessary precaution against predators.

Typical river meadow animals, also present in the undergrowth in the vicinity of settlements, are lynxes, badgers, beech martens, weasels and otters. In the upper Pyandsh valleys, and probably elsewhere, there are still wild boars. It is surprising that reports about this animal, as with those about the wolf, which were very numerous a few decades ago, should now be so sparse. It is possible that both animals have recently been strongly eliminated due to the economic crises: the former for the table and the latter to protect declining livestock numbers.

Rickmers, in 1930, could observe, among other birds, bearded vultures, crows, pigeons, seagulls, hoopoes and geese (1930: 49). Curzon listed 120 bird species in the secondary literature. He personally observed wild geese and wildfowl of many descriptions on the lakes of the Pamirs, as well as quails, eagles and bearded vultures (1896: 23). From the literature, Curzon specifically mentions the *shikor*, a bird resembling the French partridge, which, he says, was quite numerous in the Pyandsh valley. He also mentions the common seagull, as well as snow-cocks or snow-pheasants. Machatschek (1921) mentions among the larger birds the bearded vulture (*Gypaetos barbatus*), Egyptian vulture, as well as goshawks and falcons as being present in large numbers. The latter are still used by the Pamiri in Darwâs for hunting. Cranes supposedly also traverse the area in substantial numbers. The golden eagle (*Aquila chrysaetos*) should be mentioned, as well as some high-mountain species of song-birds: e.g. *Eremophila alpestris*, *Motacilla citreola*, *Chaimarrornis leucocephalus* (Dor and Naumann 1978: 33).

For the sake of completeness, the reptiles, amphibians and insects of the region should at least be mentioned. Frogs and toads can be found in large numbers in the wet areas of the Eastern Pamir. Snakes, on the other hand, are rare according to the majority of sources. However, scorpions are supposed to be numerous around Murghâb town (von Schultz 1916: 213). In Khorog there may formerly have been tarantulas, and also a species of centipede growing up to 5 cm in length. Olufsen was also bothered by scorpions and spiders in Wakhân (1897b: 713), whereas from 1995 to 1998 and in 2003 we did not catch a glimpse of even a single scorpion.

Insects are numerous in Western Pamir. However, in the high valleys of Eastern Pamir, apart from butterflies and mosquitos, they are rare. In early summer, the latter are capable of chasing people away from Pamir's lakes. What had forced Sven Hedin away a century ago made our stay at each of the lakes to take pictures almost impossible for several days.

Concerning the minerals of the Pamir region, the literature is strongly dominated by mention of the ruby deposits in Shugnân and the nearby lazurite (lapis lazuli) mines.[13] Both mining areas have until now rarely been visited by travellers, as they lie quite out of the way in the mountains between Pyandsh, Shakhdara and Shugnân. Yet the mention of rubies is very old and goes back at least to Marco Polo (*Encyclopaedia of Islam*, see 'Badakhshân').

Lazurite is called *ljadshuar* in the Pamir area. The deposits along the river of the same name, Ljadshuar-Dara, were, according to Russian sources, only discovered in 1894 (Agachanjanz 1980: 56). Reclus, however, already mentions the mining of lapis lazuli in 1881, even though this was constantly interrupted by martial unrest in Shugnân. In his time, between 500 and 1,000 kg were being mined per year and sold on the markets of Bukhara, Kabul and Kashgar (Reclus 1881: 574–576). Since enormous blocks of high-quality material were found still *in situ* by the Russian expeditions, the earlier production could not have come from a lazurite mine but rather from gathering scattered blocks of stone that had to be carried on foot over mountain trails several dozen miles into the Shakhdara valley. Grevemeyer also stresses the small economic role played by lazurite and the other important precious or semi-precious stones of GBAO, particularly the *la'l*, a kind of ruby, though he gives the difficult situation of the mines and underdeveloped mining techniques as reasons (1982: 13).

However, lazurite from the Pamir region has been traded since Antiquity. According to Haussig, lapis lazuli from the Wakhân valley came along the southern silk road to the Sumerians in Mesopotamia and to Egypt (1983: 36). Sarianidi also assumes that during the Harappa Period, that is in the third millennium BC, lazurite from Badakhshan was already traded in a large part of the ancient orient (1986: 111). However, this material is most probably from the veins on Afghani soil on the left bank of the Pyandsh.

In 1930, the Tajik veins were officially rediscovered by Soviet geologists. It is only since 1972 that it has been mined on an industrial scale (cf. Agachanjanz 1980; Luknizki 1954: 216). Mining has been interrupted anew since the beginning of the 1990s. Thus only for special occasions, such as the visit of the Aga Khan in 1995, has new raw material been produced – in part in a very adventurous way by foot caravan from Ljadshuar. The mineral polishing factory at Porshnev, formerly the buyer of the mine's produce, is idle due to lack of raw materials.

Following Marco Polo, Wood reports on the ruby mines of Badakhshan, which he situates somewhat imprecisely some 20 km away from Ishkashim, in the north of the district of Garah (Gharah, Garan), on the right bank of the Pyandsh. The mines had supposedly been easy to open and there had been more adits dug in the sand(stone) than there had been broken cliff. In his time, work at the mines had come to a standstill as the population had been enslaved, possibly by Kunduz (1872: 206). Gordon, too, was unable to visit the mines (1876: 195).

Whereas Reclus even gives a plan of Badakhshan with the approximate position of the ruby mines in his work 'L'Asie Russe' from *Nouvelle Géographie Universelle* in 1881 (p. 475), Schulz generally doubts whether rubies were mined at all in that region near the small hamlet Ku-i-lal. Although shallow older shafts were still present, they were abandoned and worthless serpentine was all that could still be found (1916: 149). Olufsen, however, reports explicitly in this context that spinell is found in 'Kuh-i-lal', as he calls the above-mentioned village (1904: 48). Luknizki as well, the second discoverer of the lazurite deposits in Shugnân, speaks of the red spinell of Goran (1954: 215), by which he means the area around Kuh-i-lal. Red spinell is sometimes seen as a less-precious form of ruby, even though it is something else entirely from the mineralogical point of view.

According to our information, the presence of true ruby deposits in Garan and in other parts of the Pamir is certain. Even if travellers well into the twentieth century never saw the actual deposits, the stones themselves are well documented. The picture of a single particular mine is probably false. Areas with numerous ruby deposits must exist everywhere in the mountains between the Shakhdara valley and the Pyandsh, particularly between the village of Tusyan and the region of the Wakhân range, which were in the past more or less systematically mined. Rubies can also be found in other parts of the Pamir.

Other raw minerals found in the Pamir include scattered emerald deposits[14] and all sorts of semi-precious stones (malachite, quartz, amethyst). Atkinson speaks of nephrite with a special dark-green colour and strong banding, also of silver and lead (1860: 270). Olufsen mentions garnets practically as a footnote, citing that they were very numerous (1904: 48), which we can confirm. As the deposits lie concentrated in the above-mentioned areas in Shugnân where rubies are found, it is possible that there was often confusion between the two in the literature, as both stones have a superficial similarity.

Finally, there are gold deposits in the Pamir that have not so far proved economic,[15] as well as copper near Porshnev north of Khorog. Luknizki mentions the numerous crystal quartz, asbestos and iron ore deposits near the Wandsh river that have been mined using artisanal methods, as well as other rare metals, mica and quartz (1954: 215). Bituminous and brown coal are present in the Murghâb and were apparently mined for a while on a small scale. Sulphur, saltpetre and cooking salt are further potentially interesting economic resources. If access to the quarries could be eased, high-quality marble could be exported.

Landscapes of the Pamirs from a cultural-geographic perspective

In common with other authors, so far we have frequently spoken of districts such as Darwâs or Shugnân without defining these terms more precisely. Yet these units are not only elementary for the understanding of the geographical division of GBAO but also for cultural, historical and ethnic differentiation. It is especially important to be familiar with the status of the districts or sub-regions of GBAO in order to be better able to attribute the relevant ethnographic information.

The political subdivision currently comprises seven districts (rayons) and the city of Khorog. These are, from east to north-west: Ishkashim, Roshtkala, Shugnân, north-east of which is Murghâb, then Roshân to the west, then Wandsh and finally Darwâs in the north-west. Khorog is both an independent entity and the main city of Shugnân. Geographically, as well as from other points of view, the city may remain in parentheses. In the geographical description Roshtkala will be treated together with Shugnân, as the valley of the Shakhdara river had until the administrative reforms of the Soviet regime always been part of Shugnân. For the same reasons, the Wandsh valley as well as the Yasgulem valley will be treated together with Darwâs.

Wakhân is nowadays, from the point of view of population centres, a relatively small strip of land on the right bank of the Pamir-Darya or, looking at it from Langar, of the Pyandsh. The area has been strongly formed by the river. The plains are sandy and full of pebbles. In the vicinity of the river there are sometimes even true sand dunes. The soil is of medium quality in the lower-lying areas. Some of the villages lie on the slopes of the Wakhân range with a view of the different mountain ranges of the Hindu Kush. In some of the side valleys with a northern orientation, there is some meagre agriculture. Since it rains here more than in the Murghâb there are a few good grazing grounds and islands of farm land on the slopes. The farmers often have to walk 20 to 30 km to cultivate barley in the isolated advantageous zones and to cut fodder for the winter. Although in its upper course the Pamir-Darya is not much more than a brook, the guarded border prevents transhumance across the various borders. This would otherwise probably occur for economic reasons.

The climate of the Wakhân region is raw, with very cold winters. The buildings are therefore centred on the interior, being traditionally practically windowless. Stalls for livestock make up an important percentage of the buildings (cf. Geiger 1887: 143–14). The hay stores piled high on the roofs is a special aspect of this district.

There are basically two means of access to the Wakhân valley: the partly asphalted main road from Khorog that passes through Ishkashim to Langar and then continues up the Pamir-Darya valley, and the trail over the saddle between Wakhân and the southern Alitshur range. This second route can only be travelled using all-terrain vehicles, yet has the advantage of reaching the road from Khorog to Osh that passes close to Murghâb town rather quickly. In this way, Murghâb has become an important export centre for some Wakhân agricultural products such as potatoes.

The old capital city of the once-united area, including the Afghan part (today the Wakhân strip established by the Pamir Convention of 1895) is Kala-i Pyandsh that lies on the left – that is, the Afghan side – of the river. On the GBAO side, Langar is the most important place nowadays. Afterwards comes Wrang, an important large village.

Ishkashim borders the Wakhân valley to the south-west. The valleys and the flat lands along the Pyandsh are broader here, so that one may speak of a rich agriculture. However, the villages, such as Namadgut and naturally Ishkashim city, are very large, which reduces the available area. Still, the kolkhozes of Ishkashim were somewhat profitable, which has in the end made the privatisation of land here especially difficult. The soil is much better than in the upper course of the river, but some areas are prone to inundation. Ishkashim is the most important potato production region in GBAO and therefore had particular importance for development strategies: both for the privatisation of land as well as for increasing productivity.

The city of Ishkashim (altitude about 2,500 m) is the regional market centre and also profits from the large garrison of Russo-Tajik border troops stationed there. Being lower than Wakhân, fruit production is beginning to gain importance in Ishkashim, with apricots in first place. On the other hand, the steep Wakhân range limits available land behind the villages so that, for want of proper grazing lands, there is less livestock here than in Wakhân. Ishkashim is, theoretically at least, linked to Murghâb through Wakhân by the above-mentioned trail. In practice, however, all the traffic uses the asphalt road to Khorog.

The district of Garan (Garân), often mentioned in the literature and which borders Ishkashim to the north, now basically belongs to **Shugnân**. The same was true for the entire populated Shakhdara valley which today forms an independent Rayon. Because of this, the district of Shugnân had a very heterogeneous character. The upper Shakhdara valley especially is a very raw region, which strongly limits the number of fruit trees (because of the high altitude) and agriculture (because of the short growth period). Both constraints result in high risks and low productivity. The agricultural areas are often tiny due to the narrow valley. For these reasons, animal husbandry predominates in the upper part of the valley, at an altitude of 3,000 to 3,300 m, with a strong tendency to transhumance. However, this lifestyle is tempered by highly uncertain potato and barley cultivation. Surprisingly at this altitude, there is even some rye.

The natural vegetation of the middle Shakhdara valley is more pronounced than in other populated valleys, perhaps because the population density and therefore the need for wood is lower. Starting at about 2,800 m, fruit trees are cultivated on a larger scale. In the lower part of the valley, the meadows open up and more gentle mountain slopes are separated by side-valleys. Here, below 2,500 to 2,200 m, there are broad areas for cereal cultivation, which also stretch out along the slopes on the plateaux.

The Gund valley, beyond the mouth of which Khorog lies in the Pyandsh valley, is very similar to the Shakhdara valley in its most important points. At the highest altitudes there is practically no agriculture, the people living traditionally off transhumance herding. Under 2,800 m, fields become more common. The valley is in some places 1 kilometre wide, but at others it can also be so narrow that the river and the road take up all the space. This leads to high variations in the amount of land available from one village to another. Formerly this was balanced by the fact that kolkhozes and sovkhozes owned land beyond the villages, as was also often the case in the Bartang valley. But since privatisation, owners must sometimes travel long distances to reach their fields.

The natural vegetation in the Gund valley corresponds to that in the Shakhdara valley. Wherever a bit of earth has accumulated, there are wild roses, barberry, thorny copse and clematis, and among them many other flowering plants (in spring and summer). Wild pear and apple trees, currant and blackcurrant bushes and raspberries are also to be found in some of the more sheltered ravines (cf. Olufsen 1911: 22–23).

Because of the still adequate asphalt road from Osh to Khorog, the Gund valley is easily accessible. The Russians had already built a dirt road along the same route from 1898 to 1899 that linked Pamirskij Post with Khorog. At the top of the list of important villages is the former Soviet transport station Jelondî, then Shasîd and Vîr. Very few villages are far from the main road. But it is also typical of GBAO that even when most houses basically look onto this transportation axis, some hamlets are still practically unreachable. Even nowadays, at least some isolated villages on the plateaux and in the side-valleys are accessible only by foot.

Between Khorog and Roshân lie the wide river plains of the Pyandsh, that are of only average quality for farming (very stony, problems with salinisation). Here too lies Khorog airport, the only one besides the seldom-used airfield at Murghâb to at least be visited by small civil and military planes. The mountains of the Roshân range are not very steep for the first few kilometres to the north, so that agriculture and villages can thrive on the terraces at their foot. A typical example is the large village of Porshnev. In the other direction, that is to say towards the south, Shugnân is limited to a mostly narrow strip above the Pyandsh. These villages have few flat areas in their vicinity and have to farm tiny patches of land in the small side-valleys. The same is true for the side-valley branching off to the east, the Garm-Tshashma Darya.

A few kilometres upstream in this valley lies the small village of Shund, which possibly hosted Marco Polo about 730 years ago during his sickness. Here, at an altitude of about 2,600 m, are the most impressive hot springs of Shugnân. Olufsen mentions hot springs and geysers that form limestone or sinter terraces (1904: 27–31). The water is rumoured to have a temperature of up to 55.5°C. A pool as well as a small bathing complex with individual tubs has a temperature of 42°C. Because of the temperature of the water and its minerals (lithium, sodium, calcium and zinc), the place has been visited for a long time for cures. The remoteness of Pyandsh, however, speaks against Marco Polo having been there.

The area along the Pyandsh belonging to Shugnân is also linked to Khorog by an asphalt road. The former capital of Shugnân, Kala-i Bar-Pyandsha, however, lies to the left of the Pyandsh river on Afghan soil. On the basis of an old agreement, the nowadays poorish village receives electricity from the Tajikistan side. This cable represented the only link between the Soviet Union and Afghanistan for hundreds of kilometres.

Khorog, with about 20,000 inhabitants, has in the meantime become a true city that sprawls over several kilometres between the mouth of the Gund into the Pyandsh and the mouth of the Shakhdara into the Gund. In 1898 and 1899, there were only about a hundred Cossacks there, along with a few fortifications and a village hardly worth the mention. Around 1950 the city had 4,000 inhabitants who received electricity from a hydropower station, not only for illumination but also for heating. The steam bath in Khorog was one of the few in the Soviet Union to be electrically heated (see Satulowski 1953: 306).

At that time there was already a theatre, two cinemas and the unique botanical garden above the city. Since then, industries have been brought to Khorog, and apartment blocks with full water and electricity services were built for government employees working at the central water and energy units. Recently, even a university has been established in Khorog, which is lodged among other places in the former Communist Party buildings. After the civil war and before trade slowly recovered in 1998, the city was more or less entirely dependent on humanitarian aid. In 1995, food was grown in the city park and front gardens.

Murghâb is the name of the largest rayon of GBAO as well as of its capital city. Its other main population centres are Rang-kul, Kara-kul and Toktomish. The rayon stretches from the Trans-Alai in the north to the river boundary of the Gund in the south-west and the Chinese border to the east. Murghâb town was founded in 1893 by the Russians as Pamirskij Post. Until the 1930s there were, besides a small (military) fort, no more than two dozen houses. Although the relative shelter at the foot of a mountain and the presence of water and some meadows are some of the reasons for founding the post there, the place never achieved a viable autonomous economy. All the achievements of the Soviet period (see Luknizki 1957: 103) were possible only with external financing.

The region is extremely sparsely populated west of Lake Kara-kul and the main road to Murghâb town. Some areas are completely empty of people because of the harshness of the place and the rugged landscape. Others such as the lower Murghâb river valley up to Lake Sares are populated, but only sparsely due to severe climatic conditions. This pattern of sparse, widely separated populations may have given rise to legends that in central Pamir above the Wandsh and Yasgulem valleys there exists a people who are completely cut off from the rest of the world (see Rickmers 1930: 111). This is not quite correct, yet the fact is that inhabitants of this region, threatened as they were by Kyrgyz raids, never betrayed the position of the passes to the east or to the north, thus conserving a natural barrier against the nomads. Rickmers also thought it possible that individual passes became blocked by ice in the course of time (1930: 119), thus at least making access to the populated valleys more difficult. Otherwise the passes could have been buried by earthquakes, which would only have increased the attraction of the legend of the lost or cut-off people.

From the point of view of sustainability, the Murghâb rayon is, despite its low population density, still overpopulated. Agriculture has not progressed beyond the point of small experimental areas up to altitudes of 3,600 m, and the grazing grounds are very limited, though nutritious. The best sort of economy would be transhumance, even if only semi-nomadic. If there are permanent settlements there today and only some of the Kyrgyz still travel with their herds, this is as a result of the Soviet period. The fixed settlements assume there are enough permanent jobs in the area – but this seems unlikely even in the mid-term future.

Apart from the main road between Osh and Khorog, another very good dirt road was opened in 1989 which leads through Toktomish into China. However, it has not yet been opened for public use due to the lack of a bilateral border agreement. The settlements and base camps of the Kyrgyz in the Pamir valleys are generally easily reached as the landscape is good for dirt roads. It is even possible to drive directly over the bare steppe with a truck. To the west towards Bartang or Roshân (Sari-kul region), on the other hand, there is just a single precarious, steep trail that represents the only access to several smaller villages. These are consequently cut off from the outside world for eight months of the year.

Roshân is a more heterogeneous district and therefore only partially wealthier. The villages in the sometimes wide valleys on the banks of the Pyandsh have access to a relatively large area of farmland and to grazing grounds at the foot of the Roshân range. However, these farmers often have to fight against salinisation. Floods are another important risk and explain why some land is not used even though it would make good farmland.

The capital of the rayon is the town of the same name, Roshân, at an altitude of 1,790 m. The town was formerly called Kala-i Wamâr (see Plate 3.5), basically a fort for the formerly autonomous regional ruler. One of the Begs of the Khan of Bukhara had resided there since 1895 (see Olufsen 1900: 146). Apart from the fort there must have been what was for the region an immense town. Forsyth speaks of 'hundert Häusern und Obstgärten' ('a hundred houses and orchards') (1877: 19). Today, mulberry trees (*tût*) predominate in the lower altitudes of Roshân, the fruits of which are conserved in various ways and are even baked in times of need, just as apricots are.

South of Roshân city, the largest tributary of the Amu-Darya in Tajikistan, the Bartang, throws itself into the Pyandsh. The Bartang valley is reputed to be the wildest of all of Western Pamir and remained the least accessible well into the twentieth century. Whereas in the lower part of the northern source river there are still wide, mostly unpopulated valleys, the Murghâb valley already narrows above Lake Sares. Below the confluence of Murghâb and Kudara (Tanimas), to form the actual Bartang at an altitude of some 2,800 m, the river valley is seldom more than 300 m wide and is often limited to the river itself with vertical cliffs rising on both sides. Many villages lie on small cones of alluvial land above the river, where side-valleys feed into the Bartang.

Roshorve, formerly Oroshor, is an exception. Lentz calls it one of the largest villages in all of Pamir (Rickmers 1930: 222). If Roshân as a whole has been considered isolated in the literature until well into the Soviet period on the basis of its inaccessibility, then Roshorve is, apart from the above-mentioned hamlets in the western Murghâb and the region of Tanimas, the most isolated settlement in all of Pamir. The older descriptions given by travellers of their successful, or vain, penetration into the Bartang valley from the Pyandsh read like adventure novels, even in the twentieth century: an entire populated valley to which there isn't even a continuous donkey trail, but in some places only ledges, or on some cliff overhangs a few wooden planks – all of it some few or even several hundred metres or more above the raging waters of the Bartang, trails along which people even have to carry their animals on their backs. Only at specific times could horses be brought into the Bartang valley by using trails along the banks of the river at low water, and often changing banks by swimming across (see von Schultz 1916: 157–206; also pp. 185–186, this volume).

Rhoshorve is perched considerably above the river on a high plateau that falls steeply away on two sides and leans in the other directions on mountain massifs (including the imposing Pic Revolutija). Despite the impressive height of 3,000 to 3,100 m, the scattered settlement subsists primarily on agriculture, mostly wheat, barley and potatoes. Amazingly, tobacco and some vegetables also thrive there, but cultivation of fruit (apricots) and nuts (walnuts) only starts in the lower settlements such as Barshediv and Nisûr. After agriculture, livestock constitutes the second most important basis for survival. Roshorve therefore owns grazing grounds reaching well into the Murghâb region.

Within Roshân another much smaller side-valley should be mentioned, namely that of Khûf, about which Andreev has published important ethnographical works (1953, 1958). Although it is only 50 km away from Khorog, the small valley is so difficult to reach that it was only 'discovered' by the Russians in 1907. This is probably due to the fact that only one small trail leads into the valley and thus to the village. Fifty years ago, by which time the inhabitants had long been attached to a kolkhoz, there was still no other access (see Luknizki 1957: 310). Since then the settlement has shifted closer to the main road, such that newer buildings are not in the older part of the village but have been built directly above the road to Khorog because of the better transport situation. This migration from the mountain to the valley is a surreptitious phenomenon that is characteristic of many settlements in GBAO.

The Yasgulem mountain range separates the Bartang valley and Roshân from Darwâs district. The latter consists of three parts: the valley of Yasgulem, the Wandsh river valley and the region of Kala-i Khumb (Kalaîkom). The latter is also the capital of the rayon, an old regional princely seat and in the nineteenth century the seat of a representative (Beg) of the Khan of Bukhara. The sub-region of Darwâs on the left bank of the Pyandsh, which was attributed in 1895 to Afghanistan (in return for which the latter definitively gave up the parts of Wakhân, Shugnân and Roshân lying on the right side of the river), was administered from there. De Rocca (1896) reports important military contingents stationed in Darwâs at the end of the nineteenth century. An early photograph shows the 8th Bukhara battalion parading in honour of the traveller (see Plate 3.6).

Kala-i Khumb lies at 'only' 1,350 m, which is why the surrounding farmland can already be farmed under subtropical conditions. There are, apart from the usual plants of the Pamir, also a lot of grapes, plums, melons and even pomegranates. The area is rich in water, yet because of this and the clearly higher average temperatures is already susceptible to malaria.

The two valleys of Yasgulem and Wandsh are entirely different worlds, at least in their upper regions. They correspond in part to the valleys of the Gund,

Plate 2.13 Above the banks of the Wandsh river lies the most remote village of the area, Poi Masûr. The alluvial slope developed over millennia by the small conflux can be clearly seen (1997).

Shakhdara and even the Bartang: zones of average valley width alternate with extremely narrow ones where villages are reduced to establishing themselves on the alluvial deposits of inflowing brooks (Plate 2.13). In such a situation, violent landslides or mudslides have buried at least 24 homes in the past few years. The trails in the Wandsh valley lead in part through rivers, so that some villages are cut off for a time when the water is high.

Since the valleys begin at quite low altitudes – at about 1,500 m above sea-level – they are favoured in the agricultural sense. Apart from plants that are very susceptible to frost, the people there can plant practically anything that can be farmed in the appropriate zones. Some villages, however, were specialised in the Soviet era in fruit cultivation, which very much limited the basis for autonomy after 1992/3. Since then, field cultivation has predominated everywhere in Wandsh.

The population of Gorno-Badakhshan

The ethnic differentiation of the Pamir population, along with their languages, will be considered in Chapter 4. Here it can be briefly mentioned that in this book the population is divided into Kyrgyz and Pamiri (plural Pamiris).[16] Only those individuals speaking an Indo-European language belong to the latter group. When reference to all of the inhabitants of the Tajik Pamir is meant, they will be designated as the population of GBAO.

A brief overview of the size of the population and of settlement patterns within the individual rayons and river valleys shows that most people have settled in the deep river valleys of southern and western GBAO. The best settlement areas were the old river terraces along the Pyandsh or, in narrower valleys, the flat alluvial deposits discharged by mountain streams as they join the main river. One can hardly assume that the upper river valleys, at altitudes of over 2,500 m, or even the more inaccessible side-valleys, were populated other than in times of need.

The villages lying there today probably owe their existence to two basic factors: on the one hand expanding populations forced a search for new cultivation areas, while on the other repeated raids probably forced people to look for regions that were easily defensible and therefore very difficult of access. It is not known when these population movements took place as the historical sources permitting clear differentiation only appear in the eighteenth century. When Bobrinskij, Schulz, Lentz, Zarubin or even Andreev did their research, it was already too late to attempt a reconstruction of history through oral tradition. Moreover, after the Russian occupation of the Pamir at the turn of the twentieth century secured protection against raids, it was already too late for the high mountain populations to return to lower altitudes as all the farm land there was already divided up and cultivated.

In pre-Soviet times – at least since Antiquity – the high valleys of the Murghâb, and certainly the river valleys of the Tanimas and Murghâb as well, were simply grazing grounds for nomads or transhumance farmers. Nothing is known of permanent settlements in this region. The sparse resources forced the Kyrgyz to adopt a life of nomadism for subsistence. In this sense, the Alai has always been a reserve region for times when fodder failed in Pamir. It is very probable that the Alai-Pamir zone, divided today among four countries (Kyrgyzstan, Tajikistan, China and Afghanistan) should be considered as having always existed as a single entity. Depending on rainfall and the consequent prognosis for grazing grounds, the Kyrgyz moved from one region to another. In some regions, though, (for example in the Alitshur-Pamir), there was competition with the settled Pamiris who were already bringing their herds there in summer in the nineteenth century.

Permanent settlements, apart from Pamirskij Post (Murghâb town), only evolved in the 1920s or 1930s. In the large village of Konakurgan not far from the city, now boasting 1,005 inhabitants (1998), there were only five or six households in 1935 – and they only settled there for the winter. Permanent houses were probably first established shortly before the Second World War in the context of the kolkhoz. At least for some families, the erection of a small school in 1935 could have been the reason to settle.

That today there should live in Konakurgan over 240 households, of which only 15 families with yurts lead a nomadic life for part of the year, is incomprehensible in view of the practically nonexistent local resources. Even less logical to the visitor is the existence of the town of Murghâb with its more than 7,000 inhabitants. Both settlements, as well as all the other permanent villages in Murghâb, are clearly the product of unrealistic Soviet policies between 1935 and 1990. Although the importance of livestock for the Murghâb was constantly underlined and the only yak-kolkhoz in the whole of the Soviet Union was there, the fact that the people who practised animal husbandry were unable to support themselves but had to rely to a great extent on subventions (state loans, free energy, delivery of fodder, etc.), was covered over. The remaining population lived as government administrative personnel, permanently employed artisans or other state employees. With the disappearance of the subventions for the kolkhozes and the thousands of unemployed former state employees, at least half the population of the Murghâb became dependent on humanitarian help or were forced to emigrate.[17]

The total population of GBAO consists of about 209,000 individuals (1998). Only 13.7 per cent or 28,656 are 'urban' (figures from 1/1997). The annual rate of population growth is quite high, at over 3 per cent per annum. This doubles the population every 25 years and therefore poses a serious problem for economic growth. Table 2.1 shows the population of GBAO per rayon for 1997.

In the course of the last ethnic classification before 1989 it was determined that 90.9 per cent of the population were ethnic Tajiks, 5.2 per cent Kyrgyz, 2.0 per cent Russians, 0.7 per cent Ukrainians, less than 0.3 per cent each Uzbeks, Tartars and Kazakhs, and less than 1 per cent altogether Germans, Poles, Armenians and Balts.

It is interesting to glance at the population over the last hundred years or so (see Table 2.2). The figures are in part taken from the Russian and later Soviet censuses and are not entirely consistent.[18]

As there is doubt as to the quality of the early data, one must be careful in offering an interpretation. However, one should assume that the reduction in population between 1910 and 1926 was caused by emigration because of the Soviet occupation, and was later compensated for by fresh population growth due to higher security. Thus the estimate for 1910 may be too high. Should the data for 1940 be correct, however, then the data for 1910 would also be correct but the estimates for 1926 and 1929 too low. Corresponding to the historical facts is the diminution of the population in the Second World War and after it. During this time some of the villages became poorer (for want of Soviet support?) and part of the population emigrated or was even involuntarily resettled. The numbers for the following years seem logical and show an important rise in population at the height of the Soviet system in GBAO.

Table 2.1 Population of GBAO per rayon for 1997

Rayon	*Inhabitants*	*Remarks*
Darwâs	23,932	
Wandsh	28,472	
Roshân	24,817	
Shugnân	37,531	Not including Khorog
Roshtkala	24,545	
Ishkashim	25,536	
Murghâb	15,480	Figures for 1/1997
Khorog	28,656	

Source: oblast administration, 1998.

Table 2.2 Population of GBAO, 1910–86

1910	*1926*	*1929*	*1940*	*1956*	*1970*	*1979*	*1986*
33,000	28,924	29,000	73,000	62,000	97,800	127,709	148,500

The estimated maximum population that could be sustained in the Pamir high valleys of the Murghâb was not approached in the early decades. Curzon cites a source from 1892 according to which there were, in the whole of the Pamir highlands, 250 yurts with a population of 1,500 Kyrgyz. This estimate was reduced in the following years to around 1,000 inhabitants (1896: 18). Similar data is provided by Sven Hedin, who gives a population of 1,232 for the Russian Pamir region in 1893 (1897: 301).[19] The population supposedly rose to some 3,000 inhabitants in 1928 (see Borchers 1931: 55).

Until the Russian population censuses that began around 1900, and that obviously overlooked whole valleys (see description of Khûf on p. 40, for example), there were only rough estimates for the population of GBAO. Most of the numbers given by early travellers are based on statements from local informants. Usually the number of households or houses is given without a specific population estimate. Forsyth for example names 700 houses for the entire Gund valley, and 500 for Shakhdara (1877: 19). Olufsen around 1900 arrives at a figure of about 3,000 inhabitants for the 50-some villages of the Shakhdara valley (1911: 16) and 3,500 inhabitants for Gund (ibid.: 22). Shugnân as a whole (the Afghan part included) was supposed around that time to have approximately 20,000 inhabitants (see Paquier 1876: 176) of whom, however, a good part must have lived in and around Kala-i Bar-Pyandsha. The 1,500 houses in Forsyth's report seem in any case to be too many even when the 400 soldiers quartered in the capital of Shugnân are included (Forsyth 1877).

Wakhân must have been practically depopulated in the 1870s due to raids from Afghanistan. The capital Kala-i Pyandsh would have had hardly more than 150 inhabitants. Olufsen, who provides a detailed list of all the villages, comes to 253 houses in the whole of Wakhân on the right bank of the Pyandsh (1904: 56–57). Between the present Ishkashim, which at that time did not yet exist, and Khorog, he counts only 33 houses. Olufsen calculates 5.0 to 5.2 people per house; this means that about 1,455 to 1,500 people lived between the upper Murghâb-Darya and Khorog.

Roshân was definitely more populated, as Forsyth attributes 100 houses to Kala-i Wamâr. In 1911, Olufsen remains somewhat imprecise as to the division of the regions when he speaks of 2,500 inhabitants in about twenty villages, not including Vartang (Bartang), and later of 2,000 people including the Bartang valley in a further 30 villages (1911: 28–30). Altogether that would give about 4,500 inhabitants.

For Darwâs de Rocca's numbers for 1896 are available. Including the subsequently heavily populated Afghan region, he comes to a figure of 40,000 to

55,000 individuals divided among 350 villages and 6,000 houses (1896: 260). In 1900, all of Yasgulem had only 200–300 inhabitants in some 15 small villages (Olufsen 1911: 32). On the other hand, the Wandsh valley supposedly hosted the seemingly high number of 4,000 inhabitants in some 50 villages (ibid.: 34).

If we combine all of Olufsen's data we arrive at some 16,750 inhabitants, to which the 1,250 inhabitants of the Murghâb and some of the inhabitants of Darwâs listed in de Rocca have to be added. If we assume that one-third of the Darwâs population lived on the right bank of the Pyandsh, we arrive at 13,300 to 18,300 people. If the some 4,000 inhabitants of Wandsh and Yasgulem are then removed, 9,300 to 14,300 people are left. Thus, Gorno-Badakhshan would have had a population of between 27,300 to 32,300 inhabitants in 1900. The higher number fits especially well with the numbers in the table for 1910. It is worth noting that, using agricultural techniques that following the collapse of the Soviet system are once more rather primitive, about seven times the number of people living in the area in 1900 must today be fed on about the same area of land.

3

HISTORY OF THE PAMIRS

During research on this book it became clear that at no time has even summary treatment been accorded to the most important eras and their events in the earlier history of the Pamir region, especially before the time of Russian expansion and the Great Game.[1] We shall therefore begin with a brief survey of the successive settlements and overlordships and their consequences, with a view to establishing at least a rudimentary historical background for discussion of the cultural tradition of the Pamiris. As for the dispute between Russia and British India, so much in the forefront of public interest at the time, it will suffice to append a few basic observations on the so-called 'Great Game', together with references to the extensive literature on the subject. A cultural history of the Pamirs will, of course, not be complete without looking at the Silk Road and its significance for this mountainous region.

The Pamirs and the Silk Road

In the geographical introduction to the region we have expressed the opinion that the snowfall and sudden changes of weather on the periphery of the Pamir range must have meant that the Pamirs could not have been a good route, but in fact offered the only possible way through the central Asian mountain ranges from north to south and east to west. Only the central highlands of the Pamirs correspond with Forsyth's description: not many steep passes, good paths in general and easily fordable streams and rivers (1877: 52). According to this description, the Pamirs could only have been relatively easy to reach from the north-east and from the Chitral and Gilgit area (formerly British India).

Although the sources state firmly that the famous Silk Road of ancient and medieval times partly crossed the Pamirs, there is in the literature no generally recognised route or path exactly kept to by the caravans. Only the gateways of Kashgar and Yarkand in China and the formerly very important city of Balkh (ancient Baktra) in Afghanistan, which at certain times belonged to the Emirate of Bukhara, are clearly defined as the most important destinations of the east–west Pamir route. In between it seems more likely that there was a network of more or less frequently used routes.[2] The same is true of the north–south route, where only

Kashgar and Yarkand are the undisputed departure points, while destinations to the south have also changed over time. The safety factor probably played an important role here.

Essentially two old trade routes through the Pamirs are known, connecting China as the source country for the Silk Road with the west and south. The northerly route began in Kashgar and ran via Irkestam through the flat and narrow Alai valleys across some dangerous passes into the Ferghâna valley.[3] One variant also went via Irkestam and Karategin to the Amu-Darya. The southern caravan route was the well-known Pamir route, which went from Kashgar and Yarkand through Tashkurgân, on the present-day border between Tajikstan and China, and which led across the Wakhân. At Ishkashim the route split into a southern path, which brought travellers over high Hindu Kush passes directly into the present-day Chitral valley, and an easier western route (see Grevemeyer 1982: 94). On the far side of the mountain chain, the latter led along the Pyandsh to Faizabad and on to Balkh.

Those who wanted to travel from Ishkashim to Darwâs with pack animals before about 1930 could not go along the right bank of the river, along the route of the present-day metalled road via Khorog to Kala-i Khumb, but had to take the same path via Faizabad in order to get further east along the river via Kulyab (currently Tajikstan). Only those on foot could traverse the paths on the riverside cliffs of the Pyandsh.[4] In this respect the map drawn up by Haussig, one of the best authorities on the Silk Road, is correct in showing the route westwards as proceeding along the left bank of the river on the far side of the mountains in that area (1983), and not along the right bank, as claimed by other writers.

The route from Kashgar over the Pamirs at this point is, however, not shown on Haussig's map as going through the Wakhân. Rather, the route goes from Kashgar to the south-west right through the high Pamir valleys in the direction of the present-day town of Murghâb where it follows the route of the existing metalled road over the Naisatash pass directly into the Gund valley and at Khorog crosses the Pyandsh to Afghanistan. In earlier times there must have been a kind of ferry over the river, for example in the form of rafts, to make the crossing with camels and perishable goods possible. This route through the Murghâb and Gund valley is also corroborated by Zelinsky (1965). Another route north of the Gund valley, for example through the present-day Bartang valley, is completely out of the question as in pre-Soviet days this route was even more difficult than that along the right bank of the Pyandsh through Shugnân and Roshân.

It is highly likely that the Pamirs were only a transit area during the heyday of the Silk Road and not even a junction for caravans (i.e. an unloading and distribution centre). This meant that the population of the Pamirs only profited in a very limited way from the traders passing through. They may have sold food and animal fodder, but local produce is not known to have been sold or goods bought on a large scale (see Abaeva 1964: 93–94).

The connection between the various fortresses in Shugnân and Wakhân and the Silk Road remains unclear (Plate 3.1). Many of them are ascribed to the Kafirs

Plate 3.1 Ancient fortress in the upper Shakhdara valley near the village of Javshangoz. It was built to protect Shugnân against the Wakhân area (1997).

(Siya-ponsh), the 'Unbelievers', i.e. a pre-Islamic people. Were they built partly to protect the caravans, which were operated by the central powers of the time? Did the sometimes extensive fortresses offer refuge to travellers in times of unrest? Or were they perhaps a sign that the economic importance of the Silk Road was so great that feudal overlordships developed here in particular because of mutual rivalry.

The pre-Islamic period

The Neolithic period

The oldest period of settlement of the Pamir region known up until now is a so-called 'mountain Neolithic period', characterised by scree artefacts (seventh to second millennia BC). This is subdivided into the Gissar and East Pamir cultures. Coarse ceramic ware with cloth imprints has been found in the former area, while in the East Pamirs no stoneware is yet known of, at least not in this early period (see Rickenbach 1989: 14). From this it may be inferred that the early Neolithic inhabitants of the area were hunters and gatherers. The kind of stone artefacts found there suggests that the mountain Neolithic period is the continuation of an older, Palaeolithic culture. However, as yet, there is no conclusive evidence for the latter.

Kurgâns and Sakas

Bronze Age kurgâns are known in the Aksu from the East Pamir region. According to Jettmar *et al.* an 'ancient bridle bit' (a snaffle?) and animal-style bronzes have been found (1966: 60). Daggers and arrowheads come from other sites, which according to Jettmar make a connection to nomads in east Turkestan possible. In at least one case pieces of iron were also found in a kurgan.

With reference to those who excavated the sites, Litvinsky ascribes at least some of the kurgâns to the Sakas. This would indicate that the burials took place over the period between the sixth and third centuries BC (1984: 13–14).[5] Rickenbach tentatively dates the first Saka kurgâns to the eighth century BC (1989: 23). If this dating is correct for all the bronze finds in the Pamirs, then the Neolithic period might have been superseded directly by the metal culture of the Sakas only at a very late date in this area – no earlier than the eighth century. However, this hypothesis is improbable and only persists due to the absence of archaeological finds: on both sides of the southern Silk Road bronze had been known at that period for at least two millennia, and copper for even longer. Near Balkh at least, very extensive hoards of weapons and implements were found, which can be interpreted as stores for trade and which date back to the early centuries of the second millennium BC. So it is highly unlikely that the inhabitants of the Pamir region in the second and first millennia BC did not possess at least a rudimentary stock of metal objects.

In a side-valley of the Pyandsh between Ishkashim and Khorog as long ago as the 1950s, stone chest graves were discovered, which contained individual copper or bronze funerary gifts. The fate of archaeological finds from later excavations is not known in Khorog. The items were said to have been 'removed' to Moscow. These finds, now lost to Tajikistan, might possibly close the chronological gap between the mountain Neolithic period and the Saka period.[6]

The stoneware containers in the Saka kurgâns of the Pamirs are remarkable. About 70 items were known up until the late 1970s, all of which show unusual characteristics for Saka ceramic ware. The round bases, which do not exist elsewhere in the Saka cultural region, are distinctive (Litvinsky 1984: 69, 71). Is it a coincidence that well into the twentieth century the later ceramic ware of the Pamiris likewise has predominantly round bases mostly with distinctive handles, just like those in the Saka kurgâns (see Plate 3.2)?

Research into kurgâns and palaeobotanical investigations have also established that there was a great deal more wood in prehistoric times than there is today. In the Eastern Pamirs there were probably even extensive forests, which would have disappeared for the most part during the first millennium BC, but must have still yielded enough wood for wooden grave coverings to be usual during the seventh to fourth centuries BC. Because of this Litvinsky concludes that the nomadic people of that time must have encountered somewhat more favourable living conditions than the later Kyrgyz (1984: 76).

The Saka, the oldest historically accessible people of the Pamirs, were Indo-Europeans and spoke an eastern Iranian language. They are documented by Greek

Plate 3.2 Earthen jar from Shugnân, on display at the permanent exposition of the Gorno-Badakhshan historic museum in Khorog (1998).

and Chinese sources which tell of a Saka race of Komaroï (Gr.) or Hiu-mat (Chin.) in the Wakhân (see Patzelt, in de Grancy and Kostka 1978: 270). One writer even claims to have localised the settled area between Ishkashim and Kala-i Pyandsh as that of the Komaroï (ibid.). It is a matter of dispute whether the Saka were exclusively nomadic or also lived in permanent stone houses. There is every reason to believe that at least in the Pyandsh valley there were permanent settlements.

Rock engravings

Several writers tell of numerous sites with rock paintings, particularly in the Afghan Pamirs. The paintings tend to feature ibex and hunting scenes with bow and arrow (Breitenbach 1978: 32–33; Gratzl, in de Grancy and Kostka 1978: 311–343). They have not yet been dated, but we can assume them to be old as there has been no hunting with bow and arrow here for generations. It is doubtful, however, whether the paintings are of prehistoric origin, as these motifs have traditionally been continued right up until recent times. The second group of engravings in the Pamirs, Arabic-Persian inscriptions and symbols with religious or magic import, are, however, completely different from the animal paintings and hunting scenes. They can mostly be dated to the nineteenth century and the early twentieth (see Plate 3.3).

Plate 3.3 Ancient rock engravings near the main road from Khorog to Ishkashim showing what are probably some Ismaili magic symbols (1998).

Persians

The advance of the Achaemenidean king, Cyrus, into the steppes between the Pamirs and the Aral Sea in the middle of the sixth century BC was successfully fought off by the peoples living there. His son, Darius I Hystaspis, succeeded, however, in subjugating extensive tracts of central Asia and in instituting three satrapies (see Maahs and Bronowski 1979: 17). The Pamir region belonged, at least officially, to the most north-easterly of these satrapies.

Alexander the Great

In the years 329 to 327 BC, Alexander the Great's troops extended their conquests to the east of the Oxus. Alexander himself may have come as far as Kala-i Khumb (ancient Roxanaca; see Tomaschek 1877: map 1) in the Darwâs district after previously advancing to the Syr-Darya and ravaging the Ferghâna valley, before turning away with his army from central Asia towards the south once more in the direction of the Indus valley. It may be assumed that it was only Greek reconnaissance troops and envoys that came into the Pamir valleys, but it is likely that their influence spread to some extent as far as the highlands. The Greeks were, in fact, able to hold their position in the south of Tajikstan under the Seleucid empire for about seventy more years before the independent Hellenistic Bactrian empire arose from its ruins (Tomaschek 1877: map 1).

Plate 3.4 'Owring' or footpath on the Afghan side of the Pyandsh near Kala-i-Khumb, built completely in and on the rocks of the river bank (1997).

Kala-i Khumb is linked in many respects with Iskander (i.e. Alexander the Great). According to legend the town was founded by the Macedonian king himself (Geiger 1887: 150; also oral tradition). At times it is supposed to have been called Iskander Sindona; that is, Alexander's prison (von Hellwald [1875] 1880: 272). Many very skilfully engineered paths along the cliffs on the left bank of the Pyandsh (Plate 3.4) are said by local people to have been the work of the conquering Greek army. In all probability they are significantly older, and quite definitely they would be unsuitable even for a small army.

Alexander's influence was felt right into the nineteenth century in at least one further important way. In Darwâs, as well as in other parts of present-day GBAO, there was a tradition that continued to survive, whereby local rulers would cite Alexander in matters of ideology and would claim that their own families were his direct descendants.

Bactria

At the end of the fourth and at the start of the third century BC, the Pamir region was probably one of the former north-eastern Persian satrapies, which were taken from the Seleucids under the satrap Stasanor, and fell to the Indian Maurya empire in 304 BC after only a few years of independence (Albaum and Brentjes 1972: 79). The Hellenistic empire of Bactria,[7] important in the third century BC, which extended from Bukhara across the Ferghâna valley as far as Kashgar and included large parts of Afghanistan, must have regained the Pamir lands from the Maurya people and absorbed them into its territory, though the mountain lands may not have actually been militarily occupied and thus opened to cultural penetration. In any case it is completely unthinkable that Bactria should not have had control of the southern Silk Road, if the areas in the north and south of present-day GBAO already belonged to it. However, there are no coin finds from that period; at least they are not documented.[8]

In 183 BC, under Demetrios, Bactria achieved its maximum expansion, following the conquest, at least temporarily, of southern Aghanistan and the Punjab. For this period at least, it can be taken that the Pamir region was not independent of Bactria. It is not known what form any co-existence or confrontation between Bactria and the Saka took during this period; the latter were then occupying at least the Eastern Pamirs and Wakhân.

China

After the empire had become weakened and before Kushan rule was established, the eastern territories of Bactria, and thus the Eastern Pamirs, doubtless fell for a time to China, which achieved its maximum expansion there in the first century BC (see Machatschek 1921: 110). From the annals of the two Han dynasties (206 BC to AD 23 and AD 24 to 220) we learn of the 'Onion Passes', as the Pamir region was called at the time. Paquier does however point out that the reports are superficial (1876: 32), and as Chinese sources are usually very precise, this indicates that the occupation was not long or intensive.

The confrontation between China and the Parthians as auxiliary troops to the local people is interesting from a historical and military history point of view. This took place in an area which the Tochars had gradually been pushing into (see p. 57). Obviously the Chinese had largely withdrawn eastwards out of the Tamir basin. However, in 36 BC, the Chinese set about reconquering the Tarim basin and thus also Kashgar (and the Eastern Pamirs?). In all probability the Chinese lost the conflict – at least, great losses are verified (see Haussig 1983: 121).[9] In any case the overlordships of the Tarim basin remained for a long time outside real Chinese sovereign territories. These conflicts had, however, no discernible lasting negative consequences on trade on the Silk Road.

The Yüe-chi and the Kushan empire

During the time in which the Bactrian empire continued to fall apart, the Tochars, who tend to be equated with the Yüe-chi, settled in the upper Amu-Darya valley after 129 BC. Evidence has been found near Balkh, Termez and Kunduz in present-day Afghanistan (see Haussig 1983: 124), which indicates that they could have at least been present in the Darwâs district of the Pamirs, especially as they had immigrated from the east, probably either directly via the southern Silk Road or via the circuitous route through the north-east Pamirs/Alai valleys and Karategin.

It was also the Tochars who repulsed further Parthian advances under Artabanes I (from 127 BC) into the region between the Hindu Kush and Amu-Darya. The Parthian king was killed during one of these campaigns, thus permanently preventing an advance of the Parthians in the footsteps of the Achaemenideans.

During the first and second centuries AD the Tochars, or Yüe-chi,[10] penetrated further into ancient Bactria, especially along the left bank of the Amu-Darya. AD 45 is considered to be the year in which the Kushan empire was founded under the Yüe-chi Kadphises. Did the present-day GBAO belong to this Kushan empire (1st to 4th centuries AD)? If this really did stretch, at least temporarily, from Afghanistan to Xinjian (Sinkiang), then the Pamir peoples of the time undoubtedly could not have escaped this vast domain for at least part of that period. There is evidence that at the beginning of the second century AD, troops of the Kushan emperor advanced across the Pamir passes into Yarkand, which they occupied for a time (see Haussig 1983: 121). During this period at least, the Eastern Pamirs must have belonged to the Kushan empire. This was also the time of the greatest expansion of Buddhism in Bactria and Afghanistan (Gandhara culture).

Sassanids

Between 242 to 272 parts of former Bactria and the Kushan empire of the time were conquered by the Persian empire under the Sassanid emperor Shapur I. It is certain that present-day southern Tajikstan fell to the Sassanids. Nothing specific has been said in the sources about the fate of the Pamir region. It is also not clear what role was played at the time by the Sogdians, who occupied Badakhshan (see Albaum and Brentjes 1972: 162).

Hephthalites

Towards the end of the fifth century the political map of central Asia changed fundamentally. Coming down from the Altai, the nomadic Hephthalites or White Huns invaded Sogdia and Bactria and conquered nearly all the territories of the one-time Kushan empire (see Rickenbach 1989: 17; Yule 1872b: xxvi). The Hephthalites ruled up until about 560, at least in the western territories adjoining the Pamirs, and advance for a time into Afghanistan (see Machatschek 1921: 110). Kunduz, on the western edge of Afghan Badakhshan, was for a time their heartland.

According to Albaum and Brentjes the Hephthalites accomplished their advance by sending on ahead one of their tribal groups, which penetrated into the Pamirs in around 450. This tribe's kings ruled in the Kabul valley and the Ghazna region from 460 to about 560 (1972: 162). There is some uncertainty surrounding the origins of the Hephthalites. Grousset assumes that they were a Turko-Mongol or even Mongol ethnic group, spreading first of all from the Altai into the later Russian steppes (1952: 110). However, the Hephthalites were probably not a Turkish ethnic group, as had previously been assumed, but an east Iranian Indo-European group.

This also explains why the civilisation of the Kushan empire continued to flourish without strife.

In 562 the Hephthalites became the victims of a war on two fronts with the Sassanids and Turkish ethnic groups. In 588 the victorious Turks advanced south and, in a sustained process between 590 and 630, seized parts of Sogdia and Tocharistan from the Sassanids. There are indications that at least the campaigns against Badakhshan (Sogdia) were carried out at that time through the Pamirs. Chinese intervention from about 600 prevented a prolonged Turkish occupation of the geographic area around the Pamirs (Grousset 1952). However, in the middle of the eighth century there were renewed invasions of Sogdia, when Muslim conquests from the west heralded a new historical period. The Chinese stayed (as part of their front-line defence?) in the region for a few decades, occupying Transoxania in 659, and in 661 the land between the Oxus and the Indus. The Pamir passes probably served as one deployment zone amongst others. In 674 attacks by nomads from the Tibetan highlands finally forced a Chinese withdrawal lasting three-quarters of a century (see p. 59; also Albaum and Brentjes 1978: 15).

Up until the time of the Islamic conquest there is remarkable continuity in the history of the area we have dealt with. From the Saka, the Yüe-chi and probably the Hephthalites as well, to the inhabitants of Sogdia, we are dealing here with east Iranian ethnic groups, all belonging to the Indo-European family of languages. Continuity is also demonstrated by the fact that most conquerors of the region started as nomadic horsemen, settling after the empire was founded and creating an outstanding civilisation either from nothing or by building on the cultural legacy of earlier rulers. A third cultural continuum is Buddhism, which spreads into the area from the second century BC and is the dominant religion up until the fourth century, only definitively being displaced during the Islamic conquest (to find out about the role of other religions, see pp. 237–238).

From Islam to the eve of the Great Game

In the middle of the seventh century Arab Muslim armies, with the indirect help of the Byzantians and Turks, had destroyed the weakened Sassanid kingdom within a very short space of time and continued their advance towards Central Asia over the following years. In 663 Baktra (Balkh) was captured by an Islamic army. In his book *Das Arabische Reich und sein Sturz* (The Arab Empire and its Fall), Wellhausen describes on the one hand how successfully the Islamic armies were able to advance towards the north-east, and yet how great their defeats – caused by internal unrest – continued to be (1902: 265–270, 292–294).[11] Around 700 essentially all territory gained by conquests had been lost, until once again campaigns of conquest – which also had the aim of permanently establishing Islamic rule – were carried out systematically under the possibly most well-known military leader in the north-east, Qutaîba bn Muslim.

In 712 the Ferghâna valley fell into the hands of the Arabs, thus marking the greatest geographical extent of their power. The few united regional rulers, whose military strength was determined by the inhospitable terrain, continued to defend their independence for a long time in the mountain lands. It was the profusion of fortresses which made the war drag on (see Albaum and Brentjes 1978: 15). This does not explain at all the Pamir region's conversion to Islam. If we take into account the reports on the culture of the 'Kafirs', particularly in Wakhân, as well as the history of the neighbouring, later British Indian border areas, then there must have still been a boundary between Islamic and 'heathen' peoples for centuries, here and in Afghan Badakhshan (see pp. 221–225).

In their defensive action against the Arabs the local rulers were again supported by the Chinese for a period in the eighth century. However, the latter were crushingly defeated in 751 near Talas, and in the north of the Pamir region they withdrew permanently eastwards for several hundred kilometres. The culture of central Asia, which up until then had been mainly Buddhist, subsequently slowly altered into a culture shaped by Islam. However, the struggle for independence by the small principalities went on for generations. In Wakhân sagas give numerous accounts of the defence of local fortresses against Islamic armies, and how they were finally conquered.

An important period in the history of that time is the Tibetan advance (with the collaboration of the Arabs?) around 740 into the upper Oxus valley, where they took up position, amongst other places, near Sarhad on the Wakhân-Darya. Sir Aurel Stein, citing the Han annals, devotes an essay specifically to the Chinese countermeasures; his account is of interest to us in that it delivers proof that it was possible in the year 747 for an army of 10,000 soldiers, though in several subdivisions, to march through present-day GBAO along several different routes (Stein 1922). The ultimately victorious Chinese army marched at that time in three columns from Kashgar, via, among other routes, the Murghâb route of the Silk Road, already described, through the Gund valley into the region of present-day Khorog. As the right bank of the Pyandsh was impassable, the path led the troops through the Shakhdara valley and over passes onto the upper Pyandsh, from where some of them marched to Ishkashim.

If we interpret Sir Aurel Stein correctly, the Pamiris of the time were to a large degree independent of China in spite of the military expedition: 'the natives do not conform to the imperial orders' (1928, II: 878). The Chinese were first and foremost interested in securing the territory militarily in front of the main battle line. The inhabitants of the 'four Pamir valleys' are said to have lived in caves. Furthermore, there is mention of five valleys under different rulers. Already at that time the inhabitants of Shugnân had a bad reputation. They were said to be warlike and to carry out raids (ibid.).

In the confusion of the struggles between the Chinese and Turkish campaigns of conquest, it appears that some of the local nobility in Sogdia made peace with the Muslims, who after 730 advanced again into central Asia and in 740 brought the Ferghâna valley under their control. Many inhabitants converted to Islam at that time, and in 749 upper Tocharistan (i.e. Badakhshan) fell under Islamic rule (see Albaum and Brentjes 1978: 16). As present-day GBAO did not directly belong to Tocharistan, it is at least a reasonable supposition that Islamic influences only penetrated slowly into the mountain areas, which were probably largely under the influence of the Zoroastrian religion.

In the ninth and tenth centuries (874 to 999) the Samanids, based in Bukhara, were the most influential power in central Asia. During this period the towns became more and more Islamified and west Iranians, Turks and the families of mountain tribes came to Sogdia and Tocharistan. During this period Sogdians and Tochars merged with the west Iranian settlers of the ancient Bactria region and became the Tajik 'people'. The west Iranian language, 'Dari', was recorded in written form and became the language of court and literature. The poet Firdaûsî from Tus (934 to 1020), the physician and scientist Abû 'Alî al-Husaîn ibn 'Abdallah, called Ibn Sina (Avincenna, 980 to 1037) and the scientist and historian al-Birûnî (born 973) can be loosely assigned to this early Tajik cultural sphere.[12]

Under the protection of the Shiite Buyids, who exercised control in Baghdad as viziers over the Abbasid Khalifate, the Twelver Shia began to gain influence at this time in central Asia (see Haussig 1983: 252), and in view of their reputed liberalism set about proselytising the last remaining adherents of Buddhism and Zoroastrianism. The Sevener Shia of the Ismailis also grew in importance. In fact the Samanid ruler Nasr ibn Ahmad Samanî even went so far as to profess his faith in the Ismailiyya publicly. Badakhshan belonged at that time to the Samanid empire, and so it is quite possible that the foundations were laid for the Ismailiyya in GBAO and beyond the Afghan border at that time. There are, however, sources which say that the conversion to Islam took place later (see p. 62).

The years between 1220 and 1365 are marked in the whole of central Asia by the Mongol empire under Temujin (Genghis Khan) and his descendants. Brutal massacres and the displacement of large parts of the population of Transoxania during that period damaged the economy of central Asia to a considerable extent. Daftary assumes, however, that the mountainous area between the Pamirs and the Hindu Kush was not influenced by the Mongols ('escaped the Mongol debacle'; 1998: 165). This is, however, rather unlikely. At any rate, the domain ruled by Ulu, the second oldest son of Genghis Khan, clearly stretched from, amongst other areas, Kashgar to Bukhara and Samarkand, the southern border going along the Amu-Darya. It is unthinkable that the southern Silk Road, which at that time was still functioning in spite of considerable economic problems, should not have been under the control of this part of the Mongol empire.

Between 1369 and 1526 central Asia was shaped by the Timurid Mongol empire. When Timur, called Timur Lenk or Tamerlane, himself no Mongol but of Turkish origin, ascended the throne of Balkh on 10 April 1370, it is likely that the Pamirs belonged to the new Transoxanian empire (see Yule 1872b: xxxiv). At least after the death of Timur, the border between Transoxania and the Khanate of Djaghataï, at first internal, went roughly along the line where the old Soviet-Chinese and also Soviet-Afghan Wakhân border goes today. Strategic border positions are seldom no-man's land and it is likely that at least the Pamir passes were controlled. It has been proved that Darwâs was directly controlled by the son-in-law of the ruling emir and descendant of Timur, Abdoullah Khan (1538–1597) Shah Kirgis. The (renewed) foundation of Kala-i Khumb, or at least the construction of the fortress there, is said to date back to him (see de Rocca 1896: 264).

At the end of the fifteenth century Kashgar and Yarkand belonged to the Emirate of Dûghlat, which in its turn had been brought under the control of Yunus, the Khan of Western Mongolistan, who thus rose to become the most powerful ruler in central Asia. From here the Khan got involved in the quarrels of Timur's last descendants in Ferghâna and Transoxania (see Grousset 1952: 546), and it is likely that the Pamirs could have played a decisive role in this as a transit route.

In the sixteenth century the areas west of the Pamirs fall into the hands of Uzbek Sheibanids. Thus present-day GBAO gradually came under the influence of Bukhara, at least during the next few decades. A young nobleman from the Ferghâna valley, called Babûr, driven out by the Uzbeks in 1500, went on to conquer Kabul after his flight in the year 1504, and later founded the Moghul empire in India (see Spear [1965] 1990: 21–22; Yule 1872b: xxxv). For the next 150 years, however, he and his followers did not give up his claim to his old homeland and all the land lying in between, including the Pamirs, which they continued to try and reclaim. It was only in 1647 that the Moghul emperor finally ceased his attacks, and as a consequence all of the land on the far side of the Hindu Kush, and thus present-day GBAO as well, fell to the Uzbeks. From then on the Great Moghul Shah Jahan and Nader Mohammed, Khan of Bukhara, established the Hindu Kush as a border between the two empires. Luknizki says, on the other hand, without naming a source, that in 1572 – 75 years earlier – Wakhân, Shugnân and Roshân, together with Karategin, were said to have fallen to Abdullah Khan, the then Emir of Bukhara, and to have been governed by his stepson, Shah Kirghiz of Darwâs (1957: 211).

Certainly, local sources, as well as the historical records of the Emirate of Bukhara, tell of repeated conflicts with Badakhshan and with the Pamiris in the period following (see Grevemeyer 1982: 21–22). These conflicts may well have been because Bukhara wanted to secure its rule in Badakhshan by appointing a direct local ruler, Mahmud Bi Ataleq, over Kunduz and Badakhshan, in 1650. The conflicts themselves might have been started by the Uzbeks, because the followers of the Bukharan Resident, Ataleq, shamelessly plundered the land instead of protecting it. The fragmented rulers in Badakhshan, maybe with the exception of Shugnân, had, however, little in the way of military means to counter the Uzbeks (see Holzwarth 1980: 189).

It is possible that the Uzbek conquest created a decisive turning point for the inhabitants of Transoxania and Badakhshan, including the Pamir region. On the one hand, it could have been the seizure of the lands lying on the plains by the Uzbeks which drove the 'Tajik' people further up into the mountain valleys (see Kussmaul 1972: 16). On the other, Uzbek despotic rule and increased insecurity in the country might have offered people greater safety in the higher mountain valleys, without them having been actually driven from the plains.

During the early Islamic era, and particularly during the Mongol period, the Pamir region all but lost its previous importance. During the Hellenistic Bactrian empire, the era of the Yüe-chi, and particularly during the period of the Saka, it had played a specific role in that people from each of these empires had settled there. In fact there are virtually no further accounts of the inhabitants, and it is likely that the role of the Pamirs was reduced to that of a transit area between the various domains or to that of an unimportant – in terms of its potential as an area to settle – connecting link within the same domain. However, the Pamir region, even as a transit area, probably always belonged to whichever dominion had the power at the time, so that others did not occupy it and use it as a gateway to their own land. There were certainly no fortunes to be made here, even if some writers continue every so often to circulate vague accounts about the ruby mines of Shugnân.

The history of Shugnân is to a certain extent an exception, as there are some more specific older sources on this area, which must nevertheless be treated with caution. Using writers from the Middle Ages as his reference, the Tajik writer Abusaîd assumes that this district was not only independent in the tenth and eleventh centuries but that the ancient Arian religion was still being practised (1997a: 49). In the tenth century contemporary sources even call Wakhân and Shugnân 'the countries of non-believers' (ibid.: 50). It appears that Islam, in the form of the Ismailiyya, arrived here in the middle of the twelfth century. Daftary, who produced the most recent summary of the history of the Ismailis (1998), assumes that Ismailis took over political power there at the same time. A so-called *dâ'î* (summoner) from Alamut, named Sayyid Shâh Malang, is said to have set himself up as ruler of Shugnân, followed by a second *dâ'î* named Mîr Sayyid Hasan Shâh Khâmûsh. These summoners are said to have founded a whole succession of dynasties of religious rulers, who are said to have ruled Shugnân, Roshân and the adjoining districts as Pirs and Mirs right up until recent times (Daftary 1998). There is a certain contradiction in the fact that rulers who claim to be of Arab origin claim at the same time to be descended from Alexander the Great.

The negative image that Shugnân, and thus also Roshân (which at some periods was seen as part of Shugnân's lands), had with the neighbouring peoples, particularly in the eighteenth and nineteenth centuries, may not just have been due to the warlike or rapacious behaviour of the Pamiris. The Shiite-Ismaili Pamiris were attacked by Islamic-Sunni peoples, specifically because of their, from the latter's point of view, 'heretical' belief. So some of the alleged Shugnân raids could really be seen as defensive, and the rapaciousness or lawlessness as the result of deliberate defamation by the 'real' Muslims. As far back as the seventh century there were similar accusations from the Buddhist traveller Hiouen-Thsang, at a time when the Shugnânis probably still practised the ancient cult of fire (see p. 83).

It cannot be said with absolute certainty, in the centuries following Uzbek dominance in central Asia, whether Shugnân and other areas on the right bank of the Pyandsh were autonomous in the seventeenth century and the early eighteenth, or whether they continued to come under the jurisdiction of Bukhara, or at times that of the central Afghan state. In order to buy relative peace, individual local rulers may even have recognised two different dominions and paid taxes to two different potentates, which might have been cheaper than having to be the battleground for border disputes.

In the middle of the eighteenth century Badakhshan was integrated into the Afghan domain, newly constituted in 1747, under Ahmad Shah. After only a few years all parts of the country up to the Pyandsh were violently subjugated. The occupation also clearly shows ideological features. It was a question of 'exterminating and subjugating the shameful Shiites and false Ismaelites, who lived in those regions of Badakhshan and Chitral' (Kreutzmann 1996: 79).

The Afghans clearly took advantage of a period of extreme weakness in the Emirate of Bukhara; their advance enabled them in 1768 to carry out an official transfer of the present-day Afghan part of Badakhshan from Bukhara to Afghanistan (see Grevemeyer 1982: 64). The agreement was repeatedly challenged, but with the exception of Darwâs, which in 1895 was divided by the Pamir Agreement between Russia and British India, the Pyandsh from now on remained a border, albeit a flexible one, between Afghanistan and Bukhara, or Russia as the case may be. Although relationships between the groups of peoples on both sides of the Pyandsh, and above all trade, were kept up, as many reports suggest, it is not absolutely clear whether Roshân and Shugnân were politically united at that time. Grevemeyer assumes that in the middle of the nineteenth century the regional domains were extended beyond the river (1982: 76). It is also possible that regional rulers for their part were under a commitment to two dominions, for instance the part of Roshân to the left of the Pyandsh to the Shah of Afghanistan, and the areas to the right of the river to the Emir of Bukhara.[13]

However, the Afghan government, at least, was not able to establish its authority permanently in Badakhshan. From the end of the eighteenth century the Afghan parts of Badakhshan, and, with the exception of Darwâs, certainly also the present-day Tajik parts, had been more or less independent regional principalities (see Plate 3.5). Unlike Afghan Badakhshan, which was united under the strong local prince Mir Mohammed Shah between 1792 and about 1820, there was no unified leadership in present-day GBAO, although Shugnân had supremacy. Internal disputes, as well as raids from outside, were common. While Badakhshan on the left bank of the Pyandsh for its part experienced 30 years of economic prosperity under Mohammed Shah, the story of the present Tajik districts at the same period is one of internal dissension between local rulers.

Afghan Badakhshan only enjoyed peace for a short time. One aim of Murad Beg's accession to power in Kunduz in the year 1815 was the definitive subjugation of Badakhshan. After 1820 there were serious conflicts with Kunduz, as a result of which the Badakhshanis were crushingly defeated. Tens of thousands of people died and about 100,000 are said to have been deported into the marshes near Kunduz and Hazrat Imam. By 1840 the population had been reduced to about

Plate 3.5 Kala-i-Wamâr, the most important stronghold in the Roshân area. The picture was taken about 1900 (Khorog Museum archives).

a third of its former size (see Holzwarth 1990: 75; Kreutzmann 1996: 80). Murad Beg's power was clearly so great that in the middle of the nineteenth century a khanate in its own right, that of Kunduz, was also spoken of in European literature – for instance, in Dubeux and Valmont's widely read work (1848: 91). In this work Badakhshan and Shugnân, as well as Wakhân and Darwâs, are named as parts of Kunduz.

Wakhân was, however, apparently able to keep itself out of the conflicts for a while. 'Distance and poverty had hitherto been his security', remarks Wood, referring to the Mir of Wakhân. But in the end the district was subjected to a punitive expedition by the Afghan commander of Badakhshan, Kokan Beg. He was, however, betrayed, consequently losing his life. This secured the independence of Badakhshan and Afghanistan for the local Mir of Wakhân, Mohamed Rahim Khan, at least until Wood's visit a few years later in 1838, although the entire population of the upper reaches of the Pyandsh was estimated at the time to be not more than a thousand (see Kreutzmann 1996: 81).

The area lying to the right of the Pyandsh remained nominally under the sovereignty of Bukhara, in spite of the internal conflicts described here.[14] There is, however, no report of a military presence of the troops of this emirate along a line east of Darwâs, at least not in sources known to us. That could be because the Bartang valley, or in general the right bank of the Pyandsh, were not accessible to larger numbers of troops, for known geographical reasons. As a result of Bukhara having lost Afghan Badakhshan, the sections of the Silk Road on the other side of the mountains along the Pyandsh from Faizabad to Ishkashim and in the Wakhân were also closed to Bukhara, making it practically impossible to reach Shugnân and the eastern districts from the west any more. Bukharan troops would have had to march across the Ferghâna valley and the Murghâb, but that belonged to the Khanate of Kokand.

In the middle of the nineteenth century a new Afghan invasion of the territory on the left bank of the Pyandsh began. This led to later attacks on the territory of Bukhara and Kokand and to Russian countermeasures, but these were already part of the 'Great Game' (see pp. 67–74). The state of affairs in Darwâs and Shugnân at the start of this Great Game is briefly described here: the parts of Darwâs on the right bank of the Pyandsh were then a permanent part of the Emirate of Bukhara; the central area, however, retained its autonomy until 1878 under its own shah. Its external dependence was documented by an annual tribute (*tartuk*). When this was refused in 1877 it led to a short war, with heavy losses for the people (200 dead) and to the direct occupation of the district by Bukharan troops (Plate 3.6). As a consequence Darwâs was put under the direct control of a representative of the Emir and a 500- to 600-strong militia.

A further uprising in 1881 was effortlessly suppressed and the district remained with Bukhara until the dissolution of the khanate by the Soviet Union. Thus Darwâs is the only part of the Pamirs which was, *de jure* and *de facto*, deprived of all autonomy at the end of the nineteenth century. This fact is clearly due to the relative accessibility of the area, which could be reached on horseback and, if need be, with cannons during at least four to six months of the year. Even before 1900 this resulted in relative prosperity, after the network of internal dependencies and taxes had been replaced by a unified tax and by a central administration which was clearly moderately just, and at any rate superior to the former system of government (see Michell 1884: 492).

Plate 3.6 The 8th battalion of line from Bukhara in Kala-i-Khumb. Original photograph by Félix de Rocca (1896: facing p. 240).

In the nineteenth century Shugnân included Roshân, with the Bartang valley and Shakhdara, as well as the Gund valley and the plains and side-valleys of the Pyandsh on both sides of the Gund estuary. Roshân was traditionally governed by relatives of the Shah of Shugnân, while in Shakhdara, as oral tradition confirms, a dependent, autochthonous family had power (see Holzwarth 1980: 203). It is known that the Shah claimed descent from the Ismaili emissaries of the thirteenth century. As a result of the already mentioned internal disputes, as well as armed conflicts with the neighbours and the resulting butchery, enslavement and mass flight of the people that this caused, the populations of Shugnân and Wakhân are said to have fallen steeply in the nineteenth century. However, the inaccessible mountain valleys, lacking in resources, were only extremely sparsely settled, and even without war Holzwarth, referring to Russian writers whose texts are not available to us, assumes that in Shugnân there were only 250 warriors, who were bound to their masters by oath (ibid.). If this is true, then we can imagine that living conditions at that time were extremely hard. Military conflicts must have affected all the villages and nearly all families in the area.

Nevertheless, we should not see the people of Shugnân only as victims of war. In spite of all the calumny, it is certain that they were often perpetrators as well, attacking Wakhân and repeatedly laying waste to valleys in Afghan Badakhshan. If the people of Wakhân sometimes had to make cave dwellings above their villages into hiding places, this was not just as a defensive measure against the Kyrgyz (Olufsen 1904: 90) but above all against attacks from Shugnân (see Stein 1928, II: 865, 870). Even the Kyrgyz, excellent though they were at putting up a fight, sometimes came off worst in conflicts with the people of Shugnân. In 1866, for example, after a serious conflict with the people of Shugnân, the Kyrgy had to leave the high valleys of the Murghâb for a time.

Not much is known about Kokand's authority over its territories in the Pamirs. In the last decades before the Russian conquest it can safely be said that it was non-existent, or very nearly so. Certainly a direct uprising by the Shah of Sari-kul against the Khan of Kokand in the 1860s had little success (see Shaw 1872: 47).

The Great Game and the Russian occupation of the Pamirs

Once Peter Hopkirk's bestseller, *The Great Game: On Secret Service in High Asia*, was published in 1990, this term became generally known outside specialist circles. In the wider sense 'Great Game' denotes the dispute over the central Asian border area between Russia and British India, conducted in part at secret service level. The action concentrates on the country between the Punjab of northern India, Kashmir and Afghanistan, on the one hand, and the central Asian khanates of Kokand and Bukhara on the other, with Chinese eastern Turkestan and even Tibet sometimes involved. Fraser-Tytler's contention that the Great Game really began when the East India Company was set up in 1599 and only ended when India and Pakistan gained independence (see Kreutzmann 1997: 170) grossly overstretches the issue both geographically and chronologically.

In the narrower sense, the Great Game can be identified geographically with the regions of the Hindu Kush and the Pamirs, and temporally to the few decades of direct confrontation between Russia and British India. For each of the two sides the question was where a line should be drawn to mark the limits of expansion directed by the respective national interests, and to mark a strategically satisfactory territorial border. In this respect, in the early years, establishing a border along the Pyandsh river and deciding to whom the Pamirs should belong were only secondary points. In British India, on the basis of what was initially only superficial knowledge of the area, the upper reaches of the Oxus (Pyandsh) were originally thought of as a possible border. With slight modifications, namely creating the Wakhân strip and assigning it to Afghanistan as a buffer zone, this proposal was finally implemented in the Pamir Agreement of 1895. Meanwhile, because of new findings by the intelligence gathering agencies of the Great Game, considerable differences remained and these led at times to the brink of military conflict.

The early focus of the British on the Pyandsh as a possible border on the far side of the Hindu Kush passes limits the actual territory which was the subject of the Great Game *de facto* to the wider Pamir region, and thus also to a particular period. For instance, the early history of Russian expansion into central Asia forms too wide a framework here. In the narrower sense the Great Game only deals with the years between the Russian conquest of Tashkent in 1865 and that of Kokand from 1871 to 1876 respectively, and the Pamir Agreement of 1895 in which Afghanistan also took part as a junior partner. Hayit describes the years between 1869 and the first Pamir Agreement in 1873 as 'wars of words', because there were 109 exchanges of notes and statements about border issues in central Asia between Great Britain and Russia (1971: 115).

From the British point of view the Russian advance on central Asia was of course seen as the cause of the conflicts.[15] The advance began in the 1840s in the region between the Aral Sea and Lake Balkhash. Disquiet was caused on the British side by the conquest of Tashkent in 1865, in which the Emirate of Bukhara was affected as a direct neighbour of Afghanistan. The latter country was seen in this context as a part of the wider British empire in India. Russian conquests to date were also formally annexed by the creation, in 1867, of the general governorship of Turkestan. In 1868 Samarkand was occupied, and in 1871 Kokand, which in 1876 was put under direct Russian administration by deposing the Khan. Thus the Eastern Pamirs were *de jure* incorporated. In 1873 the conquests in central Asia were largely completed by the occupation of Khiva, even if Bukhara was able to continue to eke out an existence as a protectorate under its Emir until 1917 or 1921 (*de jure* even up until 1924).

The British occupation of the Chitral valley (see Knight 1893), the less successful attempts to bring Afghanistan 'into line', and the already previously completely failed attempts to make an alliance with the Emir of Bukhara typify the British part of the expansion into central Asia. From the Russian point of view the takeover of the rights of the East India Company by the British state (after the mutiny in 1857), as well as the repeated occupation of Afghanistan, were, naturally, seen as expansion. In spite of this there is no doubt that there were forces in Russia in the 1870s and 1880s that aimed to draw up a border south of the Hindu Kush and which were, therefore, objectively seen to threaten British interests.[16] It has been shown many times that Cossack troops carried out reconnaissance expeditions in the Chitral valley, attempting thereby to stir up the inhabitants against their neighbours, who were still the British at that time (see Knight 1893: 352–353). Russian intervention in Persian affairs was not without expansionist intent either.

The 'Russian Threat' caused the British to become more involved in the Pamir region. Many so-called researchers between the 1870s and 1890s were nothing more than army officers or civil servants working for the Indian administration, either British themselves or subjugated nationals from the Indian subcontinent. The reports, generally known from the scientific literature and in particular the specialist geographic journals of the time, only present some of their discoveries. Many writers drew up secret dossiers for the British or British Indian government, or used public interest in Great Britain in the 'Central Asian Question' to stir up opinion in favour of intervention. Kreutzmann alone cites around twenty English-speaking writers whose books are known from the time of the Great Game, amongst them key players such as Curzon (1896), Gordon (1876), Forsyth (1875, 1877) and, above all, Younghusband (1896).

G. J. Alder, who deals with the topic of the Great Game concisely and yet in detail in the context of British India's northern frontier from 1865 to 1895, sees six main phases (Alder 1963): during the first phase, which can be dated to between 1869 and 1873, he suggests that there was an understanding on both sides not to accord too much importance to the border question and to leave the actual creation of the border open for the time being. The British were working here from two premises: the first one was that Afghanistan ended at the upper reaches of the Oxus and the second that the Oxus could be a suitable border line between Russian and British zones of influence. This position reflected the inadequate state of knowledge of the geography and history of the greater Pamir region at that time. Nevertheless, it was incorporated in an agreement made between the British and the Russians in 1873.[17]

Exploration of the area soon showed that these assumptions were not well founded. First, it was quickly realised that Shugnân, Wakhân and also Darwâs were not clearly divided by the Pyandsh. While Darwâs possessed territories on the left bank of the river, the latter also providing protection, Bukhara lay on the side of the river which the British considered to be Afghan, and Afghanistan claimed the areas of Shugnân (including Roshân) and Wakhân along the right side of the Pyandsh as its own territory. So contrary to earlier assumptions there was no clear divide between the British zone (Afghanistan) and the Russian zone (Bukhara).

Thus the second premise was also rendered partly invalid. It became completely invalid when it turned out during reconnaissance of the Pamir region that the course of the river Pyandsh could not itself be clearly defined. There were three possible alternatives for a border along the Pyandsh: (1) along the Wakhân-Darya, which clearly represented the Russian interpretation; (2) through the Pamir-Darya, which meant that there was a tract of land between Afghanistan and China not clearly assigned; and (3) that it was not the Pyandsh above Roshan which was the source of the Amu-Darya but the Bartang, which was of a similar length and sometimes with a greater volume of water. This version was the one accepted at times by the British (see Rawlinson 1875: 310–312). This brought in the Khanate of Kokand, to which the Eastern Pamirs belonged, under attack from the Russians and ultimately to be annexed by them. Russia was totally opposed to Bartang, Murghâb and Aksu as a border.

During the second phase of the Great Game, from 1873 to 1888, the too-hastily drawn conclusions on the geography of the Afghan–Russian border region were largely called into question by further research on both sides. The most important discoveries without a doubt were made by Forsyth's expedition (1875). The so-called 'Pundits', for the most part trained surveyors, gained particular 'distinction', proving to be highly qualified researchers. 'The idea of using native explorers to carry out clandestine surveys of the lawless regions beyond India's frontiers had arisen as a result of the Viceroy's strict ban on British officers venturing there', writes Hopkirk ([1990] 1992: 329–330).

This idea came from a young officer working for the Survey of India, Captain Thomas Montgomerie of the Royal Engineers. Montgomerie's plan was accepted and a number of Indian explorers, including Mirza Shuja, Abdul-Subhan, the 'Havildar' and others, were dispatched 'in great secrecy' across the frontier (Hopkirk [1990] 1992: 329–330). 'Because discovery, or even suspicion, would have spelt instant death, their existence and activities had to be kept as secret as possible. Even within the Survey of India they were known merely by a number or a cryptonym', according to Hopkirk.

This caution, which was in fact only necessary locally in order to enable them to cross safely across the Indian border areas towards the Pamir region (in fact similar missions were also heading at that time towards Tibet), destroyed the Indians' chance of becoming known to a wider public as discoverers, along with Shaw, Forsyth or Gordon. On an international level the journeys did not, however, remain a secret at all, as the results were published in all the specialist geographical journals of the time, and by Forsyth, Gordon or Yule themselves. On the one hand the results of these geographic recordings increased British fear of a Russian invasion of north India across the Pamirs, when it became clear that the passes were relatively easy to traverse. On the other hand it later allowed the relatively meaningful establishment of a borderline, for example by the creation of the Afghan Wakhân Corridor.

As early as 1885/6 Ney Elias submitted the draft of this borderline, on the basis of the geographical knowledge of the course of the Pyandsh, which in the meantime he himself had also established, and also of the border between Kokand (i.e. Russia) and China.[18] The Emir of Afghanistan was told by the British that no one would object to him extending his territory as far as the Chinese border. But it is likely that the British confronted the Emir with the fact that it would be necessary in the long run to cede the parts of Badakhshan on the right bank of the Pyandsh to the Russians, in order to secure their acquiescence in the other parts of the plan (see Alder 1963: 221). As already mentioned, both sides could have saved themselves the next ten years of the Great Game with its confrontations, as the Elias plan contained exactly what was endorsed as the Pamir Agreement in 1895, and even today this still determines the border between Afghanistan, Tajikstan (formerly Russia) and China.

But all sides still wanted to achieve more, and troops of the Emir of Afghanistan remained deployed on the present-day Tajik side of the Pamirs. The third phase of the Great Game lasted from 1888 to 1891 and is described by Alder as a 'prelude to crisis'. It also served eventually as a foundation for the Pamir Agreement, as in early 1891 what was considered initially to be an additional problem was removed: namely the surprising fact that China did not at first lay any claim to those areas up to the planned border to Afghanistan (Wakhân). One of the most important players in the Great Game, Sir Francis E. Younghusband, is generally credited with having brought about the closing of the gap.[19] In spite of this 'success' the Great Game had, however, not yet come to an end, but went into its fourth phase in which everything it had achieved was lost again.

In August 1891, during an expedition into the Eastern Pamirs, Younghusband came upon a Russian mission which gave the British information on the Russian annexation of the Pamirs. What originally need not have been a problem, as British India had fully expected this move, became the Pamir crisis of 1891–2 because the Russians claimed, at least at that time, precisely those territories for itself (Greater and Lesser Pamir, Aksu valley and Taghdin-bash) which were supposed to be allocated to Afghan Wakhân or China. Alder describes the exact events (1963: 226–247).

That also applies to the fifth phase of the Great Game, the second Pamir crisis of 1892–3; during this crisis, at the same time as the continuation of the Russian–British confrontation which was still being carried out by diplomatic means, an open conflict broke out between Chinese and Afghans, which from the British point of view ended unfortunately with the Chinese retreating from the Wakhân. Now Russians and Afghans confronted each other in the Wakhân without an eastern border. It resulted in a short military confrontation, during which the Russians held their position roughly in the present-day Russian–Chinese–Afghan border triangle. Whether under supposed British pressure, or because he himself no longer wanted to fight the Russians, the Emir of Afghanistan withdrew his troops to present-day Afghan territory beyond Wakhân. The border, which had been closed with difficulty under British influence, continued to be open along a line 100 km long, and what was even worse was that the Emir's troops continued to be stationed on the right side of the Pyandsh in Shugnân and Roshân, which was seen as a provocation to the Russians and completely thwarted British plans.

The sixth and final phase of the Great Game (1893–5), which Alder entitled the 'Third Pamir Crisis and Final Solution of the Problem', started with rumours about an imminent advance of Russian troops, which evidently was called off by St Petersburg at the last minute (Alder 1963: 263). After internal wrangling between the Russian Foreign Ministry and War Ministry a negotiated settlement was put to the government of British India. At first Russian insistence on the handing back of Afghan-occupied territory to the right of the Pyandsh aggravated the crisis, as Afghanistan was not yet prepared to give up Roshân and Shugnân to the right of the Pyandsh. The idea of getting parts of Bukhara from Darwâs in compensation had not yet been proposed. Inside the Foreign Office in London it was, however, independently decided in July 1893 that it was not worth going to war with Russia over present-day Tajik Shugnân and Roshân. In the end the British succeeded in convincing the Afghan Emir to give up Roshân and Shugnân on the one hand and on the other to keep the Wakhân Corridor, which was almost worthless to him and hard to control. The British had made certain concessions to him in return for this on the Indian–Afghan border. Although no border agreement between China and Russia came into being – which is the reason why some areas in the Pamirs between China and Tajikstan are still disputed today – the repeatedly cited Pamir Agreement was signed in 1895, which was unable to establish, *de jure*, the entire border, but which is, *de facto*, still respected today.

What did the Great Game do for the respective parties between 1873 and 1895, and what did it do for the people in the area of reference? As far as the latter are concerned, the agreement thoughtlessly divided up an area inhabited by the same ethnic groups and with a connected cultural history, with the result that right up to the present day communication between the Ishkashims, Shugnânis or Roshânis to the left and right of the Pyandsh is almost impossible. The Chinese

Pamiris and Kyrgy are hermetically sealed off from their present-day Tajik relatives in the same way.

As for the Russians, they proved unequivocally during the course of the Great Game that it was possible for the Tsar's empire to advance towards India across the Pamirs. But the difficulty of crossing such a mountain range, and the impossibility of carrying out such an enterprise with a large army, also became clear. That seems to have been the reason for the increased acceptance of the later Oxus border by the Russian government in the years between 1893 and 1895. From the British point of view, the Pamir Agreement was a great success, as thc originally desired borderline was agreed on, for the most part, with the additional creation of the 'neutral' Wakhân Corridor between the two empires. 'India gave up the chance of direct control to the north of the passes, but maintained the glacis free from Russian occupation', was how Alder summed it up (1963: 285).

For local rulers the result was less satisfactory. The Afghan invasion of the right bank of the Pyandsh in 1883[20] had caused the local rulers of Shugnân to turn to the Emir of Bukhara and the Russian Governor-General of Turkestan simultaneously for help, with the result that after the Pamir Agreement the Afghans did withdraw, after some hesitation – but not the Russians. The territory gained through Russian expansion in the Pamirs, which had begun with the conquest of Kokand, where the Russians regarded themselves as its legal heirs, could now also include the territory formally belonging to Bukhara; that is, Roshân und Shugnân. Either way Bukhara was the loser, as on the one hand it did not gain much from the new areas, which were co-administered by the Russians and not by Bukhara alone, while on the other hand it had to give up, on the left of the Pyandsh, the parts of Darwâs which up until then it had controlled itself.

The Pamir Agreement settled relationships between British India and Russia, although conflicts continued locally for some time. Even though Russia could claim a right to the Western Pamirs from 1868 onwards after the defeat of Bukhara, and from 1871, after the conquest of Kokand, to the Eastern Pamirs as well, it only formally took possession of the area in 1893, though without any permanent occupation. Only in the Murghâb was a military outpost set up in 1892, the 'Murghâb Guard' ('Pamirskij Post'), the present-day Murghâb town. It was fully occupied only after the Pamir Agreement. The small village of Khâruk (present-day Khorog) became the headquarters of the Russian troops at that time. In 1894 there was a skirmish between the Afghans and the Russians near Kala-i Pyandsh, and, in spite of the fact that the Emir of Afghanistan had accepted the Pamir Agreement, attacks on what was now Russian-Bukharan Roshân and Shugnân took place up until at least 1896.[21] As for the Eastern Pamirs, the Russians did not immediately occupy Wakhân, on the right side of the Pyandsh, after 1895, with the result that even as late as about 1900 Afghan incursions threatened the region.

The Afghan invasion of those parts of Roshân and Shugnân on the right side of the Pyandsh from 1883 to 1895 clearly only represents one small detail in the Great Game, but it was long remembered by the inhabitants of the affected areas, as large parts of the land were laid waste. In Said Haidar Shah's 1912 history of Shugnân, which exists in manuscript form in Khorog, it says, 'the lives of people in Shugnân were never worse than at that time'. The Shugnânis did, however, repeatedly put up resistance to the Afghans, without Russian support. According to Becker the population of Roshân went down by 50 per cent during those years (1968: 215, note 14). Refugees from the war attempted to escape into Chinese territory (see Younghusband 1896: 274).

Russia and Bukhara's 'condominium', joint sovereignty over the Pamirs, lasted 28 years – between 1893 (official annexation of at least the Eastern Pamir region) and the dissolution of Bukhara from 1921 to 1924. At first Russia only placed the Pamir Highlands and the Oroshor District (western high-mountain range country, including the upper Bartang valley and the Murghâb valley) under its own Ferghâna district military rule. Administrative headquarters were at first in Pamirskij Post. Shugnân, Roshân, Ishkashim, which had been named as a distinct entity for the first time, and Wakhân, all were formally put under the control of the Emirate of Bukhara. The Emir protested against this, however, and said that the territories had only been bestowed on him against his will, in exchange for the lost Darwâs territories on the left bank of the Pyandsh (see Hayit 1971: 114). The fiction of Bukharan rule, at least for Shugnân, was soon brought to a close by the transfer of the Russian military administration in 1897/8 to present-day Khorog, even if the civil administration remained under Bukhara's jurisdiction right to the end.

The first Russian settlement in present-day GBAO is Murghâb town, where in 1892 a small fort was built. The Earl of Dunmore, who was one of the first foreign visitors to what was then Pamirskij Post, came across a troop of 180 Cossacks under two officers, who had made themselves very comfortable here in this extreme climate (1893b: 394). Further troops of unknown strength were positioned on the present-day Chinese border and in the Wakhân. As little as 15 years later, Russia seems to have been absolutely confident of its new territories. Schultz, who travelled the length and breadth of the Pamirs several times between 1904 and 1912 for the purpose of ethnographic research, finally found only 100 infantry soldiers and the same number of Cossacks, with some artillery and machine guns, in Khorog, Pamirskij Post, as well as in the villages of Njut (Nut) near present-day Ishkashim, Langar in the Wakhân, and also in Rang-kul and Kisil-rabat in the Central Pamirs. The troop strength referred to included the posts on the Chinese border and on the Pamir passes (1916: 221–222). Other posts on the Bartang and Pyandsh were only occupied in the early years, which indicates that all was quiet in Afghan Badakhshan.

Not much is known about larger Russian projects to develop the region before the First World War. Sir Aurel Stein, who travelled from Ishkashim to Khorog along the Pyandsh in the summer of 1915, does mention a bridle-path, which had been made with Russian help shortly before, and which made this direct route possible using pack animals (1916: 217). A connection between Khorog and Darwâs, on the northern side, does not seem to have been attempted at that time.

The Bukharan civil administration also did little more than institute, from about 1900, a very cursory census which provided a basis for taxation. It is interesting to note that already at that time the special status of the high mountain valleys was taken into account. A farmer's wealth was measured according to the weight of his crop and not according to the absolute size of his holding (see Holzwarth 1990: 151).

There is no account of resistance by the Pamiris to the Russian occupation of the region. On the whole administration by the Tsar was considered by many of the newly subjugated peoples of Central Asia to be well organised and not too oppressive or tyrannical, in spite of its harshness. Security and religious freedom under Russian rule were emphasised (see Debelak 1875: 120). Another source speaks, however, of the Tsarist empire's hostile policy towards Islam, which caused disaffection in Ferghâna, amongst other places (Hayit 1965: 35).

In the climate of the Cold War after the Second World War, and with a lack of knowledge of earlier social history, W. P. and Zelda Coates, however, tell of Russian colonialism and racism towards the central Asians, of brutal military commanders and of general stagnation brought about by the deliberate obstruction of agricultural and industrial development (1951: 52–61). 'The Tsarist conquest of all the Khanates and the Turkoman country did not improve the hard lot of the peasants (*dekhans*) or of the craftsmen of the towns', and 'literacy varied throughout the Khanates and provinces of Turkestan from 1 to 2 per cent – considerably worse than in India at that time' (ibid.: 54) and, worse still, 'taken by and large, the lot of the natives was hard under the Khans, but it became still more arduous under the new conquerors . . . The Tsarist Government not only helped the Emir against his own people, it understood also how to flatter his vanity' (ibid.: 59).

This description is perhaps true of parts of western Bukhara, if it is not pure invention as regards the Russian side – but it is not true of the Pamirs. The Soviet writer Pavel Luknizki – himself certainly not at all unpartisan – probably reflects reality more accurately when he describes the people's joy encountered by the Russian captain Vannovsky in 1893 when the Russians withdrew back down the Bartang (1954: 218). The problem here – and probably elsewhere too – was not the Russians themselves but the fact that under the protectorate treaty they were not allowed to interfere in Bukharan administration. There was repeated unrest amongst the population, which complained to the Russians about the way the Bukharan regime continued to behave[22] and wanted to be annexed by Russia. The Russian military administration did at least insist that the population of the Wakhân be exempt from taxation for a time (Luknizki 1954: 220).

Consequently, during the period between 1895 and 1921 the old regime of despotism by local rulers in traditional Afghan and Bukharan style continued, though with less brutality under Russian influence. It was to be expected that Russian annexation would be welcomed, at least by ordinary people, regardless of whether it was in the name of the Tsar or the Soviets.

The early Soviet period

In the run-up to the October Revolution of 1917 the Bolsheviks repeatedly declared themselves in favour of detaching non-Russian areas from Russia, including the recently occupied central Asian areas. The social revolutionaries and constitutional democrats, on the other hand, went a step further than the Tsarist government regarding the future of the conquered territories by demanding the incorporation of the Khanates of Bukhara and Chiva into Russia. As a result, there was sympathy for the Bolsheviks' October Revolution in many parts of central Asia, at least from local nationalists.

Partial disillusionment set in when the Bolsheviks took control in Tashkent and former Tsarist Russian officers or civil servants exclusively replaced all natives. On 19 October 1917 Muslim organisations were even explicitly excluded, by declaration, from taking part in the first Soviet congress (see Hayit 1956: 61, 74). The Autonomous Republic of Turkestan, which had in the meantime been set up by nationalists, and to which the Eastern Pamir region belonged,[23] was brought down in February 1918, paradoxically by the same Soviet government which had previously supported its independence through its propaganda (see Hayit 1962: 27). The nationalists, who up until then had still looked favourably on the new system for social reasons, now woke up to the real strategy of the new government in Moscow.

It was precisely the anti-socialist former nationalists who were to be found, however, in the organisation of the Communist Party right up to the 1930s. Many of them belonged to the former upper echelons. The Bolsheviks, bearing in mind the autonomy of the former khanates, clearly seem to have looked on them as 'softer' opponents when compared with the 'imperialist' socialist revolutionary and democratic groups. The former nationalists were themselves only expelled from the party under Stalin from the mid-1930s onwards, some of them being eliminated because they refused to take action against the Kulaks amongst their own people, and against religious institutions.

But the Soviets, knowing of the anger caused amongst the peoples of central Asia by the Tsarist policy towards Islam, were at first ready to compromise in cultural matters and particularly in the matter of the Islamic religion. The new government returned to the city of Samarkand an important, ancient copy of the Koran, which had earlier been stolen by Tsarist troops, and the initially sequestered estates belonging to Islamic foundations *(aûqâf)* were restored to the Islamic authorities in June 1922. In 1922 Islamic Sharia law was reinstated. This Soviet policy of rapprochement towards Islam only started to change from 1926 onwards (see Hayit 1965: 36–37), and was definitively replaced in the 1930s by Stalin's ruthless anti-Islamic policy.

In general the Soviets' policy towards each nationality, as laid down by Lenin and practised in the 1920s, was, in spite of the inconsistencies encountered by non-Russian groups and national minorities, on the whole beneficial even in non-religious matters. Although the Soviets had laid the foundation of present-day conflicts between states in central Asia by separating Tajikstan from Uzbekstan in 1929 in a way that virtually ignored the actual settled areas of each individual people,[24] cultural autonomy was encouraged and, for example, the national language promoted. There are no figures for Tajikstan, but in neighbouring Uzbekstan right into the 1930s lessons were still being taught in schools in 22 different languages (see Simon 1982: 49). Regarding the traditional role of women at that period, the Soviets supported a policy of equality in central Asia from no later than 1924 onwards. National women's groups were supported and serious conflict with conservative clerics was thus concurred with (see Halle 1938: 146–152). Campaigns against wearing the veil were particularly successful. This affected Uzbek areas especially; less so Tajik areas where the veil was seldom worn.

From September 1920 the Soviets took charge of events in the Sultanate of Bukhara, which was only abolished *de jure* in 1924. Bukhara was then added to Uzbekistan, while the Pamir regions were added to the Autonomous Socialist Soviet Republic of Tajikistan – separated from Uzbekistan in 1929 – first of all as 'Special Pamir Oblast', then as 'Gorno-Badakhshan' ('Mountain-Badakhshan') (see Kreutzmann 1996: 118). As far back as 1921 an agreement was made between Great Britain and the Soviet government not to carry out mutual indoctrination of the inhabitants on the other side of the borders.

The October Revolution and the ensuing years of famine probably did not have serious economic consequences for GBAO, as there was enough to subsist on because producer taxes had been significantly reduced. Khorog, where around 1930 about 2,500 people lived, became the capital of GBAO, subdivided into six district committees (district soviets): Shugnân, Roshân, Bartang, Ishkashim, Wakhân and Eastern Pamir (Murghâb). Literature on the subject does not indicate to what extent GBAO was influenced by the internal power struggles in East Bukhara, which had not ended with the suppression of the Autonomous Republic of Turkestan. There are accounts of floods of refugees in 1920 into north-eastern Afghan territories (Holzwarth 1990: 78), which may not have had much effect on GBAO.

In contrast to the period of Russian military rule after 1893–5, distinct economic progress began when the Soviet system was set up in GBAO and, in particular, the infrastructure was improved. In 1928 Sir Aurel Stein writes about Khorog 'where civilizing Russian influence manifested itself not merely in extended cultivation and flourishing orchards but also in electric lighting and a well-frequented Russian school' (1928, II: 878). The first generator had been installed as long ago as in Tsarist times (see Gawrilyuk and Yurotshenko 1987: 119), when the town had only a few dozen, mostly Russian, households. The caravan road from Osh to Khorog via Murghâb had already been widened for horse-drawn carts in 1900. Bridges were now built, and at the end of the 1920s the caravan road was widened to become a proper road for vehicles. The Ak-baîtal valley thus became the highest pass open to vehicles in the Soviet Union. Because of extremely difficult conditions, road connections along the Pyandsh remained poor right into the 1930s, and those in the Bartang valley until the 1950s. There are still no cross-country connections for normal vehicles between Wakhân and Shakhdara, Murghâb and Roshân and Murghâb and Wakhân even today.

Education improved appreciably. In 1925/6 a primary school was set up in a traditional house in the village of Tusyan. By 1930 it already had its own school building. A school was even set up in 1936 in the remote village of Roshorve, and in 1937 a film projector was installed. In Vîr, where fewer than two dozen families lived, a school consisting of two classes was also set up in 1930, and in 1936 a completely new school was established, with seven classes. There were also attempts in the 1930s to offer an education to the Kyrgyz, who at that time were still mainly nomadic. A school was set up in their yurt encampment in Konakurgan in 1935. In fact, the investment in education went so far that in 1936 a teacher was employed just for the four children in Jelondi in the upper Gund valley.

There were, however, considerable inconsistencies in the education system in the whole of central Asia: 'First we studied in the Farsi language, then in Latin and then there was a muddle', an old man told us in Sejd (Roshtkala). What he meant is that in 1928 the Latin alphabet was introduced for lessons in the Tajik language, replacing the Persian one. Finally in 1940/1 the Cyrillic alphabet became compulsory. According to Hayit this latter move was a serious setback for the entire education system, and led to large numbers of the population of Turkestan becoming illiterate again (1956: 316).

Due to the diversity of languages, the consequences were less far-reaching in GBAO, because Tajik, alongside Russian as the important foreign language, did not attract any hostility during Stalin's campaigns of Russification from 1933 to 1938 (see pp. 98–103). In 1931 the Soviets had gone so far in their concessions to the people over education as to allow Shugnî to be used in official school lessons for the first time. A Latinised script was developed especially for Shugnî. Use of that language in lessons was, however, prohibited again in 1937 (see Kreutzmann 1996: 181). Since then only Russian and Tajik have been taught, as well as Kyrgyz in some schools in the Murghâb, although, with a few exceptions, there are native speakers of both these languages only in Khorog and Murghâb town.

The general policy on nationalities continued to foster the inconsistencies in the education system between phases of unusually preferential treatment of (even unimportant) national languages and other phases of strict Russification. At certain times local cadres (i.e. party functionaries) were promoted, only to be replaced again, wherever possible, by Russians. On the one hand the homogeneous Soviet people were promoted (*sovjetskij narod*), but on the other hand ethnic, religious and cultural differences, though reduced to folklore status, were also to be promoted, expressly in order to keep ethnic minorities as part of the Soviet people (see Kreutzmann 1996: 162–164). However, as numerous national cadres were able to stay in top party positions into the 1930s, it can be assumed that they did use the available options to the advantage of the Pamiris.

However, establishing the Soviet system in the Pamir region did not go quite as smoothly as is claimed by Gawrilyuk and Yurotshenko (1987). Revolts against the Russian government which had started before the October Revolution (from 1916 onwards) in many parts of central Asia also continued after the Soviets' victory. The most important movements were the Alash-Orda amongst the Kazaks and the Basmatshi (Basmachi) movement amongst the Uzbeks, Tajiks and Turkmens, which repeatedly involved the Pamir highlands. The repercussions of the Basmatshi Uprising and its defeat were particularly felt in the Murghâb area. Starting in 1918 in the Ferghâna valley, the uprising had spread in 1920 to the Afghan border on the Pyandsh. Well into the 1920s incursions and clashes were recorded in the Eastern Pamirs. While there are no reports of Pamiris fighting for the Basmatshi, it appears that numerous Kyrgyz fought against the Soviets after the dissolution of the Autonomous Republic of Turkestan, the burden of which was substantially borne by the Turkmens. There were still reports of uprisings in Badakhshan and in the Pamirs in 1936 and *c.*1950, seen by Hayit at least as bearing the hallmark of the Basmatshi (1956: 188, note 530).

The background to the Basmatshi Uprising is still obscure. One hypothesis considers the Emir of Bukhara to be the founder of the movement, which continued long after his flight to Dushanbe in 1920 and then to Afghanistan. While the Basmatshi are generally described as bands of robbers in Soviet literature, a clearer distinction is necessary today between the first phase of the uprising from 1918 to 1920/1 and the years that followed. The requisitioning of food from the Islamic inhabitants of the Ferghâna valley had caused a widespread famine in 1918, during which an estimated quarter of the population died. As a result anti-Soviet, mixed groups of partisans, consisting of Tajiks, Uzbeks and Kyrgyz, previously insignificant, became popular, gaining the support of the rural population in their resistance to the Soviet regime.

When, on Lenin's instructions, pressure on the rural population was eased in 1920 (land returned to native people; a huge reduction in requisitioning, which was completely stopped under the 'New Economic Policy' in 1921; reopening of bazaars; reintroduction of Islamic law, etc.), the Basmatshi revolt died down relatively quickly. In the opinion of many Russian and some Western writers it was practically over by 1923, except for a few remaining cells which had established themselves in the Murghâb and other places (see Figes 2001: 750–751). In 1936, however, the chairman of the People's Commissioners' Council of Tajikstan, Rahimbaev, was forced to admit that the movement had only been definitively stamped out in 1935. The last Basmatshi might even have been just refugees or simply bandits, who, after minor campaigns, managed to withdraw across the border between China, GBAO and Afghanistan, which at that time was not as closely guarded as it was later on.

It is clear that some Pamiris opposed the Soviets independently of the Basmatshi movement, in spite of the improvements brought about by the new system. The first elections to Soviet bodies are said to have been carried out only in 1927 – and then only under military protection (Plate 3.7). The period after 1930 in particular is the subject of much contention: on the one hand, Russification and Stalinist violence (especially from 1937 onwards); on the other, material progress and efforts to develop the area. At all events education in the 1920s and 1930s suffered. During

Plate 3.7 Soviet troops entering Pamir territory in order to establish Soviet control (probably about 1930); in Krist (1941: Plate 52).

the period of Stalinist terror from 1937 to 1939 literate adults were persecuted as 'Kulaks' in GBAO by hardline Communist Party members.

It is not clear how far the forced resettlements of Pamiri populations in the cotton-growing regions of western Tajikistan – implemented, according to Kreutzmann, in the late 1920s and early 1930s – can be held to have contributed to latent resentment against the Soviet system (1996: 182; 1999: 96). Our own investigations have only shown that there was migratory movement, from the upper Bartang valley in 1954 for example, because of continuing drought; however, nowhere is there any mention of forced settlement. The people interviewed tended instead to criticise agricultural collectivisation since the 1930s and Stalinist suppression of religion after 1937.

Seasonal migration in search of work is mentioned rather than forced settlements. In the early days of the Soviet system at least, it is clear that no lasting improvements in local living conditions were made. But economic alternatives did lie elsewhere. Ignoring the question of the forced settlements, the Pamiris were tolerated and even encouraged as seasonal workers in the low-lying cotton fields of Tajikistan and Uzbekistan, where production had dramatically increased under the Soviets. Yet people had to walk hundreds of kilometres on foot to the cotton-growing areas in the 1920s, as there was no other transport (see Rickmers 1930: 52).

Most people interviewed describe the years following 1937 until after the Second World War as particularly hard. They coincide with the worst years of Stalin's reign of terror. The literature of the period stresses the purging of the Kulaks and the fight against Islam. On top of that comes collectivisation, which not only caused loss of property but also caused harvests to fail, thus resulting in considerable loss of livestock amongst herdsmen. The losses were caused by attempts to force nomads to settle, as well as to collectivise farming, and this virtually destroyed their traditional method of feeding livestock. In central Asia all three measures led to mass starvation, with hundreds of thousands of refugees and people actually murdered. These measures began as far back as 1934/5, when religious education was prohibited and Islamic functionaries were arrested, and continued in 1935/6 with a purge of party leaders. Measures to secure the 'home front' were only relaxed when the Soviet Union entered into the Second World War.

In GBAO, where amongst the Ismailiyya – apart from their holy places – religious buildings are traditionally inconspicuous, it was mainly the clerics, the *khalifas*, who were affected by suppressive measures. They were forced to hand over all religious works. Continued possession would bring the death penalty, though this did not stop people hiding some of the holy books in safe places. Apparently they were only taken out of hiding in the 1980s, for the most part undamaged.

To what extent 'Kulaks' were murdered in the Pamirs will probably remain a secret, as the children of perpetrators and victims alike are still reluctant to discuss the subject. On the other hand agricultural collectivisation, started in 1929 (according to some sources only in 1933) and forced through and completed between 1937 and 1941, has been openly criticised since 1995. A *kolkhoz* (abbreviation of *kollektivnoe chozjajstvo*, 'collective economy') is equated with the expropriation of the foundations of agricultural life, although the idea at first meant no more than the pooling of means of production, livestock and agricultural products for common use (see Kreutzmann 1996: 172).

Practically the only criticism of the Soviet system expressed by many people interviewed was the collectivisation of land and livestock. One could say that most families did not lose out under collectivisation, in view of the poverty of the time. On the other hand there had been a reduction in absolute poverty, even if in the 1920s, as already said, material conditions had not been revolutionised. By the end of the 1920s many families possessed a cow and a small herd of goats and sheep for the first time. Some additional arable land was in use, and even possessing a small amount of land was a bonus to the people as they were no longer subject to the extortionate taxation from the time of the khanates. People now felt that these gains were likely to be lost in a few years.

In spite of Stalinist intervention, or because there was no chance of getting out of military service, many Pamiris served in the Red Army in the Second World War. Nothing is known about the number of victims of the war, nor about whether Pamiris joined the ranks of about 500,000 deserters who fought as part of the German armed forces against the Soviet Union, most of whom were later killed on Stalin's orders. However, many Pamiris were awarded Soviet medals for their service on the front line, and rose up through the ranks to become officers, which suggests the absence of concerted opposition to the Soviet system during those years.

The Pamiris are indeed aware of the negative aspects of the Soviet system as described here, but these are set against their previous living conditions. Apart from forced collectivisation and the Stalinist excesses already mentioned, which were not considered to be an innate part of the Soviet system, there was very little fundamental criticism. The standard of living had somewhat improved, the despotic rule of the khanates had been removed and in many areas (e.g. communication and employment) there was definite progress. Things which might be seen by an outside observer as inconsistency in the education system, Russification or even colonialist policy directed from Moscow, were of little interest to people who previously had never gone to school.

We must also consider the other part of Badakhshan: to the left (that is, the Afghan side) of the Pyandsh time had more or less stood still during the first two decades of the Soviet era in GBAO. While a subsistence economy had (re-)established itself almost everywhere in Badakhshan during the nineteenth century because of the continuing state of war, the mass of the population did not achieve any economic development beyond subsistence level right up until recent times. On the contrary: because the population had increased, land became increasingly scarce and more and more former smallholders had to work for big landowners because they could not pay off their debts (see Grevemeyer 1982: 176–179). (Permanent) economic migration became another way of securing an existence.

Plate 3.8 A man stands in Tajikistan and looks across the Pyandsh to Afghanistan. Mountain Tajiks are separated by only the 50 m width of the river, with unbelievable consequences (1995).

A negative picture emerges from this period on the whole; that is, the standard of living of people to the left of the Pyandsh continued to deteriorate. If you travelled on the new roads by lorry or bus on the Soviet side you would see, 100 metres beyond the river, villages which were only accessible on foot or by donkey, their mud houses – windowless or with wooden shutters – heated only by meagre amounts of firewood (Plate 3.8). Living conditions inside the houses were no secret either, as the border had not yet become as difficult to cross as in later times. In view of such circumstances, all the many drawbacks of the Soviet system probably counted for little.

Travellers on the 'roof of the world'

The history of the Pamir region also includes the history of its exploration, associated with famous names such as Marco Polo, John Wood, Sven Hedin, Sir Aurel Stein and Ole Olufsen. Less well-known are the early Chinese travellers, the Russian explorers from about 1870, and the Indian surveyors already mentioned in the context of the Great Game, who, prior to Olufsen and Russo-German studies, supply most of the information on the inhabitants of the region from about 1900 onwards. Without writing a complete history of exploration I now want to summarise at least those expeditions of ethnological and ethno-historic relevance in or across the Pamirs.

Geiger and Olufsen both claim that the Pamir region was probably first mentioned in the Awesta, the holy scriptures of the Zoroastrians (probably in the sixth century BC; see Geiger 1887: 3; Olufsen 1911: 9–11). On the other hand, Herodotus and the geographers of the ancient world, possibly with the exception of Ptolemy (second century AD), had no real idea of what the upper Oxus was like; they could at most tell the difference between Amu and Syr-Darya.[25] Eratosthenes, who in about 200 BC summarised all the material available in the ancient world from the era of Alexander the Great and the subsequent century, gave only a rough account of the peoples of the region. Ptolemy names a few places, for example the Vallis Comedarum, which could refer to the valley of Roshân (see Paquier 1876: 37). On the other hand, Severtzov thinks this valley is more likely to be a part of the Ferghâna region (1890).[26] In the context of the Silk Road, there is somewhat more specific evidence in the ensuing years in the already mentioned Han Annals (206 BC until AD 220).

The first European traveller known to actually have crossed the Pamirs appears to have been the Macedonian merchant Maës Titianus, who was probably a contemporary of Ptolemy (see Capus 1890a: 10–11). The only thing known about his journey from surviving records is the actual route, as he named the valleys he crossed. Similarly, the second-known traveller, the Chinese Buddhist priest Fa Hián, who crossed the Pamirs in AD 399, only names his actual route.

The first specific accounts of the Pamiris (for example on irrigation) come from a Chinese envoy called Sung Yün, who crossed the Eastern Pamirs in 519 on the way to India (see Lentz 1931: 186–187). The Buddhist monk Hiouen-Thsang[27] gives the first of these accounts in more detail. His description of his journey between 629 and 645 is available in a comprehensive French translation from 1857, which also has explanations on the Pamir region by writers ranging from Schlaginweit-Sakünlünski (1880: 307–309), Saint-Martin (appendix to Hiouen-Thsang 1857, II: 251–428) to Sally H. Wriggins (1999).[28] According to Saint-Martin, the Chinese Hiouen-Thsang came to Badakhshan on his way back from India, traversed Ki-li-se-mo (= Ishkashim, the old settlement left of the river) and continued through the Pyandsh valley in the Wakhân (In-po-kièn) towards the north-east. The nearby kingdom of Chi-khi-ni is explicitly mentioned in his account, and according to Saint-Martin this is actually Shugnân (op. cit., p. 425). Like most travellers, Hiouen-Thsang then continued past the Sir-i-kol (Sari-kul) and across the passes of the Po-mi-lo (Pamir highlands).

Although his descriptions of living conditions in Shugnân are precise, they already anticipate the negative remarks made about the inhabitants in the eighteenth and nineteenth centuries:

> On récolte beaucoup de légumes et de blé, mais peu de riz. Les arbres des forêts sont clair-semés; les fleurs et les fruits sont rares. Le climat est glacial; les hommes sont farouches et intrépides. Ils commettent le meurtre de sang-froid, et s'abandonnent au vol et au pillage. Ils n'ont aucune idée des devoirs prescrits par les rites, et ne savent pas distinguer le bien du mal. Ils ignorent le malheur et le bonheur à venir, et redoutent les calamités de la vie présente. Leur figure est commune et ignoble; ils portent des vêtements de peau et de laine . . .
>
> (Hiouen-Thsang 1857, II: 205–206)

Some information does indicate that Chi-khi-ni was in fact an area inhabited by Pamiris: the cold climate, the cultivation of wheat and vegetables and, above all, the woollen and leather clothing (cf., even nowadays, our Plate 3.9 on the subject). It is likely that the Shugnânis continued to adhere to their ancient fire religion, in which case they would not necessarily have been familiar with Buddhist rites. Our pious traveller clearly did not like this at all. This information, and other information on violence and hints of fatalism, comes not from Hiouen-Thsang's observations, nor even his experience, but from the people in the Wakhân, who are known to have often been involved in disputes with the Shugnânis.

Arab writers of subsequent centuries are mostly ignored in descriptions of the history of exploration. Khordadbe (about 865), Ibn Dastah, Mas´ûdî (tenth century), al-Istakhrî, Ibn Haûqâl, Mokadassî (about 1000) and al-Idrîsî (twelfth century) deserve at least a mention here, along with the compilers al-Jaqûtî and Abulfîda (thirteenth century), and also Ibn Battûta (fourteenth century), who passed through Balkh on his travels, continuing on through the Hindu Kush (see Geiger 1887: 6). Al-Birûnî also mentions Badakhshan explicitly, and the kings of the part-kingdoms of Shaknán Sháh and Wakhán Sháh (Yule 1872a: 475).

Plate 3.9 Farmer from the Bartang valley wearing the same clothes as described by the Buddhist traveller Hiouen-Thsang in the seventh century (1997).

Marco Polo's journey across the Pamirs is the one most comprehensively described in literature, although in 1933 Lentz investigated whether this journey really did take place. 'Marco Polo was not in the Pamirs', he concludes, basing this on a detailed analysis of the texts and a comparison with the geography of the area. He thinks it is more likely that Marco Polo bypassed the Pamirs on the northern side (1933b: 30), though still managed to gather some authentic information on the country and its people, which means that his account is still useful. What is certain is that Marco Polo was at least in the vicinity of the Pamirs in 1271/2.[29] His description of his itinerary is in fact open to different interpretations:

> And when you leave this little country [Wakhân], and ride three days north-east, always among mountains, you get to such a height that 'tis said to be the highest place in the world! And when you have got this height you find a fine river running through a plain clothed with the finest pasture in the world; insomuch that a lean beast there will fatten to your heart's content in ten days. There are great numbers of all kinds of wild beasts; among others, wild sheep of great size, whose horns are good six palms in length . . . The plain is called *Pamier*, and you ride across it for twelve days together, finding nothing but a desert without habitations or any green thing . . . The region is so lofty and cold that you do not see even any birds flying . . .
>
> (Stein 1928: 859–860)

If Marco Polo really travelled from Wakhân or even Ishkashim towards the north-east, the comments on the altitude could be accurate, but the description of the pasture land is completely exaggerated. The subsequent description of the desert could, however, be of the border area between present-day GBAO and China. The mention of the wild sheep with the big horns, which were called *Ovis Polii* after Marco Polo, does not necessarily only refer to the Eastern Pamirs but would also apply to the Alai valleys. Lentz assumes in fact that Marco Polo went from Ishkashim northwards along the Pyandsh and then in Darwâs crossed the foothills of the Western Pamirs, continuing east through the valley between Alai and Trans-Alai towards Kashgar. Anyone driving through the Alai valley today is more likely to accept the description of the pasture land as applying to this area rather than to the barren country in the upper reaches of the Pamir-Darya or even the Aksu. Agachanjanz, who has studied a total of five alternative routes, considers the question of the actual itinerary to be still unresolved and indeed probably insoluble (1972: 57).[30]

Marco Polo tends to give only brief descriptions of the inhabitants in the area he travelled through, but this is not surprising in view of the huge distances travelled:

> The people [of Wakhân] are Mahometans, have a distinct language, are civilised in their manners, and accounted valiant in war. Their chief holds

> his territory as a fief dependent upon Balashan [Badakhshan]. They practise various modes of taking wild animals.
>
> (Marco Polo 1997: 48)

There are no accounts of journeys over the next 330 years, though there may be yet-undiscovered accounts by Islamic, Christian or Buddhist travellers, or simple merchants. The next known journey is that of the Jesuit Benedict Goës (probably) in 1602 or 1603 across the Pamirs, but this provided no important information. Serious scientific records on the regions of central Asia start about 230 years later with the travels of William Moorcroft (1824, published in 1841) and Alexander Burnes (1832, published in 1835). The latter presents information on Badakhshan based not on direct experience of the area but on information received as a result of enquiries.

A controversial manuscript in the archives of the Topographical Department of St Petersburg might, however, provide the first physical description of the Pamir region made by an eyewitness since that of Goës. A German nobleman is said to have reached the upper Oxus from India in 1806 and to have continued on to Kashgar. In the 1870s, during the Great Game, maps, historical accounts, statistical data and also ethnological information were published in Russia; their authenticity had however already been called into question by Rawlinson in 1875 (pp. 224–231). Apparently no mention of the writer concerned was found in the British Indian archives, although he was supposed to have worked for the government there.

The credit, according to accepted opinion, for instituting real exploration of the Pamirs is given therefore to the Briton Captain John Wood, who explored the Wakhân in 1838 starting from Badakhshan and was the first person to give an account of the headwaters of the Oxus:

> at five o'clock in the afternoon of the 19th of February, 1838, we stood, to use a native expression, upon the Bam-i-Dúniah, or 'Roof of the World', while before us lay stretched a noble but frozen sheet of water, from whose western end issued the infant river of the Oxus.
>
> (Wood 1872: 232)[31]

Wood was the first to describe the country and the people systematically, especially Ishkashim (Afghan Badakhshan) and the Wakhân: he describes religious conditions; the language; the different ethnic groups, including the Kyrgyz; feudal society and its effect on the people, such as slavery, clothing, housing, agriculture, etc. Much remains unverified and it is clear that Wood is first of all an officer and to a much lesser degree a scientist. His information is however highly valuable in the analysis of social change, as 30 to 35 further years elapse before the journey of the pundits Manphúl and Faiz Bakhsh in 1869/70, and the next expedition of any importance to the Pamir region under Douglas Forsyth and Colonel Gordon in 1873/4. With all the time that has since elapsed, we can gain no more than an indirect knowledge of the area by studying Robert von Schlaginweit-Sakünlünski (1856/7; report only in 1880) and the Britons Johnston (1865) and Shaw (report in 1871/2) and Hayward (murdered in 1870, like Shaw a member of the first Forsyth expedition in 1868/9).

The first in a long line of secret 'scouts' in the Great Game were Abdul-Mejid and the pundit Manphúl, whose short account of his journey (before 1867) was only published by Yule (1872a: 440–448). He describes the various stages of the journey and gives some basic information on the people, their religion, language and agricultural products. I do not know of any publicly available account by Abdul-Mejid. Paquier does, however, mention a government report: 'Report printed in the political records of the Indian government' (1861; see 1876: 109).

Paquier also draws attention to the contribution of a merchant named Mohammed-Amin, who explored the upper Pyandsh valley and the Eastern Pamirs in 1868/9 (1876: 111–113). It is likely that the so-called 'Mirza', well-known from British literature, is manifest proof of the longest period spent in the region around the Pamirs after Marco Polo (1868–70). Mirza Sudsha worked for the Trigonometrical Survey and carried out systematic surveys of the terrain between Badakhshan and Kashgar.

The Wakhân was explored by Faiz Bakhsh (Bukhsh) Munshee in 1865 for the first time; as part of the first Forsyth mission; and on further trips in 1867, 1869 and 1870 he travelled through the upper Oxus region for an on-the-spot study (Yule 1872a: 448–473). His remarks also include comments on Kirghiz politics and on more recent Kirghiz migrations.

Further British Indian exploration was carried out by Abdul Subhan in about 1870 with the help of the 'native assistant explorer' Ibrahim Khan, and subsequently after Abdul Subhan by the 'Havildar' Subadar Haider Schah in the Western Pamirs as far as Darwâs from 1870 to 1873 (see Forsyth 1877; Geiger 1887; Paquier 1876). This provided very detailed information on, for example, the number of inhabitants in the areas between Ishkashim and the Bartang estuary. Precise details are also given on the fortresses and troops stationed in the area.

The wide-ranging British Kashgar mission of 1873/4 under Sir Douglas Forsyth produced mainly geographic information, as well as various political complications, and when Colonel T. E. Gordon's book *The Roof of the World* (1876) was published that also provided economic and ethnic information. Gordon, like Forsyth himself, provides geographic information, as well as details on the political and military state of affairs in the context of the Great Game.

The journeys of the famous Russian explorer Fedshenko took place in the years between 1868 and 1871; he explored the Pamirs starting in the north and mostly studied the flora and fauna (see Paquier 1876: 97–105). Kostenko was the first European to reach the Kara-kul lake in 1876 as part of a military expedition against the Kara Kyrgyz of the northern Pamir/Alai, and in 1877 Mushketov began geological research on the Pamir plateau; in 1878 he was joined by Severzov, who had made a name for himself with his exploration of the Tien-shan range of mountains (see Geiger 1887: 10–13; Schlaginweit-Sakünlünski 1880). It is worth mentioning the journeys of Oshanin, who was the first to explore the high-mountain range of the Western Central Pamirs. In 1881 the German-Russian Albert Regel resumed Russian explorations in the Pyandsh valley. He visited the ruby mine in the Gharan district and the hot springs of Garm-Tshashma. Paquier also mentions the contribution of the Russian scholars Veniukoff and Mayef in the exploration of the Pamirs (1876: 91–107).

In the years 1880 to 1882 three Frenchmen undertook a journey. Two of them, Guillaume Capus and Gabriel Bonvalot, independently published wide-ranging books on central Asia and the Pamirs. The book *Du Caucase aux Indes à travers le Pamir* by Bonvalot (1889) is one of the most finely crafted publications on central Asia, but it reads more like an adventure story, apart from occasional passages about the Kyrgyz and the Wakhân. In his book *Le toit du monde (Pamir)* (1890a), Capus goes into much more detail on the region and its history, describing for example Russian and British attempts at expansion. Further publications by Capus deal with the relationship between Chitral and the Pamirs, the Kyrgyz, as well as the Kafirs and the 'Siahpouches' (1889, 1890b, 1890c). Though seldom quoted, the most exhaustive study is a book by a Frenchman, Félix de Rocca, who took part in a Russian expedition to the Pamirs in 1893 to survey the borders and who gives accounts of the Kyrgyz as well as conditions in Darwâs (1896). Some very old original photos are by him.

Lastly, it is worth mentioning the journeys of the Earl of Dunmore and a Major Cumberland, who subsequently published wide-ranging accounts of their travels. However, these only provide information on the Kyrgyz (Dunmore 1893a); Cumberland 1895). At the same time the Russians Ivanov, Bendersky und Putyata were engaged with geographic and hydrographic investigations, which extend Forsyth's explorations. The Danish lieutenant Ole Olufsen was, however, the first to make substantial contributions to the ethnology of the Pamir region, leading two expeditions into the Bukhara area and across the Pamirs in the years 1896/7 and 1898/9. This is the first time that systematic information had been gathered on the living conditions of the Pamiris, and documented photographically (see Olufsen 1904, 1911). Until then exploration of the region had concentrated primarily on its geographic importance and had focused more on landmarks and river systems than on a detailed investigation of living conditions. Bearing that in mind, present-day readers can admire the achievements of von Hellwald ([1875] 1880) and Elisée Reclus (1881) all the more for producing substantial contributions to the general knowledge of the culture of the Pamir region at that early date.

Before the turn of the century exploration of the Pamirs was the monopoly of the British (including native surveyors and geodesists from British India) and the Russians, except for the Frenchmen Bonvalot, Capus and Félix de Rocca. After Olufsen, interest spread to other nations. Although over the following decades Russian, and later Soviet explorers, fill in most of the gaps in scientific knowledge left unresolved by earlier less-detailed exploration, Germans also start to take an interest in the region. As well as climbers in the German–Russian and later German–Soviet expeditions from 1913 onwards (see contributions of von Ficker and Rickmers), Arved von Schultz in particular, led the way in providing geographic contributions (1916), in addition to his purely ethnographic study on the material culture of the Pamiris (1910, 1914); and there was also Wolfgang Lentz, a linguist, who had joined the climbers. The last joint Pamir expedition in which Germans took a substantial part was in 1928 (see Luknizki 1957: 10–11). Subsequent exploration of the Pamirs was continued until 1937 exclusively by Soviet scientists, in a total of 72 separate scientific departments, under the title of 'Pamir-Tajikstan-Expedition'.

Apart from the Germans mentioned above, the ethnology of the region was mainly studied by the Russians Bobrinskij: 'The Ismaili Sect' (1902) and the *Mountaineers of the Upper Pyandsh* (1908); Semenov: *History of Shugnan* (1916); and especially Zarubin (Sarubin): various contributions to regional ethnography and linguistics (1918, 1936, 1937). The Soviet monopoly on research continued after the Second World War. Until the 1990s the border triangle between China, Afghanistan and the Soviet Union had remained closed to foreign researchers, with the exception of a few Eastern European climbers, as it had become extremely sensitive politically with the start of the Soviet–Chinese border dispute.

However, further ethnographic studies were published by Russian and, more recently, Tajik scientists, the most important one being Andreev's ground-breaking publication *The Tajiks of the Khuf Valley* (1953, 1958) and L. F. Monogarova's study *Changes in the Way of Life and Culture of the Iranian-speaking People of the Pamir* (1972), the latter being the first to focus deliberately on change. Because of travel restrictions Western research on the Pamirs had to be restricted to the Afghan part of Badakhshan after the Second World War. Since the 1960s wide-ranging research has been carried out in this area, in particular by German and Austrian scientists and the Frenchman Rémy Dor. Most recently such work was done as part of the German Research Association's special studies on the Pakistan–Afghan region of the Hindu Kush (see Kreutzmann 1996).

4

ETHNOLOGY OF THE PAMIRIS

Up to the beginning of the 1990s, experts on Gorno-Badakhshan had to accept the fact that developing an ethnography of the Pamiris would soon be a task for cultural historians. Yes, one could assume that certain traditional religious elements would continue to be perpetuated over a long period of time. Yet no one could have expected that outdated agricultural, handicraft or irrigation techniques would still play a recognisable role in GBAO. Anyone wishing to predict that these relicts would retain any economic importance for the future would have been laughed out of the room.

The last ethnographic study dealing with the material culture of the Pamiris was published in the 1950s. Even this was only a reconstruction of a local culture and at the most an inventory of the forgotten contents of attics and of the dusty corners of old sheds (see Andreev 1953, 1958). A land in which at the end of the 1960s even the most remote settlements had electricity (Hemmo 1970: 182) seemed to be without doubt well on the road to modernity.

The collapse of the Soviet Union, the independence of Tajikistan and the resulting civil war not only interrupted the supposedly inevitable trend of modernisation but even brought an apparently lost world back to life. In order to be able to survive economically people in many areas had to revive techniques which had been discarded sometimes as far back as pre-Russian times, but anyway before the Second World War. Our sections that deal with agriculture (pp. 103–129), crafts (pp. 130–141) and the household inventory (pp. 172–175), respectively, are thus based on the one hand on previous publications, mainly from between about 1870 and 1930, but also on personal observation of practices during the years 1993 to 2003 such as when speaking of the wooden hoe, threshing with a team of oxen or spinning with a wooden wheel. The often overused 'ethnographic present tense' is therefore to be taken quite literally here. So as to make it possible for the reader to differentiate between the traditional pre-Soviet culture of the Pamiris and current practice, statements still valid for the present will be clearly declared as such.

Indo-Europeans in the Pamirs

The last Soviet census from 1989 gives the following figures for GBAO: 90.9 per cent Tajiks, 5.2 per cent Kyrgyz, 2 per cent Russians and 1.9 per cent other nationalities (the census lists about two dozen such nationalities). Due to the emigration of practically all people not native to the region after the collapse of the Soviet Union, the percentage of Tajiks had risen by 2002 to about 94.5 per cent and that of the Kyrgyz to 5.5 per cent. This chapter primarily deals with the former group. Chapter 5 focuses on the Kyrgyz population of the Murghâb.

Today, there is no doubt that GBAO is part of an independent Tajikistan, at least once the short-lived move for secession that arose after the civil war of 1992–3 was abandoned. However, the term 'Tajiks' poses a problem for the population of the Pamir when one is not strictly speaking of nationality.

In the literature, a variety of terms is used to designate the Iranian-speaking population of Pamir. Lentz reminds us that in the early Russian publications the term 'mountain Tajik' is used to distinguish the Tajiks living in the mountains from those living in the plains (1933: 15). These 'Tajik montagnards' are already known to de Rocca (1896: 255), and this term is particularly used in the first decades of the twentieth century (for example, in Olufsen 1904 and 1911).

Often, the Pamiris were also designated as Galtsha (Galcha, Galtscha). Goës is probably the first to refer to this term when he spoke of *popoli di Calcià* on both sides of the Pyandsh (see Lentz 1933: 11–12). Whether a region or a population is meant remains unclear. The term 'Galtsha' was, according to Krader (1962: 56), Lentz (1933a: 11) and Olufsen (1911: 22), at least formerly known to the Pamiris. Shaw, in his article 'On the Galchah Languages', also believes that the word 'Galtsha', as used by the Turkish-speaking neighbours living around them, was a term in their language that described the Pamiris (1876: 139).

Both meanings given by Krader for the origin of the word (1) from the Iranian *gar* (mountain) or (2) in popular etymology as 'the hungry crow' which retreats to the mountains – are not really convincing. Probably equally false is the meaning given by de Rocca, according to which 'Galtsha' derives from a special sort of shoe (1896: 255). More convincing is the origin given by Tomaschek, who disagrees with meanings such as 'small person' (from the Turkish '*ghalcha*') or a designation of a population based on the words 'rough', 'common' or 'uncultured', and instead bases himself on the local designation of 'mountains' (*gairi, ghar or gor*) (1880: 5). Galtsha would then designate an inhabitant of the highlands, a meaning found also in the above-mentioned designation as 'mountain Tajik'.

Younghusband mentions the term 'Sarikoli' for the Pamiris on the other side of the current Tajik border in the Afghan Wakhân and in China (1896: 274), though this seems to be unknown today.

A further designation, given by Lentz (1929: 149), 'Pamirtadschiken' ('Pamir-Tajiks') already brings us closer to the name the people in the Pamir region give to themselves. Here, we will speak neither of mountain Tajiks nor of Galtshas, but of Pamiris. The assertion 'I am a Pamiri', however, only applies collectively regarding the non-Kyrgyz indigenous population. Moreover the same question would, if posed in the Gund or Shakhdara valley, be answered more specifically with 'I am Shugnî' and along the Pamir-Darya with 'I am Wâkhî'.[1] The foreign or personal designations of course say very little about the ethnic identity of the Pamir population, only that the people themselves do not see themselves primarily as Tajik. To rephrase this statement more clearly, they do not identify themselves with the Tajiks of Kulyab or Khatlon (West Tajikistan).

Still, in the literature the search for the roots of the Pamiris has up until now always begun with the Tajik language group. It is certain that population groups speaking an east Iranian language had lived in the Pamir area before the Turkish expansion and also survived it (see pp. 52–58). However, the earliest one can speak of Tajiks is in the seventh (Krader 1962: 54), eighth (Akiner 1983: 303) or, more realistically, in the ninth century or even only in the tenth, when urban life evolved under the Samanids with their seat in Bukhara (874–999).[2] And that Tajiks alone, under the different designations such as Tát, Tájik, Sert, Galsha or Parsiwán, were the 'founders of civilisation in Central Asia', as Rawlinson says (1875: 244), is also questionable.

Lawrence Krader believes that 'the Tajiks have a record of continuous residence in Central Asia over three millenniums, possibly longer. The present-day people bearing that name, however, were not a single, coherent body during the early part of this period' (1962: 54). This restriction is certainly applicable not only to the early period, but well into the Middle Ages. Barnett R. Rubin reflects the general opinion of scholarly circles when he maintains that Tajikistan had never existed as a territory nor Tajiks as a society. It was simply the Soviets who clumped all speakers of Persian and related languages into the 'nationality' of Tajik. That the Soviet Republic of Tajikistan, founded later on in 1929, was in no way identical with the area of dissemination of the Iranian-speaking population of central Asia has already been mentioned. Moreover, the core habitation areas of Iranian-speaking groups were formerly ruled, not by autochthonous rulers, but by Turkish dynasties. Finally, the inhabitants of Bukhara, Samarkand or even Kabul and other Afghan cities have never called themselves Tajiks (see Rubin 1993/4: 73–75).

Particularly confusing is the contrary fact that for a time the term 'Tajik' did not designate the Iranian-speaking population at all, but was used by the latter to designate Arabic-speaking newcomers who streamed into central Asia in the wake of the Islamic conquests (see Kreutzmann 1996: 42–43):

> In Mittelasien wurden die islamischen Eroberer als Tadschiken bezeichnet, später wandelte sich der Begriff zu einer allgemeinen Benennung für Muslime. Mit diesem gewandelten Inhalt wurde er von den turksprachigen Bevölkerungsgruppen auf ihre Nachbarn angewandt, die zumeist iranischsprachig waren, und etablierte sich als Terminus für die Untergruppen der 'Nicht-Turksprecher'.
>
> (Kreutzmann 1996: 43; cf. Schurmann 1962: 73)

This change in meaning, which, in Bukhara for example, had probably already taken place around the Samanidic period, only evolved in Afghan Badakhshan in the seventeenth century.

In this book, the earlier designations will be applied to the current Tajik territory: thus 'Tajik'[3] will designate that part of the population that speaks an Iranian language, is sedentary and Muslim:

> In medieval times (i.e. the 13th–14th centuries), the word Tadjik (then usually written Tâzik) meant Persian-speaking Muslim, sedentary people, as opposed to the nomadic or semi-nomadic Turks and Tartars. For medieval Muslim historians, the Tadjik were the inhabitants of 'Irân' and the Turks the inhabitants of 'Tûrân'. The *Irân wa Tûrân* duality was not thought of so much in territorial as in cultural and ethnic terms.
>
> (Schurmann 1962: 73)

B. Fragner, quoted by Kreutzmann, also does not equate the term *tajik* as used in central Asia with an ethnic group, but primarily with a socio-cultural category used to describe certain sedentary peasant or urban social strata with an Iranian cultural background (1996: 43). These latter characteristics certainly apply to the Pamiris as well, yet in the literature they are more or less clearly differentiated from the Tajiks with terms such as 'mountain Tajiks', 'Pamir Tajiks', 'galtshas' or, indeed, 'Pamiris'. But as there are obviously no 'ethnic Tajiks', many of the arguments based on a cultural difference between the Pamiris and the Tajiks are no longer convincing. Within the category 'Tajiks' as it was defined above, the Pamiris meet the criteria just as well as the current population of Gharm, Kulyab, Dushanbe, Samarkand, Bukhara or those also answering to that name in Afghanistan.

The fact that some live in mountain valleys and others in plains, or that the one are Shiites, the others Sunnis, is not a fruitful argument – for agriculture, as it is practised in western Darwâs, resembles that of the Tajik core lands more than it does that of the high valleys of the Shakhdara or Pamir-Darya. In the same vein, the population in Darwâs is primarily Sunni, that of Shugnân and the other rayons, except for Murghâb, Shiite.

Much more illuminating is a completely different argument that rests rather less on cultural differences but introduces physical and physiognomic aspects. Although culturally the Pamiris may very well belong to the wide palette of Tajiks, ethnically they represent a completely different unit which has as little to do with any other subdivision of the 'Tajiks' as these possibly have to do with each other. The decisive argument for a representation of the Pamiris as a separate group is that we obviously have to do with an especially old subdivision of the Indo-European subgroup, which remains, despite ethnic mix, independent compared with other populations, and which may be considered separate within the east-Iranian language branch.

A good argument for differentiation between Pamiris and western Tajiks is also the fact that they speak entirely different languages. Alfred Janata points out that the actual Tajik language (that is, the written national language of the state of the same name) is related to the west-Iranian language group whereas the languages of the Pamir population should be attributed to the north-Iranian group (1975: 19). We will go into this aspect in further detail later (see pp. 98–102). In any case, one cannot agree with Olufsen when he designates the population of Shugnân and Wakhân as Tajiks 'without any noteworthy intermixture of foreign elements whilst the greater number of Tajiks in the lowlands west of Pamir are more or less strongly intermixed, especially with Turkish elements' (1904: 217). It is not the amount of intermixture that makes the difference but the fact that we have to do with two different peoples, which do, however, have the same roots.

It is difficult for non-linguists to judge to what extent the conclusions about the inhabitants of the Pamir drawn from linguistic history are justified or not. To my knowledge, the very early interpretation of Tomaschek (1880) has never been disproved. This maintains that the original population of the Pamir, including the Hindu Kush and the western Tarim Basin, represents something between the Caucasian and Masanderanic mountain peoples on the one hand and the Tibetoïd peoples of the Himalaya on the other. According to the author, the autochthonous populations merged with Indo-European groups in the course of the latter's migration around 1,500 BC.

This theory – namely – that the Pamiris are, with or without slight influence from an earlier indigenous population, more or less pure descendants of these Indo-European migrants – can be found throughout the scientific literature and is probably not to be disproved. The surprising thing is that this also confirms that, ever since the Indo-European migrations, the Pamiris have mixed relatively little with other population groups of, say, Turkish or Mongolian origin. Thus, the Pamiris represent 'einen fast "reinen" Typ der europiden Rasse mit allen deren Merkmalen', as Maahs and Bronowski put it (1979: 14). However, the 'europidic' characteristics are not always defined in the same way. In an appendix to Olufsen (1904), Hansen takes the view that the population he found there at the time 'is identical to-day with the widely dispersed Celtic race of Europe' (p. 218). Sir Aurel Stein, on the other hand, describes the Pamiris as 'pure Homo alpinus' (1916: 214; 1928, II: 863, 885; 1933: 281). The purest type is supposed to have survived in Roshân (1928, II: 885) which was known to be historically the least accessible to invaders.

The central European look of the Pamiris diminishes from east to west, or rather from south-east to north towards the Tajik flatlands. Sir Aurel Stein noticed about the people in Wandsh: 'I could well observe the gradual change in physical appearance, houses, ways of living, etc., of the people, bearing testimony to the historically attested conquest of Turki tribes and the influence by the civilisation of the Turkestan plains' (1916: 219). In any case, Olufsen also observed that in the more eastern areas some people 'have a partly Indian stamp of feature' (1904: 58). The people of the Pyandsh valley, on the other hand, were 'doubtless principally unmixed descendants of the old Iranian people, who, as far back as we can trace, have formed the principal part of the population of Transoxania, Turkestan, and the mountains south of the Hindu Kush' (ibid.). This supposedly was especially true for the populations of Ishkashim and Garan.

Modern cultural anthropology is very hesitant in employing the term 'race', and concentrates instead on cultural characteristics. Yet one must still record the fact that, for visitors to central Asia, the contrast between the Pamiris, at least between those specimens considered 'typical' of this people, and the surrounding ethnic groups has always been very noticeable. So it was for us as well, when, in the middle Wandsh valley, in Roshân and also in Ishkashim, we met people, usually women and children, who one would have labelled without hesitation 'German' or even 'Danish' (Plates 4.1, 4.2). Yet at the same time these people are exceptions. More predominant are those whose looks correspond to the dinaric type in Europe (Plates 4.3, 4.4). In the valleys of Yasgulem and Wandsh, as well as in other areas of Darwâs, we met people whose looks would seem to us more typical of Iran – and thus from a place not too far from Pamir – or of Turkey (Plates 4.5, 4.6).

Living conditions have an important influence on the looks even of the middle European ethnic type in Pamir. Even among members of the same family, those living in relatively comfortable conditions, for example in Khorog or in the flatter valleys, have much lighter skin and are less shaped by the rough climatic conditions than those living in the high mountain valleys, such as those of Roshorve (Plate 4.7). These people, in order to survive, must practise agriculture at an altitude of 3,000 m and must graze their herds between 3,100 m and 4,000 m.

In general, we should consider that 'the' Pamiris as pure Indo-Europeans do not exist. Krader is of the opinion that 'of the indigenous populations of Central Asia, there are none at present who are wholly European in appearance' (1962: 53). The quote is not absolutely true, as our pictures from 1995 prove. Yet the very fact that up until the twentieth century slavery was still common in the Pamir, and that important families frequently immigrated there – such as, for example, the Ismaili 'messengers' from Syria in the twelfth and thirteenth centuries who supposedly later became the local aristocracy – must have led to at least a partial mix of the population with non-Indo-European ethnic groups. It is also known that the Pamir has frequently served as a sanctuary for refugees (see Capus 1890a). These included not only farmers driven out of the plains by the Uzbeks but certainly also members of Turkish or Mongolian populations.

Before we come to the language of the Pamiris, it should be mentioned that there are other groups also known as 'Pamiris'. These are ethnic groups typologically related to the Pamiris, for example in north Pakistan (Lentz 1933a: 12–13; Grötzbach 1964: 281) or in China (Kreutzmann 1996: 44, 189–234, 249–52). There, the above-mentioned Sari-kul doubtless represent an Indo-European enclave in a primarily Turkmen settlement area who are quite closely related to the other Pamiris (among other things, they are Shiites). Shaw, among others, mentions similarities in appearance with some Kashimirs (1872: 22). The same goes for people in former Kafiristan (see Capus 1890a: 6), of whom legend says they are descended from soldiers left behind by Alexander the Great.

Plate 4.1 Young fair-haired girls from the middle Wandsh valley (1997).

Plate 4.2 A 15-year-old fair-haired girl from the middle Wandsh valley, in the village of Bunaî (1997).

Plate 4.3 Some girls from the Yasgulem valley, showing a 'Dinarian' physical type (1997).

Plate 4.4 Older women from the village of Porshnev, Shugnân District (1995).

Plate 4.5 Two village elders from the Darwâs area near Kala-i-Khumb with some Iranian and/or Turkish features (1997).

The language of the Pamiris is not the modern Tajik or Darî, even if the latter won ground in the Soviet era as a lingua franca next to and nowadays even superseding Russian. Yet whereas Tajik (Darî) belongs, along with Kurdish, Balutshî and Persian, to the west-Iranian language group, all the Pamir languages belong to the east-Iranian, more precisely to the north-eastern subgroup. The latter is made up of Ossete and Pashtu, as well as the seven different Pamir languages (see Kreutzmann 1996: 41).

Historically, between the second millennium BC and the seventh century AD, Parthic evolved from Middle Iranian, and Middle Persian from Sogdic as well as, among others, Baktrian, both languages thus going separate paths. The Pamir languages have definitely not evolved as far from Middle Persian as, for example, Tajik. Today the differences between the language groups are greater than those between English, French and German. A Tajik from Dunshabe and a Pamiri cannot understand each other any more. This is also true for the different Pamir languages, which have only a small common vocabulary.

According to Lentz (1933a: 20–21), around 1920 the various languages of the Pamir were represented as shown in Table 4.1. This gives us a total of less than 18,500 individuals. As there were in 1910 around 33,000 and in 1926 some 28,924 inhabitants in GBAO (see Table 2.2), less than 3,000 of which were in the Murghâb (Borchers 1931: 55), some 10,000 inhabitants are not linguistically attributed. Could this represent the majority of the population in such places as Ishkashim who no longer speak their ancestral Pamir language, but Shugnî or even Tajik?

Plate 4.6 A farmer from the upper Wandsh valley with an Iranian appearance. This ethnicity is supported by the turban, which is very rare in the Pamirs (1997).

Akiner (1983: 377) gives the numbers shown in Table 4.2 for each ethnic or language group. At that time (early 1980s), there were also 6,930 Kyrgyz as well as 764 Russian, and in all 788 members of other ethnic groups. The latter, and with them their languages, are now almost completely gone from the Pamir. Concerning the figures given by Lentz and Akiner, the smallness of the Ishkoshûmî-speaking population is noticeable. Whereas in Roshân, Shugnân and Wakhân the old native tongues are still used, most of the 25,000 people living in Ishkashim today have abandoned their old language. This could be due to the fact that, according to our

Plate 4.7 Older men from the village of Roshorve showing the effects of rough living conditions in a high mountain area (1995).

informants, Ishkoshûmî is very different both from Vakhî and Shugnî, whereas apart from Wakhî the other languages, Sari-kulî included, are more closely related (Roshânî and Shugnî are also clearly related). Therefore, the inhabitants of Ishkashim have taken to using the lingua franca of this micro region, namely Shugnî.

Yasgulamî also represents a language of its own, whereas in the Wandsh valley as well as in Darwâs, at least, Tajik is the main or even only language used. Yasgulamî is so obviously different from Shugnî and Roshânî that people visiting one another from these different language areas are forced to speak Tajik or Persian. The old language of the Wandsh valley must be considered to have completely died out. In the 1920s, Lentz could find no one who could still speak this Pamir language (1933a: 23–24). Zarubin, who in 1915 met two old people who still knew a few words, was clearly the last visitor to be able to record something of this ancient language.[4]

We are uncertain whether, within the Roshânî language, one should also differentiate between the actual Roshânî along the Pyandsh, a Bartang language, and one spoken only in Roshorve and three other villages in the upper Bartang, or if these only represent dialects. Lentz assumes that 'Shugnî', as a general term, designates the actual Shugnî as well as Roshânî (Rushânî) and the languages of the populations of the Bartang and of Roshorve (written Oroshor) (1933a: 20–25). This does not, however, explain how different each of the four languages (dialects?) are from each other. Our translator (from the core region of Shugnân) told us from

Table 4.1 The various languages of the Pamir, *c.* 1920s

Language	*Geographical area*	*Number of individuals*	*Year*
Ishkoshûmî	Ishkashim	100	1917
Wakhî/Vukh	Wakhân	2,224	1920
Shugnî	Shugnân	7,968	1925
Rushnî	Roshân	6,139	1925
?	Bartang	700	1925
?	Oroshor/Roshorve	333	1925
Yasgulamî	Yasgulem	About 1,000	1920

Table 4.2 Numbers in each ethnic or language group, 1980s

Language/ethnic group	*No. in group*
Shugnî	20,000
Rushanî	7,000–8,000
Wakhî	6,000–7,000
Bartangî	3,000–4,000
Yasgulemî	1,500–2,000
Khufî	1,000–1,500
Ishkashimî	500

Source: Akiner (1983: 377).

Note: Spellings are Akiner's.

experience that she could with confidence understand the people in the Roshân region, but that she was not certain she could translate correctly in the Bartang valley. There, our conversations were carried out in Shugnî, which all dialect-speakers spoke well.

The linguistic border between the dialects of Roshân and Shugnân (that is, Shugnân in the geographical sense) lies at the village of Khûf, which still belongs to Roshân. However, it would be incorrect to say that its inhabitants use a separate language (see Akiner 1983: 377) for one must remember that all the languages mentioned above may be pronounced differently from one village to the next.

Within the core region of Shugnân (villages along the Pyandsh river, Khorog, Gund valley and Shakhdara), different dialects of Shugnî are spoken. In the upper Gund valley, the influence of the resettled population from Sares (see Chapter 2) who brought their own language from the upper Bartang or the Oroshor language area (today the area around Roshorve) with them is recognisable. Supposedly, an entirely different dialect is used in Shakhdara than in Khorog and along the Pyandsh.

Lentz had already correctly remarked in 1933 that the Pamir languages ('Pamir dialects') were retreating in favour of Persian (in fact Tajik) (1933a: 31). This retreat is partly due to the fact that, with the exception of a short Soviet trial period from 1928 to 1937 during which Shugnî was used in lessons (with a Latin alphabet?), none of the Pamir languages has their own alphabet or literature; instead, Persian is used for written communication.[5] However, most people, especially women and children, spoke no Persian. Lentz reports that in Oroshor (Roshorve) Persian was used in a more or less broken form at family feasts; that is, at weddings, during illnesses (religious-magical ceremonies are probably meant) and at funerals (1933a: 34–36). It is curious that the children themselves obviously barely understood the rhymes they recited in Persian to the German linguist.

In this context, the problem of traditional written education is apparent. Olufsen mentions wandering teachers (*mullah*) who occasionally taught the children, as well as professional teachers in the larger villages. Apparently, the lessons were already taught in Shugnî – 'in these schools the children learn to read the language of the country, sometimes also a little writing and arithmetic . . . The language the children learn to read and write is Shugnan (the Tajik)' (1904: 138–139). Therefore, whoever went to school around 1900 could write their own language, at least in Shugnân. Olufsen explicitly points out that, in Wakhân, the children were not able to use their own language in school and therefore, if they didn't go to school, were fluent only in Vakhî.[6]

In more recent times both Tajik and the Pamir languages have been influenced by Russian. The only available study concerns Tajik, yet it showed that a great part of the Marxist vocabulary and that of Soviet political culture was taken over from the Russian, as were terms having to do with modern economy and communications. On the other hand, medical, biological and mathematical terms have remained mostly untouched by foreign influences due to the importance of these fields in the Middle Ages (Bacon 1966: 196). The vocabulary lists for the Shugnî and Wakhî given in Hjuler show that, as in all cultures influenced by Islam, Arabic terms have crept into common speech and not merely in areas concerning religion. That religion (*dîn*) or prayer (*salat*) should have come from the Arabic is to be expected. But the words for the cardinal points (for example south = *jenû'b*, east = *mashrik*), midwife (*dâya*) or bride (*arôs*) also come from Arabic (see Hjuler 1912).

Finally, for the sake of ethnographic correctness, it should be mentioned that older Pamiri informants do not accept the designations for the populations and regions of Pamir that are given in all the publications. Many terms which we know are russified. In fact, the following designations are correct: Pamir = Pomêr, Pamiri = Pomerê (pl. Pomeriên), Shugnî = Shugnenê (really correct Khugnenê, pl. Khugneniên), Bartangî = Bartangê, Ishkashimî = Ishkashimê, Darwâs inhabitants = Darwosê, Wandsh inhabitants = Wandshê, and Yasgulemî = Yasgulemê. The Murghâb also has a different name among the Pamiri – namely, Marghow or Murghow, and the inhabitants are called Marghowê (pl. Marghowiên).

Economy

The Pamiris' traditional means of subsistence is agriculture, which is replaced by herding only at the highest altitudes of the valleys. Farmers also have animals, if only because they need draught oxen – but they play a secondary role in their subsistence. Equally, the herdsmen primarily survive on agricultural produce, which they receive in trade against their livestock or animal products. Below 3,000 m the farmers almost everywhere also grow fruit, but this occupation extends beyond subsistence in only a few villages. Crafts and trade have always had comparatively little importance in GBAO and are only practised in a limited way. Mining and industry are almost entirely absent in the traditional economy.[7]

Traditional agriculture and cultivation methods

In the Pamir, as a general rule, agriculture predominates below 3,000 m. At higher altitudes, up to 3,500 m, and in a few scattered fields in protected valleys (supposedly even up to 3,820 m – see Geiger 1887: 51), wheat and barley are mostly grown, as well as a few cooking herbs. In Jelondî, in the upper Gund valley at 3,500m, the risk of harvesting only headless stalks is about 50 per cent or higher, so that there only luck allows one's own grain to be plentiful enough to be baked into bread. The harvest usually only serves as a dietary supplement for livestock. In 1998, 450 kg of wheat was harvested from 250 kg of seed and 80 kg of potatoes from 20 kg of seed potatoes. Only those who can afford to fertilise their fields – that is, those who do not need all the dung for heating, and who can protect their fields from the icy wind with walls – can achieve yields of two to three times the quantity of seed used. We know that a hundred years ago the land there was not cultivated; in fact, no one even lived there permanently. Only in Wakhân along the Pamir-Darya do good farming conditions exist at this altitude.

The most important cultivated plant in Pamir is wheat, after which come barley and legumes such as peas, beans (Vakhî: *baqla* = horse beans) and lentils (Vakhî: *mojuk*). Among the formerly widely distributed kinds of cereals are millet (Vakhî: *arzen*) (Olufsen 1897a: 338; Shahrani 1979a: 9), rye in Shugnân and Roshân, and, especially in Darwâs, maize.

Von Schultz reports that mustard seed was also sown, as well as hemp or flax (Vakhî: *zaghir*), both for oil. Mustard oil was used to soak pine torches for use in lighting (1914: 24). Lupine (*patuk*) is mentioned for Wakhân (Shahrani 1979a: 9). The fodder plants (alfalfa and clover) were always important and in some (sometimes amazingly high) areas also tobacco (for example in Roshorve). Whereas Olufsen rarely saw tobacco smoked in 1900, but merely the leaves used for decoration, it is nowadays often chewed and sometimes smoked. Potatoes appear to have been introduced by the Russians – in Wakhân probably only in the 1970s (on the ambivalence of their new role in the present, see Chapter 9).

One must also count among the cultured plants for Darwâs the presently no-longer-cultivated cotton, known in central Asia since Antiquity, as well as other subtropical plants such as melons, pomegranates and guava.

Almost everywhere, sparse alluvial soil serves as the basis for agriculture. There are basically two types: first, the old river terraces found along the Pamir-Darya, Pyandsh, Gund and Shakhdara that in some places are high above the current flood level. The material in the terraces comes from quite far away and is relatively fine, so that the earth is quite fertile. However, irrigation is difficult in these areas, for long canals are required. Second, in the narrower cleft valleys (parts of Bartang, Pyandsh, Wandsh), rubble cones resulting from silt deposits from smaller tributaries are used for agriculture (see Plates 2.6 and 2.13). Due to the coarser material, the quality of the earth is not as good but irrigation is much easier. One simply taps the tributary itself (see von Schultz 1914: 23).

Traditionally, an agricultural village relies on three to four different categories of land, which to some extent still applies today. The best land lies right next to the houses and is primarily used to cultivate vegetables. Around the core of the village or, depending on the site, next to it are the fields and orchards. Often several kilometres away and on the slopes of side-valleys are less productive areas, usually used for barley and occasionally for wheat. These areas are often just at the limit of productivity, barely yielding double the amount of seed. The fourth category includes the good village grazing lands (as opposed to wasteland), which can sometimes be quite scattered and distant.[8]

Vegetable gardens, formerly also important for the daily menu, played an especially important role during the Soviet era as they were the only places that could be cultivated privately. The owners of the 500 to more than 1,000 square metres did so intensively. 'The gardens (*gulistan*) are situated near the houses, and are irrigated by small channels which lead the water to the fruit trees, vegetables and flower beds', writes Olufsen on the subject (1904: 119). Today all the kinds of vegetables for which seed is available are cultivated. Even as late as 1900, potatoes, cucumbers and tomatoes were supposedly only known to the Russian troops (von Schultz 1910b: 253). Such vegetables are now widely distributed in the middle and lower altitudes and are even conserved, as are cucumbers, pumpkins and carrots (salted).

The produce planted in the gardens can be divided into three groups: the first of these consists of the classic vegetables, including, apart from those already mentioned, onions, garlic and different sorts of radishes. The Darwâs area also grows eggplant, zucchini and melons.[9] The second group is made up of cooking herbs which are used extensively in soups, including spring onions, leeks, parsley and large amounts of dill. Mint is also occasionally cultivated here. In the third part of the garden, various food staples are cultivated, especially potatoes, wheat, corn and rye. This represents an innovation that was encouraged when supplies of these staples became scarce. Gardens were, especially during the Soviet era, absolutely the most valuable pieces of land, at least from an individual point of view. Although gardens often make up only 2 to 5 per cent of all available land, one-fifth of agricultural production occurs in them. But as the gardens were not a priority for the kolkhozes and sovkhozes, despite their importance, cultivation methods have not changed since the Middle Ages. Neither mechanised equipment nor sprinkler systems nor chemical fertilisers are known. The earth is worked with a plough (see pp. 107–108) when larger areas have to be tilled. Otherwise the spade and hoe are used (see Andreev 1958: 44). Each potato is individually harvested with a spade or plough (Plate 4.8), a chore that is shared by men and women.

Plate 4.8 Women from the village of Porshev (Shugnân) harvest potatoes with a hooked implement (1997).

Despite their poverty, the Pamiris have always enjoyed flowers, for which they dedicate at least a few metres of valuable ground around the house. Olufsen names hollyhocks, hemp, mallow, marigolds, yellow carnations, fox-tail and yellow tobacco, and emphasises that 'the caps of the Pamiris or their turbans are often adorned with flowers stuck into them' (Olufsen 1904: 121).

Agriculture has also always been very intensive in Pamir, at least in the areas near the village. Kreutzmann, who assessed Russian sources from 1902 and 1904, arrives at an average size of 2.35 ha for the plots which, with an average household size of about ten people, gives an area of only 0.23 ha per head. The smallest plots were in Roshân, with an average of 1.56 ha each, and the largest in Wakhân with 3.81 ha. Yet the decisive consideration was not the size but the climate and the quality of the land. This definitely favours the smaller farms in Roshân compared to those in Wakhân (1996: 170–171). In all, only 2.6 per cent of all families were declared 'rich' with over 8.72 ha,[10] but 74.8 per cent were declared 'poor' with less than 4.36 ha. In order to arrive at the actual, very low average, one can imagine that many families owned very little land at all. However, only 2.8 per cent were categorised as entirely landless (ibid.).

The productivity mentioned above for Jelondî refers to an area at the upper threshold for harvests, where agriculture does not in fact make any economic sense. According to Russian studies, climatically favoured Roshân produced eight times its seed in 1903, Shugnân six times, and in the distinctly higher Wakhân four or five times (Chalfin, quoted in Holzwarth 1990: 151). Yet microclimatic conditions and the above-mentioned land quality were decisive factors for the actual harvest of each family. Whereas in Tusyan at altitudes of 2,450 to 2,650 m, on private garden land for example, a harvest of 20 to 30 times the amount of seed planted was gathered in 1998 (the conditions may, due to the lack of chemical fertilisers, be compared with those prevailing in Europe a hundred years ago); in the same village, on remoter new land on a steep slope, only 2.5 times the amount of seed was harvested. Some fields even gave only straw. Generally, the Russian figures should be considered with caution as the farmers, with an eye on taxes, certainly gave numbers that were too low. These typically reflected yields from fields lying at very high altitudes and/or in bad years. Traditional agriculture has, according to older men in Tusyan (Shakhdara), Wîr (Gund) or Namadgut (Ishkashim), always produced more than ten times the seed even in pre-Soviet times.

The amount of seed sown is indirectly given as a traditional land measurement. Von Schulz summarises the more important grain measures: the main measure is, according to him, the greater *por* at about 15 kg wheat grain. A greater *por* consists of two middle and four lesser *por* or 12 *dsham*, the latter being the amount of grain that fits into a cap. The cupped hands make 1/48 of a greater *por*. Two and a half greater *por* are sown on a *samin* or *lup-undr*, which is divided into two smaller *undr* or four *chidgor*. According to von Schulz, a middle-class family around 1910 owned about 20 *samin* of land (1914: 24–25). On the basis of the numbers we can calculate that for 20 *samin* 50 *por* or 750 kg of seed was needed, so that in Roshân, based on the Russian figures, an average of 6,000 kg of wheat

– based on our own information more than 7,500 kg of wheat – was harvested. However, less than 23 per cent of the households obtained such a large harvest. What is more, not all the land was planted with wheat, as fruit trees and gardens must be subtracted from the total agricultural area.

Apart from intensive farming, land poverty also forced the cultivation of areas situated far away from settlements. In such places, summer houses were often erected in earlier times where the family stayed from planting-time at the end of April/beginning of May until the harvest in August or September. While in Soviet times the only buildings outside the village were herdsmen's huts, in the last few years summer homes have once more been erected so that maximum use can be made of available land.

The beginning of the agricultural year depends on altitude. Whereas in the highest parts of a valley, ploughing and sowing do not take place until May, around Khorog and along the Pyandsh in Shugnân and Roshân, work begins in March when it still freezes at night.

Earlier, before mechanisation following the Second World War, wooden ploughs were used (*plug*), as Andreev illustrates in his monograph on Khûf (Roshân) (1958: 41). Unfortunately, the author usually gives only the Russian terms for each component and not the Pamiri. After 1992/3, the old ploughs were taken out of the mothballs they had been laid into for so long and new ones were built, based on older examples. Plate 4.9 shows a wooden hook plough with an iron share in the shape of a shoe slipped onto the sole in front. Ploughing is done with a team of oxen, which well-to-do families own themselves. Poorer families either have to

Plate 4.9 A young man using a traditional wooden plough. It is obvious that the man has only a little experience with this uncommon technology (1995).

pool their animals, or a group of neighbours (= *tabaq*; also *amtabaq*) keeps up one team. The team is kept in a private barn, but each family in the group contributes a certain amount of fodder or must serve as herdsmen during the summer.

After ploughing, the earth is broken up and levelled with a harrow board, which is also pulled by oxen (see Kussmaul 1965b: 48). Olufsen reports that larger clumps of earth are broken up individually with a truncheon (1904: 114). The banks to form the irrigation ditches (*wez*) are raised up afterwards with the help of a wooden board hitched to the draught oxen.[11] Where necessary, a spade (*zigandor-phaî*) can also be used. As the fields are irrigated using both the surface flooding and furrow methods, they must sometimes be cut through with ditches. In the first case the whole surface is sown, in the second only the mounds (*waltsh parra*) between the ditches. If we have observed correctly, nowadays mostly potatoes and legumes are irrigated using irrigation furrows whereas grain and fodder are irrigated using the surface method. In the latter case, the surface must also be divided into irrigation squares formed by raising small banks around their perimeter (see Andreev 1958: 67). On steeper slopes, ploughing is done along the contour lines, thus making it necessary to use the ditch irrigation method.

In Soviet times, when motorised pumps could be used for many things and water consumption was not a problem, all the larger areas were ploughed, harrowed and finally furrowed with a tractor. It is understandable that the surface was rarely well levelled, thus resulting in huge water loss. Today, when water has to be supplied almost entirely by gravity from the river, farmers are much more careful that the fields are well prepared. This entails much more work that was at first too great a burden for many farmers. Many had never worked in the fields before or else, as simple agricultural workers, had never had to carry out complex operations; they had previously simply been used as manual labour by the kolkhoz engineers. We therefore often observed farmers at their wit's end trying to control the water that flowed everywhere around the landscape except into the irrigation ditches they had dug. This leads us to suggest that the often-mentioned lack of water does not, in many villages, reflect a general lack of water resources but rather a lack of water in the fields.

About a hundred years ago the fields were only occasionally fertilised. Whoever had enough land let the earth rest every two years (see von Schultz 1914: 25). Due to the general scarcity of wood, cattle dung was primarily used as fuel and thus was not available as fertiliser. Thus, fertilisers were restricted to incidental compost, old straw, chicken droppings and some goat dung, and – as later usage shows – were mostly used on the vegetable gardens.

At the beginning of the agricultural year, barley is sown first, then legumes and wheat last (see von Schulz 1914: 25). Supposedly, the Pamiris formerly treated their sown fields with little care and did not even bother to keep grazing horses and cows away from the sprouting seeds. On the other hand, von Schultz also reports how much trouble was taken to scare the birds away from the fields while the crop was ripening (1914: 25–26). We could, in the hard times from 1995 to 1998, observe several techniques used mostly by children to protect the harvest by day and during the night. Thus, sticks were used to drum on empty oil cans or the children ran with slings through the fields to occasionally frighten away a flock of birds with stones (Plate 4.10). However, we had the impression that more grain was 'threshed' by the stones than was eaten by the birds. Luknizki reports that tambourines were used at night to protect the harvest, causing much disturbance (1957: 235). Finally there are also scarecrows made out of straw, or wooden frames hung with rags or else sticks with banners. Raunig further reports that catapults ('Kugelbögen') (see p. 176, Plate 4.36) were used to protect the harvest (1978: 283), to which von Schultz, though, gives a range of only 25 m (1914: 44). Much more effective are the slings, with which even small girls can still cover a field 50 m away.

In Soviet times, large areas were harvested using a threshing machine, in some areas even with a combine harvester. Smaller land units were harvested with the Russian scythe. This method of harvesting is known to lose a lot of grain. Traditionally, the Pamiris only had a relatively thin sickle curved through a right angle which, according to von Schultz, was brought in from Russian Turkestan at the turn of the nineteenth century. We were told, however, that the forms common in the Pamir are typical for the area even now. They correspond to the *zirf* illustrated in Andreev (1958: 44, fig. 8).

Plate 4.10 A young girl in Namadgut (Ishkashim District) using a sling to drive birds away from ripe wheat fields (1996).

Harvesting, before the Soviet era as again today, no doubt suffers especially from insufficient manpower. Based on our experience in Egypt, one person needs about 17 days to harvest one hectare of wheat (see Plate 4.11). Even today, all the members of the household, even the elderly and the children, have to help out. In some villages, especially in Roshân, part of the masculine population is on the road for weeks during this period to work in fields far away from the villages. In this case they complete the full harvesting cycle at the field and only come back when the threshed and winnowed wheat has been packed into sacks. The grain harvest is a welcome opportunity to lend a neighbourly hand (*tabaq*-groups). Such work is begun by several neighbours on one field and goes on daily until all the fields belonging to group members have been harvested.

After the harvest, most fields used to remain unploughed and served as stubble pasture. An intermediate harvest was apparently only introduced by the Soviets, and then only at the lower altitudes.

Processing of the harvested ears and straw was formerly, and is again since the collapse of mechanised agriculture, strictly manual work. The ears are nowadays, as in the Middle Ages, set out on the floor and threshed with a team of oxen. This is achieved by prodding four to six oxen round in a circle (Plate 4.12). Ears are added continually with pitchforks. According to our estimates, it takes about eight hours for enough ears to be threshed to fill a 100 kg sack with wheat grain. If 2 hectares of wheat were sown, then after the 34 days needed for one person to cut

Plate 4.11 Older women in the village of Tusyan (Shakhdara valley) cutting wheat with sickles (1997).

Plate 4.12 With all sovkhoz machinery out of order, a boy from the Shakhdara valley leads a team of five oxen round a threshing floor in order to thresh wheat (1996).

it, assuming 15 quintals yield per hectare, another 30 days are needed for threshing alone. The work lasts so long, the farmers in the Shakhdara valley explained, that it starts freezing again at night before all the grain is in the barns. That means that six weeks after the harvest the people are still occupied with the follow-up work. Using a similar technique, the legumes such as beans, peas or lentils are threshed. When the harvest is small, a threshing stick is put to the same use. As a curiosity, it should be mentioned that in 2003, during a visit in the Tajik Gharm valley, we often found ears spread out on the main road. There, the cars driving through took over the threshing.

Yet even after all this there remains important, physically strenuous work to be done, namely the winnowing of the threshed grains to separate them from the chaff. A day with strong wind is needed for winnowing, so that one must often wait a long time before the cleaning process can finally take place. For three to four days strong young men throw the grains in the air with the winnowing forks (*zekund*; see Andreev 1958: 41, figs 5–7), until the estimated 30 quintal have been cleaned (Plate 4.13).

Naturally, the grain threshed by oxen on outdoor threshing floors is at first still full of impurities, although we did not observe that shovels were still used, as they had been a hundred years ago, to catch the oxen dung before it fell on the threshing floor (see von Schultz 1914: 26). Pebbles and small clumps of earth also get mixed into the grain so that it cannot be immediately poured into sacks. Various impurities are first removed using sieves, work done mostly by women using large sieves

Plate 4.13 Men from Tusyan (Shakhdara valley) use *zekund* (wooden pitchforks) to separate spelt grain from its straw in the wind (1997).

(Plate 4.14). Occasionally, part of the grain is winnowed again, the women letting it fall from a shovel in strong wind (Plate 4.15), or from their hands into baskets. For 30 sacks of wheat, another 15 days is spent in this work.

Only once this last step is finished can the grains be filled into sacks and stored in the granaries (see p. 173, Plate 4.35). This represents one last wearisome step, for one man with a donkey needs another five whole days to transport ten sacks which he harvested in a side-valley 15 km away from his home. The poor have to carry their sacks using a carrying frame strapped to their backs, something we have been able to observe occasionally within the last few years. In Langar in 1997 we helped a farmer drive some 70 kg of wheat 14 km to his home, which he would otherwise have had to carry the whole way. If we tally up all the work that our sample household, having sown 2 hectares of wheat in the year 1997, must do (concurring with figures from 1900, the epoch of Olufsen and von Schultz) we arrive at a post-harvest work programme of some 90 days per person in the household or three days of work per 100 kg sack of wheat.

There remains one more aspect of farm work that has been completely ignored in earlier publications: choosing the seed. For the farmers do not simply set aside some sacks from the harvest at random to be used for seed, but pick out, as early as possible during the cleaning of the grain, the better (larger) grains by sifting, to store them separately for the next sowing season. Nowadays, this is done with much more care than in Soviet times, or even before that.

To be able to bake wheat, barley or rye into bread one still needs to grind it. There is in this respect both in Pamir and in the surrounding regions (Afghan

Plate 4.14 A woman in Sejd (upper Shakhdara valley) cleans the wheat in a soil-filled sieve (1997).

Plate 4.15 A young woman from Roshorve (Bartang valley) cleans the wheat in a final stage before it is stored as bread grain (1997).

Badakhshan and in the Kafir region of north Pakistan) a very old tradition of village water mills, of which there are still a great number in GBAO:

> Jedesmal stehen in der Nähe der Siedlungen an den Bächen entlang Reihen solcher kleinen Mühlen. Jede Sippe hat ihre eigene Mühle . . . Die Mühlen sind aus Holz gebaut und etwa 2,50 × 2,50 × 2,70 m groß. Das Mühlrad liegt horizontal und bewegt 2 Mühlsteine gegeneinander. Ein darüber aufgehängter konischer Wollsack enthält das Getreide; eine selbsttätige Vorrichtung und eine Rinne sorgen für die Zuführung der Körner.[12]
>
> (Voigt 1933: 84)

What Martin Voigt observed in Pakistan in 1928 (see extract immediately above) may, with but few restrictions, also apply to the mills (*khadurdsh*) in the Pamir valleys. Only there the mill building is of clay and instead of the sack there is a wooden funnel in which the grains lie (Plate 4.16). The mill is powered by a paddle wheel (*tsharkh khona*) which lies horizontally in the water below the millstone and turns in the current. The upper millstone (*tîrğîr*) is linked to the paddle wheel and revolves, whereas the lower millstone (*bîrğîr*) is stationary and embedded in the floor.

The water current is not only obtained by the natural slope of the canals but is also enhanced by down pipes. These direct the water of the mill streams, usually

Plate 4.16 A man from the Ishkashim District (Wakhân valley) operates a small traditional water mill. Our plate shows the upper millstone and the wooden funnel with the refilling mechanism at the lower end (1997).

some 3 metres deep, into the 'turbine canals'. An elevation drawing of a mill from the Afghan Wakhân can be found in Patzelt and de Grancy (1978: 235–238, fig. 10).[13] The technique is also described there. A good drawing which can be proved to relate to the mills in GBAO is from Andreev (1958: 89). In his fig. 1 the mechanism allowing the grain to flow from the funnel to the millworks becomes evident. A small stick hangs on a string which leads through the supply opening underneath the wooden funnel. Here, the string is linked to another which keeps the closing mechanism shut when the mill is at rest. If the wheel begins revolving faster, the stick hits the upper millstone and receives a jolt, which then pulls on the other string somewhat, thus allowing some grains to pass. The faster the wheel turns, the quicker the jolts follow one another and the more grain is freed for milling.

The speed of the wheel may be controlled by using an elevating mechanism (*shargo*) to raise or lower the paddles in the water. This requires much strength from two men, who raise or lower the entire frame either entirely with physical strength or with the help of levers. Stones of different sizes serve as supports for the wheel: smaller ones if the wheel should be low in the water and larger ones to keep it as high as possible.

The mills are mentioned for the first time by de Rocca (1896: 232) who designates them by the local term *teguerman*. The performance was of seven *batmans* in 24 hours, although the measure is unfortunately not explained. Our enquiries in 1998 revealed that only 70–100 kg of flour could be ground in a 14-hour day; this, however, is due to insufficient grasp of the technique. Similar mills, for example in Egypt 50 years ago, could grind 250 to 400 kg of wheat a day. The important thing is the quality of the flour, which is specifically described by Olufsen: 'the flour is not at all badly ground, even from a European point of view' (1904: 122), which we can definitely confirm.

For a while the mills of GBAO were, with a few exceptions, out of use after modern electric mills were introduced in the 1950s or when grain was delivered from other parts of the Soviet Union in the form of flour. Since 1995 those mills still in sufficiently good condition have been rehabilitated, often by cannibalising the more derelict structures. Thus, five mills are once more in use in Roshorve today. A problem over the medium term is that no one now knows how to make millstones.

Traditionally, the mills belong to private individuals. Formerly, a miller ground for third parties in return for payment, which was a certain percentage of the grain to be milled. Today, milling is generally free for neighbours. To what extent the current stand of not taking anything in return for milling ('in times of need, we cannot take anything for the grinding of flour!') will persist is questionable.

A healthy diet would hardly be possible in Pamir from only the produce of the fields. Vitamin requirements alone call for dietary complements. Fruit represents an important contribution – in conserved form for the long winters. In the highest altitudes of Pamir, up to a little over 3,000 m, apples and apricots are cultivated. In Wakhân the only fruits apart from wild berries are basically apricots. In the middle altitudes, such as Khorog (around 2,200 m), a few grapes already appear next to the dominant apricots and apples, as well as plums, cherries and pears. Mursajew [1956] found the grapes served in the village of Shidz (altitude of 1,900 m) still rather sour.

Mulberry trees were formerly used to support sericulture. The fruits were, next to apricots, often the most important source of vitamins in the middle altitudes (and are once more since the crises of 1992/3!). In times of need, bread used to be baked from dried mulberries, or else these would be mixed in with the dough (Plate 4.17). De Rocca gives the name *tout-talkan* for mulberry powder (1896: 262). Tout (*tût*) is the Arabic word for mulberries. Black mulberries, white ones when these aren't available, are eaten dried or used ground as a sugar substitute. In Roshân and some other places, a mild spirit is distilled from mulberries.

In the middle and lower altitudes another important tree is the walnut, whose nuts are eaten dried or else pressed for oil. The oil yield, representing 20 per cent of the weight of the nuts, is rather low due to primitive pressing techniques. Walnuts are especially useful, for they store and travel well and thus make ideal travel food. Below 2,000 m we also found the first figs, which are therefore mostly to be found in Darwâs (see Mursajew 1956: 272).

The 'lowest points' of the Pamir around Darwâs, still at an altitude of over 1,600 m, are already mentioned as a favourable region in earlier publications. Olufsen even speaks of the region as a 'hot-house' (1911: 117). Here, wine grapes

Plate 4.17 Woman from Shidz (Roshân) preparing mulberry flour from dried mulberries by pounding them on a rock (1997).

predominate, and the ranks of the above-mentioned trees are swelled by peaches, almonds, pistachios, plums and the aforementioned figs, as well as by subtropical fruit such as pomegranates and guavas.

The Pamiris – and the Tajiks west and east of the Pamir in general – are known for being good fruit growers (see Grötzbach 1964: 286). In Afghanistan, fruit from Badakhshan was known and appreciated even in the markets of Kabul.

In order to survive long winters in the high mountain valleys, extensive food storage is necessary. Apparently, sun-drying is the only traditional method known for conserving fruit. The making of preserves goes back to Russian influence and only imposed itself in the Soviet era. A basis for its introduction was the availability of sugar in large quantities, which was not available before 1900 and again until four or five years ago.

Our Plate 4.18 from 1996 shows an old farmer setting out thin apple slices, previously cut by the women, on old sacks. The uppermost row had been set out two days previously. Formerly, mats were used to set the goods out to dry, or else they were simply put on stones. In all, the people do not make much of an effort to dry fruit properly. Thus, only especially good apricots were pitted or apples laid out as rings without the core or skin. The dried fruit thus has a commensurately low value, and formerly rarely came onto the market. Even today it can be found in only small amounts on the market of Khorog. However, pains are taken to preserve the fruit from impurities. Apricots and mulberries, which are harvested ripe and burst easily, are often shaken down from the trees by men using sticks.

Plate 4.18 Older man from Khorog laying out apple slices on old sacks to dry them in the sun (1996).

But clean spreads are previously prepared so that the fruit does not fall onto the ground.

Even in the fruit harvest, people generally give themselves little trouble. Apples and pears are also shaken from the trees so that they are bruised and go bad the very next day. Why this loss of value is accepted, even in goods that we found offered in the last few years on the Khorog market, is unexplainable.

Animal husbandry of the Pamiris

What Nazif Shahrani remarked for Wakhân – 'There are non-Wakhi pastoralists in the Wakhan ecological zone independent of their agricultural counterparts' (1979a: 63) – also applies to the few other Pamiri villages that primarily breed livestock in other districts. Vice versa, farmers show a predominantly 'paleotechnic ecotype, where even poorer agriculturalists keep a few cattle, sheep, and goats for traction, transport, milk, fleece, fuel, manure for their fields, or cash', not to mention, in some cases, for taxes. 'In the lower valley, the animals are generally kept in the agricultural settlement year round and are pastured nearby with a communally hired herder' (ibid.). In the higher altitudes, without such good pastures and where the limited fertile land is needed to support human subsistence, the animals are led to summer pastures that are sometimes quite far away, so that it is possible to speak of a transhumance similar to the alpine economy. In the case of Roshorve, the pastures lie nowadays near Aktash, some 140 km away.

Olufsen (1904: 117–119) reports on the different domestic animals of the Pamiris. Thus, around 1900, there were two species of cattle, a smaller one with short horns and a larger one with larger, curved horns. Both supposedly gave little milk, which is also true of the majority of cows today. Yaks cannot be found in the valleys, although in Roshorve and other villages at the higher valley altitudes a few households owned some of these 'grunting oxen'. They are handed over to herdsmen who make sure they are fed throughout the year in the actual Pamir high valleys.

There also supposedly existed two separate species of both sheep and goat, with a pygmy race of each. The animals gave wool of good quality, which would still be true today if there were any means of adequately working the wool. Whereas Olufsen found the larger breed of both animals in Wakhân, only the pygmy races were present in southern Shugnân, at least at that time.

Horses were formerly rare and have again become so, for although they facilitate transport they compete with cattle for fodder. Thus the donkey is more common, and was praised by Olufsen for its efficiency.

Poultry has always been rare in Pamir. Olufsen (1904) mentions a dwarf chicken breed laying eggs the size of pigeon eggs. Apart from that, household animals include only watchdogs and tiger-striped cats, the latter being comparable to the European house cat. Other sources mention mules and Bactrian camels, the latter only to be found in the eastern edge of GBAO along the Chinese border. It has become rare even there.

Cattle, sheep, goats and yaks mainly serve as sources for milk and meat. Yak butter is especially important as a cooking fat. The wool and leather from sheep and goats are used for fur coats, pants, bags, etc. The wool is spun by hand or using a simple spinning wheel (see p. 139, Plate 4.27), and was formerly used for weaving and knitting, but nowadays only for the latter. Cattle leather is used for straps of all sorts, especially in agriculture, and shoes. Shoe soles are once more made separately from yak leather, as they were in the past. Oxen serve as draught animals. Especially important is cattle and yak dung, which, as already mentioned, is used more for fuel than as fertiliser.

The number of animals in the Pamir was dependent in part on rank, or on the household's ability to arrange for winter fodder. According to Russian sources, an average household around 1900 owned six to seven head of cattle and 25 smaller animals (sheep and goats); for 1908, nine head of cattle and 44 small animals are the numbers given for Shugnân (see Holzwarth 1990: 154). More than a fifth of the cattle were working oxen (1917: 3,292 out of 14,101 animals). Another survey found that only 4 per cent of households did not own any animals at all, around 16 per cent did not own any cattle and 23.5 per cent owned no working oxen.

There are no recent official data available for comparison, but the percentage of households without domestic animals is higher than it was 100 years ago and the number of animals relative to the population has diminished (75,200 cattle in 1990 compared to 70,800 in 1997; 329,600 sheep and goats in 1990 compared to 225,400 in 1997 [our own survey from 1998]).

Animal products are an important source of nutrition for the population in the Pamir, especially milk and butter (fat). Meat, on the other hand, as in all agricultural societies with greatly restricted resources, is seldom eaten. In all, the productivity of the animals is amazingly low, which is due to the difficult ecological conditions in the Pamir. With a vegetation period of not more than four or five months, stall feeding, and thus the accumulation of fodder reserves, is a matter of life and death for stockbreeders. This was and is achieved in two ways: first, through the cultivation of fodder plants, almost always by irrigation, whereby the cereal fields in the vicinity of the villages are lightly sown with clover or alfalfa so as not to come into competition with the bread grains; second, through gathering wild fodder. In the end, the availability of fodder and of working hands in the family to gather wild herbs carries more weight in deciding whether to own livestock than their actual income. Even today, women and children are mainly the ones entrusted with cutting fodder. In Soviet times it was a favourite way of putting the Young Pioneers and Komsomol youths to work.

The fodder, sometimes gathered far away and brought into the village in heavy loads by back, was dried and then stored in huge piles on the roofs (Plate 4.19, around 1925). Based on the amount of fodder, it was and is possible to appraise a family's wealth of livestock, just as in the villages of Murghâb, as well as other areas, the dried dung heaps set as fuel in front of the houses could also be used as indicators of the amount of livestock a family possessed. However, even good provisions were no guarantee that all animals would survive. If the winter came early and ended a few weeks late, then even households with enough hands had a shortage of fodder and the animals would be brought to the nearest spring pasture half-dead – if they survived the winter at all.

In a fair number of houses, one can see even today in the disposition of rooms how closely man and beast used to live together in the winter. Whoever did not have a separate stall annexe in the house basically had to go through the stall area to reach the family's living quarters. As the only oven in the house was often to be found here, young animals were often kept in a corner of this living room during cold winters.

The past presence of nomad Pamiri is, on the whole, not very likely. There is also no record that the herders on the summer pastures would have, at any point in the past, set up tents like those that can be observed among the Tajiks in Afghanistan (see Andrews 1997: 235, 404–406). Only von Schultz says that they used to have yurts such as the Kyrgyz use (1910b: 252). In the literature, when the theme of alpine economy or transhumance is addressed, only 'summer settlements' are mentioned. This, based on present remains, means nothing more than that the herdsmen built small and simple, but sturdy houses out of stone and clay. Such houses are quite comfortable and, because of the cool nights even in summer, equipped with ovens. We found them up to an altitude of 3,800 m in the valleys between Wakhân and Shugnân/Murghâb, as well as between Roshorve/Tashkurgân and Lake Kara-kul. The term 'settlement' is usually an exaggeration. In view of the scarcity of pasture, however, two or three herding families do live together.

Plate 4.19 Enormous stack of hay and dried herbs on the roof of a Pamiri house for use as cattle fodder during the winter (photo from about 1925 in Rickmers [1930], Plate facing p. 65).

The highest pastures observed in the Afghan Wakhân lie at 4,600 m (see Grötzbach 1964: 294). In GBAO we never found the 4,300 m limit surpassed.

An alpine economy requires both men's and women's work among the Pamiris. Whereas men guard the herds in the dangerous areas – there are slopes that open directly into wedge-shaped valleys with cliff walls several hundred metres high – the children and older girls watch over the goats and sheep near the summer camps. Women take care of milking and making milk products.

During Soviet times communication between the summer camps and the herdsmen's villages of origin was better than it had been in the past and is again today. In 2003, just as in Olufsen's time around 1900, the animals' departure meant being cut off from civilisation for several months. When the pastures are not too far away, and 'not too far' may mean 60 or 70 km on foot, the men sometimes visit their wives and children in the summer. The current lack of transportation means that no milk can now be brought from the pastures into the villages. Thus, at the end of the season only butter fat and dried cheese, prepared and stored in the previous months, can be brought back.

We were surprised to observe in several villages of the Roshân district that, for want of alternatives, ancient butter-making techniques that are known from publications from around 1900 were being revived. The tools used for this were similar to those known from European folk art or craft museums for the nineteenth century. Andreev (1958: 142) and Olufsen (1904: 82) illustrate the device, comprising a clay pot (Olufsen) or, more realistically, a wooden jar (Andreev) which can hold about 15 litres, and a beater:

> In this pot is placed a stick with wings at the end; at the mouth of the pot the stick plays through a couple of pieces of wood in which are round holes, these pieces of wood being fastened to a pillar. A string is tied around the upper end of the stick, which is made to revolve by pulling each end of the string alternately as it winds on the stick.
>
> (Olufsen 1904: 108)

More common, according to Olufsen, is the technique of making butter by shaking cream in a bladder.[14] What is more, butter is (was) a luxury in the Pamir. It remains only to be said that butter-making is women's work.

The gender division of labour in agriculture

In some cases we have already seen examples of gender division in work. Unfortunately, this theme has never been systematically investigated and it would be presumptuous to try to reach conclusions on the traditional division of labour based on observations in the present after 70 years of Soviet influence. Thus the following remarks, based on works on life in the Afghan Wakhân and Shugnân on the left bank of the Pyandsh (Kussmaul 1965b: 47; Shahrani 1979a: 71–72), are only leads as to how things might have been.

It can be assumed that all areas of agriculture (fieldwork, garden work, fruit cultivation and animal husbandry) occupied both sexes and that a division of labour only occurred for individual tasks. Two such tasks were without exception men's work, something that did not change during Soviet times: (1) working the earth (that is, ploughing and harrowing as well as cleaning irrigation canals and ditches), and (2) all irrigation work (including canal building and upkeep). When, according to informants, women also took part in 'canal building' from 1995 to 2003, it invariably turned out that in fact they brought water to the working men and cooked food.

Sowing, possibly with some exceptions, is done only by men even today. Weeding, on the other hand, is more, but not exclusively, the work of women and girls. Many wild herbs are gathered for fodder at these times and then carried home. Women also spread dung on the fields when fertilisation is practised at all, and protect the fields from birds. Recently, we have as often as not seen the latter task being done by boys. Earlier, harvesting grain may have been reserved for women (see Plate 4–11), but today all available hands share in the work. Transportation to the threshing floors, mostly with the help of donkeys or with carrying-frames on the back, and later on the full sacks with the harvest to the farmsteads, is men's work. It is also the men alone who winnow grains or beans/lentils. Women in the meantime concern themselves with cleaning the grains with the help of sieves. Straw is mostly carried to the house by women.

Gardening is nowadays no longer exclusively the province of women. If, for example, potatoes or carrots are planted in large numbers, the men take care primarily of the preparation of the earth and irrigation: weeding and harvesting is done by both sexes. What formerly had no role – that is, the selling of vegetables or potatoes – seems to be the women's domain once more.

The division of labour on the pastures has already been described. Though Shahrani, looking at Afghan Wakhân, describes haymaking as being in the men's domain, for GBAO this is true only for the systematic cutting of meadow herbs in especially good areas. When such cutting takes place on the slopes or at the side of the road with the sickle, we saw only women and children at this task in the period 1995 to 2003.

The ownership of livestock is an interesting study. Although the animals were obviously the property of men in the past, though this may only be implicitly gleaned from the literature, today they are the 'property of the family'. If an animal is to be sold, this is supposedly discussed among all the adults together.

The conservation of fruit and vegetable harvests seems to have been women's work in pre-Soviet times. Even today, one definitely sees more women than men at this work (such as cutting up and setting out apples to dry); yet men certainly take part.

Land laws

Traditionally, it seems that pastures (except irrigated clover fields), areas with bushes (such as *tersgen*) used as fuel, as well as water not held in canals (lakes and streams) were the collective property of a village and were controlled by the village community. Farm land, gardens and all other productive areas (such as orchards) were, on the other hand, private property. This agrees with classical Islamic law, often applied in central Asia in the nineteenth century. 'Suivant la coutume, la terre devient la propriété de l'intéressé lorsqu'il entoure son terrain d'une clôture, construit une maison, aménage un jardin et sème de la luzerne' (Moser 1894: 195). Decisive in this is certainly not the fence nor the alfalfa, but the public demonstration of the development and use of the land. An area could thus be fenced in, but if it was not used for several years the rights to that land were lost, at least in pre-Soviet times.

Thus there is in Islamic land law no unlimited property right, but rather a right to exclusive use of the land for as long as that use is continued. According to Moser, this also applies to government land: 'Tout droit de possession et d'usufruit d'un terrain entraîne l'obligation de le cultiver' (1894: 195), although land having a house before it is an exception, but again not unlimited. If the house falls to ruins, another person may under certain conditions take possession of the land. How long the land must remain unused before someone else takes possession is decided by local common law. The three years cited by Moser is certainly not the rule everywhere – rather five, seven or even ten years. The question as to whether a stranger could take possession of land was unfortunately not addressed in the literature known to me. After 1992/3, refugees were generously allowed to practise agriculture, though on farmland of lesser quality, which hints at a flexible tradition within GBAO.

With the Russian occupation of Turkestan, the legal foundation changed substantially. Articles 119 and 120 of the statute of the Russian military government provided that all land should belong to the state and that the farmers would only be allowed its use. While there was no dispute as such over ownership of the land, in practice only wasteland, and all the land having previously belonged to the khans and emirs, was considered government property (see Machatschek 1921: 145).

Cultivated land was accepted as being the property of the one using it, and the water needed for irrigation was ceded to the population 'according to habit'. Nomad land, as for example the high plateaux of the Pamir, became *de jure* and *de facto* government land under the Russian occupation, which was however handed over to the Kyrgyz for a low per capita tax for their otherwise free and 'perpetual use' (Machatschek 1921: 145). There are no reports for the Pamir of 'Russian arbitrariness'; that is, the removal of land in favour of their own colonists, as was supposed to have taken place in the oases of Turkestan.[15] This may have been because Russian settlers never had to fight with possible former titleholders for land.

In 1922 Russian land law in Turkestan was confirmed by the Soviets in its basic substance. Buying and selling land was prohibited, something which in any case was already *de jure* impossible. Yet all people over 16 were explicitly promised the right to the use of land and water, which was also to be made possible by the distribution of land (see Hayit 1956: 268). The planned land reform was hampered until 1925 by the Basmatshi Uprising.

If land reform occurred in GBAO before collectivisation, which began in 1933[16] and only ended after 1937, it could only have affected very few areas as the number of farmers with land significantly larger than the subsistence limit was very small. The area to be distributed would also have been very small. In reports, therefore, land distribution is not cited as the great achievement of the early Soviet period, but rather the possibility of being allowed to use existing land relatively free of taxes.

In GBAO there were, apart from farmland, also communal village areas that could be used by all inhabitants. If the users of such land in a hamlet belonged to a single *qûm* (approximately 'lineage'), one could speak of property ownership within a kinship group. Unfortunately, we found no one who could still tell us how things were settled in villages comprising several lineages. Did each lineage have its own piece of communal land or did the land belong to the village community as a whole?

Irrigation

In the Pamir, farming was in the majority of cases dependent on irrigation. The digging and upkeep of the irrigation facilities therefore represent the most important social organisational achievement in the country, having survived even the modernisation of the Soviet era and continuing even to this day. Thus, the inhabitants of GBAO, as well as those of Afghan Badakhshan, have dug canals for hundreds of years under extremely hard conditions in order to irrigate fields, gardens and orchards.[17] Krader dates the beginning of irrigation agriculture in central Asia to about 1000 BC (1962: 25). Walter Raunig, however, believes that in Pyandsh irrigation (for wheat and barley) can be attested for as early as 1550 to 1200 BC (Bactro-Margianic archaeological complex) (1982: 128). Mursajew has this to say about the achievements of the older canal builders:

> Zuweilen kann man hoch in den Felsen an einem Gebirgshand einen Aryk sehen, der irgendwo Dutzende von Kilometern weit entfernt talaufwärts von einem Fluß abzweigt, und begreift nicht, wie Menschen an senkrechten Felswänden diesen Kanal anlegen konnten. Die Erbauer mussten sich an Seilen von den Bergen herunterlassen und in der erforderlichen Höhe . . . das Gestein sprengen, mit primitiven Geräten den Kanal reinigen und seine Außenwand zementieren.
>
> (Mursajew 1956: 262)

Our Plate 4.20 shows an *aryk* (the Russian term; Shugnî: *wirth*) running some 100 metres above the Pyandsh along an erosion slope. The canal branches from the river about 5 kilometres above this place. A canal is begun by diverting the river by rolling boulders into the water at the river's edge so that water begins to accumulate at that point (see Kussmaul 1965b: 38, fig. 7). This causes the water to run into the small canal. The latter has a more gentle slope than the river itself so that the further it goes, the higher it lies in relation to the river (see Andreev 1958; also our Plate 4.21). After a few kilometres, the *aryk* may run some 100 or 200 m above the river. Smaller branches lead from the main canal according to the same principle. It is thus possible to irrigate all the land between the canal (on top) and the river (at the bottom) (see Machatschek 1921: 142). This land may comprise large cultivable areas but also, in difficult terrain, merely smaller arable islands.

The problem is that in the narrow valleys of the Pyandsh and its tributaries farmland is very scarce. It might only be present on a large enough scale high above the river, where it is often impossible dig a canal. According to the principle of gravity irrigation, a canal can only 'rise' slightly per kilometre in relation to the incline of the river. As such a 'rise' is seldom more than 1 per cent, almost one kilometre of canal is generally necessary to serve land that is only 10 metres above the river. Accordingly, when the land is higher, it is necessary to begin the canal a good way upstream. Because of this, it can happen that cliffs, slopes (consisting of eroded material) and side-valleys have to be crossed or bridged over. This

Plate 4.20 An irrigation canal about 100 metres above the Pyandsh river crosses a scree slope. The canal shows damage caused by a landslide (1996).

explains how a situation such as Mursajew describes can come to pass. Andreev uses a sketch to show how even smaller side-valleys can be bridged by water pipes (1958: 295).

A canal on a scree slope like that in Plate 4.20 is especially difficult to construct and prone to damage. At every movement of the geologically active terrain a landslide could destroy a part of the canal, so that someone must set out five, ten or 20 times a year to repair the damaged area. When landslides are especially large, a summer's harvest may be destroyed because the canal could not be repaired in time.

Although the wider side-valleys almost always boast small brooks, these often cannot be tapped as they dry up in summer, meaning that bridging solutions must be found. Andreev illustrates one such aqueduct in which a pipe (formerly a half-pipe out of wood) is mounted on columns and planks. Through these means the canal is extended over the valley (1958: 295). In practice, the canals almost always look rather amateurish and leak in several places, but the achievement behind this is impressive and the system is anything but primitive, as Machatschek explains (1921: 254).

The Russian geobotanist Stanjukowitsch also gives the early canal builders their due. Today, so he says, holes are bored and the cliffs simply sprung, but formerly years of hard work were necessary. On the cliffs, a large fire was lit, warming the stone, and then cold water poured onto the heated cliffs, causing them to split. This was repeated several dozen times until a few metres of canal were created

Plate 4.21 Beginning of a small irrigation canal in the lower Shakhdara valley near the intake (1995).

(1961: 173–174). In actual fact, of course, the work was not yet done. Protrusions had to be removed with a hammer, and afterwards the bottom levelled and a side wall erected so that the water could flow through the channel.

Irrigation was either through surface flooding or using ditches. In the first technique, water is channelled into small square or rectangular fields dammed on all sides. Once one field is submerged, the dam to the next lower one is broken and this is allowed to flood. With ditch irrigation, the water is channelled from the canal into parallel ditches between which the cultivated plants stand on higher ground. This way, the seed is not washed away after sowing (see Kreutzmann 1996: 60–61); also the plants themselves, that unlike the others cannot tolerate flooding, remain healthy.

The irrigation workers, both in the past and today exclusively men, must be present in the fields during the entire procedure. They open and close the small walls around the fields and channel the water through the ditches. Their only tool is a wooden spade (*zer-phaî*) with a very long handle (200 cm and more; see Plate 4.22 and Andreev 1958: 44). The art of irrigation resides in the ability to channel enough water out of the main canal so that the plants receive sufficient water, yet also not too much (water velocity as well as total quantity) so that the irrigation works and fields are not washed away. In the past few decades, knowledge pertaining to efficient irrigation has markedly decreased. During our studies after 1995 we often observed dams breaking and flooded land. A great problem in irrigation is the fact that the slope of the minor canals can be very steep, so there is a risk of erosion if the canals are not finished with cement.

Plate 4.22 Irrigation in progress in a field in the Roshân District. The man uses the typical shovel with its long handle (1995).

Practically nothing is known about the traditional organisation of irrigation, the building and upkeep of the canals, as well as the water laws. Lentz mentions that in the 1920s in Oroshor (Roshorve), every day a different person was responsible for irrigation (1931: 185). Based on our knowledge of the region, this can only mean that the landowner assigned someone to work under his supervision and not that one person at a time irrigated their fields themselves. For this, the areas were too big, even 80 years ago.

In Afghan Wakhân in the early 1970s, there was a '*mirea*' who was responsible for the management of the irrigation systems (Gratzl 1974: 46). The work of the water supervisor was and is especially crucial in spring and autumn when there is but little melted water in the streams, for a scarce resource must be fairly distributed. On the other hand, in many places a farmer may take as much water from the canals as he considers necessary in the summer.

In addition to the distribution of water, those responsible for irrigation in Roshorve were also responsible for the upkeep of the canal systems. Since time immemorial, no new canals have been built in Roshorve, only repairs made. Only in 1995 was a new canal project launched with the help of the Aga Khan Foundation and international financing. But even upkeep, in view of the canals' length, sometimes over difficult terrain, can be very complicated. The supervisors (these were never women) had to organise a watch capable of reporting damage, which could mean at times a daily patrol of 10, 15 or more kilometres of canal along steep slopes. In case of landslides, one had to mobilise many men to repair the canal quickly. If a canal is out of order for several days in summer, it could sometimes mean and still can mean the loss of the entire crop. What is more, in many villages the *aryk* was also a source of drinking water. In this case, a leaking or broken canal means that inhabitants are completely cut off from their drinking water.

The *khalifa* of Roshorve told us that the current canal construction was, apart from the modern techniques using tractors and explosives, organised in much the same way as in the past. The neighbourhoods of a village (*amtabaq*) each make up one work group (in Soviet times and even today referred to as a 'brigade'), each working in alternate one-day shifts on the construction site. On that day the women of the neighbourhood also cook food for the workers.

The main tools were the traditional spades, hoes and heavy hammers. Canal slope was checked using the water of the canal itself as there weren't any surveying instruments. One can imagine how slowly the work progressed when it had to be done with simple tools over a smooth cliff face. This work was and is not without danger. In Roshorve two men died in 1997 while they were working on a very steep and, due to pebbles, very slippery slope. They slid for several hundred metres before falling into a v-shaped valley half a kilometre deep. In answer to our questions, we were told that with ropes and safety devices work gangs of 20 to 30 men could no longer be used. Certainly over many centuries many men have lost their lives during the construction of those canals, that are now referred to by some visitors as 'primitive'.

Crafts, industries and trade

Before the Soviet era, there were never in the whole of the Pamir region craftsmen such as were developed through its apprenticeship schemes. None of the settlements in GBAO existing around 1900 could have been capable of feeding a craftsman properly.[18] This is also true for specialised trades such as that of smith, whose products are needed mostly by farmers. Thus, the smith was first of all a farmer who worked at his forge (*kurga*) only when he had an order from a customer. Only during the land cultivation (ploughing) period and while haymaking was there so much to do that the smith could have been occupied the entire time. But as the smith himself had to take care of his fields, it was precisely during those periods that problems arose with repairs.

While some crafts can be reconstructed from current practice, others have more or less disappeared. To the latter category belongs pottery-making which, even in view of the necessity after 1992/3, could not be resuscitated due to the loss of tradecraft knowledge. Similarly, for lack of tools, weaving has not been revived either. We also searched in vain for a wood turner, whereas the traditional woodworking techniques of the joiner, including making boards using only a hand saw (!), have been revived. The traditional smithy has also been reactivated with success. The quality, though, remains low, for there had not been an artisan smith in GBAO for decades.

Continuity rules in textile techniques such as spinning and knitting, in artisanal woodwork and in the fabrication of musical instruments. The trade of house carpenter was never in any danger in Soviet times due to low state resources for house building. On the other hand, after the crises, catastrophe loomed when it turned out that there was not a single artisanal shoemaker left in the entire country and that the traditional leather production techniques had been also forgotten. Some brief notes about each of the crafts now follow:

Iron extraction and ironworking

Von Schultz reports that in 1910, on the left bank of the Pyandsh in Roshân, a very poor iron for hoes, sickles and knives was still being produced by Afghan Tajiks, but that this was already being supplanted by Russian items (1914: 37). Firearms had never been produced in the Pamir, but had been imported from India, Pakistan or Turkestan. According to von Schwartz, the iron industry 'of the Galtsha of Darwâs and Badakhshan' (it is uncertain if the Pamiris of GBAO or the population of all of Badakhshan is meant here) was on an equally low level, but weapons were produced (1900: 402, 440).

De Rocca reports that iron ore was extracted in Darwâs, but only from the surface. The smelting ovens were also said to be primitive, but quite widespread ('chaque maison a un fourneau pour la fusion du minerai' (1896: 246)). Most famous was the iron from the Wandsh valley, which one could find in the entire eastern part of Bukhara. The smelting ovens probably looked much like those recorded by Kussmaul at the beginning of the 1960s in Afghan Badakhshan (1965b: 69, fig. 21).

Contrary to the affirmation of von Schultz and despite the apparently primitive iron smelting, the knives from Wandsh enjoyed great popularity on the markets of Bukhara, being in fact very ornate (de Rocca 1896: 247). Finally, Gordon not only allows that they 'smelt iron more successfully than any people in the East' but also that the art of iron casting was mastered (1876: 168). Once more it remains unclear whether the inhabitants of Afghan Badakhshan only or also those of modern GBAO are meant.

After the Second World War, artisanal smithcraft fell more and more into disuse until the dire situation of the early 1990s forced people to re-establish long-disused smithies (*kurga*). Indeed, there were also smiths on the sovkhozes, but these were accustomed to using soldering machines. That today there are again at least a few specialists, we could observe especially in the villages of Roshân but also in the Wandsh valley.

The equipment of these 'new' smithies is identical in every detail to those Andreev found in the middle of the twentieth century in Khûf (1958: 183): the forge may be found in a separate mudbrick building and is fed by two goatskin bellows (with the fur still on, called in Andreev '*dâm*'). The metal is worked on an anvil set into the ground (*sindôn*). The basic equipment is simple: a pair of tongs (*ambur*), with which the object being worked is thrust into the fire and held fast during hammering, and a heavy hammer (*koleb*). A stone trough filled with water is used for cooling. More tongs, hammers and chisels already belong to a deluxe kit with which the artisan nowadays, in addition to plough parts and knives, mostly makes agricultural implements (spades, hoes, sickles, etc.), household cutlery and metal fittings as well as nails. The knife from Khûf illustrated in Andreev (1958: 190) is approximately comparable in quality to today's production.

Occasionally, metal pots such as jugs (see Raunig 1978: 299, fig. 25) or cauldrons are illustrated in the literature. Simple pieces soldered together from several sheets of iron were probably formerly made by the Pamiris themselves. Higher-quality work, usually water pitchers with silver inlay and/or incised decoration, are probably Tajik products from Bukhara, Tashkent or Samarkand. Although they are used only by the richest in Pamir, they were still being produced by the thousands at the beginning of the twentieth century. One can only speculate about the origin of the copper cauldrons sometimes holding 30–40 litres or more.[19] Von Schultz attributed them to Afghanistan or Chitral in north Pakistan (1914: 38).

Pottery production

Ceramic production techniques can only be studied through older sources, as pottery making in the area of Soviet GBAO lapsed decades ago. With the few examples from the museum in Khorog, 23 samples from Khûf illustrated on two plates in Andreev (1958: figs 66–67) and a small spherical pot which we found after intensive searching in a shed in Tusyan in 1998, we do not even have enough pieces to establish a typology.

The spectrum of forms is, in any case, very limited. Dishes (*gidora*), small cooking pots with grips instead of handles (*beshakdor beg*), bowls, full-bellied jugs with a handle (*guzdon bog*) or a handle and a spout (*naîdor bog*) make up the selection. Hardly any decoration is used, apart from a few dots or lines in the wet clay (see von Schultz 1914: 38). The common characteristics of the forty or so pieces illustrated in the literature are uneven firing in low to middle temperatures, very thick walls, irregular forms, and bulging lips and handles. Most of the pieces are distinctly small. The water, oil or grain storage pots found en masse in neighbouring southern and south-eastern countries seem to be completely absent. The biggest pot we know of can hold 5–7 litres. These clay wares from Pamir are thus very similar to antique models of the Saka period (see pp. 52–53; also Plate 3.2).

We can only comment on technique based on parallels from Afghanistan (see Kussmaul 1965b: 71, fig. 23) and on the basis of the ten or so pots we saw. Thus, the pots were made by women[20] using the coiling technique (i.e. the potter does not use a wheel but forms the pot first from a ball of clay and then adds 'sausages' of clay to continue the walls). A slab of stone or clay served as a work surface, itself placed on a stone slab so that the women could turn it more easily in the course of their work. We do not know whether, as adaptations of the original coiling technique, they continued to work with rolls or whether only the hands or else mould boards were also used. However it does look as though some of the vessels were polished with a stone after moulding. Firing probably took place in field holes rather than in true pottery ovens, as the pots are sometimes very irregularly fired. Kussmaul speaks of 'open fires' in a similar context (1965b: 71, fig. 23).

It could be that, also to the right of the Pyandsh in GBAO, ceramic production was not practised everywhere, but rather by the women of particular villages. In Afghanistan, such centres did (and still do) exist, at least in Wakhân and Shugnân.

Woodworking

The woodwork of the Pamirs is highly evolved, yet without the finesse of, for example, the Swat valley in north Pakistan.[21] One must differentiate between true house carpentry for home construction and the decoration of the beams within the house, and the making of interior furnishings such as cupboards, chests or cradles as well as small objects like kitchen implements of all sorts, storage boxes, lamp holders, etc. Within the field of construction work belongs most specially the building of the roof with its lantern (see pp. 170–171), including the five supporting posts in the living quarters so typical of the Ismailis. The same craftsmen also carve the decorations on doors, wall cupboards and the transverse beams over the entrance to the living quarters, the latter being, even today, the most widespread decorated element within the house.

To the second group of woodwork belong the formerly painted built-in cupboards along the walls of the living quarters and between the entrance to these quarters and the raised divan, forming a sort of closet there. The most common wooden objects, even today, are chests made from the trunk of the walnut tree. In pre-Soviet times they served as hidden clothes closets and were still occasionally produced at least two or three decades ago. They were decorated on their front face with carved geometric shapes and then brightly painted. This *sandûq* (Arabic) is a typical element of a bride's dowry and is imported today from Osh in Kyrgyzstan or Dushanbe.

Much smaller and better proportioned, as well as decorated on all sides, is a further group of wooden containers, seldom larger that 40 to 60 cm in diameter. They are also made out of walnut and almost always have three legs. An especially fine example is exhibited in the Khorog museum (see Plate 4.23). Flower patterns and other geometrical shapes are chip-carved all around the actual container as well as on the entire lid. These lovely wares were, formerly at least, in no way as rare as von Schultz implies and definitely did not come from Bukhara; at least for the rougher types, they were mainly of local production. A few especially fine examples were certainly brought in from Chitral or the Swat valley.

The cradles are especially magnificent and may be even today the most widespread traditional wooden object of local production. The relatively simple example shown in Plate 4.24, from Roshorve, is very carefully worked in cherry wood. There are much coarser pieces that are typologically similar to the previously described decorated walnut containers. A few very decorative examples from Khûf, illustrated in Andreev, supposedly came for the most part from Afghanistan (1958: 360). One example, designated as a 'doll's cradle' by Raunig (from Afghan Wakhân) is also of walnut and shows the same floral-geometric decoration (1978: 292, fig. 13). Similar pieces are also shown in Andreev (there called *guk*; 1958: 359). The same author also illustrates wooden toys (camel = *akhtûr*, horse = *wurdshak*).

Within the kitchen inventory, big wooden plates (arab.: *tabaq*), bowls for tea (*pela*) and dishes (*nugulmaî*) predominate (see Andreev 1958: 361). A large rectangular dish (*akhikht*) serves as a trough for the preparation of bread. Dubeaux and Valmont also mention large wooden vases and storage vessels for flour (1848: 95). The latter are not registered, at least in the Khorog museum. The pieces on display there are for the most part of small to middle size and turned from walnut. In some households we were shown relatively new pieces that invariably came from Afghan Badakhshan. Despite the closely watched border, in 1997 a trader from Afghanistan exchanged a large dish in Roshorve against three times what the dish contained in wheat.

Such dishes are probably made by professional wood turners who, at least formerly in Afghan Badakhshan, used water power for their work (see Gratzl 1974: 51). There must have been both production centres, where the pieces were fabricated en masse for sale by traders, and travelling turners who plied their trade in the client villages. The turned woodwork was, at least in the past, very valuable

Plate 4.23 Wooden (walnut) container for fine clothes such as scarves, kerchiefs and perhaps some jewellery (Museum of Khorog, 1998).

and thus saw prolonged use and repeated repairs. This was done by 'sewing' cracked places together with wire or riveting pieces of metal foil onto them (see Raunig 1978: 299).

Finally, all the stirring, serving and eating spoons used in the kitchen must be counted among the woodwork (see Gratzl 1973: fig. 15). Metal was much too valuable for such use, so that a household owned dozens of wooden spoons, usually large. Andreev differentiates between small spoons, in part in an artistically whittled

Plate 4.24 Cradle for small children in Roshorve (Bartang), made in earlier times from the wood of a cherry tree (1997).

style (*tshebbitz*), and normal eating spoons (*tsheb*) (1958: 357). Unlike our spoons, the latter have the bowl at right angles to the handle rather than in its axis, so that one can only slurp out of them.

The making of musical instruments enjoys an old tradition in GBAO. Even more than the different drums and tambourines (Farsî: *daf*), the *rabâb* (*rabôb*), a stringed instrument, represents the most important instrument of the Pamiris. The sound box is made out of apricot wood and covered with stretched horse skin. The instrument has a total of five longer and one shorter string (see Gratzl 1974: 56). Roshân is the centre of production today, but in the past pieces were also made in Shugnân. Plate 4.25 shows one of the last instrument-makers in Shidz (Roshân) scooping out a thick wood-block previously seasoned for several months, which will become the body of a *rabôb*. First, the wooden block is roughly sawn to size and then hollowed out or sculpted with a pick. Finally, it is polished with files and paper pulp.

Another sort of woodwork is represented by wooden clogs, somewhat similar to those common in the Netherlands. However, these have much higher heels. A few pieces are still used by older folk. We were even able to buy a pair of clogs ourselves in Tusyan.

Andreev illustrates a sample of the traditional woodworker's tools (1958: 188). Among these are burins, borers (*akhavdsh-mikh*), different coarse and fine saws (*arra*) and various picks (*randa*). The latter are coarse and of a very primitive type

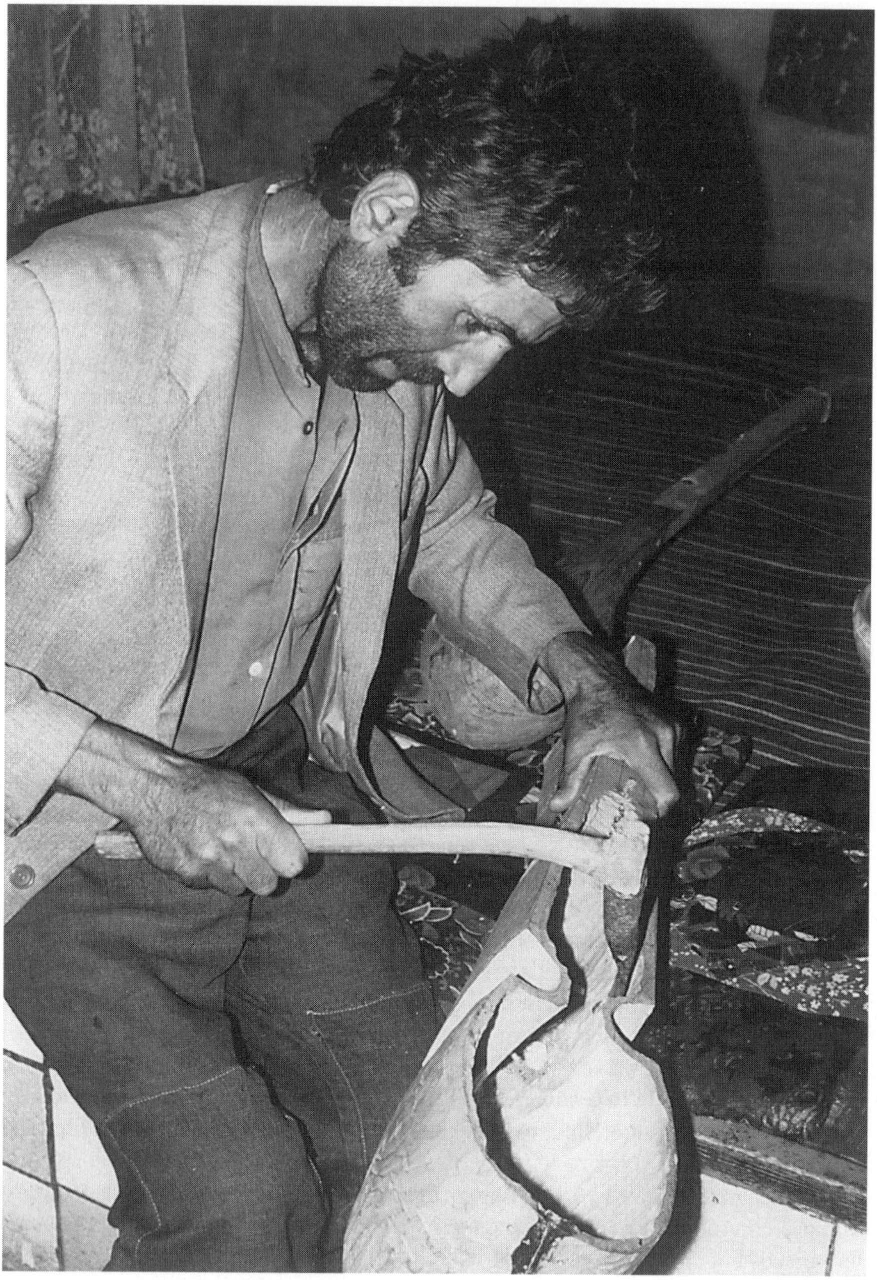

Plate 4.25 One of the last men in the Pamir region to make the famous *rabôb* (from Shidz, Roshân) (1997).

(local production). With their socketed hafting, they are very similar to African iron tools. Yet the artisans were very skilful in using these tools, being capable of finishing 95 per cent of a *rabôb* sound box with them. Simple yet practical were the planes (*dosrand*), differing greatly from the Russian ones that are comparable to our Western types.

Textile techniques

Textile types will be introduced later on in another context (see pp. 178–182). Here, the technical side of clothing manufacture will be presented, which, however, we could partly deduce only from older publications. Only spinning and knitting are still widely distributed, largely because GBAO was built up by the Soviets as a regional centre of the modern textile industry.

Whereas in the Tajik lowlands cotton is quite common and was expanded by the Soviets into Tajikistan's most important agricultural product, the area currently called GBAO, with the exception of Darwâs where cotton was also used, uses practically only local sheep or goat wool. More rarely, ibex, camel or yak wool was used, the latter also being used to make ropes. The quality of the sheep and goat wool of Pamir can be very good, approximately comparable to Cashmere wool.

Sheep's wool is cleaned with the aid of a large wooden bowl with a gut string (see von Schulz 1914: 40–41, fig. 11). The wool is placed in a heap on a horsehair sieve and, by beating the wool with the string, it is freed from dust and dirt. After the wool is cleansed and washed, it is spun either on a hand spindle (*tshalak*), which consists of a wooden rod with a perforated stone, or on a wooden cross as a crank (Olufsen 1904: 104; Andreev 1958: 208; also Plate 4.26, this volume).

The work goes faster when using a spinning wheel. We found one such wheel still in use in the village of Shidz (Roshân). It was dug out of the barn in 1995 and repaired, not having seen any use for 30 years. Yet the owner still recalled the technique taught to her as a little girl by her mother and grandmother and had no trouble using the contraption (Plate 4.27). An exact description of the tool described here as *tsharkh*, and of the spinning technique, can be found in Andreev (1958: 208–210).

Spinning, at least with the spinning wheel, was women's work in the past, yet Lentz illustrates a man spinning in public (1931: pl. facing p. 289). Von Schultz confirms that among the Pamiris, men also (at least in the past) worked the spindle (1914).[22] Before the wool was knitted or woven after being spun on the spindle, it was spooled with the help of a rotating construction (*tsharkh*; see Andreev 1958: 208) into balls of yarn. Spooling was automatic when the spinning wheel was used.

We searched in vain during our trip to GBAO in 1995 for a loom. In the last few years the loom has no longer been used, despite the growing shortage of clothing, since the complicated technique has been lost. Old devices, which could still have been repaired with extant know-how and once more set to work, were

Plate 4.26 Woman from Jomdsh (Shugnân) spinning with a spindle (1995).

nowhere to be found. We could only discover that weaving was formerly (mainly?) men's work.

In the Afghan Wakhân, the Austrian Hindu Kush expedition was able in 1970 to observe one of the last weavers at work in a village on the left bank of the Pyandsh. There, wool was woven on a horizontal mechanical loom, from which a strip of cloth only 30 cm wide could be obtained; meaning that, for example for coats, several strips needed to be sown together. Kussmaul illustrates in his report on the Afghan Badakhshan a technically much simpler vertical loom on which, however, bands 70 cm wide could be woven (1965b: 70, fig. 22).

Plate 4.27 Woman from Shidz (Roshân) using a rebuilt spinning wheel inherited from her grandmother (1997).

Generally, it seems that the weaving technique used to the right of the Pyandsh, as described by Lentz (1931: 39–40) and most recently by such as Andreev in the 1950s in Khûf (Roshân) (1958: 208), was equivalent to the first, more developed technique. Despite what Olufsen says (1904: 104–107), the Pamiri loom was not the simple mechanism illustrated by Kussmaul and formerly used in GBAO among the Kyrgyz, but was instead a mechanical loom such as the one used in Afghan Wakhân (see Andreev 1958: 202–203, figs. 35, 36). However, it is also possible that finer cloth bands were made for clothing with the mechanical loom and coarser rugs with the vertical loom. Thus, comparatively simple looms could also have existed in GBAO. In some households we found rugs that were sewn together from two to three bands of 60 to 70 cm cloth. However, they had not been locally produced but had, in some way or another, been traded from the Afghan side. Only once, in 2003, in Namadgut (Ishkashim), did we receive indications of current household weaving.

The working width of the loom from Khûf (Roshân) illustrated in Andreev is, as in the first Afghan example, 30 cm. Very probably, some looms must have allowed for weaving broader pieces. Thus, von Schultz mentions that the cloth woven on the local mechanical loom in Pamir was 40 cm wide and some 10 m long (1914: 40). Another kind of loom, according to Olufsen, consists only of a wooden frame on which the coarse woollen yarn is stretched, and another yarn is then simply interwoven with it (1904: 107).

Most of the hand-woven cloths were made using undyed wool, meaning that the colours ranged from beige and brown tones to the black of goat wool. Whether in the current area of GBAO, as seems to be the case on the Afghan side, weaving was only done by men, is beyond our knowledge. On the other hand, it seems certain that the final working of the cloth bands into clothing was done both by men and women (see Gratzl 1974: 50).

Knitting and crochet, however, has always been women's work and this holds true today. Knitting is not 'work' but was, like spinning, done on the side, perhaps while watching the herds or waiting for customers at the market stand. Previously, long tights, gloves and mittens were knitted. Sweaters and shawls have only been produced since the Second World War. The traditional tights of the Pamiris, though coarse, are very warm and, according to von Schultz, traded all the way to the cities of Turkestan (1914: 41).

At the beginning of the twentieth century, only wooden sticks were used to knit, just as wooden crochet needles were supposedly used. In the Soviet era, iron needles took over. Contrary to the woven cloths, dyed wool was sometimes used in the past for knitting and crocheting. The examples on display at the Khorog museum show an evolution from natural colours to combined colours and in the last decades to very bright colours. Despite the difficulty in obtaining dyes for dyeing wool after the civil war of 1992/3, very bright green, red and orange tones are a fashionable must for knitted wares today.

Leatherworking, wickerwork and other crafts

Usually, the coarse leather boots, today homemade once more because of the crisis, are the leatherwear most frequently cited in the literature. Supposedly, they were formerly dyed red – but we did not find any surviving examples. On the one hand, the boots are quite practical, for they are soft and do not skid on the cliffs; however, they wear out quickly despite their yak-leather soles. Von Schultz reports that, after each march, the Pamiris sat around the fire, on long evenings, mending their boots (1914: 35). In winter, the above-mentioned wooden clogs were apparently bound with thongs over the leather boots. In view of the somewhat bulky clogs, one finds it difficult to imagine that the people could walk very safely or even very fast.

No doubt the most important leatherwork next to shoemaking was for agricultural purposes: the leather straps needed for harnesses and to complete the attire, for which yak and cattle leather was used. The hunter wore a solid belt (*kamar*) with all sorts of hooks (*tshangak*) which allowed him to carry a powder horn (*tirdôn*), knife, small leather bag for kindling, etc. (Museum of Khorog exhibits; see also Andreev 1958: fig. 44). The crampons and snowshoes (*tshapâr*) of the Pamiris were of leather with iron nails (Andreev 1958: fig. 43).

In the literature, wickerwork was usually only mentioned as an afterthought. Yet baskets woven from willow boughs seem to have been quite common. Perhaps their fabrication does not count as a craft, as even small children learn to weave simple baskets. Still very widespread today are the large woven carrying baskets with which the men transport the harvest and the women the hay. One kind of small satchel (*siptak*), illustrated in Andreev, is especially elaborate with different coloured patterns, among others a zigzag ornamentation and an animal motif (donkeys?) (1958: fig. 62).

Apart from a short mention in von Schultz (1914: figs 31–34), we know of no source that has concerned itself with Pamiri painting. Yet this is definitely of interest and can be found today on the wooden chests, some of the beams of the houses, and on the doors and side walls of the living quarters. However, opinions differ as to their age. The works we saw, in which animals were a popular motif, date no earlier than 1960, and older people told us they hadn't known such fine painting before. This information corresponds to that of the German ethnologist who only illustrates simple line drawings with symbols, stylised animals and people, and hands.

Finally, stonework is only mentioned once, in Dubeaux and Valmont (1848: 95) ('lampes de pierre . . . ressemblent pour la forme à un soulier, comme les lampes antiques'). Today, no such lamps are known.

Mining

Indications for the economic importance of mining for GBAO are sparse. Most explorations did not take place until the Soviet era. The ruby mines mentioned in Chapter 2, which are situated near Bashâr (Shugnân) were supposed to have employed some 30 people at the beginning of the 1870s. Their production was sent to the Emir of Kabul (Forsyth 1877: 65). In the past, gold was supposedly panned from many of the tributaries of the Pyandsh, but the statements of the German scholar von Schultz on the importance of this practice are contradictory. Thus, 'some lone' Tajiks practised gold panning, but in the next sentence he says that this occupation lured 'numerous' Tajiks. His indications do, however, speak for a considerable importance for gold panning:

> Im Spätsommer und Herbst, nach Beendigung der Ernte, kommen die Eingeborenen mit langen Schöpfeimern her und schöpfen den goldhaltigen Sand, der in Ziegen- oder Schaffellen geseigert wird, wobei das schwerere Gold in den Haaren hängen bleibt.
>
> (von Schultz 1914: 45)

The author mentions another technique used by the inhabitants of the Bartang valley. These people had erected masonry frames (dams?) on flat areas along the Bartang which were flooded in summer. When the water level dropped in the autumn, the sand deposited on the frames would be scraped off and washed out. There is no information on yield, though, as people were afraid of taxes. Von

Schultz estimates the daily yield at 0.50 to 0.75 German Marks (ibid.).[23] On the slopes of the Alai as well, at least in the past, gold was retrieved by the Kyrgyz using the simplest methods. The gold-carrying sand was, according to Rickmers, rinsed on a tilted surface bedecked with felt. Tiny gold flakes – there was rarely more than that – remained caught in the felt (1930: 149). Both reports, by the way, are reminiscent of the saga of the 'Golden Fleece', perhaps an indication for this sort of gold prospecting from river sand.

Trade

In the nineteenth century the Pamiris maintained trading relations both with the Kyrgyz in the Murghâb and Alai, and also with the trade centres of Afghan Badakhshan. Kunduz and Kabul are also named as important trade partners, and Chitral in north India (current Pakistan) as well. Thus, in 1897 Cobbold met a fair number of Pamiris who had been in Chitral themselves (1900: 178, 263).

Trade relations with Afghanistan, and even reaching all the way to Chitral, should not blind us to the fact that the mountain dwellers' trade contacts with their neighbours both near and far were very limited, even in earlier times. There was but little money, and the conversion, for example, of wooden products to grain etc. represented little more than petty trade. Pamir, if we interpret the historical sources correctly, had no currency of its own. Around 1900, Russian silver currency was used in parallel to the main currency of the Bukhara Emirate. Chinese coins were only grudgingly accepted (see Cobbold 1900: 174). Until Russia occupied the Pamir with larger military forces (that is, after 1900), there was on the whole very little money in circulation within the subsistence economy.

Thus, even in 1910 there were no more than three small markets in the Pamir region: Khorog, Murghâb town and Tashkurgan on the Chinese side. Von Schultz reports that the Kyrgyz traded felt rugs for grain from Pamir. Before the Russian occupation, lively trade trafficked between the Pamir and the Afghan Badakhshan. Iron and iron tools, salt, cotton and wool cloth was traded by the Pamiris for coats and shirts. Copper cauldrons, dishes and pitchers from Chitral and wooden utensils from Afghanistan (Sebak) were traded against the felt they received from the Kyrgyz (1914: 55).

Internal trade seems hardly to have existed within the subsistence economy, as everyone in essence produced the same things. Trade may have taken place on a personal level without the need for middlemen. In the course of our questions, we stumbled on a phenomenon already known to us from the Egyptian oases of the Western Desert – namely, that the trading of agricultural products within the village was considered unseemly. This means that whoever has more than he needs of one product may give it to his neighbours, but not sell it or part with it for a direct return service. This has led to the fact that, even after the collapse of the Soviet Union and the dissolution of state shops, a market for local products has evolved only grudgingly. From as early as the 1960s comes an interesting report from a certain Mrs Belkina, who writes:

> The Pamiris do not even know how to trade. In Khorog a bazaar has been built, but it is always empty. It is said that in the Pamirs for a long time it was impossible to find shop managers and they had to be brought in together with the merchandise from the great outside world.
>
> (Belkina 1966: 228)

This view fits well with a saying cited by the same author: 'Why trade? The law says: give your spoon to your neighbour if he needs it, and eat with your fingers' (ibid.). However, starting in 1994/5, very slowly and mainly in Khorog and Murghâb city, a selection of local produce has started to establish itself in the markets. In the villages, even in the summer of 2003, practically no local agricultural produce is sold.

Power and administration

The traditional political system

Typical for early Gorno-Badakhshan is an extreme fragmentation of authority, meaning that little could be undertaken against the Uzbek raids starting in 1657, basically signalling the bankruptcy of the traditional regional political system (Holzwarth 1980: 189). Accordingly, the land to the right of the Pyandsh always remained under external rule until the Russian invasion, allowing the local princes more or less autonomy as long as they paid the corresponding tribute.

Grevemeyer speaks of a system of graded authority: there was 'imperial sovereignty', by which Bukhara or the later Afghan kingdom is meant, the province (Badakhshan), and regional sovereignty such as Wakhân or Shugnân (1982: 108ff.) Shugnân, for its part, had much greater importance in the nineteenth century than the current district borders suggest. The valley of Shakhdara and Roshân, together with the Bartang valley, today separate districts, were dependent regions ruled by close relatives of the rulers of Shugnân (Roshân) or by autochthonous dynasties.

At the same time, the whole of Shugnân's dominion should not be overestimated: at the end of the nineteenth century there must have been only some 1,500 to 2,000 households with no more than 250 armed men in this immense area (see Holzwarth 1980: 203). One can deduce from the literature that the local rulers had (small) standing war bands. However, in view of the humble resources even in the ruling courts, these could not have exceeded one or two dozen armed men in peacetime.

The regional units, as we have seen not necessarily identical with the current districts, generally had a *shah* (local: *shoh*) or *mir* at their heads. For a time, the *mir* of Faizabad (current Afghanistan) was the ruler of a unified Shugnân, itself possessing under-*mirs*. Atkinson describes the ruler of Badakhshan as *khan* (1860: 257). The difference seems to be purely linguistic: whereas *khan* comes from the Turkish (along with the occasionally used term *beg*), *mir* and *shah* are Iranian terms. The title *padishah*, a word familiar to us as designating the ruler of the

Osman empire, seems only to be used in reference to the Afghan king, but is often used in Pamir fairytales to designate a ruler (see p. 192).

Mullah (*mulloh*) and *mirza* are often honorary titles without political meaning, whereby the former designates an Islamic educated person and the latter any other educated person (see Olufsen 1904: 139). *Mullah, pir* or *sayyed*, however, are also used in reference to religious dignitaries, whereby *pir* still designated in 1900 the Ismaili functionaries and *mullah* the Sunni clerics. Whereas today the latter title has come back into use, *pir* has been replaced by *khalifa*. The Arabic title *amîr* hardly ever appears any more in recent publications as a designation for a political leader, just as *hakim*, which formerly sometimes designated a second-in-command, has similarly disappeared.

Grevemeyer gives a list of other titles for political functionaries. The *qazi* (probably from the Arabic *qâdî*) is the judge; *wazir*, a 'minister'; *hakem* (*hakim*), also a doctor; and *mirza*, a scribe. The military entourage seem to have been designated by *nokar* (1982: 128).

It is often mentioned in the literature that the regional rulers, especially in Badakhshan to the right of the Pyandsh, saw themselves as descendants of Alexander the Great.[24] Such traditions are recorded for Wakhân, Shugnân and Roshân as well as Darwâs. This is in part a blatant contradiction of a second ideological justification, namely the claim of many princes to be the descendants of the Prophet Muhammad.

Their authority was based for the most part on a combination of ideological legitimacy (descent) and actual power. From a political perspective, this was supported by a client and kinship system in which political loyalties were important: the underlings were under obligation to support the ruler through contributions and military service, in return for which the ruler was under obligation to honour the loyalty of the local elite (see Grevemeyer 1982: 110ff.). This system was actualised in the form of hospitality, presents, Islamic alms (*zakât*) for the poor and certainly also through the division of booty in the case of war. Grevemeyer even speaks, in the context of great rivalry for political power, of a 'theft economy', which would have given those involved the means to prove their loyalty. As we shall see, the consequences of this political system, which shows some anarchic features, were sometimes quite horrible for the simple folk, for human life was hardly worth a thing and children were taken as booty without a second thought. Sexual misdemeanours seem to have been rather the rule than the exception.

It is possible to speak of a partial takeover of the administration by the Russians starting in 1892. On 30 June, Pamirskij Post, now Murghâb town, was founded as a military and administrative post. The Pamir expeditionary forces took control of Shugnân, Roshân and Wakhân. Out of the north-western parts of the region the Oroshor District was formed, and from the eastern area the Pamir District. Both districts were made dependent on the Ferghâna administration. Darwâs was handed over to the administration at Bukhara.

Village administration and justice

Below the level of the *mir* or *shah* there were liegemen whose role still remains unclear. Andreev reports that at the turn of the twentieth century in Khûf (Roshân), with its 70 or so farmsteads, there were eight such liegemen of the *shah* (*nûkaran*) who were exempt from taxes. They probably saw to the delivery of taxes in Khûf and served as soldiers, or rather as the leaders of the local militia, in case of war. Andreev speaks also of the *aqsaqal* ('whitebeards'), otherwise known from Kyrgyz areas, who were supposedly formerly the elders of the sub-district of Shugnân. For their part, they had *arbab* and *mirdah* below them (1953: 37).

The term '*aqsaqal*' is also known in Wakhân to designate the administrators of the four sub-districts (see Holzwarth 1980: 212). Their duties comprised tax collecting and the organisation of military service, as well as settling disputes that could not be solved at the village level such as those that concerned conflicts over water and land rights between two villages. Works requiring the cooperation of several villages (for example the building of canals, roads or bridges) were also coordinated by the *aqsaqal* (ibid.). In other places, *aqsaqal* are mentioned as village leaders.

Even in the Russian period, the post of *mingbashi* ('Lord over a thousand') is still mentioned in Badakhshan to the left of the Pyandsh (see Lentz 1931: 194; Olufsen 1904: 99; Stein 1928, II: 887). In Roshorve, in pre-Soviet times, this was what other authors have designated *aqsaqal*, a sort of regional chief. In the 1920s the people of that village gave that title, long ago repealed by the Soviets, to their local overseer.

In more recent times, at least in Afghan Wakhân, local chiefs chosen by the population ruled with the council of the old men (*aqsaqal*) (see Raunig 1978: 274). These old men are also the heads of the local lineages. The Ismaili clerics, the *khulafa* (plural of *khalifa*) must be considered another generally accepted authority at the village level.

The governance of the village, as exercised by the liegemen of the one in power under supervision of the *aqsaqal*, was naturally not limited to tax collection and the carrying out of the works ordered by the *aqsaqal*. Thus, they also took care of most local affairs and smoothed over conflicts. They ran the local guesthouse as well as, in the Sunni region, overseeing the upkeep of the mosque. Grevemeyer reports that in regions with difficult paths, which are famously common in the Pamir, an escort was arranged for caravans and, in border regions, their protection assured (1982: 147).

Below the *aqsaqal* in the sense of a sub-regional overseer or village head, as Olufsen understands it (1904: 144), there were judges (*kasi, kazi*) responsible for trying petty crimes and who gave sentences of fines or beatings. Although the death sentence could, according to Olufsen, only be imposed by the Emir of Afghanistan himself, even the 'lighter' sentences were hard and gruesome. For simple theft, beatings were considered fitting. After the third case of recurrence there was the threat of losing one or both eyes or hands. However, the defendant did have the right to defend his innocence and, using Islamic judicial practices regarding proof as our guide, the latter could only be given by eyewitnesses.

In case of a killing (Islamic law does not differentiate between murder, manslaughter or only accidental homicide), the *kasi* generally ruled a death sentence, confirmed by the Emir, which took place in the village itself by stabbing with a knife, beheading with an axe or stoning (Olufsen 1904: 145). According to Islamic law, if the family of the deceased agreed to it, a high blood price could also be paid, after which the murderer was let free.

Just as between the rulers and their local liegemen, the client–patron relationship between the local elite and the plebs or farmers was probably not merely of an exploitational nature. Whether the distribution of food in hard times was part of the arrangement cannot be gleaned from the available literature, but military protection of the subject population would have represented an important return.

Tax system

De jure, taxes were only paid by the ordinary populace in Badakhshan. The liegemen of the regional rulers did, however, pay voluntary contributions, such as an ox or two coats, for which they received gifts in return. In this case we are dealing more with reciprocal exchange relations to cement the links to one another than with taxes.

Thus, the simple farmers had to pay the most. Holzwarth lists the taxes that each household had to pay yearly towards the end of the nineteenth century in Wakhân: a leash, a piece of leather for one pair of shoes, one horseshoe, one cup of butter, one wether and one sack of flour. In neighbouring Ishkashim, there was additionally one day of unpaid work per person twice a year for the *mir*. This also required them to bring certain extra things with them, such as butter, flour, fuel and two loads of firewood (1980: 201). One must also work on the assumption that the population had to labour on the land of the *mir* unpaid and give over the entire harvest.

According to de Rocca, in Darwâs in the late nineteenth century every person had to hand over seven pounds of iron (from the local mine in Wandsh), and the households added among other things a wether or goat, a coat (*khalat*), one pair of boots, one bowl of butter, one chicken, etc. (1896: 256). The *zakât* (a tax that was later distributed to poor people as required by Islamic law), otherwise usual in Bukhara, was not collected in Darwâs at that period because of the poverty of the people. However, a base tax of 10 per cent on grain and mulberries also had to paid, as well as a contribution at weddings. The taxes seem plausible to us nowadays, but we should consider that a humble family could itself in one year afford to slaughter only one wether and that wheat production barely sufficed for its own needs.

Added to the taxes paid to the political leader, there were also contributions for the Ismaili clerics. According to the same source, these represented another tenth of the grain, one-fortieth of the livestock, as well as animal products (butter, for example).[25] Added to this was also labour deployment on the private land of a *pir*, called *zamin-e shahi* (Holzwarth 1980: 202). Whoever refused this contribution *de facto* switched over to the Sunni faith. Information about comparable services in the Sunni region are lacking.

One must label the above-mentioned contributions as 'normal' taxes. Added to this came various special services to the parish and repeated war contributions, either to the victorious opponent or to their own overlords (cf. Shaw 1877: 97; Olufsen 1904: 86). These arbitrary taxes were collected with great harshness and when the population, continuously living at the existential minimum, could not pay, people, especially beautiful girls, were seized and sold into slavery (see pp. 150–151).

The Russian occupation of the Pamir was received at first without resistance, later even with some excitement, as it led to a definite reduction of taxes. After 1905, only half of the previous land tax and one-third of the livestock tax (measured by the rates for the Emirate of Bukhara) were collected. As for the harvest tax, the Russians even took only 5 per cent of the former amount (see Holzwarth 1990: 159–160). However, informal contributions continued – for example, for the building and upkeep of the village guest house or unpaid labour or goods and services for the village community (for example the building of canals), or for the district (for example the building of roads and bridges).

Pamiri society

Current observers in GBAO remark on the widely distributed tendency towards as egalitarian a treatment of people as possible, which among other things was expressed by an equal consideration of all households for humanitarian help from 1994 to at least 1997. Also, all the households should take part in equal measure in communal investments. In relation to the state farms, it was considered a matter of course in sovkhoz management that each labourer had to receive a share of the land. This position is a product of the Soviet era. Formerly, society was strongly differentiated; sometimes the gap between rich and poor was immense.

Traditional social stratification

Olufsen is the first author to speak openly of a caste society in Pamir, in 1900 already in part a thing of the past: 'During the time of the former Shahs or Mires, caste existed, so that all offices were inherited, and the poor man, whatever his talents, was as a rule forced to remain in the same social position which his father had occupied.' In his time, 'the only ones who can occupy the leading positions in the villages' were the descendants of the former administrative class (1904: 145).

Luknizki also speaks of the previous existence of a caste system in current GBAO and in Badakhshan in general. The highest caste (*shaná*) was that of the Khans. They were followed by the Seiïdes[26] (*pir* and *khalifa*), who were considered 'servants of the living god' and seen as 'representatives of the prophet' (1954: 218–219). One caste rung below that stood the representatives of the Khan from the caste of the *mir*. To the fourth caste belonged the 'Akobyres' (that is, the war leaders of the Khan), and to the fifth, lowest caste, the 'Rajats' or 'Fokirs', belonged the farmers who had to strive to feed all the higher castes (ibid.). Holzwarth differentiates only between two main groups, the aristocracy (*khawass*) and the humble folk (*'awam*) (1980: 197). Numbered among the ruling class or aristocracy were the relatives of each *mir*, his liegemen (*nûkaran*) and the local aristocracy, designated as *akabiran*, 'the great ones'.

The upper class and the plebs can be differentiated not only by real or attributed descent but also by the fact that the former did not pay any taxes while the humble folk, as we said, fed them through taxes and all sorts of other special contributions. Some doubt may be expressed about the reciprocal services, comprising among other things the military protection of the simple folk. The Shugnî rulers could not protect their people against the Afghans nor could the Wakhî potentates protect theirs from the repeated raids of Shugnî bands.

In perusing the knowledgeable work of Grevemeyer about the political history of Badakhshan, one notices that, on the one hand, the change of rulers is stressed (between Kokand, Bukhara, an autonomous Badakhshan and the Afghan kingdom) and, on the other, that a remarkable continuity in the privileges of the upper class may be observed. This means that, despite all the wars and repeated new overlords, the *sayyids, mir, pir*, or however they are named, as well as the liegemen in the sub-regions and villages, managed to retain their places at the upper end of society and thus their privileges as well (1982: 126–152).

Shahrani, in his work from the 1970s, delivers a critical view of Afghan Wakhân society, which probably differs little from the situation in the nineteenth century (1979a: 55–58). Thus there are six descent groups, the highest-ranking of which are the *sayyeds* (the descendants of the Prophet Muhammad). However, we do not learn anything about their material situation. The *Khuja*, as second group, trace their ancestry back to the first Khalif of Islam, Abu-Bakr. At present, they are the religious leaders.

The descendants of the old lords (*mir*), as a third group, lived in relative comfort in his day. Because their ancestors married women of a lower caste, the *Sha-ana*, formerly belonging to the *mir* group, make up a fourth level. A very small fifth group are the descendants of the courtiers of the earlier *mir*. To the sixth and biggest unit by a landslide belong the *Kheek*, who, as the socially lowest group, retain only few links with one another. How far the delimitation between the first three and the last three groups (intermarriage forbidden) still existed in the 1970s remains a mystery due to the author's use of the ethnographic present.

In the work of Andreev on Khûf, published in 1953 and 1958, it is also unclear about which period the author is speaking when, in contrast to what has been said above, he assumes a very egalitarian society. Supposedly, on the border between Shugnân and Roshân there were neither landless people nor serfs, and all households including that of the *khalifa* or the so-called notables took part in farming.

Economic and social stratification may have diverged here. Whether in Khûf there was a social impermeability similar to that in Wakhân, however, we do not know.

Poverty

One consequence of the caste system in the current Tajik Badakhshan until the beginning of the twentieth century based on the exploitation of the lower classes, was poverty – indeed, the complete impoverishment of the humble folk. This can well be imagined even today based on the few remains of the earlier residential constructions, such as we found in Roshorve on the upper Bartang in 2003. There, abandoned and in ruins, we found a mudbrick structure with a single small room of some 4 by 5 metres, no windows apart from a smoke hole in the ceiling, the household inventory consisting mostly of mudbrick benches. Such a structure housed five, ten or more people, a few scrawny goats or sheep, and of course various tools and provisions.

'Die Bewohner lebten hier das primitivste Leben in armseligen kleinen Steinhütten, hatten nur einigen Fell-Lumpen im Haus, worauf sie ruhten, und primitive Hausgeräte aus Thon und Holz', reports Olufsen about similar living conditions in a village north of Khorog near Kuh-i-lal (1900: 145). As the traveller was riding along the Pyandsh in Ishkashim and Wakhân in 1896, he remarked on the numerous caves, inhabited owing to the unusual poverty and disturbances that were prevailing in the provinces (1904: 86). In any case, cave habitation seems also to have a certain tradition in that area, as signalled by Aurel Stein, basing himself on Chinese sources (1928, II: 878).

According to scattered references, the living conditions of the Pamiris had worsened mostly due to the Afghan invasion of 1883–95. Yet the poverty of most Pamiris is one of the things that the first European visitors Wood and Gordon had already remarked upon, in part long before the Afghan invasion: 'In former times Badakhshan was noted for the social qualities of its inhabitants,' Wood remarks, 'but few have now the means of being hospitable.' Whoever needed a place to stay 'will not have to complain of any want of attention, . . . but for a meal, he must look to the really charitable' (1872: 178). The last means, of course, those who can afford to sacrifice a meal to travellers.

Luknizki reports that it was even the practice in the Pamir (for want of other options) to pay contributions with children, especially young girls of the lower castes (1954: 219). Whether this was only true in the context of the aforementioned war contributions, or if it was in fact usual among the poorest, remains unclear. What is certain is that this remark does not merely reflect Soviet propaganda, as we will see when we view the question of slavery.

Substantive numerical data about the social stratification of the Pamiris are only available beginning with the Russian occupation of the Pamir at the end of the nineteenth century: almost three-quarters of all farmsteads or households were classified as 'poor' and only 2.6 per cent having more than 8.72 hectares of land were considered well off. In 1917, on the eve of the Revolution (and thus probably at the beginning of the Soviet era a few years later as well), the proportions were similar: 5.9 per cent of the farmsteads were considered well off, 27.2 per cent as middle-class and 66.9 per cent as poor. From the latter, some 60 per cent owned less than a hectare of land and almost no livestock (Kreutzmann 1996: 171).

Holzwarth (1990: 151) provides corresponding numbers, based on Russian sources, for Roshân, which was considered to be especially poor, at least in the Bartang valley area. According to this, from 670 families in all, none were classified as rich, 14 (or 2.1 per cent) were considered middle-class, 652 (or 97.3 per cent) as poor and four (0.6 per cent) as landless. However, only four families were entirely landless. On the other hand, this points to the extremely low yield in agriculture achieved by most families, if they were poor despite owning land.

Even if this classification system does not report the absolute poverty situation, one can impute from it that the national poverty categories used here in no way employed rigid criteria in classifying a household as 'poor.'[27]

A possibility, apparently already common in the nineteenth century, of fleeing the absolute poverty in the Pamir was offered by work migration, which was only possible, however, under extremely difficult conditions. Rickmers mentions hundreds of Pamiris going to Ferghâna on foot as migrant workers (1930: 165). In the middle of the 1990s this tradition was revived, though with different migration goals.

A brutal method in fighting poverty was the forced resettlement of the Pamiris organised by the Soviets in the 1920s and 1930s to the cotton-producing regions in western Tajikistan, which was revived shortly again in the 1950s.[28] Another possibility for survival existed, apparently earlier as well, as paid workers for the Kyrgyz nomads, in which, according to Kreutzmann, the Pamiris served as herders (1996: 151). In a similar way, some Pamiris in 1995 to 1998 period again did unskilled work in Kyrgyz settlements, for example building houses.

Slavery

Luknizki writes in 1954 most vividly about the former practice of slavery in the Pamir, when, for example, he points to the fact that among the state and party functionaries active in his time there were still women who had been sold as wares in their childhood (p. 219). The girls of the lowest castes had been bartered for in the markets of Kabul, Chitral and Peshawar, probably also in the north to the Kyrgyz.

The Soviet author is in no way the only one to address the issue. Wood already reports that one source of income for the Wakhân ruler was his slaves (1872: 244). Stein points to the earlier enslavement, especially of women and children, by the *mirs* in Shugnân (1933: 276). Kreutzmann mentions the caravan route between Kabul and Yarkand through which the slave trade with Pamiris from Shakhdara and Sari-kul (that is, the Chinese Pamir) passed (1996: 81).

Grevemeyer mentions former slavery practice several times, based on local and Russian sources. Thus, the rulers of Shugnân used to enslave people from the neighbouring areas, but also unscrupulously their own people, although they were Ismailis (1982: 105–106, 114). Later on, the author mentions that between Roshân and Khûf, and from another neighbouring region, 100 to 150 young men and women were seized yearly and sold in Afghan Badakhshan or even in Kashgar. Children descended from *sayyeds* were supposedly spared (p. 155). This information concerns the first decades of the nineteenth century.

Thus, when in older sources it is sometimes said that mostly unbelievers (*kafire*) were enslaved, one should not forget that in the eighteenth century and the early nineteenth the power-holders of the Pamir apparently did not bat an eye when Muslims were also enslaved, whether Shiites or Sunnis (see von Hellwald [1875] 1880: 264).

According to Olufsen, slavery was widespread only until the middle of the nineteenth century; however, every judge or *aqsaqal* at that time had both male and female slaves. Bobrinskij says, on the contrary, that it was in the middle of the nineteenth century that the use of slaves as tribute or presents to more powerful rulers or as income increased (1908: 62). Thus whole families were sold, though the children between 8 and 12 years of age were preferred. These were captured in raids on neighbouring regions, thus of the Shakhdara people on Wakhân or the Shugnî on the Kyrgyz of Eastern Pamir.

Yet the enslavement of those they were actually supposed to protect did not stop. According to Andreev, in the nineteenth century the village of Khûf was also a frequent victim of the rulers of Shugnân who, for example, had seized one child from every household in one raid (1953: 29–32, quoted by Holzwarth 1980: 209). According to another source, sometimes as many as two-thirds of all youths were enslaved by collecting them as taxes as if they were sheep or goats (based on Holzwarth 1980: 209).

Capus later explicitly says that around 1890, in the Afghan region, slavery was still quite widespread, but that to the right of the Pyandsh on the Bukhara side it no longer existed (1889: 239–240). Yet in Darwâs, supposedly even at the beginning of the twentieth century, ‘sehr hübsche Jungfrauen’ (very beautiful virgins) were offered to the German Rickmers for 200 Marks ‘bei sofortiger Lieferung gegen Kasse und zum dauernden Eigentum’ (to be delivered immediately against cash and as permanent property) (Rickmers 1930: 101–103). Certainly the tradition of giving over daughters of a third party (probably against their will) as a ‘gift’ in securing economic alliances should also be considered a contribution to slavery common in those times.

Following the earlier slavery, the area now suffers from modern sex slavery which evolved after the civil war of 1992–3. This is still practised today by bands who regularly sell girls from the Tajik heartlands into prostitution in at least Uzbekistan, and possibly in other places.

Household life

This part describes daily life in a private household as reported from pre-Soviet times. However, many of the old rules, habits or traditions reach into the present – for example, concerning the elaborate hospitality of the Pamiris.

Kinship and solidarity

Very few sources are available on the kinship system of the Pamiris, perhaps because it appeared to be of little interest apart from the already mentioned division of the population into descent groups or castes. Concerning the mass of the population, neither clans nor lineages are especially marked, and even in the early Soviet times researchers were unable to gather any interesting information on genealogy any more. After 1990, even the founding stories of most settlements could hardly be reconstructed from the oral tradition.

Traditionally, the village (*kishlak*) is the basic social unit in the Pamir (see Krader 1963: 163–167). Larger villages in the Western Pamir valleys, already numbering 30 to 40 homesteads in the nineteenth century, were organised in groups of patrilinear and affinial families of five to ten homesteads each. In smaller villages, the village community and the kinship group were often identical (see Holzwarth 1980: 210).

In Ishkashim and in other places, a kinship group (also called a lineage) was called *qoum* (*kaum*) or *konda* ('trunk'), in Wakhân *tokhm* (literally 'seed') and in Shugnân *goruh* ('group'), even when they seldom numbered more than ten households (Holzwarth 1980: 215). Today, the families can seldom name their ancestors past two or three grandfather-generations. But, according to our information, the tradition of maintaining a *nisba*, the genealogical lists cultivated in the Islamic world, was not very widespread even in the past, except within the *sayyid* families. Even in the more traditional Afghan Badakhshan, ancestors' names are rarely known past three or four generations (Kussmaul 1965b: 75).

Communality among family groups existed and still exists in large villages in many forms: for example, the founding and upkeep of the irrigation system as an important basis of the economy – but also as a collective activity (long before the Soviet era) concerning, for example, the building of houses, common rituals or festivities connected with religion, initiation (circumcising the boys) and life cycles (weddings, funerals) etc.

Within the village, 'the large patriarchal family, often in its later form of an undivided family (*ibyna, ashgol* or *vokh*) consisting of two or more married couples usually of two to three generations, was, as a rule, a primary social and economic unit of society in the nineteenth century' (Monogarova 1978: 298). Families with a common line of descent worked closely together: 'they rendered mutual help (*kyryar*) in agricultural work, pasturing cattle, battue hunting, construction of dwellings and farm premises, etc.' (ibid.). Perhaps this cooperation has more far-reaching reasons, as L. Monogarova believes that until the middle of the nineteenth century land was not privately owned but was the indivisible property of the patrilineage, and that only afterwards, with the multiplication of users, did it become private property.

There were and still are communities of interest between non-related families as well, such as the *amtabaq*, already mentioned concerning the keeping of draught animals, a form of cooperation that clearly supersedes the usual grade of neighbourliness. *Tabaq* means 'plate' in Arabic, and in many countries, *amtabaq* designates the group 'eating from the same plate'. Yet it is precisely this tight cohesion which is expanded in the *amtabaq* by the cooperation also of non-related households. This means that, in the Pamir, solidarity and tight cooperation is in no way restricted to the family.

Traditional family authorities at the clan level (*konda*), such as Friedrich Kussmaul still met with on Afghan soil in the 1960s (1965b: 75), have not existed in the Tajik Pamir region for generations. For this reason, truly wide political participation on the village level of all the households exists today, which very much simplified the recent founding and work of Village Organisations for self-help.

Gender in pre-Soviet times

An extreme lack of clarity about gender roles in pre-Soviet times prevails in the literature. In the early travel reports, Pamiri women were on the one hand often considered reserved, even extremely shy (for example in de Rocca 1896: 244, or in Cobbold 1900: 192). Though they left the house unveiled, they would hide from any strangers they met in the alley. The reasons for this conduct remain puzzling, for it is often mentioned in the same context that a cloistering of women founded on Islam had always been unknown in the Pamir. On the contrary, many, though probably unmarried, women were supposed to have lovers among the Russian Cossacks (see Cobbold 1900: 192, 197). In the same context, it is also clearly emphasised that adultery was very common, yet the men did not know jealousy (and thus feelings of revenge).[29]

We were able to record an interesting comment by a farmer on this theme in 1996. To the question of what he would do if he found out his wife was unfaithful, he answered: 'Do not pay attention to rumours. And even if it's true, don't do anything about it. Don't quarrel or insult your wife. Don't be jealous. When you're on the road for days with the animals on the grazing grounds, it would drive you crazy otherwise. Don't even think about her.'

Other sources, on the other hand, emphasise the poor position of women, because for a long time girls especially were basically considered a ware. Women were considered for a long time to be the private property of men (fathers, husbands or else older brothers), and were even given over to important people as 'presents'. Certainly there was, beyond this, for a time a tradition of wife stealing, and concerning slavery, girls are mentioned more often than boys and/or men.

Considering the sources in chronological order seems to confirm that older sources show the woman's role in a much more negative light than more recent ones. Thus, one may proceed on the assumption that until well into the nineteenth century women were clearly disadvantaged compared with men. But this did not result from the Islamic religious tradition and was definitely not justified by Islamic rules.

Even before 1900 the situation must have improved drastically, even if poor women (like poor families in general) certainly still took on a socially lower position for a long time. A more nuanced picture is offered by Olufsen for this period. If there was a school in the village, both boys and girls went there. If a father did not send his children to school, the village elders spoke to him about it (1904: 139). Poor people forced to hire out their children to the rich supposedly did this only with boys, not with girls.

Around 1900, according to Olufsen, most of the marriages were monogamous (1911: 288), yet the question arises as to whether this was due to an improvement in women's status or impoverishment of the men. The author emphasises that the women did not strictly adhere to the rules of Islam, and a series of usages from the Avesta religion were still kept alive in his time. This fact, as well as that the women were not veiled, seems to point to a certain amount of personal freedom but does not confirm their social position.

On the contrary, von Schultz, who also describes conditions at the beginning of the twentieth century, emphasises that the men were not good spouses and that women were watched and hidden by their men (1910b: 253). The early marriages, or even child marriages, of that time certainly do not speak for girls' freedom in planning their lives (see von Schultz 1911/12: 26). However, von Schultz also confirms the sexual freedoms occasionally taken even by married women, an absolute exception in the Islamic world. It seems, moreover, that the obsession with virginity of other Islamic societies obviously never existed in that form in the Pamir (see Monogarova 1978: 300). This, though, does not mean that sexual promiscuousness before marriage was widespread. Even today, according to our informants, most girls emphasise their wish to be wed a virgin and justify this with Islamic moral rules, even in Khorog.

It is undisputed that women as well as men had to work very hard and, apart from a few chores such as ploughing and irrigation work, worked in all areas of agriculture (see Olufsen 1904: 130). This is true, with a few exceptions (for example, women seldom drove tractors), throughout the entire Soviet era and may also be observed for the present. When Olufsen remarks that women possibly had a greater personal freedom than in other Islamic countries, because, for example, a man would not decide on anything before asking his wife first for counsel, this points to a certain equality in family matters. One should not, however, ignore the fact that in other Islamic countries such as Pakistan, where women possess little to no public decision-making power, in many places they take either equal part or, concerning spending, in some places even dominate in the decisions concerning domestic affairs.

Reports explicitly underlining the freedom of the Pamiri women are usually of a more recent date and it is not always clear which period is being alluded to.

Certainly they do not predate the beginning of the Soviet era. Since then, however, one has to agree with Monogarova (1978) and Bekhradnia (1994) when the authors underline, among other things, the participation of women in the whole of public life in Gorno-Badakhshan. This is in complete contradiction with some of the surrounding countries. These liberties express themselves, among other things, in their participation in public social events and in festivities. It is explicitly pointed out that women had taken part in village councils when their husbands were absent, that they had even been present during evening parties, that they had taken over religious functions and, in this case certainly an allusion to pre-Soviet times, that they were equals in the case of vendettas for killing crimes (Monogarova 1978: 300). The last is, once again, an absolute exception within Islam-influenced societies.

However, Monogarova also mentions areas in which women were in no way men's equals: thus, a married woman was under the authority of the head of the house, first her father, then her husband. 'A husband for the woman is her god, her tsar, and then – her husband' (1978: 301). Also, a daughter only inherited one-quarter (of a man's portion?), and never the land, which only went to male heirs. However, it can be easily explained why a son having sisters inherited more livestock than they did: he had to pay expenses for his sisters' weddings.

Polygamous marriage had its positive and negative aspects: from the point of view of inheritance it had the distinct advantage that the children of both wives collectively had the right to equal parts: 'If one wife had only one daughter and the other had many children, the property and land were divided into two equal parts – one part was inherited by the single daughter, the other was successively divided among the second wife's children' (Monogarova 1978: 301). In the case of an only daughter, patrilocal residency was waived. Her husband had to move to her parents' (mother's) house, becoming a so-called *primak* (husband living in the wife's family).

In the early Soviet days it was already attempted to introduce a general equality for women. This worked very well in economic life, in the employment area and in public administration, though the women's role as the only one responsible for the household and child raising has hardly changed in the end.

The extent of the merits of the Soviet system is clear only when one compares the women's situation in GBAO in the twentieth century with that of their sisters in Afghanistan or north Pakistan. In those places there are also Shiites, among whom is an impressive percentage of Ismailis. Yet women, apart from their 'equal' role in heavy farmwork, are held strictly cloistered. It needs only a comparison between the illustrations in the literature for it to be clear that outside of GBAO women rarely appear in public (see Snoy 1975, in whose 119 photographic illustrations from Gilgit and Hunza in north Pakistan not one woman, not even a girl, is shown). It is particularly emphasised in the literature that women usually play no role in public life.

Customs and laws

In the last 150 years, mostly positive habits have been attributed to the Pamiris in the literature. In the *Nouvelle Géographie Universelle*, which usually avoids going into much detail, Elisée Reclus stresses their egalitarian tendencies and their good manners. Even children moved among adults with dignity and showed them respect. Women were industrious and took good care of their households (1881: 477). Olufsen completes the picture in saying that sons always carried out their fathers' orders (1904: 140). Vice versa, adults showed respect and obedience towards older people, and older men with beards were called *bâbâ*, grandfather.

Von Schultz, one of the most knowledgeable men on Pamir society at the beginning of the twentieth century, mentions the honour of the Western Pamiris and their love of their homeland, their sense of family and their love for their children. They were also conservative and respected the old manners and customs (1914: 19–20). To strangers, the Pamiris were polite and obliging and left a pleasant impression. Morals were lax, by which the above-mentioned sexual liberties are certainly meant. However, the author has extreme prejudices against the people of Ishkashim, compared with the neighbouring Wakhî who were raw and strong, industrious and energetic. The former, though, are represented as quarrelsome, deceitful and false; thus the author's informant very probably came from Shugnân. In earlier times, there was much tension, even escalating to open war, between the two districts, and even today the inhabitants of Ishkashim and Wakhân reproach those of Shugnân for their previous raids.

Lentz, who worked in the 1920s in the Bartang valley, emphasises the humour of the Pamiris there, their absolute honesty and their reliability. The people there also had a subtle feeling for fairness. The reproaches of his Turkmen caravaneers that the people were liars and morally depraved seemed to him completely implausible (1929: 158–159). The author takes the inhabitants of the Bartang valley expressively under his wing, even concerning reproaches about their supposed amorality, and considers that a conflict between the Turkmen Sunnis and the Ismailis of the Pamir lies behind the reproaches.

What's more, the inhabitants of the Bartang reciprocally had good memories of the German expedition. The name of Lentz and that of their expedition leader Rickmers is known to all the older informants of Roshorve. It is proof of the education in the out-of-the-way Pamir valleys in the Soviet period that today some men have even read the publications of the Germans in the original language(!).

In most reports, the generous hospitality of the Pamiris is mentioned. This only decreased somewhat in the feeding of strangers because of impoverishment during the second half of the nineteenth century. Accommodation in the guest house or a private household was and still is mandatory. This is also true for food, when this is at all possible. Today, as 100 years ago, in case of doubt a goat or a sheep will be slaughtered even by the poor. If special guests arrived, these were greeted before the village by the *aqsaqal* and *kasi*, together with the village elders, during which bread, fruit and eggs were presented (see Olufsen 1904: 143). Today, in similar cases, guests are greeted by the dignitaries of the village, while girls present bread and salt and a group of musicians usually plays.

We have already touched on the subject of law in the context of political administration and the exposé on gender. To complete the account: according to Olufsen, in earlier times violence and especially capital crimes were very rare among the Tajiks (1911: 290). On the position of judge, de Rocca says that in Darwâs at least the people voted for the *kasi* themselves to serve for an undetermined period of time and presented him to the Emir of Bukhara for confirmation. The latter then officially named him and presented him with an honorary coat (*khalat*) (1896: 267). There is also something to be added on inheritance laws: a settlement which is at first gender-neutral but as a rule favours men is the divergent principle of the above-mentioned inheritance laws, according to which that child inherits who takes care of the parents. Often this was not the oldest but the youngest son, and very seldom (if sons were also present) a daughter.

Surprisingly, traditional irrigation laws have been completely unnoticed by the literature. Today, no one can inform us any more as to what rules were true for the pre-Soviet era. From general works on central Asia (e.g. Moser 1894), as well as the instructions of Islamic law, we can suppose that the following rules also applied to the Pamir:

- Free access to water for the building of a canal; that is, the inhabitants of a village lying upstream had to allow a village lying downstream to build a canal going through their territory – if need be, even through their fields.
- Vice versa, the owners of the canal had the responsibility of making sure that the canal did not leak and that it did not cause any damage to the fields of those upstream.
- In the case of damages, a complete compensation at the least had to be paid.
- Concerning the building and upkeep of the canal, all the users were obliged to take part in all the works.

Life cycle

As mentioned earlier, the Pamiris have always been fond of children and as large a number of progeny as possible was considered a blessing of God. Reciprocally, a childless marriage was seen as divine punishment. According to Olufsen, boys were preferred to girls (1904: 135). This remark has, however, been disputed for later times. In every village there was a traditional midwife, who stood by together with other women from the family of the mother-to-be. Men were not allowed to be present during birthing. After a successful birth, the event was announced with rifle shots (see Lentz 1931: 230).

According to Olufsen, breast feeding only started on the third day after birth; until then the infant was fed only fat. It was then nursed until its third year, assuming the mother did not give birth again in that period. On the third day the child also recieved its name. To celebrate this, a feast was given (1904: 135–136).

Lentz reports a feast on the seventh day on which the infant's head was washed and guests were received. Later on there was another feast when the child was laid in the cradle for the first time. For this, the *khalifa* was called for and a festive meal with meat was organised (1931: 230).

Cradles (*shnak*; Shugnî: *ghök*) are widespread in all of central Asia and even today are rarely absent from any Pamiri household (see Plate 4.24). Children had the entire body wound quite tight and bound fast in the cradle which is rocked to and fro, often by older siblings, at astounding speeds. In any case, this seems to please the babies, as we could often observe.

In Tusyan they told us that, today, naming takes place on the seventh day, when the chosen name is whispered into the ear of the newborn by a child from among its kin. Child, mother and the five pillars of the house are then sprinkled with flour as a blessing.

Between the ages of four and twelve, the boys had to undergo the Islamic circumcision (*khonâ sûr*), which is still true today. Formerly the *ustô* was responsible for this, but since the Soviet era a visit to the doctor from the nearest hospital is usual. According to Lentz, the *ustô* received for his work the pelt, head and guts of the feast wether slaughtered for the occasion.

Today, in religious families, both boys and girls are taught the Ismaili prayers (*namoz*) for the first time at about the age of five. In the majority of the families, however, this takes place a few years later.

Children are free to play. In times past, however, they were obliged to help in the house or on the pastures at an early age. Already in the nineteenth century many villages did their best to house travelling scholars for the education of the children (boys and girls). In larger villages, even before 1900, there was a teacher who could at least teach the children to read and write. This was generally done in the Shugnî tongue (see Olufsen 1904: 139).

In pre-Soviet times, marriage in the Pamir took place at an early age. However, many very poor people could not afford to marry at all for the entire length of their lives. Olufsen reports that on the other hand the sons of well-to-do families supposedly married as early as 12, whereby the girls were even younger (1904: 190: 147). This is confirmed by more recent studies in the 1960s in Afghan Badakhshan where the rule among girls was 14–16 years, with the exception of 10- to 12-year-olds getting married happening frequently (Kussmaul 1965b: 76). These age groups are also confirmed for the 1970s in Afghan Wakhân by Gratzl, who says that men normally marry around 18 and girls from 13 to 14 (1974: 51). With very young girls, though, the rule was that the formal marriage was not consummated until her sexual maturity. This is the usual way of doing things in the traditional Islamic cultural area.[30]

At that age, the girls especially could hardly have been in any position to make a free choice. Therefore, von Schwarz's remark that Pamiri women had married according to their own free choice is not truly believable (1900: 440). Even if the girls had had a pro forma right of veto, one can hardly believe that a 12- or 13-year-old would have refused to marry the boy chosen by her father. Since many girls were also married to much older men, one must suppose a lot of forced marriages.

Olufsen mentions that wife-stealing had once been quite widespread in the Pamir (1904: 131). Whether this always meant a kidnapping, or rather an elopement of the young people (which in a judicial sense is also theft, as the *kalîm* is forfeit in this case), remains unclear. In any case, this wife-stealing was still common at the end of the nineteenth century.

When authors such as Olufsen speak of bought marriages or purchasing of brides ('Die Frau wird durch Kauf erworben'; 1900: 147), what is really meant is that the boy's father negotiates the bride price (*kalîm, kaling, kaleng*) with the father of the bride that must be paid to her family. The bride price is usually counted in livestock (cattle), or with poorer people in the form of articles of clothing (for example a dress, a shawl, shoes, several headscarves and perhaps some jewellery). This bride price (Arabic: *mahr*), is the usual way of dealing in Islam, which in no way represents a purchase in a judicial sense, even if it negatively influences the chances of sons of poor families marrying.

In some ethnic groups, the negotiated money may compensate the girl's family for the fact that, with the wedding, they are giving up a productive member of their household to another family. More often, in the Islamic cultural sphere the *mahr* represents a sort of dowry that is paid by the groom's household to the girl's father but which is then passed on by the latter to his daughter, often together with other goods. Therefore, the *mahr* also serves to support the woman in the case of a future divorce.

The question of preferential marriage partners must remain open. Krader claims that among the Pamiris, contrary to most other ethnic groups of central Asia, the majority of marriages were endogamous (1962: 143). Von Schwarz supposes that the Pamiris only married within their 'clan', which would allow for both endogamous and exogamous marriages (1900: 440). The fact that on the one hand polygamous marriages were allowed, but on the other only rarely practised on economic grounds, has already been mentioned.

Traditionally, the marriage was sealed by appointment in the presence of the *khalifa* (Ismaili) or *mullah* (Sunnis). Formerly, the festivities lasted several days and the entire village took part (as a social duty). The family of the groom also contributed, and still contributes, the greater part of the costs of this wedding feast, which is reduced today to two days: one feast in the house of the bride's parents and one in the groom's house, during which the move to the man's parents' house or else a newly built house takes place. In pre-Soviet times, on the first day of festivities there was a festive procession with musicians and men who accompanied father and son (on a horse) to the bride's house. During this, rifles were fired into the air, which in similar situations is supposed to drive away evil forces. In the bride's farmstead a feast was arranged with music and dance, in which both men and women took part; a second procession on the next day accompanies the bride and her father to the groom's house where there was a second feast. On this day, riding games were also organised (see Olufsen 1900: 148).

It remains to portray the death and burial ceremonies, which are only seldom mentioned in the literature. In the case of a death, according to Olufsen, the judge and *aqsaqal* first officially certified a person dead, whereupon the family members held a sort of funeral dirge and a *khalifa* or a *mullah* read from the Koran or the holy writing of the Ismailis (1900: 149). According to Lentz, the dirge was in no way merely wailing by women, such as is usual in other Islamic countries, but consists of the singing of mourning and love songs in the Persian language. The women accompanied this with tambourines and men with the *rabôb* (see pp. 188–189). There was also dancing (1931: 248).

The burial takes place even today according to Islamic rites on the day of death, or, when this occurs during the night, on the next day before sunset. The corpse is washed, enveloped in white clothing and carried to the cemetery on men's shoulders. Before closing the tomb, at least in previous times, hands, feet and face were freed from the shroud. If one forgot to do this, so it was believed, the animals and kin of the deceased would follow soon after. The graves were and are still oriented so that the deceased's head is placed to the north with the eyes looking towards Mecca (Olufsen 1900: 149). Apparently, no difference was made between men and women or children and adults.

Today, the neighbourhood men sit together with the *khalifa* the whole night after the funeral and remember the dead.

Daily nutrition and starvation diet

Existence since the collapse of the Soviet Union is seen by the population of the Pamir as a humanitarian catastrophe; in their own view, they had been very well off during the Soviet era, at least after the Second World War. However, as we have seen, hunger had formerly often been a reality in the Pamir. As Rickmers says, in the Bartang valley a corpulent person would 'mehr Aufsehen erregen als ein Elefant in Masuren' ('raise more attention than an elephant in Masuren'; 1930: 99).

What kinds of food were actually available to people in pre-Soviet times is a topic of scholarly discussion. Holzwarth bases himself on a Russian source of that time when he allows a consumption per capita of 147 to 260 kg of grain and legumes (1990: 158). These numbers appear rather high and it is unclear whether this represents the amount of food actually available or rather the entire harvest from which one must subtract seed (at least one-sixth!), taxes, and in winter also fodder for the animals. Another tenth of grain must been subtracted through milling/grinding loss. One must also consider that the grain consumption is complemented only meagrely by fruit and vegetables and practically not at all by meat. Occasionally, the literature speaks more of foods to stave off extreme hunger than of food for the well off. Especially towards the end of winter, grasses and wild herbs have to fill the bellies in many families (see von Schultz 1914: 34). One of the typical 'better' starvation diets consisted of 'lengthening' the bread with mulberry or pea flour or by serving pea noodles (cf. Regel 1885: 174 and von Schwarz 1900: 363).

According to Lentz, in the 1920s the staple food in the Pamir consisted of a meal of soup with bread and a little bit of fruit (1931: 229). On the summer pastures, milk products were mainly consumed along with bread, which is also true today. Contrary to the diet of families in the village and generally in the winter, this food was very rich in fat. Since otherwise there was a general shortage of fat in the villages, Pamiris still tend to eat a lot of it when it is available: Olufsen mentions the pleasure occasioned by an entire cup filled with melted fat (1904: 122); we also observed many times a man eat a whole bowl of cream to himself.

One must agree with Olufsen that bread was by far the most important food in the Pamir: 'Bread is not, as with us, eaten with meat or other things, but it is eaten by itself, and generally eaten hot' (1904: 123). This still holds true today, with the consequence that it was and is very difficult for the development aid agencies in GBAO to convince people that the cultivation of plants other than grain is much more useful to them on the nutritional level.

One can conclude from the literature that bread was baked almost daily. For this, the dough is prepared even today in a bowl. After that, the loaves are formed and laid out to rise (Plate 4.28). The loaves are afterwards baked in a *tandûr*, a mudbrick oven standing in front of the house (Plate 4.29). Because of the extreme scarcity of fuel nowadays baking is only possible every few days, so that the loaves' (*nôn*) particularity – namely their excellent taste when warm – can only be appreciated on the first day.

Plate 4.28 Young woman in Roshorve (upper Bartang valley) prepares bread (*nôn*). The work is done in the living room of the house (1997).

Plate 4.29 Baking bread in a mud oven. The woman has already made a fire with shrubs. The blaze beneath the oven (*tandûr*) allows the preparation of about twenty loaves of bread (*nôn*) (1997).

Complicated dishes were formerly extremely rare. Grevemeyer describes how usually, when bread alone was not eaten, water was simply brought to boil and (bean)flour scattered in the pot. Any passer-by could take part in the frugal meal, which was only enriched for special guests (1982: 160).

Plov (a rice-dish pilaf), also *ôsh* or *palô*, is, on the other hand, already considered a luxury food, served to guests during festivities, especially weddings. For the *plov*, a lot of fat is needed and if possible also a bit of meat, which is why this traditional food has only recently begun to return to the menus.

Gratzl remarked that in the 1970s in Wakhân meat was boiled and not grilled as in other parts of the orient (1974: 49). This is not without reason: if one were only to grill meat, one would lose the good meat broth which is almost more important than the meat itself – in any case it is much richer. For the *plov*, some of the boiled meat is occasionally roasted afterwards.

Mulberries (*tût*) play an important role in the winter diet, either dried or as flour (*pikht*). Previously – and perhaps again after 1992/3 – the flour often also replaced sugar (see Olufsen 1904: 104), in baking for example. Pressed mulberry flour represents practically the only traditional sweet of local production. Apricot pits were also hoarded for the winter. Traditionally, the above-mentioned dried apricots and apples are also winter supplies.

Some of the streams contain trout (Rickmers 1930: 57), the lakes various other fish as well, yet fishing does not seem to have been very widespread in the past.

Only slowly did fishing appear as a consequence of the economic crises of 1992 to the present. Especially on the upper Shakhdara, fish rather than meat represents an important nutritional supplement in some families.

The country population of the Pamir eat nowadays three times a day. In the morning before work, around six to seven, there was breakfast (*saraki khardj*) which was almost always made up of *tshirtshoî*: tea with milk, salt and fat in which the bread was crumbled. The midday meal (*mathor khardj*) took place between one and two o'clock and was made up simply of the former ingredients. Supper, between seven and eight (*wega khardj*), is the main meal of the day. Whoever can afford to supplements bread and a simple soup with fried potatoes or serves a good *shurpo*, a potato soup with herbs and, when possible, a few pieces of meat.

Traditionally, food is eaten with the hands. Big wooden spoons are carved for soup. *Plov* has been eaten with a spoon only since Soviet times. Most of the dishes presented are served on a wooden board or in a dish and the whole family, including any guests' eat from the same container.

From a nutritional-physiological point of view, potatoes are perhaps the most important element of nutrition. They were probably unknown, though, before the Russian occupation of the Pamir. Indeed, potatoes were introduced by the Russian army, at first for their own use but afterwards also for general cultivation (see von Schultz 1916: 218).

We have compiled the following short list ourselves to give a more complete view of the Pamiri menu for the last 100 years:

- *Osh* (Shugnî) is wheat noodles in a soup, prepared only with a bit of salt.
- *Rughan kharwô* is a liquid porridge made out of flour, butter, water and salt for daily use; similar, but without butter, is *kothsî*.
- A more solid porridge out of the same ingredients is called *bât*, only this latter is sweetened.
- *Khikhts* is a similar porridge made out of white flour and thus is considered a wedding dish.
- *Shîrbirindj* is cooked rice porridge, sometimes with dried apricots.
- *Katlaman* is a warm layer cake made out of flaky pastry soaked in fat (Rickmers 1930: 146).
- Salads of all kinds, prepared with many herbs, especially dill.
- Yoghurt and cream, eaten with bread.
- *Nonî ghugân*, crumbled bread covered with melted butter and milk and a bit of salt.

A hundred years ago, tea was still a luxury and only to be had in the wealthier households (see von Schultz 1914: 33); it has only enjoyed wider distribution since the 1960s. Today it is served at every occasion, and it should, if possible, be black tea. Green tea, which is cheaper, is considered to be especially healthy for older people, which is why younger people do not necessarily enjoy drinking it. Tea should have a lot of sugar in it, but since the economic crises families tend to serve unsweetened tea instead. Apart from tea, it is water which is mostly drunk and, when it is available, milk in the mornings.

Drugs

Alcoholic beverages have apparently been known in the Pamir for a long time in the form of mulberry eau-de-vie. High alcohol consumption, however, is nowhere mentioned in the literature. Vodka was only introduced under the Russians and is used moderately in social life, mostly in Khorog. According to our informants, one can speak of a certain amount of alcohol misuse only since the economic crises.

According to Rickmers, the Pamiris were supposedly heavy smokers of opium and hashish (1930: 69) in the past, which makes one wonder given the current lack of opium in local agriculture (though not of the transport of opium or heroin from Afghanistan to the neighbouring countries of central Asia or a limited consumption, especially of heroin, in Khorog). However, there was and is in Wakhân some general poppy cultivation for the manufacture of opium, today both for personal consumption as well as for export (see Shahrani 1979a: 78).

Lentz illustrates an opium-smoking woman (1931: 289). Our Plate 4.30 also shows a group of female opium smokers (around 1900), who seem to be extremely young. This opium consumption has been remarked upon by many visitors to the Pamir. Olufsen reports that in his time practically every household cultivated poppy

Plate 4.30 Group of women and girls smoking opium (historical photo from about 1900, Khorog Museum archives).

(*kuknar*) in their own garden and that many people used opium (*afiun*) themselves: it was either smoked or else the capsules were ground to powder and dissolved in water (1900: 144). In a later publication, however, the author paints a different picture, according to which in Shugnân specifically, and in its eastern outskirts of Garan, opium was smoked by everybody, though in Wakhân only by poor people.

Leaving aside the negatively judged social and physical consequences of drug consumption, a glance at the economic importance of opium especially is quite interesting. On the one hand, in Afghan Wakhân (and probably also in the other regions of Badakhshan lying left of the Pyandsh), poppy cultivation has a certain economic value for the farmers. On the other hand, there are obviously many opium consumers who do not plant poppy themselves and thus are forced to exchange a part of their meagre wheat supply for tea and, yes, opium (see Kreutzmann 1996: 148).

With heroin (see pp. 336–338), the consequences on both sides are much greater, especially in their inequality: here, in a time of extreme penury, one may weigh on the one side the huge incomes of the drug smugglers in the 10,000 to 100,000 dollars and more, and on the other side the ruinous expenses of the drug addicts. Both take place in an economic situation where practically nobody earns even half of the Tajik minimum required to exist.

Inventory of material culture

Villages and castles

In the general geographical overview (Chapter 2), the predominance of silt deposits as zones for settlement and cultivation was mentioned. These alluvial deposit areas, which in some valleys such as the Bartang or the upper Pyandsh represent the only possibilities for settlement, are known to have been formed by the deposit of alluvial silt by smaller side rivers and streams over thousands of years. The continued existence of those streams, that have a year-round water debit, thus represents the most important basis for survival. There are also a number of high plateaux with good soil in the Pamir, which could theoretically be used for cultivation and settlement, but many of them lack water, making them practically impossible to settle and useless for fields.

Depending on the geographical conditions, the traditional settlements are either scattered widely across the landscape on, for example, the few inhabited high plateaux where each farmstead lies surrounded by its garden (very easily recognisable nowadays, for example in Roshorve on the upper Bartang), or else the houses stand huddled against one another. The latter pattern may be found when cultivation surfaces and habitation ground are in competition with each another, such as in many villages on the upper Pyandsh or in the middle Bartang valley. In this case, one also builds on wasteland or above the fields. Especially in the current Afghan Badakhshan, one may observe from the Tajikistan side, some 200 kilometres upstream from Khorog, how the villages there are practically inserted into the mountain slopes and merge into them.

The village core may become more dense when the families of the first settler lineages multiply and group their living quarters around the oldest houses. In Wakhân, homes were built close together mostly to facilitate resistance against enemies. Some former castles (*kala* = castle), must have been nothing more than a closed front protecting such residential buildings against the outside world.

In one of his first reports on Badakhshan, Olufsen writes that at the end of the nineteenth century most of the farmsteads in western Wakhân, or even practically all of them, were equipped with towers and embrasures (1897b: 713). In this region, often vulnerable to raids by the *Kafirs*, later also by the Shugnân authorities, there were also about a dozen true forts, among which Olufsen describes that of Kala-i Sirgyn in more detail: a closed complex raised out of wood, stone and mudbrick some 4 metres in height, with corner towers looming over the walls by that height again. Before the gate a breastwork provided additional protection (1904: 94–97). A system of watchtowers in Ishkashim was, in the past, supposed to offer further protection against raids, on which signal fires were lit to warn the population of impending raids (Grevemeyer 1982: 90).

In his time one of the largest castles at Kala-i Pyandsh on the confluence of the Pamir- and Wakhân-Darya still boasted a permanent garrison of 300 soldiers. The largest of all the Pamir forts, Kala-i Kaka near Namadgut not far from Ishkashim, was, however, already in ruins by 1900. Here, in previous centuries, 1,000 soldiers could probably be stationed, based on the available space. There were also some castles, though smaller ones, in the west, such as Kala-i Wamâr at the site of the current Roshân, the castle of Roshtkala ('red fort') in the Shakhdara valley and the main fort of the former Afghan Shugnân, Kala-i bar-Pyandsha, not far from Khorog on the left bank of the river.[31]

A typical Pamiri village with its traditional mudbrick houses on a silt deposit cone, in the middle of gardens and fields, offers to the observer a picturesque view. Compared with Afghanistan, where the buildings still have empty window frames even today because there is no glass to be had, the standard of living in such a village in Soviet times truly was very high. There was a nursery school, almost always a primary school (occasionally, the children had, and have, to walk to a neighbouring village), formerly also a shop and, until the beginning of the 1990s, also enough fuel.

In extreme contrast to these modern achievements lies the water supply and sanitation situation. The hygienic conditions in the villages thus remain, up until today and despite the general progress made in the health sector in Soviet times, completely unsatisfactory: only larger villages have a piped water supply system. Moreover, in many villages, even though water for all uses (drinking, cooking, washing, etc.) should be taken from upstream of the village, yet on grounds of convenience most people go no further than their front door. Thus, in 2003 there was the same drinking water supply situation here as in Soviet and even pre-Soviet times.

The same goes for sanitation. Awareness of hygiene is not very evolved in GBAO – and this is generally the case in central Asia. Only in larger villages does one find even latrines on the farmsteads or in the gardens. Waste water is, as it was 100 years ago, simply thrown into the court, on the nearest field or – in the worst case – flows back into an *aryk*. Accordingly, in the Pamir water-borne diseases including typhus were and are common. However, the 'persian Typhus' in the past was not spread through water but carried by a tick (Rickmers 1930: 34).

Of further relevance to the theme of health: in the Wandsh valley, due to iodine deficiency, goitre was quite widespread. Supposedly, in 1929, 3,000 of the 3,500 valley inhabitants were prey to this condition (Rickmers 1930: 116). Here also it is probably not a water-borne problem; but the fact that it is so prevalent proves that the health consciousness and the knowledge of the Pamiris are very limited.

Residential houses, furniture and devices

For reasons of space, a detailed description of the fascinating living culture of the Pamiris, showing many parallels to surrounding areas (such as Chitral and the Swat valley) must be waived. Instead, a short systematic sketch of the most important basic ideas and architectural elements of residential buildings, as well as the immovable and movable inventory, will be given. An important part of the information comes from the author's interviews. More detailed presentation of residences can be found, for example, in Olufsen (1904), von Schultz (1914), Andreev (1958), Kussmaul (1965a, 1965b), Gratzl (1974), Kuschel (1978) and Patzelt and de Grancy (1978).

The Pamir house was formerly, according to Lentz, usually a primitive construction of stones and mudbrick: 'Höhlen ohne Fenster, nur mit einem Loch in der Decke, durch das im Winter Schnee und Kälte eindringen' (in Rickmers 1930: 222). This representation is confirmed by other sources (for example, Kuschel 1978) and our own observations in Roshorve (see p. 149). The most remarkable thing about these constructions is their tiny size. Even the residences in Wakhân described by Olufsen in 1904, which were in no way considered to be especially poor, are relatively small, with about 30 square metres of living space for an extended family. However, here there were at least a separate kitchen and stalls.

The newer building in Plate 4.31, built in 1960 in the traditional style, already sports a ground area of about 80 square metres, among which are two living spaces, each about 25 or 20 metres square. In the illustration, one can recognise the typical look of a Pamiri house in the eastern rayons of Wakhân, Ishkashim, Shugnân and Roshân, whereas in Wandsh and Darwâs newer buildings almost always have a pointed roof of corrugated iron. The building is rectangular or is made up of several rectangular elements strung together. No windows can be seen, for they are small and few in number, oriented towards the river (Plate 4.32). Not until the 1970s and 1980s, when there was for a time no lack of fuel, did the windows become larger. In the traditional house, though, they are almost entirely lacking.

Plate 4.31 Typical traditional Pamiri house with small light dome (*tshor khonâ*), Pyandsh valley (Shugnân) (1995).

Light comes through the small opening discernible on Plate 4.31 in the roof. Traditionally, such structures remain open in the summer and are covered part of the time in the winter.

The house contains the central living space (*tshîd*), recognisable in the picture by the glass roof over the light opening, a smaller living space or hallway (*poga*), a kitchen, an entrance hall (*dâlis*) and stalls. The living area is separate from the stalls nowadays, and the latter have a separate entrance on the other side of the building.

The buildings are of mudbrick, the walls occasionally also built with stones plastered with mud. The ceiling (Figure 4.1) is stratified, with supporting beams (1), strong sticks (2), smaller branches or thatch (3), and a mud or clay layer some 30 cm thick (4). After each winter it needs to be patched, though this is not too much work. Such roofs were accessible and in the past served to store fuel and fodder (see Plate 4.32).

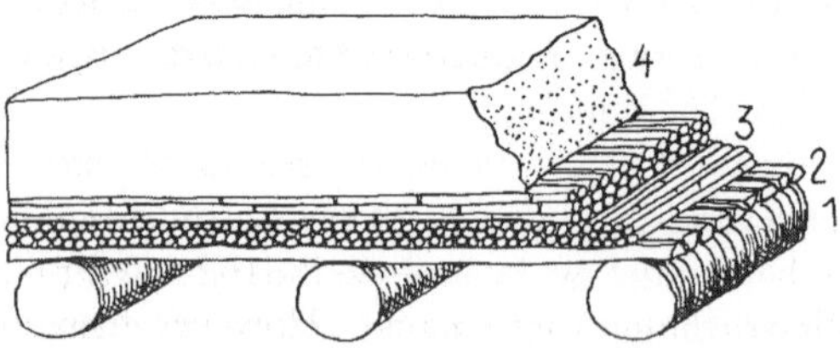

Figure 4.1 Section through the roof of a Pamiri house: (1) poles carrying the ceiling, (2) cross beams, (3) two layers of reeds or small branches, (4) clay finish. (With kind permission of the author, F. Kussmaul, 1965b).

Plate 4.32 Traditional Pamiri house in Vîr with small stock of fodder on the roof (Gund valley, Shugnân) (1996).

Few buildings today have a terrace in front of the entrance. Before, rich farmers at least had a sort of terrace across the entrance side of the house. Artistically carved wooden columns and a frame ornamented with carvings (*owakhk*) supported a roof. To the left and right of the entrance, guests could rest on platforms covered with mats. We still found such old terraces in, among other places, Basîd in Bartang. A newer variation has, instead of the open terrace, an anteroom with a glass window front. With the energy crises, this 'winter garden' has, in winter at least, lost its function as a brightly lit living room.

The core of the traditional house is the living room (*tshîd*), the roof of which is supported by five pillars with a cupola constructed out of four layers of beams in its centre, a square opening in the middle. The layout of this room, which makes up the Pamir residential house, goes back to the legend that the people of Medina mocked the Prophet Muhammad because he had no home. Thereupon, he put his arms around his daughter Fatima, his son-in-law Ali and their children Hassan and Hussein and said: 'This is my home.' This is what the five pillars are supposed to recall, of which three are on the entrance side and two on the opposite side of the room and thus surround a central space around which are grouped raised floors on three sides (see Andreev 1958: 423–470).

The pillars are named after the 'Prophet's house': on the left next to the entrance is Ali, to the right Fatima and on the far right Hassan, on the opposite side the often somewhat thicker column Muhammad, with Hussein to the right. The pillar Muhammad is sometimes also called *hasitan* 'king's arrow'. However, there are certain differences of opinion as to the identity of each of the pillars, and during the Soviet period no importance was attached to distinguishing the king's arrow.

The raised part of the room on the left side (*tshorsî-ga*) served, and serves, for hosting guests (in some houses also on the right). On the right (or left) side (*paskitîn*) is the stove (*tîn* or *kitsûr*) set into a hole in the raised floor. On this side, household activities are carried out and the family members sleep. Opposite the entrance is the third raised area, called *tshalak*, which formerly served to wash the dead but is today a normal part of the living space. Naturally, this ideal scheme was often broken, for in smaller houses all the space was needed so all could find a place to sleep. Yet nowhere did we find in a traditional house, whether old or new, the basic plan with the pillars and platforms ignored.

The same goes for the opening in the ceiling or roof. Figure 4.2 and Plate 4.33 show the core part of the ceiling schematically, a construction recognisable only from outside as a cupola because of the mud covering, made up of four square rows of beams one on top of the other, leaving in the middle a small, equally square opening.[32] This cupola or roof dome is called *tshor khonâ*. It allows the entrance of light and has an important symbolic meaning which probably goes back to Avesta times. This is why it cannot be made up of however many beams strikes the fancy, but of exactly those four rows, the lowest of which represents the earth, the second water, the next fire and the highest air – that is, the four basic elements.

The light opening does not merely give the Pamir house a festive flair when the sun's rays fall through. At the beginning of spring, the first rays of the sun fall on a specific spot on one wall, which is marked in older houses and wanders further each day in the course of the year, so that with the help of the light slot an annual calendar is formed. Lentz devotes a separate work to the time reckoning of the

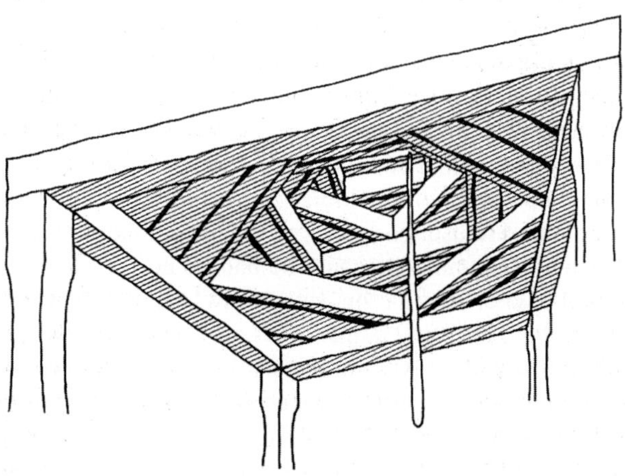

Figure 4.2 'Lantern' roof of a Pamiri house with four layers of wooden poles symbolising the four elements. On the top, during Soviet times, a glass construction became common in GBAO. (With kind permission of the author, F. Kussmaul, 1965b).

Plate 4.33 *Tshor khôna* seen from the interior of a Pamiri house. Four layers of timber symbolise the four elements: earth, water, fire and air (Namadgut, Ishkashim) (1995).

Pamiris (1939), and Andreev clarifies the basic idea using a drawing (1958: 164): different points in the house make up, abstractly, a human being whose body parts are hit by the sunrays: 'leg', 'between the legs', 'intestines', 'heart', etc. are some such body parts. If the first rays of the sun illuminated the 'leg' one day, then the Pamiris knew, at least in former times, that a specific date had been reached. Today, only a few old men can name elements of the old calendar.

There are other symbols in the Pamiri house. The meaning of the great transverse beam lying on the five pillars in no longer known, but the 12 transverse beams roofing the side opposite the entrance are still designated today as the '12 helpers in need', 'Good spirits' or the 'sinless saints'. Another interpretation calls them the '12 murdered imâms'. Occasionally, there are also 13 beams instead of 12, and the inhabitants of the house find another explanation.

Over the entrance between two of the pillars is always a transverse beam (*butshkighîdj*) decorated with carvings and often brightly painted. The ornaments show floral patterns as well as geometric chip-carvings (see Kussmaul 1972: 59). Some old men remember that it used to be called Abdullah, after the Prophet's father. On this transverse beam, good luck symbols may sometimes still be found, such as the 'corn maiden/bride' out of braided ripe ears of wheat called *arûsa al-qamh* ('bride of the wheat') in Arabic. Similarly ornamented beams could be found over the terraces of the residences in Khûf (Andreev 1958) or in Basîd (Bartang).

In newer houses, the living areas are often divided somewhat by fitted closets. Plate 4.34 show the 'family side' of the room. One can still discern on the bottom left the entrance to the oven (*kitsûr*). On the end wall lie shelves for household effects, a closet and a television set. To the right, a small fitted closet is discernible, dividing up the space between the pillar and the wall. Its name, *shkâf*, indicates that this is a tradition taken over from Russia. With the help of another closet on the other side, a small separate room is created where provisions and personal effects can be stored.

In the past, in some regions of the Pamir, for example in the villages of the Bartang valley, separate granaries, called *sidôn* (Shugnî), *wûrth* (Roshân) or (*ğiw*), were raised to store provisions (Plate 4.35). As a protection against rodents, the mudbrick constructions were built on a platform of stones and wooden beams. Inside there were two to four separate small chambers for wheat, maize, onions, etc. All the granaries are fitted with a wooden door and a lock. Many of them are still used today. They appear to be peculiar to these regions as no similar buildings are known to have existed in other parts of central Asia, nor does the literature mention any. The granaries of the Bartang Valley are similar in their basic structure to those common among the African Sahel cultures. With its divided chambers, a granary in Roshorve is strikingly similar to corresponding Dogon buildings in Mali.

Félix de Rocca describes the inventory of a Pamir house at the end of the nineteenth century as being of the simplest kind: 'Très primitifs les ustensiles. Ni

Plate 4.34 Interior of a newly (1980) built Pamiri house in traditional style showing common furniture (Namadgut, Ishkashim) (1995).

Plate 4.35 Old but still used granaries or storage houses in the village of Basîd (Bartang) (1995).

tables, ni chaises, rien qu'une pièce de toile ou de laine' (1896: 259). This is without doubt accurate, when the visitor is accustomed to European seating furniture. However, in a Pamiri house, seating furniture is traditionally unknown – as elsewhere in the Islamic Orient – and is replaced by felt coverings and carpets on the floor. Several layers of felt mats make up the base, over which originally hand-woven carpets of sheeps' wool, later Soviet industrial wares out of artificial textiles, are spread out. To sleep on, skins were used in the past, yet since the Soviet era more and more often quilts serve both as cot and as blanket.

Olufsen (1904) and von Schultz (1914) described what movable furniture they found in Pamiri houses around 1900 in detail. In one picture in Olufsen, a wide choice of objects is illustrated (p. 105). From the middle of the twentieth century we have the very detailed information in Andreev (1958). Finally, our knowledge of household effects was greatly enlarged by Austrian Wakhân expeditions in the 1970s (Gratzl 1974; de Grancy and Kostka 1978).

These report that the greater part of the household furniture was made up of wooden and clay wares. Metal objects were for the most part imported from Afghanistan. Wooden bowls, dishes and plates represent the greater part of the kitchen inventory (see Andreev 1958: 361), to which must be added cooking pots of clay, wooden spoons (a typological list is illustrated in Andreev) and, only among the well-off, big metal cooking vessels. Practically a luxury good were Bukharan pitchers out of copper or brass in which water was served and special guests received water to wash their hands before the meal.

The basketry wares of the Pamiris appear to be too simple to have occasioned the notice of visitors. Apart from the woven bags (*siptak*) illustrated in Andreev (1958: 290), there is practically no mention of the products, their basketry techniques, or the decoration.

In place of the modern closets, wooden chests were used (*sandûq*). The cradle was perhaps the only piece of 'furniture' in the European sense. Plates and spoons were stored in wall frames. The bedding was simply piled on one side of the room and covered with a brightly embroidered sheet. Carpets or other richly embroidered or patchwork curtains adorned the walls.

An important modern element of the household inventory is the iron Russian stove which has replaced the *kitsûr* in practically every house. This *pitshka* has the advantage that it can be carried from one room to another, the iron stovepipe is easy to take apart, and in the summer the stove can simply be put into a shed. However, families living in the country still always have a *tandûr*, a bread-baking oven, in front of the house.

For lighting, in past times there were either pine torches stuck into artistically carved wooden wall holders, or clay lamps for burning fat, with a cloth wick. Later on, the petroleum lamp (*fanûs*) was added, replacing the older versions by the Second World War at the latest. In the country, which is currently without electricity in the winter, this has once more replaced the light bulb.

Finally, part of the older household inventory included the household work implements such as the loom, spinning wheels, tools, and valuable farm implements among which are also the tack and plough (because of the expensive iron share), etc. Also stored in the house was a part of the provisions, for which storage pits were occasionally provided in the entrance area of the living space. Finally, Soviet additions to the household are freezers and television sets, which were very widespread before the economic crises.

Devices, hunting equipment and armament

The traditional plough, put back into use since the economic crises, has already been described (see pp. 107–108, Plate 4.9). Comparison with illustrations in Olufsen (1904: 115), Andreev (1958: 41), Kussmaul (1972: 37) and Raunig (1978: 279) shows that the technology has not changed in the last hundred years.

Previously, threshing was done with teams of oxen (Olufsen 1904) or, for small amounts, with sticks. This technique has been put into practice once more after 1992/3. The much more effective threshing sleds are unknown in the Pamir. Apparently, though, there were threshing floats with inlaid flint pieces such as are known from North Africa and the Middle East. We were able to observe simplified variations of such threshing floats in the summer of 2003 in the Gharm valley up to Tavildara; that is, on the border to GBAO.

For soil preparation, frame harrows were used to level the soil after ploughing. Such harrows, weighed down with the weight of the farmers and pulled by oxen, still existed 30 years ago in Afghan Badakhshan (see Kussmaul 1972: 39).

Apart from the wooden hoe that was replaced during the Soviet era after the Second World War by the tractor with iron ploughs, the main tools for working the earth are wooden spades (*zigandor phaî*), iron hoes and hand sickles (*zirw*) for the harvest. Wooden winnowing forks (*sekund*), winnowing shovels and rakes of the same material, and every sort of sieve, complete the list of agricultural implements (see Andreev 1958: 44).

Finally, limited to the Wandsh and Yasgulem valleys, we find some wooden transport sleds pulled by two oxen. They can also be found in Gharm and are quite certainly back in use after the events of 1992/3.

In the mountains, there are many places where not even beasts of burden may tread, which is why the Pamiris are used to transporting even heavy loads for long distances on foot. This is especially true for firewood, sacks containing the harvest and even whole tree trunks, which are even today transported by several men alternately over 10 kilometres or more. A wooden frame (*tshukht*) facilitates transport (of wood bundles, for example), even though it increases the weight of the burden in no small measure.

Traps used for hunting have become rare, but in earlier times they were quite widespread, especially in winter (Olufsen 1904: 126; Andreev 1958: 224). Hawking was also known. Olufsen's claim that every second man in Darwâs hunted with a falcon does seem somewhat exaggerated (1911: 105). However, there are still some hunting falcons in Darwâs as well as in Wandsh.

Concerning the weapons of the Pamiris, the numerous wars and feuds of the past were carried out with extremely simple means. In the Yasgulem valley, in Wakhân and also in other places there used to be wooden bows (Plate 4.36), which certainly looked very similar to Indian bows, but which only served to shoot stones (see Rickmers 1930: fig. facing p. 193).[33] Von Schultz ascribes a certain effectiveness to it up to a distance of 25 m, but does not believe that the bows could have been effective for hunting, except for birds (1914: 44). Stone-throwing bows could still be met with even after 1970 in Afghan Wakhân (Raunig 1978: 289). Perhaps these bows were actually only used to scare off birds from the wheat fields (Rickmers 1930: 203) and not, as Olufsen believes, to defend residential buildings against attack (1897b: 713). We saw, in any case, such a bow used in 1996 for the former purpose with little success, though this could have been due to the bowman's lack of practice after the 'weapon' had lain forgotten for 80 years.

The most 'modern' weapon before 1900 was, with few exceptions, shotguns with fuses, equipped with a fork to prop them up (Museum of Khorog exhibit; and see Kussmaul 1972: 73). The older matchlocks were almost as hazardous. They served mostly for hunting, but were also used by the indigenous militias. Whoever owns a gun usually also carries a belt (*kamar*) with all sorts of utensils. In the Museum of Khorog one such old *kamar* is shown (see Andreev 1958: 218): fastened to it are a powder horn (*tirdôn*), a hook for the bag (*tshangak*) and another pouch for small things (*sidzdôn*).

Olufsen mentions some scimitars, but knives were used as working tools not as weapons (1904: 109).

Plate 4.36 Bowmen in the Yasgulem valley in the 1920s (in Rickmers 1930, Plate facing p. 193).

Energy and environment

Though the crises of 1993 introduced an important help programme to provide nutrition, the question of energy was only discussed years later and would prove to be an equally difficult problem in the long run. While in Soviet times there were fuel subventions, usually in the form of mineral coal and charcoal, with Tajikistan's independence the deliveries were reduced and in 1992 completely stopped. Within a short period of time the people were forced to fall back on the natural resources, especially riverside trees and pygmy bushes from the mountains. These resources are extremely limited in the high mountains (Plates 4.37, 4.38). The result is extreme, not only in the consequences for Nature but also in the exponentially rising workload for people in finding wood.

A glance at the older Pamir literature, however, shows that in the current GBAO there was always an important lack of energy resources. Olufsen remarked as early as hundred years ago that it was difficult for the Pamiris to find enough firewood and that 'the poor people generally only heat the huts a little whilst the meals are being prepared, or when they have visitors' (1904: 124). Though Lentz does not speak of any lack of fuel in Roshorve, where in 1900 there was not a single tree, he does mention the immense burdens of brushwood that the women carried on their backs from the surrounding mountain valleys (1931: 168). Plate 4.38 shows two older women in the Bartang valley, who had already carried their burden for two hours and still had another 3 kilometres to go to reach Basîd. The difference is that our picture was taken in 1995.

Plate 4.37 Old woman in Roshorve (Bartang) uses *tersgen* to heat a Russian-type iron stove (1997).

Plate 4.38 Two women in the middle Bartang valley with heavy loads of dried shrubs on their long way home from the mountains (1995).

Those who own a lot of livestock, especially yaks, used and still use yak dung formed into practical dried cakes (*teyzak*) for heating and cooking. Dried brush is then used only to start the fire. However, contrary to the majority of the Kyrgyz of Eastern Pamir, only a few Pamiris own yaks or a sufficient amount of cattle. What is more, the farmers in the lower regions try to use a part of the dung to fertilise their fields. The consequence is that, with the exception of the city of Khorog and neighbouring areas which have electricity in winter as well as in summer, many Pamiri households are forced to get their fuel from nature.

Women especially are forced today, as their ancestors were hundred years ago, to search for fuel wherever there is still some to be found. Naturally, every tree in the area around the village to which claim can be laid is cut back each year to the point where it can barely survive. This fuel source, though, despite new plantings, particularly after 1995, is only a drop in the ocean, so that the distances women must travel to find fuel – as well as that of the growing number of men supporting them – are becoming longer and longer.

In Roshorve, from 1995 to 1998, we could observe how *tersgen* in particular (pygmy forms of trees found in the high mountains) were burned (see Plate 4.37). A large bush such as that shown in our illustration can, at a height of 3,500 m, have needed 100 to 200 years to grow 50 cm, only to burn up in a stove within five minutes. During our last visit in 2003 it was reported that there were no more *tersgen* to be found within a circumference of 15 km, which is why bushes of even less heat value are used. These have to be brought in ever-increasing quantities from ever-greater distances. Yet in these areas they only start heating in November when the temperature has sunk to a consistent below zero – and then only one small room.

A study done by the Asian Development Bank has shown that the pressure on natural resources due to fuel scarcity is a general problem in Tajikistan (Asian Development Bank n.d.). Attempts to curb deforestation in central Asia have a long history. Already the Khans of Kokand, who ruled for a time over the Pamir, were supposed to have tried to reduce burning for charcoal over most of their territory (Durrieux and Fauvelle 1901: 279), and the first reforestation was undertaken in 1878 in Turkestan under Russian aegis. In the Pamir, such attempts only began with the energy crises after the economic collapse of 1995. Before that, only a few trees to be used as construction timber were planted in limited numbers. The year 2003 shows a progression in the sense that the energy crises have become much worse and that a solution from reforestation is not yet in sight.

Clothes and shoes

In the current area of GBAO, clothing was very simple in pre-Soviet times. For the greater part it was made out of local materials, but despite a certain functionality it was not always appropriate to combat the extreme conditions (especially footwear; see pp. 140–141). Basic materials were wool, leather and skins for the under- and over-clothes of men and women, as well as leather and wood for shoes.

Although cotton was cultivated in the Tajik plains, the older publications report cotton clothing mostly only in Darwâs. In the eastern districts, cloth from this material was considered a luxury in pre-Soviet times, although Olufsen mentions it frequently as an alternative to woollen clothing (1904: 63–70). The author, though, had more frequent contact with hosts of somewhat comfortable means. Later on, cotton cloth became common everywhere for summer and house clothes (see Andreev 1958).

Lacking dyes, woollen clothes remained until after 1900 mostly limited to natural colours: white/dirty grey and brown tones predominate. The very colourful cloths, and especially the typical colourful Tajik 'flame' patterns for women's clothes, caught on rather late in the Pamir (Plate 4.39). However, the phase of valuable silk cloths such as were worn in Bukhara, Samarkand or other Tajik-dominated cities was skipped; that is, the change in clothing went directly from undyed wool to cloth of wool dyed with synthetics.

In the winter, the men wore thick coats of wool or fur. The *khalat*, a thick winter coat of very fine wool, which must be considered absolutely typical for the Pamir, was only worn by the notables (see de Rocca 1896: 244). The Garan men illustrated in Olufsen (1904: 60; see Plate 4.40, this volume) wear a similar woollen coat but of very coarse fabric (*chupân, gilêm*). Underneath, simple, very wide pants and shirts (*pirân*) of wool were worn (Olufsen 1904: 60; Andreev 1958: 245). Schlaginweit-Sakünlünski calls the wool coat *tshoga* (1873, in von Hellwald [1875] 1880: 271). In the summer, a thinner tunic was worn (*jaktaî*), which at least in the Western Pamirs was, as early as 1900, frequently of cotton (see Olufsen 1911: 74; Andreev 1958: 399).

Women wore dresses underneath their pants, out of somewhat finer wool, reaching down to their calves and extremely wide on top and fastened with a cord, but tight around the ankles (see Gratzl 1974: 50).

Even in earlier periods, Pamiri women went unveiled. For weddings, though, an imposing bridal veil with complicated embroidery (*ruband* or *tshashband*) was used in the past, passed on within the family (Rickmers 1930: 287). The oft-represented symbol of a red cock has been interpreted as an old Iranian motif.

Even today the woollen tights of the Tajiks (*jirâb*) are widespread (see Gratzl 1973: fig. 6.8). 'The stockings, which generally reach to the middle of the thigh, are knitted like a bag, without a heel, and are adorned with very tasteful patterns' (Olufsen 1904: 64). These stockings were highly prized, and were and are used as valuable gifts both amongst the Pamiris themselves and for strangers. Even in the years after the civil war, home-knitted stockings were the only possibility for many families to use as gifts for the road for their guests.

These entirely traditional *jirâb* are of coarse wool and rather uncomfortable. They hardly fit the foot, but are made up of a tapering tube and a funnel-shaped end which does not fit itself to the toes. Because of the scarcity of wool they are almost always closely fitted. If, based on these recent pieces, we may draw conclusions on traditional stockings, then the wearers can only be pitied.

Plate 4.39 Woman from Gharm-Tshashma (Shugnân) wearing the national Tajik dress with 'blaze' ornaments (1995).

Plate 4.40 Men from Garan wearing woollen *chupân*, 1896–9 (in Olufsen 1904, p. 60).

The motifs in the knitted pattern of the stockings are, according to Rickmers, among other things swastikas (we did not see any), tiger paws, bear tracks, branches, ducks, cocks, snakes, swords, scorpions, sheep's horns or tea kettles (1930: 287). Every district in GBAO had and has its own motifs, allowing people to recognise each other's origins (along with the men's cap).

In terms of headgear, notables apparently formerly usually wore only a turban (*salla*), most of them of wool, the very rich out of silk or at least fine wool. The simple folk wore, according to the pictorial material available to us, rather simple knitted or crocheted caps, such as Andreev shows under the term *mishoî* (1958: 405) or mentioned by Olufsen (*chelpök*). The very colourful caps widespread today (*toki, toqî, tokin, sket*) with a stiff edge, crocheted borders and silk tassel are also illustrated in Andreev. They seem, however, only to appear *en masse* since the Soviet era, probably since the 1950s, because of the dyes needed in their fabrication.

After the Second World War, hats made their appearance (*shljapa, shlap*), at least among the Party functionaries and the employees of state institutions. Workers wore the Russian 'Proletariat hats' (*kepka*). In the post-Soviet phase since 1991, traditional headwear such as turbans in Darwâs and Wandsh, as well as Pamir-hats in Shugnân and the other districts, have re-emerged.

Concerning footwear, 'they wear short soft brownish yellow tanned leather boots, or rather a kind of leathern stockings (*musa*), which, to prevent their falling off, are tied around the ankle with a string of plaited wool of different colours' (Olufsen 1904: 63). The pieces we were able to observe had an extra sole of yak leather sown on. What's more, these boots are smeared with tallow against humidity. That in the winter wooden shoes were bound under the boots as well seems hard to believe, for these would greatly limit freedom of movement and make locomotion practically impossible in the snow. However, clogs were worn separately – especially in more temperate weather. One author compares them with shoes such as were used in the Bavarian forest (Germany) around the same period (von Schwarz 1900: 439). There were also wooden sandals with leather straps.

Many poorer adults and especially children used to go barefoot, at least in summer. We also know from travel reports that the Pamiris had nothing but bad shoes and were forced to repair their boots each time a halt was called (see Lentz 1931: 163).

With the Russian occupation and a slight economic recovery starting around 1900, a change in clothing fashion may be observed, at least in the somewhat wealthier families. Von Schultz reports from his observations in 1911 and 1912 that Russian calico began to replace the traditional wool clothing. In Eastern Pamir, Kashgari products were gaining ground and it became fashionable to clothe oneself in military outfits from Afghanistan or Bukhara. What's more, silk coats from the city were often given as gifts, and in the winter one would also see at least Kashgarian, Kyrgyz and Bukharian fur hats (1914: 84–85). However, very little new footwear was introduced, except perhaps for clumsy Afghan lace-up boots.

In general, this overview shows that, although home production supplied basic items, many pieces of Pamiri clothing were, in their simple form, much too coarse and not very practical. This is especially true of footwear. In the winter, many poorer families almost certainly froze bitterly. Since Russian winter clothes have, in the last ten years, no longer been available, many people along the Bartang or other high valleys live nowadays in much the same conditions as reigned more than a hundred years ago.

Jewellery and body ornamentation

Pamiri women are very pretty according to European standards. When travellers such as Cobbold report that the girls are 'fairly good-looking' but 'fade when still young' (Cobbold 1900: 163), this is due to the extreme living conditions, which today are barely any different than they were in the days that particular observation was made – that is, a heavy workload, bad hygienic conditions and especially the high-mountain climate that is so aggressive to the skin.[34] That in Soviet times the retirement age for women in villages at altitudes of over 2,000 m was ten years below the usual age in the lowlands had its justification even after the Second World War, and despite subsequent improvements in medical care.

Despite their poverty, women and girls in the Pamir have always done their best to look attractive by wearing jewellery, adorning their hair and using other body ornamentation (for example with the generous use of antimony over or instead of the eyebrows). Natural ornaments were flowers and necklaces out of seeds, capsules or bored stones (among others lazurite). Olufsen mentions apricot pits on strings (*pyrk*) (1904: 70), such as still can be found today.

Apart from the different kinds of beads for necklaces, the jewellery of the Pamiri is limited to a few basic forms, which are hardly ever made locally. Andreev illustrates among other things a necklace with false coral (*tsamak*), an armband out of glass discs (*dast seftz*), silver (?) bracelets (*parzist*) and a pendant with coins (*tog*) (1958: 417). Small glass discs with engraved or embossed stamps of Islamic formulae (*Muhammad, Allah*) are widespread everywhere in the Middle East and probably came from there. The pendant with coins points to Kyrgyz production.

The typological list in von Schultz is much longer, but whether these represent basic types of Pamiri jewellery or only examples found here and there remains unclear. The illustrated silver filigree work (1914: 48, figs 12–14) came for the most part from travelling silversmiths and is probably of urban origin and only to be found among very rich women.[35] The same goes for silver throat pendants (ibid.: 49, fig. 15), earrings (fig. 16) or men's finger rings (fig. 21).

The variations among the necklaces, practically the only piece of jewellery still worn today, are endless. The occasional (cheap) gold jewellery has in most families been sold long ago. Among the beads, there are apparently some earlier variations out of clay or wood, and some that come from the antique tombs of the Pamir plateaux (see Litvinsky 1984: 59–63).

Especially valuable, and today perhaps even overestimated in their worth, are red corals, introduced by Chinese traders a long time ago (see Olufsen 1911: 9). True corals are extremely rare nowadays. Predominating are (good) older copies and glass imitations. Collectively, corals are designated by the Arabic term *marğŭn*. Fragments of coral are also called *piruzâ*, beads in general *marvorâ*. Since 1995, necklaces of (false) coral with Bukhara silver coins from Ishkashim have occasionally been offered in Khorog. In 2003 we found such imitations in Dushanbe, in which the silver coins were cast as replicas in recent times.

A special group of traditional jewellery consists of amulets of various materials, but which fell out of fashion in the last decades of Soviet Badakhshan. In the Afghan Wakhân they were often still in use in the period 1970 to 1975: bundles with metal objects, coins, claws from predatory animals, leather pouches, etc., which were worn mostly by women at the belt or the throat (see Raunig 1978: 302).

Women always wore their hair as long as possible, and still do. Formerly, it was either not put up or, among married women, bound in two thick plaits. Girls wore many thin braids, up to 40, going down to their hips (see Renner 1975: 57). Black woollen yarn was also braided into the hair to lengthen it (von Schultz 1914: 37). At the end of the braids, decorations such as bells, red tassels, etc. were bound. Voigt reports, based on an older source, that a long time ago the women in Badakhshan supposedly wore horns up to a metre in length in their hair (Ujfalvy 1896, in Voigt 1933: 92).

Men still occasionally dye their beards red with henna, which is said to have been common in the past (see Olufsen 1911: 84). They preferred, however, to wear their hair short or even completely shaven. Only Sufis and the descendants of holy men or *sayyids* wore longer hair.

Nothing is said in the literature about tattoos, although today at least they are occasionally worn.

Communication and transportation

In a high mountain region traversed by raging rivers and where often only narrow passes (snowed in for months in winter) lead from one valley to another, communication presents a very particular problem. This is especially true for Southern and Western Pamir. The central area of Roshân along the Bartang and its tributaries was particularly cut off for months from the outside world, thus leading to the creation of the legends mentioned at the beginning about secret passes and mysterious peoples on the other side of the mountains.

Since many visitors in earlier days had great difficulties in travelling through Shugnân and Roshân, the number of rather adventurous stories about travel in the Pamir is very high. These may be divided into three types concerning: the so-called *owringi* (sing. *owring, owringe*, also *rafak*), foot paths leading along the slopes and cliffs, the traditional flotation using inflated animal skins, and the building of bridges.

The first non-Russsian traveller to reach the Bartang valley from Murghâb and to travel to the Pyandsh from Roshorve, then called Oroshor, Ralph W. Cobbold, vividly describes the difficulties in moving along the improvised and yet only possible path, *owringe* (*owringi*). An *owring* is a path laid down by the population allowing travel along a river that stretches to the cliffs on both sides.[36] Many places could not be reached in any other way at all, before, starting in the 1930s, passable roads were built with much trouble by the Soviets.[37]

Wherever possible, the path takes the form of a trail over passable slopes high above the river. But when the cliffs, for example between Khorog and Ishkashim, between Roshân and Darwâs and especially between the town of Roshân and the upper Bartang valley, reach right up to the river, the attempt was made to make passage possible even along the sheerest sections, at least for pedestrians, with a simple path construction. This construction was the collective work of a village or, when the road was longer, by all the villages along its path.

Where the cliffs were ragged and had many ledges, a passable road could be obtained by filling in with stones, earth and wooden beams, along which sometimes even donkeys and cattle could pass. Smooth vertical faces were crossed by building bridges out of tree trunks from the nearest ledge (Plate 4.41). In some cases, no longer visible anywhere in GBAO, paths were truly ‘hung up’; that is, ropes were let down from ledges above the planned route, to which was attached a sort of suspension bridge of interwoven branches. An illustration in Cobbold (1900: 177) shows how precarious the construction seemed. For lack of good rope and wooden staves long enough to span to the gap, even the carrier ‘ropes’ of these bridges were nothing more than bundles of scrub somehow linked together. This once even brought British-born Cobbold into mortal danger when the *owring*, attached only to branches, broke underneath him.

Today it is easy to imagine how a skilled climber with good shoes and absolutely no fear of heights (for there can be a sheer drop of 50 m directly from the *owring* into the churning river) could somehow pass even the most difficult *owringi*. Yet

Plate 4.41 'Owring' on the Afghan side of the Pyandsh between the Bartang and Yasgulem valleys, also called 'Alexander of Macedon's Path' (1998).

one must not forget that these paths were the only passages to whole valleys and everything the people needed had to be carried in their hands or on their backs over the *owringi*. This includes such things as iron stoves, building wood, sacks of grain and even calves and sheep or goats to be sold or else brought back from the market. With loads of up to 100 kg, such as the Pamiris still transport on their backs, the use of the *owringi* represents an impressive, even artistic achievement.

On the road between Roshân and Darwâs, one can see *owringi* on the Afghan side, partly sprung out of the cliffs, leading over the Pyandsh for dozens of miles. Legend has it that this path was laid by Alexander the Great, which is certainly plausible. Even if the path was built only later, it remains an extraordinary feat on which hundreds of men must have worked over several years.

Passing an *owring* in times of peace was a feat. When in times of war the paths were destroyed at the most difficult passage, the enemy was almost always denied any sort of access to the region lying beyond. One should remember that other accesses to the upper Bartang valley all went through the Murghâb, a detour of some 400 kilometres. The destruction of an *owring*, however, needed to be very carefully considered, for its disappearance meant that the people destroyed all contact with the outside world until the difficult rebuilding of the paths.

The second great communication problem in Western Pamir is and was crossing rivers and their tributaries. Even in earlier times, small footbridges and wooden bridges existed, but these, built in the traditional way, could not span any great distance. Wider rivers such as the Pyandsh, Bartang or Gund had to be crossed another way. For this, the simplest kind of floats or swimming aids were used. Typical was a small float made out of inflated goatskins (general: *tursuk*, Bartang: *gupsar* or *saal*; the latter term may designate only the inflated goatskin). The float consisted of a wicker frame to which were attached three or more inflated goatskins (see Rickmers 1930: 221).

Cobbold also vividly describes larger floats which, steered by two experienced men, brought him over the Bartang without getting wet (1900: 172–174). While floats meant simply for the transport of people were often made only from a single inflated goatskin (as sometimes today as well), or two air-filled bags linked by wooden frames, quite comfortable floats also existed. An illustration in Cobbold shows a frame of wooden staves between which all of ten goatskins were attached. When a platform of reeds was laid on this construction it was possible to float down the less tumultuous parts of the lower Bartang to Kala-i Wamâr quite comfortably and, most importantly, with dry feet.

Such a float ferry linked the road from the Bukhara fort to Khorog through the mouth of the Bartang. The difficulty, however, was enormous. A float with 10–12 goatskins could just about carry two people and some baggage: 'während 3–4 Eingeborene, je einen großen aufgeblasenen Ziegenfellsack unter sich, im Wasser, am Floße angeklammert, liegen und dasselbe, mit den Füßen rudernd im richtigen Stromstrich halten' (von Schultz 1910b: 254).

Even today, with inflated inner tubes from cars usually taking the place of goatskins, the transport of people – as well as heroin smuggling over the Pyandsh – is done this way. In the years after 1995 we were no longer able to observe a true float, but instead merely improvised floats out of one or two skins bound together, which could just about aid one man and a waterproof sack to stay on the surface of the water. In any case, floating on the Bartang as well as on the Pyandsh must have at all times been an adventure due to the speed of the current and the cliffs.

Bridges over the larger rivers are relatively new in the Pamir and definitely a product of the Soviet era. Smaller tributaries, though, were already bridged prior to 1900 by technically very interesting wooden constructs or hanging footbridges on ropes. The latter were made out of two ropes, formerly out of leather or plant fibres and nowadays out of steel. These are fastened to large stones, nowadays heavy earth anchors, and then built into footbridges with horizontally placed branches (Plate 4.42; also see Cobbold 1900: 175).

Better bridges crossing rivers up to 20 m wide were and in some cases still are built in the following way: beams were laid on both banks and weighed down with stones, so that every further layer went over the one below it towards the middle of the river. The upper layers of beams from both banks joined up far out in the middle of the river, and were linked to one another with long poles, usually of poplar. Over this, rods or planks were laid down and bound fast.[38] There was (and is!), naturally, no railing. With greater weights such as that of a laden donkey, the beams in the middle would flex and spring quite a lot. Contrary to the true swinging hanging bridges of the first-mentioned type, however, these can be used without danger. The hanging bridges, on the other hand, can even swing away when an

Plate 4.42 Suspension bridge over the Bartang river made from two steel ropes tied together with branches(1995).

inexperienced person goes over them. However, we could still observe in 2003 how even old women cross such bridges without help.

Some travellers remarked that the Pamiris, though good carriers and climbers on the *owringi*, were no mountain climbers (e.g. Borchers *et al.* 1929: 90). They used the roads, travelling extremely long distances on foot, but did not climb the stone slopes nor the cliffs. For this, the earlier tools may have been inadequate. There was also no such thing then as mountain climbing as a sport.

Ice shoes (*parnom*) with spikes used to be made, allowing iced passes to be travelled safely (see Andreev 1958: 217). There were also snow shoes (*tshapâr*) with or without spikes. Coates and Coates refer to the fact that even the 'normal' travelling of some passes in the summer was difficult and dangerous (1951: 178). This was even more difficult in winter.

For their long foot marches, the people used leather knapsacks made out of skins that one, as Rickmers writes, 'einem Zicklein über die Ohren gezogen hatte' (1930: 68). These sacks were certainly waterproof up to a point, as they were, for example, taken over a river on a float.

In view of the above-mentioned communication problems, the achievements of the Soviets in the exploration of the Pamir and its sub-regions are impressive. This was, by the way, not merely for economic reasons. Among others, Coates and Coates (1951) and Gawrilyuk and Yurotshenko (1987) honour the results: the 700-km-long Osh–Khorog road, the 557-km-long link between the current

Dushanbe and Khorog which leads from Gharm over sometimes steep passes, the road between Khorog and Ishkashim and further on to Murghâb, and finally, in the last decades of the Soviet Union, the Bartang road sprung for kilometres out of the cliffs.

Music, dance, games and poetry of the Pamiris

Perhaps the love of music and dance, as well as of companionability in general, is especially pronounced among the Pamiris because of the particularly long winter in the remote valleys of Badakhshan. In any case, hardly any tradition has remained as pure as the music, handed down along with the instruments and a part of the song repertoire. What's more, the Pamiris dance often and with pleasure, not only during standard occasions such as weddings but also spontaneously. This dance seems, at least in part, to be absolutely timeless. The following overview of the musical instruments, the songs and dance can, even if older sources are also cited, exceptionally be written in the ethnographic present.

The first list of the commonest musical instruments comes from de Rocca, who mentions the *sitar* (*sitor*), a sort of guitar; the *roubob* (*rabôb*), a plucking instrument with a long neck (see Gratzl 1973: fig. 1); the *naï*, a flute made out of a tube of copper or wood and the *koughi-naï* ('chalumeau'; 1896: 260). The *rabôb* may be considered the typical Pamir instrument. It is usually carved out of well-dried apricot wood (see Plate 4.25) and has five strings. The strings are tuned using

Plate 4.43 The *khalifa* of Roshorve (Bartang) plays an old *rabôb* that he inherited from his father (1996).

pegs as with a violin. Yet the instrument is played like a guitar, without a bow (see Olufsen 1904: 129). It is often, as shown in Plate 4.43, played by older musicians – according to our questioning, only by men.

Men and women use various tambourines (*dârga*). These, like sieves, are made out of a wooden ring over which a goatskin is stretched. Before they can be played, the latter must be tightened over the fire. We observed after 1995 some tambourines stretched with strings, which serves to strengthen the sound. Plate 4.44 shows a group of girls from Roshorve gathered to greet guests.

The *naï*, whose sound is not created by using a mouthpiece but through the lips of the musician at the end of the tube, exists in different forms and materials. Luknizki mentions other instruments, a *gitshak* (perhaps a kind of *rabôb* with a shorter neck), the Pyandsh harp (a plucking instrument), cymbals (*tshang*), the *dutor*, a plucking instrument with two strings, and the two percussion instruments *doira* and *nagora* (1954: 221). Many instruments closely resemble those of the Sartes such as are illustrated among other places in von Schwarz (1900: 293). Under Soviet influence, the accordion (*garmoshka*) became another standard instrument of the Pamiris (Plate 4.45). Especially the young people regret the lack of new instruments since the economic crises.

The music achieved with these instruments may be monotonous, as de Rocca says not without reason (1896: 260), but it is also sentimental and very melodic, and the musicians overflow with energy with some pieces. Professional musicians have only existed since the Soviet era, and then just in Khorog. Yet practically

Plate 4.44 Girls in Roshorve (Bartang) with tambourines preparing to receive guests (1995).

Plate 4.45 A reception party in Nisûr with men playing accordion and tambourine, and girls with tambourines (1997).

every household has at least one instrument hanging on the wall, a tambourine at the very least, often the *rabôb* as well, and one need not beg for long before it is brought forth.

Luknizki describes the background of many Pamiri songs as nature itself, the wondrous, beautiful, picturesque gorges of the Pamir with their murmuring sources. The result may be heard in emotional songs filled with melancholy about the remoteness of the land, about love, and about the power of relentless nature (1954: 220).

The texts of the songs were published by Bobrinskij (1908), Andreev (1953) and Zarubin (1937) among others. Among the Western authors, Lentz (1931) published some of the texts. In his article on the 'Pamir dialects I', he also addresses rhyme forms (1933a). It is interesting that mostly men sing love songs in public, even when women are present, and that married women are also sung to (1933a: 67).

Next to the songs about the region and its people, religious texts are also widespread. The sometimes extremely old songs extol the prophet, and especially his son-in-law Ali. There are within the Ismaili Shia naturally also numerous texts that sing of Hassan and Hussein and lament the death of the latter. Another type of song is sung outside the Pamir, so-called 'homesickness songs' for one's mother or homeland.

De Rocca only observed men dancing in Darwâs (1896: 260). In strict Sunni areas it is still (or once more?) true that men and women dance separately at weddings. In the predominantly Ismaili areas, though, men and women have danced

Plate 4.46 Dancing girls in a Pamiri village (1997).

together as long as anyone can remember. The dance forms, though, are solitary, without anyone touching the other. The dancers make few steps, carrying out the actual dance movements with the upper body and the arms and hands (Plate 4.46). Apparently, masked dances existed formerly (Lentz 1931: 287–288).

The games mentioned in the literature are archery, *guibosi*, a kind of polo (see Luknizki 1954: 221), as well as a dance game with wooden horses (Lentz 1931: plate facing p. 288). *Buskashî* or 'ram brawl' was perhaps formerly the most widespread public game in the Pamir. A ram was butchered, the head severed, the skin removed and the carcass was thrown in a circle. On a signal, a dozen to a hundred riders threw themselves on the skin while trying to be the first to throw it over a goal line. During the game, the participants did their best to tear the carcass away from the others and to push the opponent out of the saddle (see Agachanjanz 1980: 106–107). *Buskashî* is played over several rounds and observers always wondered at the fact that nothing more than light injuries resulted.

An overview of the ethnology of the Pamiris cannot be ended without at least casting an eye on the art of poetry and stories. Lentz is not alone in pointing to the rich popular literature of the Pamir, especially in the Bartang valley, which was still creative in his time and reached a high literary level (1931, and in Rickmers 1930: 223). From the same period come the works of the important Russian ethnologist Zarubin.

In Oroshor alone (today Roshorve), at the beginning of the twentieth century, there were two experienced storytellers plus a whole list of younger men well versed both in Pamiri lyric as well as in an amazing number of stories, sagas and fairy tales. Noticeable is the spare language of many of these stories, such as that about King Behram:

> In der Zeiten Zeit war – (oder) war nicht – ein König, König Behram. Alkais war (sein) Wesir. Ein anderer Wesir war Bachtek. Er schickte sie zum Handel aus. Unterwegs fanden sie nun etwas. Darin war der Reichtum der Welt. Unter sich teilten sie (es) . . .
>
> (Lentz 1933a: 101).[39]

The fairy tales of the Pamiris are uncountable, yet a good selection was translated into German in a collection by Isidor Levin ([1986] 1997). Many motifs from *The Arabian Nights' Entertainments* appear here, just as does the motif of the poor man whose son marries a king's daughter, or the biblical and Koranic stories of Joseph of Egypt (Ysyf and Suleika). Here, the hero marries the beautiful temptress and becomes king himself (Levin [1986] 1997: 158–171).

The characters in the fairy tales are completed by scholars, hashish smokers, mullahs, wise men and many clever, as well as especially stupid, *padishahs* (kings, but also merely local rulers). Solomon, as king of the Ghosts, also appears, as well as Hassan and Hussein as the protectors of men (Levin [1986] 1997: 105). Among the women there is the wise smith's daughter and the clever Jewish girl. Many (nature) spirits are mentioned, such as *Peris* (spirit people) or *Simurg* (the magical bird). The clever fox, first among the animals, is the victim himself in one fairy tale.

The language of many fairy tales is rough, even if – contrary to the fairy tales in the most important *Arabian Nights'* collections – the motifs are not erotic. Yet body parts and body functions are clearly named. The *padishah* 'pisses', 'shits' and his 'ass cheeks' are beaten. Funny stories are, by the way, similar to those told by the wise Sufis such as Nasreddin Hodsha from Turkey or Guha of Egypt:

> Afandi beat his son and then gave him his jug and sent the son to get water. Then a woman asked him: 'Why did you hit your son, who had done nothing wrong?' Afandi answered: 'I beat him as a precaution, for if I beat him after he had broken the jug, it would be too late.'

5

THE KYRGYZ OF THE MURGHÂB

Our research work in the Pamirs has concentrated on the Indo-European ethnic groups; that is, the actual Pamiris. The people of the Murghâb, however, were regarded as another important problem group in terms of developmental politics: their completely different economic structure meant that the resources they had access to after 1995 were for a while even more restricted than they were in the lower valleys, where agriculture was possible. For that reason we visited the settlements of the Murghâb, travelling right into the furthest corners of the most remote valleys to interview representatives of the people about their problems. We concentrated on the present situation – the existing resources and how they are used – and also on possible alternatives. We did not carry out ethnographic research while doing this, concentrating instead on aspects relevant to development, for example animal husbandry, living conditions, food and social security.

With one or two exceptions, the information on the Kyrgyz people of the Murghâb[1] compiled in this chapter is therefore taken from the literature on the subject. However, this is practically non-existent on the Kyrgyz in the present-day Tajik region of the Pamirs. Monographs only exist on the Kyrgyz people of Afghan Wakhân (see Dor 1975; Dor and Naumann 1978; Sharani 1979a). It is correspondingly clear to us that the information gathered from isolated comments is far from complete. Its primary use is for rounding off and completing the picture of the Tajik Pamir region.

History and tribal organisation

Origin of the Pamir Kyrgyz

Earlier research, under the generic term 'Kyrgyz', combines the Kazaks and Kara-Kyrgyz; that is, the real Kyrgyz with settled areas stretching from the Alai across the Tien-Shan and the Issyk-kul area as far as the Murghâb and the Afghan Pamirs (cf. Dubeux and Valmont 1848: 122–149; Sommer 1842: 26–76; Moser 1885: 15). 'Kara' means 'black' in the Kyrgyz language, so we are dealing with the 'Black Kyrgyz' in the Pamirs. One version of folk etymology claims the name of this people derives from '40 virgins' (kirk = 40 and kiz = virgin). The term 'Qîrgîz' first appears in the Orkhon inscriptions of the eighth century as the name of a Turkic people who in the following century defeated the Ughur state in present-day Mongolia in 840 (Andrews 1997: 99).[2] Although later Kyrgyz are always depicted as being of Mongolian type, the earliest references to the Kyrgyz depict them as being blue-eyed and red-haired (see von Gabain 1979: 6, 15).

It was only around 1700 that Kyrgyz groups moved towards Ferghâna and Karategin, under pressure from the Kalmucks. It is likely that they had initially to pay tribute to the Khanate of Kokand (Akiner 1983: 328), but then in 1842 were able to achieve virtual independence (Lansdell 1885, I: 231) and even take over actual power in Kokand. Rawlinson says that before the Russian conquest of the Khanate 'the Khan [was] in most cases a mere puppet in the hands of the Kara-Kirghiz or Kipchak chiefs' (1875: 195).

The furthest advance westwards took Kyrgyz groups as far as Hissar, close to the present-day Tajik capital Dushanbe. After the collapse of Kalmuck rule many returned east, where they settled in present-day Kyrgyzstan, especially in the Issyk-kul area (Dor and Naumann 1978: 44). Around 1880 the Kara-Kyrgyz are said to have consisted of five 'tribes' (von Hellwald [1875] 1880: 21). In the literature these groups are also called Burut and more infrequently Dikokamennyje – 'wild-mountain' Kyrgyz – however, these are names that they themselves do not use.

At the start of the nineteenth century Kyrgyz clans established themselves in the Alai range of mountains. This is also where we find the origins of the present-day Pamir Kyrgyz. The Teyit, according to Andrews (1997), were the first people to move to the Little Pamirs (today Afghan Wakhân) in summer, for grazing. The Kesek, a second clan, is said to have come here originally in 1834: it is, however, unlikely that they came via Darwâs and Shugnân, as the writer claims (ibid.), because the route, which often went across *owringi* (see pp. 184–185) was known at that time to be virtually impassable even for individual travellers, let alone for nomads with sheep, goats, horses and yaks. So it is more realistic to assume that they came in directly from the north, more or less following the present-day road from Osh to Murghâb town; that is, across the Ak-Baîtal pass to Rang-kul, across the Aksu valley to the present-day town of Toktomish and continuing to the Wakhân (see Dor and Naumann 1978: 45–46). It is said that at that time they got as far as the Karakoram.

Evidently these advances were not attempts to gain more land, but were to determine/sort out grazing rights. As late as around 1900 it is said that the Kyrgyz whom travellers came across in the Murghâb and Wakhân did not, at that time, overwinter in the Pamirs but in the Alai (which had better grazing). However, the Kyrgyz were seen by the Russians as inhabitants of the Pamirs as early as 1892 and were included in a census. The results listed 1,055 people in 227 yurts (Hedin 1897: 302–303).

It is unclear why the Kyrgyz moved into the Pamirs. The grazing was clearly worse than in the Alai, which is supposed to mean 'paradise' in Kyrgyz, and which has much better grazing than the high-lying valleys of the Pamirs. One possible reason was population pressure in the Alai, resulting in the expulsion of individual clans, at first intermittently and then completely.

Up until the time of the Russian occupation of the Pamirs it is evident that repeated serious conflicts occurred between the advancing nomads and the Pamiris, particularly the people of Shugnân. The latter sold captured Kyrgyz into slavery. On the other hand there were also Kyrgyz attacks on Pamiri settlements, in keeping with the general reputation of the Kyrgyz at the time of being thieves and robbers.[3] Finally the Shugnî people triumphed. Paquier reports that in about 1870 the Kyrgyz had retreated north-east because of the conflicts (1876: 154–155). Forsyth also only found the remains of Kyrgyz settlements in the Wakhân and in Ishkashim, the Kyrgyz having left the area completely before 1873 (1877: 16, 45).

At the beginning of the twentieth century relationships between the two ethnic groups began to normalise, when hostilities between Pamiris and Kyrgyz were no longer possible because of the presence of Russian troops in present-day GBAO. Economic relationships were built up and extended, with the Kyrgyz buying grain and selling animals. In the years between 1920 and 1930, according to Lentz, many men in Roshorve at least understood Turkish (i.e. Kyrgyz) (1933a: 37). However, the old prejudices persisted in the way that each group characterised the other (especially Sunni disparagement of everything Ismaili-Shiite).

Even though there were repeated disputes with China, the Russian occupation of the later Kyrgyz and Tajik areas (especially the territory of Kokand) did have the advantage of allowing Kyrgyz clans freedom to travel and to enjoy grazing rights, for a small contribution, on all the grazing land where no earlier rights had been claimed. The Kyrgyz were still able to rotate their grazing land until the beginning of the 1930s, some time after the Soviets seized power, even though this was at the cost of an annual 10 per cent contribution on livestock. There were, however, repeated disputes between the Kyrgyz and the Russian authorities after the Russian occupation of Kokand, for instance in 1876 near Osh (Schlaginweit-Sakünlünski 1880: 376) and later in the Alai, where the Kyrgyz were successfully commanded by the 'Empress of Alai' Kurban-Jan-Datka (Strong 1930: 114–115).

Later on the border was hermetically sealed, and anyone approaching to within 2 or 3 kilometres of Soviet territory would be shot (Dor and Naumann 1978: 48). In this way contact between the Kyrgyz in the Soviet Pamirs (Murghâb) and those in Afghan Wakhân was almost completely broken off, though there may still have been movement at the time across Chinese territory. Nevertheless, the borders were still sufficiently porous for Kyrgyz groups to continue to escape to China from the Soviet Pamirs during the Basmatshi disturbances and also later on (see Stein 1933: 260).

During the Second World War there was a rebellion of Murghâb Kyrgyz against the Soviets for reasons no longer known, and the response was a punitive expedition. The leaders managed to escape to Afghan territory, but in the autumn of 1943 the Soviets killed 41 Kyrgyz, amongst whom was one of the two Khans of the Greater Pamirs region (see Dor and Naumann 1978: 48). It is probable that in the ensuing years some of the Murghâb Kyrgyz fled to Chinese territory, and after the Communists seized power they emigrated into Afghan Wakhân.

It was there that a refugee crisis unfolded after the Communists seized power in Kabul in 1979. Together with their Khan, most of the Wakhân Kyrgyz fled to Pakistan, where they were, however, unable to get properly established and lived in the most wretched conditions. As a result, the majority of these emigrants were resettled in Turkey in 1981 on Kurdish territory and, subsequently, in the Turkish–Kurdish conflict were exploited to the disadvantage of the Kurds (see Shahrani 1979a).

Living conditions in Afghan Wakhân were worse than in the Soviet part of the Pamirs, at least from the 1960s. Nazif Sharani, one of the leading authorities on the Wakhân Kyrgyz, assumes that the closed borders had a particularly negative effect on these Afghan Kyrgyz in the Wakhân (1979a). This comment can be accepted in principle, but it must be noted that especially after the Second World War the precarious resource situation (for example grazing) was also the result of a considerable increase in population, which went up from a few dozen yurts (less than 300 individuals) at the beginning of the twentieth century to more than 1,800 people.

Tribal organization of the Pamir Kyrgyz

From earliest times the Kara-Kyrgyz divided themselves into two groups, which are described as right (*sol*) and left (*on*) wings in the old military tradition (Kreutzmann 1995: 163). As time passed the meaning of the two traditional wings was lost and a third group developed, the *itshkilik* (*itshilik*) or 'Group of the Integrated'. Made up of part of the old wings, and including conquered and 'Kyrgyzised' peoples (e.g. Kalmucks), this group represents the original community of the four Kyrgyz 'tribes', or rather clans living today in the Afghan and probably also in the Tajik Pamirs: the Teyit, Kesek, Nayman and Kipthsak (see Dor and Naumann 1978: 49).

The Teyit, also called Tai-it by Dunmore, consist of two sub-clans, the Kara Tai-it and the Sart Tai-it, the former living near Kara-kul, for example, at the end of the nineteenth century and the latter in Murghâb and Rang-kul. The Kesek, or Kissack according to Dunmore, were or are divided into three clans: Bostan, Kiddarshah and Khandeh. The Bostan lived in Sari-kul, Taghdin-bash and the area adjacent to the Alai mountain range, that is north of Lake Kara-kul. Some of the Kiddarshah lived in Rang-kul, Murghâb and on the Alai. The Khandeh, last of all, lived entirely in the Alai (Dunmore 1893a, II: 114–115; cf. Capus 1890b: 513).

Kyrgyz clans divide into various subgroups, each of them forming a camp with their blood relatives, called an *aûl*. This term is still used today, even if a camp has long since become a permanent settlement, so that *aûl* and *kishlak* are now synonymous.

Kyrgyz traditional economy

Kyrgyz economy is based on stockbreeding and the clans continued partly nomadic stockbreeding well into the twentieth century in the area of present-day GBAO. The yurts were taken to new grazing areas several times a year, even though with the passage of time *aûl* communities in the Murghâb have now become permanently settled. Because of limited resources and the continental climate, this kind of life proved extremely hard, particularly in winter, but at least the people were able to make their own decisions.

The Soviet Union fundamentally changed the life of the Kyrgyz. From being semi-nomads with their own livestock, by the 1930s they had become state-subsidised shepherds and sovkhoz workers made to live in permanent settlements. Only the shepherds used to go with the herds across the Pamirs of the Murghâb, and they still do so today – if needs be with some members of the family. The settlements made schooling for all children and good medical care possible for the first time. People received relatively high wages: several times higher than the income of their relatives in China and Afghanistan. In addition there were large subsidies (for example fuel in winter, each family receiving generous amounts of coal).

The collapse of the Soviet Union and of the sovkhoz initially hit the Kyrgyz of the Pamirs particularly hard, because unlike the Pamiris in the low valleys they had no access to arable land, living almost entirely above 3,800 m. As well as the shortage of food the lack of fuel was especially difficult in a region where in 1995 the temperature in winter fell to below –56°C. Privatisation of livestock when state-run enterprises were broken up considerably improved circumstances for the population after 1996, so that the situation is now almost the reverse: with their valuable animals, and because many people were very well located to benefit from cross-border trade, numerous Kyrgyz families are better off now than the average Pamiri farmer.

Animal husbandry as a traditional way of life

Whether the early Kyrgyz were ever fully nomadic is unclear. In the nineteenth century those Kyrgyz who moved into the Pamirs in summer had their winter quarters in the Alai, where some of the families lived all year round. For that reason it was not correct even then to speak of a fully nomadic economy and way of life. It is more a case of typical semi-nomadism, characterised by the annual return of the shepherds to base camps.

Around 1900 many Kyrgyz families lived permanently in the Pamirs. Their traditional grazing method followed a system of horizontal and vertical migration. In the winter the animals were kept in a protected and low-lying valley, like that of Rang-kul, where in January 1900, for example, some 400 people and 12,000 small and large domestic animals lived. There were not as yet any permanent houses here, but some yurts were left up all year. Here 'low' still means between 3,800 to 4,200 metres. However, von Schwarz's comment that there were even winter camps situated as high as 4,800 m (1900: 126) is not credible, as this would have meant the existence of camps even higher than the highest pass in the Pamirs, the Ak-baîtal.

During the spring and summer many families accompanied the herds into the foothills and high-lying valleys (see Litvinsky 1984). Here they set up their yurts, for a few weeks or up to two or three months, in a place from where they could let their animals graze within a radius of up to 10 km (Plate 5.1). Herds of sheep and goats were accompanied by boys, and yaks (nowadays cattle too) by men. In 1998 we were able to establish that the migrations which followed the roughly 100-year-old tracks would involve a quite substantial height difference amounting to over 600 metres.[4] According to Litvinsky the distances between winter and summer grazing grounds were between 10 to 50 km and rarely more than 100 km (1984). This is also confirmed by Andrews with reference to the Afghan Pamirs; he even assumes migrations of only 15 to 35 km, or three to eight hours on horseback (1997: 112). Under these conditions it is perhaps better to speak of vertical transhumance than of semi-nomadism. It can also be justified on the grounds that some members of each family always remained in Rang-kul all year round.

Soviet collectivisation did not radically alter the system of transhumance, at least for the Kyrgyz of Rang-kul, as state collective livestock farms took over the grazing system. There were even distinct improvements: for example, the use of lorries

Plate 5.1 Kyrgyz 'summer' camp in late September with three yurts in the valley of the upper Aksu at an altitude of about 4,400 m (1995).

for transporting yurts, household goods and supplies instead of using yaks; the opportunity of leaving the lonely summer grazing grounds for a short time by motor bike; and the above-mentioned subsidies, which meant, for instance, that the long-standing heating problems could be forgotten.

As well as vertical migration there was also horizontal migration; that is, other Kyrgyz from the Alai came to Rang-kul, and Kyrgyz from China traversed the present-day Tajik Pamirs on their way to the valleys of the Alai. During the course of these migrations the territories of various clans were crossed. Normally the elders (*aqsaqal*) agreed on handing over a certain number of animals in return for the use of others' grazing grounds. By the 1930s this semi-nomadism had become restricted due to border closures. But in fact limited horizontal migration of animals continued, because the sovkhoz had grazing grounds allocated to them which were far apart from each other, thus necessitating movements of between 100 to 250 km.

Von Schultz's statement that the grazing system of the Kyrgyz at the beginning of the twentieth century was not arbitrary, but that grazing grounds were distributed and used systematically (1910b: 250), must have also applied to the Pamir region. Unfortunately there is no information available on traditional grazing management, which is all the more regrettable as new strategies need to be developed now that the sovkhoz have been broken up. We do know that the Kyrgyz often marked their animals (see Karutz 1911: 49–50), allowing the owners to find their property in mixed herds and also for the quick identification of unknown animals whose owners may not have had grazing rights.

Kyrgyz livestock was a mixture of sheep, goats, yaks and horses. We saw a few camels on the Aksu in 1998, but not thereafter. Sheep and yaks are the most important, as they give milk products and meat, the latter being the basis of present-day income in the Murghâb. Milk in the form of sour milk, or made into yoghurt, cream and butter is mainly used for immediate consumption.

Dor and Naumann (1978) give a good description of the livestock-based economy of the Kyrgyz in the Wakhân. The authors draw attention to the considerable care taken then, as now, with organising the search for grazing. The animals seldom graze together, as places are sought with various different kinds of vegetation, each suitable for the particular type of animal. During the summer the beasts may stay for weeks on end on the grazing grounds. At the change of the seasons and in winter they stay in stockades next to the yurts. Here they are also less subject to attacks by wolves. In extremely cold winters the sheep are still brought into the yurts at night, where man and beast have to share the confined space.

Apart from the yaks, the animals are not able to find their food under the layer of snow, even though this is mostly quite thin in the Eastern Pamirs. Each family has to store a large enough supply of fodder during the summer. Yaks are certainly the domestic animals best suited to the central Asian high-mountain ranges. Apparently there even used to be wild yaks (*Poephagus mutus*) in the Pamirs. Present-day animals are domesticated yaks (*Poephagus grunniens*), which the Kyrgyz brought with them when they moved into the region (see Dor 1976).

It is not just that yaks are hardy and survive the harsh winters better than all other animals[5] – they have many uses: their milk is very rich and is the main form of food based on animal fat; their meat is highly prized and is traded profitably across the borders to Kyrgyzstan; traditional shoes and leather harness and riding equipment are made from yak leather; the hair and skins form the basis for very tough and hard-wearing ropes, etc. Yaks no longer carry out their previous important function as beasts of burden, noted in Sven Hedin's accounts of the Himalayas. In earlier times loads were, however, transported by yak (for example the yurts with their heavy felt coverings). Dor quotes 250 to 280 kg per animal as an acceptable weight for shorter journeys of between 10 to 15 km (1976: 131).

Sheep (and goats) also produce milk, although in smaller quantities and used mainly in raising young. In fact the women like using goats' milk, as the animals are always near the yurts in the evenings, while the yaks often spend the night with the shepherds far from the camps. In order to get enough milk, the Kyrgyz separate mothers from young after bringing them back to the camps. For milking the animals are often tied tightly to a rope pegged into the ground in two rows opposite each other, and are milked by the women.

In earlier times sheep's wool was important as the basis for woven articles (e.g. Kelim rugs), coats, knitted garments and quilts. Sheep are still shorn, while the finest goats' wool was plucked, at least in the past (see Karutz 1911: 56–57). Basic goats' wool, used for example for the warp (lengthwise threads) in Kelim rugs, could also be obtained by shearing. One could reckon with between 1 and 1.5 kg of wool per animal.

During Soviet times shepherds only had a strictly limited quantity of wool made available to them, leading to Russian winter clothing replacing the traditional coats and manufactured goods replacing the felt rugs. Economic collapse after 1991 seriously reduced the use of sheep's wool and sheepskins. The sale of wool has almost come to a standstill, while local production of wool products and leather goods has remained at a low level of technological development, with only small quantities being produced. The decades in which army coats, boots and factory-made shoes were available have led to the people's own traditional skills dying out. Until about 2000 not even tannic acid was available for processing leather, or dye for wool.

Nothing is mentioned in the literature about the introduction of cattle into the Murghâb when the kolkhoz and sovkhoz were created, and the fact that it was ultimately at the expense of the yaks. The shepherds took the cattle, likewise the sheep and goats, up to the high-lying valleys in summer; however, in the winter the animals had shelter in byres in the settlements. For this purpose the sovkhoz workers had to cut and store huge quantities of fodder during the growing season. The effort involved, and the costs (transport by lorry), has always been considerable and it is doubtful whether keeping cattle in the Eastern Pamirs is a suitable kind of animal husbandry. Yet today there are more cattle than yaks in the Murghâb.

No description of animal husbandry would be complete without mentioning the horses, which every Kyrgyz family used to own in earlier times. Even today there are still several hundred horses in the Murghâb. Right into Soviet times they were the most important method of transport for people and goods, as donkeys could barely withstand the harsh climate. The most important main routes in the Eastern Pamirs and in the Alai to China or the Wakhân could be covered on horseback. It was only in the deep river valleys that using horses for transport often proved impossible. Von Schultz says, however, that around 1900 a good riding horse was very expensive and that mares were seldom kept for milk (fermented and drunk as *kumys*[6]) (1910b: 251). At any rate, keeping horses in the Pamirs involves a great deal of time and energy and is very demanding. Only the strongest beasts can survive the severe night-time frosts in the open. In addition supplies of fodder are needed.

Economic resources in the early years of the Soviet Union were significantly better in relation to the number of people and animals than they are today. In 1927/8 there were said to be 60,000–100,000 sheep in the Eastern Pamirs and enough fodder for 150,000–200,000 (Litvinsky 1984: 74). In 1936 there were also 10,000 yaks. The sharp increase in the number of animals in the Murghâb (about two-thirds of the total number of animals in GBAO: by 1992 there were 76,400 cattle and yaks and by 1991 241,900 sheep and goats) means that the limits on natural resources have been reached or even exceeded. The trend towards overgrazing is not yet too pronounced, but severe ecological problems may arise in the foreseeable future because of the additional overuse of brushwood (for fuel). The traditional, very environmentally friendly, method of grazing (see Dor and Naumann 1978: 85) also seems to be giving way to convenience. Staying in one place for a longer period of time nowadays saves the expense of moving yurts and household goods, and this is the reason why the land is grazed right down to the last blade of grass.

We know little about the traditional trade in animals and animal products amongst the Kyrgyz of the Pamirs. We do know that they traded wheat flour, peas, barley and cloth for felt, sheepskins and wool with the Pamiris (see von Schultz 1910b: 251). Later on potatoes and some vegetables (especially onions) began to appear; however, the Pamiris were only able to trade small quantities. The only food traded by the Kyrgyz was dried cheese (*kurût*).

Capus mentioned itinerant traders coming from Kashgar or the Wakhân to the Pamirs and trading animals and skins (1890c: 540). These traders were probably not Kyrgyz. However, since independence and the privatisation of the economy, the Kyrgyz of the Pamirs have made use of their cross-border contacts and have established themselves as the most important groups of traders in GBAO, ahead of the Pamiris. As they had a certain amount of capital in the form of livestock, they were soon able to trade them for goods in Osh (Kyrgyzstan) and also in China, somehow managing to get them through customs, or past customs, in spite of all the border fortifications (via Afghan Wakhân?). They then sell them in Murghâb town, and especially from 1995 onwards on the market in Khorog.

Diet and guests

Although milk and milk products are a mainstay of the Kyrgyz diet, they evidently hardly ever drink fresh milk, as is also the case with other native people across central Asia. Milk is usually heated instead and then fermented. *Aîrân*, a sort of basic food, is produced in this way. Yoghurt, cream (*keîmak*) and butter too are only made from fermented milk (see van Leeuwen *et al.* 1994: 65; Strong 1930: 130). A mixture of yak's, sheep's and goat's milk is particularly popular.

In the Pamirs cheese is not produced for direct consumption but for winter supplies in dried form. Small balls or cakes weighing from 50 to 100 g are made from thickened and salted yoghurt and these are dried on wooden frames in the sun and wind until they are rock hard. This *kurût* can be packed into sacks and stored for months in a dry place. The *kurût* is consumed after being soaked for a day in water, thus making a kind of quark, which may be further thinned. This kind of dried cheese is widespread in Kazak Kyrgyz, and even throughout the central Asian cultural area (see Sommer 1842: 58).

The present-day Kyrgyz have adopted from their neighbours in the Pamirs the custom of baking round loaves of bread in clay ovens. In earlier times, and on special occasions even today, thin unleavened loaves are eaten, which are cooked on a griddle or in a heavy frying pan. However, wheat, and therefore bread too, was never traditionally part of the Kyrgyz diet. Capus states that even at the end of the nineteenth century bread was an absolute luxury (1890c: 537). In fact, even meat does not seem to have formed such a large part of everyday diet, as could be assumed from the lists of foods mentioned in literature. 'Ils mangent plus souvent la viande de leurs bêtes crevées que de la viande fraîche', says Capus (ibid.).

In earlier times soup was made with wheat flour, pea flour and sour milk, replacing pure milk dishes in winter when the animals gave hardly any milk (see von Schultz 1910b: 251).

Bearing in mind the lack of grain, a typical present-day dish, such as the little fried rings or balls made of wheat flour often given to guests, must be of more recent date. The rings already have a lot of fat in them, but if cream or butter are offered they are dipped in it. It is altogether astonishing how much fat some of the men can eat. This may be an indication of the food crisis after 1991, as fatty food is still the exception in many households today and so everyone takes advantage of any opportunity offered. But we know from our own experience and from the literature that traditional food is also fatty. One of the old dishes still prepared for visitors today is sheep's liver served on thick strips of fat (see Borchers 1931: 210). Soup is enriched with rendered mutton fat and pieces of fat, and if a plateful of large pieces of meat is served it is not the leanest pieces which go first, as they would in Europe, but the fatty pieces. So it is quite natural for the fat-tailed sheep (*dumba'*) to predominate amongst the Kyrgyz of the Pamirs (see Etherton 1911: 59).

The slaughter of a fat sheep is obligatory even today if special guests are expected. The animal is jointed and cooked. Enormous pieces of meat are placed in front of the guests on platters, the cooked head of the beast in front of the guest of honour. The liver is first served in the manner just described before guests help themselves to sometimes entire joints of meat. If the Kyrgyz eat huge quantities of meat today this does not seem to be the result of the food crisis after 1991. This fact was also established in earlier literature (Karutz 1911: 77). After the meat, the meat soup (*shurpa*) is served – nowadays thickened with potatoes, Pamiri style. However, the herbs for soup that are so popular with the Pamiris are almost unobtainable in the Murghâb. Von Schultz says that in his day rice was also served with meat (1910b: 251).

It is seldom mentioned in the literature that the Kyrgyz roast meat differently to the Pamiris; they don't put it in the soup beforehand. In one case a young yak was slaughtered expressly for this purpose (see Borchers 1931: 209). We ourselves had the opportunity to be served roast meat from a Marco Polo sheep. For this the meat is cut into strips (Plate 5.2) and roasted with ample amounts of yak butter.

Plate 5.2 Family life inside a yurt: the housewife and her husband cut meat for dinner while the grandmother heats the Russian-type iron oven (*pitshka*) (1995).

Capus is one of several writers who say that the Kyrgyz of the Pamirs were very good hunters and marksmen. In spite of their very primitive guns and poor-quality powder they were able to shoot very accurately and often killed an animal with a single shot (1890a: 223). Officially hunting was of virtually no importance during Soviet times. The wild animals that were shot were mostly those that might pose a danger to the domestic animals. Other animals, such as the Marco Polo sheep, were probably only hunted unofficially. The economic crisis has caused this to change. It is astonishing how many (simple) guns are to be found once more, guns which formerly only a small number of selected people were allowed to possess. The result is that wild goat's meat and also the meat of the Marco Polo sheep – although it is strictly protected – supplement the menus of many households.

Guests are served their meal on the side of the yurts opposite the entrance in front of the wooden boxes and piles of covers. One sits in a circle on thick felt covers round a festive tablecloth (*dostarkhan*), in which mountains of fried specialities have already been wrapped (we experienced this in the period 1995 to 1998; see Stanjukowitsch 1961: 129). Dishes with butter, yoghurt and cream, and afterwards the bowls of meat, are put on the spread-out cloth. People eat communally with their hands out of a large wooden bowl. In earlier times the soup was also served in a large wooden bowl, the guests spooning their soup out of it with wooden spoons. Nowadays in better-off households each guest is served their soup in an individual dish.

In pre-Soviet times tea was an expensive luxury and for that reason was only served on special occasions. Nowadays it is almost the rule, whether at festive meals or at private family meals. Both green tea and black tea are drunk. Unlike the Pamiris the Kyrgyz do not look on green tea as medicine for the old. It is poured into small bowls, with only the bottom of the bowl being properly covered. But the guest has his bowl refilled every time it is finished. This duty falls to the head of the house, his oldest son, or even a neighbour sitting with them at table.

Like the Pamiris, many Kyrgyz drink or eat tea with milk, ample amounts of butter fat and bread broken into it. In earlier times, apart from milk and *kumys*, water was drunk for the most part. The Kyrgyz get their drinking water from the streams of the Pamirs; in larger settlements which are situated some distance from any streams (like Konakurgan, near Murghâb town), they dig wells.

It is clear that not much emphasis is placed on clean water, as no effort is made to fetch water upstream of a camp where the danger of pollution is less great. Maybe the women and girls who have sole charge of fetching water think that the streams are polluted everywhere by grazing animals anyway. Although they wash their hands before and after a meal, and guests have water from a jug handed to them for this purpose, hygiene in Kyrgyz settlements is primitive. Even if there are latrines, at least in Pamiri villages where they occur every few houses, most people still go off into the bushes to relieve themselves.

Housing and equipment

The traditional accommodation of the Kyrgyz is a tent made of felt covers or a yurt. In the literature the term *kibitke* is sometimes used for the yurt. Nowadays almost every Kyrgyz family in the Murghâb still has a yurt, as they are essential for transhumance. New yurts are still being made, even though these are expensive because of the amount of wood needed. However, most Kyrgyz settlements today have permanent houses. These are the result of development continued for decades, based on the assumption that energy costs almost nothing: buildings with thin concrete or wooden walls, poorly insulated, with windows that are too many and too large, allowing additional cold to penetrate.

As long as people had tons of coal dumped on their doorstep every year and were able to use a Russian stove in every room, this type of house construction presented no problems. However, by 1993 coal deliveries to private households had almost completely stopped, and these 'modern' houses have turned out to be extremely impractical. It is no wonder that nowadays the use of yurts is increasing rather than decreasing and the time spent on summer grazing grounds is being extended. After all, it is warmer in the easily heated yurt than in a permanent house. Hardly any winter camps, as described on pp. 197–198, remain, but summer camps do get used between April and November.

The yurt

As the nights are already very cold at the start and especially at the end of the period of the 'summer camp' (around –20°C), the accommodation has to meet certain demands. Yurts are astonishingly good at meeting these demands, and in earlier times were even used in the winter camps where the temperature falls as low as –40 to –50°C.

The method of constructing a yurt has often been described in the literature,[7] so a summary will be enough here, leaving us to concentrate on more recent developments. The basic frame is still made of wood; in the Afghan Wakhân this is of willow. A lattice frame (*kerege, ostakhan*) forms the base of the yurt, with bent poles arranged around this, forming a circle where the roof opening is to go. The lattice frame consists of four individual pieces which are fastened, together with the door frame, into a circle. The frame is on average 1.15 m high. The bent poles (*ûl*) form the ceiling at a height of about three metres. The dome or vault which forms the roof opening (*tündük*), is about one metre in diameter. This lets in the light, as in Pamiri houses the *tshor khonâ* does, and traditionally serves to draw the smoke out. In the days when the Kyrgyz used to believe in shamans it was thought that the shaman left the yurt through this opening, on his way up to the higher powers (see Dor and Naumann 1978: 58).

In Konakurgan we had the opportunity of watching a yurt being built, a process taking three hours. First of all bands woven using the Kelim technique are stretched over the *ostakhan* (Plate 5.3). At the point where the bent poles for the roof begin,

Plate 5.3 Construction of a yurt. The wooden frame has already been erected. Bands of long woven *kelims* are fixed on the interior side while felt mats form the outside 'wall' (1995).

a particularly fine and beautiful old band is attached. Across the woven strips a layer of rush matting is laid on the outside, then a layer of heavy dark felt covers (*tutu*), which is attached by very narrow woven tapes. Finally there comes a layer of light-coloured felt, which has to be tied down with strong ropes and pegs. A proper door frame is set into the structure to form the entrance and a wooden door is hung. The door is relatively low, so that one has to bend slightly. If the threshold of the door was touched when entering it used to be considered to bring bad luck (see Dor and Naumann 1978: 59). In front of the door a strong felt cover is hung, which has to be lifted before going in (Plate 5.1). This is to stop the cold getting into the yurt every time the door is opened.

As can be seen in our illustration, the outside of the yurt can additionally be protected against the weather with canvas, although this is a recent development. Ideally, on a typical yurt there is a device to close the opening, made out of a piece of felt, which can be raised and removed with the aid of long poles (Plate 5.1). A Kyrgyz riddle goes: 'A stork which flies away in the morning and returns in the evening. What is it?' It is this felt cover, which is removed in the morning to let air and light into the yurt and replaced in the evening to keep the cold out (Dor and Naumann 1978: 60). In the summer this cover is left off, so that in the absolute darkness of the Pamirs the stars and the moon can be seen passing overhead.

A whole yurt, with an internal diameter of from 5–6 metres, can weigh between 400 and 600 kg, which together with the basic household goods adds up to between 800–900 kg. This used to be three yak loads altogether (see Wood 1872: 215); nowadays the yurt and the significantly increased collection of household goods take up a 5-ton lorry.

Amongst the Kyrgyz it is nowadays normal that the family of the bridegroom supply a new yurt at the time of the marriage (see Andrews 1997: 111). Residence is patrilocal; that is, the young couple move into the new yurt in the *aûl* of the husband's father. The distances between the yurts of an *aûl* are traditionally greater in winter than in summer. The main reason is that the animals are more often in the camp and need room. Moreover, every yurt has a fuel store (dung and *tersgen*), and in more recent times vehicles and carts are also parked here.

The interior of the yurt consists of a large round room with the floor covered by old worn-out felt covers, then with nice colourful newer ones on top. In the middle there is an uncovered area of about a square metre for the stove, with the stovepipe going out through the roof opening. This is closed on winter nights, as described. In earlier times there would have been an open fireplace on the spot where the stove is now.

On going into the yurt one sees the kitchen area on the left, sometimes separated by a partition wall or a curtain (see Kreutzmann 1996: 59). These partition walls or curtains are called *ashkhana* and are often the pride of the housewife on account of the intricate decorations (see Breitenbach 1978: 99–100). Supplies are stacked up on the wall here, and in more recent times there is sometimes a cupboard for plates, pots and other kitchen utensils. Of course such cupboards did not exist traditionally. Instead small bags with supplies used to hang on the lattice frame, and knives and spoons used to be inserted between the wooden frame and the cloth walls (Plate 5.2).

To the right of the entrance is the 'nursery'. If there is a baby in the tent a wooden cradle stands here, as already described for the Pamiris (see p. 135, Plate 4.24). In front of that are the man's boots and possibly other pieces of his equipment, and maybe on the wall a gun too. Opposite the entrance are the woman's wooden boxes, on top of which the bedclothes are neatly piled (Plate 5.4). The wooden boxes (*sandûq*), usually colourfully painted, and some of the bedclothes are brought by the women into the household. Usually an extra cover is spread out in front of this pile for guests to sit on, and more recently cushions are also available. The man of the house sits in the middle, opposite the entrance, his children and wife on his right side. Guests take their place on his left in order of importance. The lowest-ranking guests end up sitting near the entrance if there is a large gathering (see Andrews 1997: 110). The ethnographic presence is certainly appropriate in this context, as we carried out several interviews with this order of seating being used.

And so the yurt is amazingly comfortable if the weather is not too cold. However, it must not be forgotten that this level of comfort can only be found in former Soviet areas. Yurts visited in the last years of the twentieth century in Afghanistan were much more simply furnished (see Kreutzmann 1996).

Lastly, it is at least worth mentioning the Kyrgyz types of house in the Karategin region, which can be considered as part of the Pamirs from the geographic and

Plate 5.4 Permanent Kyrgyz houses and yurts use the same furniture and household effects: facing the entrance, large wooden cases (*sandûq*) are covered with all the family's mattresses and blankets (1998).

cultural history point of view, although today the settlements belong to Gharm district. Yurts had already been replaced here by permanent dwellings by the early twentieth century. In Altin Mazar, for example, by about 1930 there were windowless, cube-shaped buildings made of mudbricks. One entered the house by an anteroom, from which there was access, to the left and right, into a small byre. The living room was straight ahead. A hole in the roof – as in a yurt the only method of letting daylight in – drew out the smoke from the cooking fire (Borchers 1931: 207).

Present-day houses in the upper Gharm valley have hardly changed, except for the fact that on the whole they have become larger, now have windows and the animals' quarters have been separated from the actual living quarters. The layout of these houses is still based on that of the yurt, as described above: opposite the entrance one finds wooden chests with the bedclothes piled on top, in front of them a rug for the occupants and guests, to the right a cradle when needed, to the left the cooking area. The walls are also hung with covers or rugs, like in the yurts. And in spite of Islam and 70 years of the Soviet Union, in 2003 we were politely asked by the occupants of the houses to *cross* the threshold into the house.

Belongings, clothing, jewellery

Some domestic equipment has already been mentioned when describing the yurt and the way it is divided up. A few more will be mentioned here and the most important ones singled out. The felt covers are the most labour-intensive items. Making thick felt covers, usually out of summer sheep's wool, is still probably the most important domestic craft amongst the Kyrgyz of the Murghâb. Simple, very heavy covers of light-coloured wool are needed to cover the yurts, and colourfully dyed, slightly lighter ones are used as floor coverings. Many Pamiris also make the latter.

Some writers say that patterns are created in the felt cover by cutting up the felt after the first stage of the process and then arranging it in patterns before continuing to make the felt. However, we found that in Pamiri households the pattern was made in advance, with all its colours, on a top layer made of coarse wool. The ones we saw were Kyrgyz patterns, which had simply been adopted without understanding their meaning; the colours were a deep red, a bright blue and green, and also yellow.

The technique is the same and we had the opportunity to observe it in 2003 in the Gund valley in Shugnân: a pile of raw wool is spread out on a firm base and a group of women and girls, usually four to six of them, each with two thin switches in their hands, beat the wool. It is further loosened by pulling at it and then it is spread out in two layers, the bottom one of worse-quality wool and the top one of softer and better wool, on a straw mat, although nowadays this is more likely to be a large sheet of canvas.

The two layers of wool now have hot water poured on them and are then rolled up in the mat or canvas. The bundle is then trodden on and at the same time one of the women rolls it slowly backwards and forwards. It is then unrolled and wool is added in some places, the whole thing has more water poured over it and is then rolled up again. This time three to five women press the roll with their forearms, rolling the carpet backwards and forwards at the same time (Plate 5.5). Karutz states that this technique is not just used for heavy covers, but also for many of the traditional belongings: saddle cloths, curtains for doors, horse blankets, and chest covers or bags in which to keep household goods, etc. (1911: 58).

The patterns used in the felt covers are also repeated in the door curtains and other decorative adornments in the yurt. Wild sheep's horns certainly form the focal point of many motifs. Breitenbach mentions figures with names like *kuyruk* (dog's tail) or *kotshkorok kötshöt* (young ram), which vaguely resemble these animals, or a part of their body (1978: 99). Karutz also mentions the horn motif several times (1911: 162–178); yet we heard many other interpretations for Kyrgyz decorations, like 'flowers', 'yak' or 'hoof'. A motif such as spirals has not necessarily developed out of the basic 'horn' motif, as Karutz claims. The author's illustrations of the decorations on woven bands in the yurt could just as easily be interpreted as stylised plants or even meander patterns (ibid.: 169–172). There is no reason why the meandering mountain streams of the Pamir valleys, which shape the landscape so markedly, should not have had some influence on traditional decorations.

Plate 5.5 Preparations to make a felt carpet *c.* 1930 (in Borchers 1931, Plate 78 facing p. 193).

Like the Pamiris the Kyrgyz know how to knit and crochet, at least nowadays. Only a few families still weave. Unfortunately the right person was never there when we asked about it in our 1995 to 1998 period and again in 2003. We were, however, given proof in the form of recent pieces of work that Kelims are still woven somewhere in the Pamirs. As we could not record this technique ourselves we will have to rely on Karutz's description (1911: 59–62).

Unlike the Pamiris, who are known to use a spinning wheel, knitting wool is nowadays only made by using a spindle (Plate 5.6). The wool is first cleaned, washed, perhaps dyed and then spun by the women.

Apart from cardigans, stockings and a few other things (some caps) there were even fewer traditional or new kinds of home-made clothing amongst the Kyrgyz than amongst the Pamiris. They have relied so heavily in the past few decades on Russian or Kazak garments, that local production has ceased altogether. Typically necessary Kyrgyz items of clothing, such as the men's felt hats or thin tent boots and shoes came via Osh into the Pamirs, where goods are now being bought again.

Round about 1900 the traditional clothing of the Pamir Kyrgyz was rather poor and home-made looking. Men and women wore cotton or woollen smocks with bands for a belt. About thirty years ago more ornate garments with mother-of-pearl buttons and sewn-on coins were certainly worn sometimes in Afghan Wakhân. The word 'kaftan' (*khalat*[8]) for men and women, mentioned so often in early literature (Sommer 1842: 62–64; Capus 1890c: 537), is only used for a very simple version of the Tajik garment of that same name worn nowadays in the Tajik Pamirs. The authentic Tajik garment of that name was very finely woven and intricately decorated and therefore only a garment for the well off, whereas the more coarse Kyrgyz *khalat* was worn by everyone.

In Kyrgyz Naryn and in the Murghâb we sometimes came across men on horseback in November wearing a heavy fur or sheepskin coat with the fur or sheepskin on the outside. There is a winter version of this coat: a double fur or sheepskin coat with fur on the inside and outside. These coats, weighing about 20 kg, are worn by shepherds on horseback checking on the herds of yaks in winter in temperatures of –30 to –40°C.

Men and women traditionally wear boots out of doors and in the yurt they wear a kind of soft-leather stocking. Poverty has forced many women to wear plastic galoshes instead of good boots, even when leaving the yurt in winter. Men sometimes still wear Russian military boots and in the 1995 to 1998 period we frequently saw them wearing home-made cowhide boots with soles of yak hide, similar to those worn by the Pamiris.

There are not many signs nowadays of the riding accoutrements which used to be the pride of every man: one still finds simple leather saddles,[9] almost undecorated bridles, also some fine felt blankets, small Kelim rugs used as saddle cloths, and almost entirely undecorated riding whips. These whips used to be made of yak tail and had an artistically decorated handle. Although the thongs were very short, one could give a hard lashing with such a whip, especially as pieces of lead had often been incorporated in the thong. The weapons of the Pamir Kyrgyz

Plate 5.6 Old woman in a Kyrgyz camp near Rang-kul preparing sheep wool twine for a pullover with her spindle (1997).

were on the whole too insignificant and plain to be mentioned in the literature: bows, knives and flintlocks or matchlocks, which were mounted on a rest when shooting, none of them decorated.

Riding accoutrements and weapons gave a man some standing, at least in his outward appearance, whereas women gained standing from their jewellery. Women traditionally seem to have worn richly decorated caps with all sorts of silver pendants on them (see Sommer 1842: 63–65). Almost all women still wear plaits on which coins used to be fastened, the old women still doing this today.

Breitenbach's illustrations from Afghan Badakhshan show large pendant earrings, fine brooches and decorated rings, sometimes even on small girls (1978: 64–65, 96–97). The Stalinist persecution of well-off families as Kulaks has resulted in few of these surviving to the present day in GBAO. By far the most valuable jewellery we came across amongst the Pamir Kyrgyz were some several-hundred-year-old coins we saw being worn as buttons on one woman's waistcoat (Plate 5.6): her future husband had taken them in 1945 from a collection in a German museum in Berlin.[10] Otherwise the only jewellery we saw was often simple silver rings or necklaces made of agate or fake coral, such as are also worn by Pamiri women. Sometimes little pendants are attached to the necklaces. The old woman in Plate 5.6 has hung her late husband's signet ring on her necklace. Some women also wore simple earrings.

Social life

Socio-political and social structure

Although the word 'tribes' is used when speaking of the Kyrgyz people, there has never been much political authority. The focus of traditional authority was the leadership of the clan (see Hambly 1975). Although people still spoke of a Khan in Afghan Wakhân in the years after 1970, the people we spoke to in the former Soviet part of the Pamirs only knew of the *aqsaqal* as communal authority and representative of the lineages.

According to Capus a socio-political structure amongst the Kyrgyz of the Murghâb was no longer very marked by the end of the nineteenth century. He said that in spite of common ancestry there was absolutely no unity, and solidarity was only shown with other members of one's household (1890a: 517). This may have been true in terms of economic aims. However, the campaigns in the Basmatshi war later on, the well-organised uprisings in 1943 and migration to China and Afghanistan suggest that there must have been a certain central authority amongst the clans and/or at least good organisation. Thus de Rocca states that the Pamir Kyrgyz acknowledged three chiefs, but leaves open whether Russia's seizure of power in 1891 meant that the tribal chiefs – probably living on Chinese territory – were cut off from their people to some extent (1896: 192). This would explain the sudden collapse of central tribal authority observed by Capus.

The older men are still aware of the idea of belonging to a clan, but it no longer has any meaning. The most important group for any family is the lineage, the oldest member of which (probably the 'Begs' mentioned by Dunmore 1893, II: 117) represents ultimate authority in a group of related people. A lineage going back to a first common ancestor three or four, and in earlier times up to six or even seven generations ago, now mostly consists of about a dozen extended families, each living in two or three different yurts. This is the result of improvements in economic conditions during Soviet times. Unlike in Afghanistan, it is not often that three generations still live under one roof in the Murghâb, as grandparents still alive have their own yurt and each married son and his family have their own too. Usually a lineage lives in an *aûl*.

It is interesting to note that in the 1930s Soviet functionaries also respected the family ties of the Kyrgyz, shown by the fact that they created kolkhoz from the lineages of a clan (see Bennigsen and Wimbush 1986: 77–78). So the functionaries on a collective farm, and thus also most local Soviets, were frequently representatives of a related group of people. However, it is said that it was not the *aqsaqal* of each lineage who were promoted to management level in the local Soviets, but usually younger men. There must be some doubt as to whether they always thought of themselves as the representatives of their *aqsaqal*.[11]

In pre-Soviet times, and in Afghanistan even now, not every old man could become an *aqsaqal*. This title and its role as a kind of camp counsellor was only given to well-off men, who were able to afford a certain amount of generosity. Dor and Naumann state that when a man received the title of *aqsaqal* it was not as the result of being elected but as a result of having his deeds acknowledged: 'The stature of an old man whose opinion turns out to be true will gradually grow and spread beyond the confines of his camp, and people will start to come to him to hear his opinion when there is a dispute' (1978: 53). The important thing is that an *aqsaqal* cannot impose his authority on other people; that is, he does not exercise power in the the Max Weber sense of the word (1922: 603–612). People tend to go to him voluntarily as a sort of referee. The 'White Beards' on the Tajik side have acted in this capacity since the abolition of the Soviets.

In Soviet times a more or less egalitarian society was created, with neither obviously rich nor poor, but differences are increasingly becoming obvious in the present-day Kyrgyz society in the Murghâb. Those who were lucky when livestock from the sovkhoz were distributed – for example, because there were many members of the family all receiving the same number of animals – were at a distinct advantage over smaller families. If they also had sufficient labour to provide the animals with enough fodder, and perhaps even took the opportunity to procure a vehicle from sovkhoz sources, then in some cases they could build up a herd of a considerable size over the course of time. If they have connections to Kyrgyzstan, they can organise a profitable trade in live animals or meat and earn a good income.[12]

Life cycle

Compared with Pamiri households the Kyrgyz nowadays have relatively few children. The average size of a household in 1993 in the Murghâb, for example, was 4.9 people, while in Roshtkala district it was 9.8 – exactly double. Today this is the result of targeted birth control, whereas formerly it just resulted from the extremely harsh living conditions. In pre-Soviet times children born in winter were certain to die, according to Dor and Naumann. Their chances rose significantly in summer, and then in winter they tried to 'wrap up' these infants – then a few months old – as well as they could against the cold (1978: 70).

In earlier times on the Afghan side of the Wakhân they were only given a name when they were ten days old, probably because of the high mortality in the first days of life. Clearly they wanted to avoid the costs incurred when an already named child had to be buried according to Muslim rites, as is the tradition in Islamic societies. Likewise they wanted to avoid the cost of the normal name-giving celebrations if the risk of death was too high. Boys' names are often still taken from the Koran, while girls are named after popular female relatives (see Dor and Naumann 1978: 71–72).

According to Dunmore, children had a relatively lax upbringing, especially the older ones, and they did what they wanted (1893a, II: 118). Karutz also says that children too often got their own way, that they were rarely stopped from doing something and that if this did happen they would play the father off against the mother, one parent always being willing to give in. Boys and girls used to have plenty of time to play, the girls for example being given numerous dolls, or making dolls themselves (1911: 88–89). It is worth noting Dubeux and Valmont's early comment on the Pamir Kyrgyz in 1848, 'on voit souvent dans leurs tentes des enfants qui apprennent à lire et à écrire, sous l'inspection d'un vieux mullah' (p. 116).

However, we noted that very early on the girls have to start helping with the housework while the boys have to help the men look after the animals. This cannot have been any different in earlier times, except during the Soviet period when individual families had less responsibility for the livestock. Although we have no empirical data on the matter, there may be some truth in the comment of one person who told us that after livestock was privatised from 1995 to 1997 in the Murghâb, boys did not go to school so often, as they had to help look after the new 'treasure'.

According to Dunmore, marriages were arranged by the oldest members of the lineage (he calls them 'chiefs of the tribe'); they did this by entering into negotiations on behalf of the young man and deciding on the dowry with the parents of the girl (1893a, II: 119). Today this is done by close relatives of the husband, usually his uncles. Courtship and all other procedures must have been relatively expensive for well-off families. Each of the matchmakers is supposed to have received a *khalat* from the girl's father, just as some of the bridegroom's friends were later on given a coat. On the wedding day ten or more sheep were slaughtered by the young man's family and taken to his father-in-law's property. The dowry itself was said to have been a sum of money and a number of animals, probably yaks and sheep (ibid.). Additionally there was the jewellery often mentioned in the literature.

Nowadays the dowry, *kalym*, still has to be agreed on. If one can generalise from the information given to us from two sources, this involves a *de facto* agreement on the marriage settlement, as in other Islamic countries. That is, the young man's family hands over a certain number of animals, possibly other goods too, to the girl's family, also providing the yurt if the newly founded family has need of one. Otherwise a room is set aside for the young couple in the living quarters, or one is added on, or another solution is sought. For their part the girl's parents provide the wooden boxes, some of the bedding and the kitchen equipment.

According to Dor and Naumann, the Kyrgyz considered that members of non-Turkish-speaking ethnic groups were quite out of the question as possible partners in marriage (1978: 73), though they no longer consistently keep to this principal. The first marriages to Pamiris have already been documented. The prohibition of closer endogamy[13] meant that in the past the opportunities of finding a partner nearby were very restricted.

Boys used to marry at the age of 18 to 20 and girls at 14 to 16. Even during the Soviet period it was unusual to exceed that upper age limit. In fact, by about 25 girls are still considered to be almost too old, at least for a first marriage. However, the age at which they marry has tended to rise in the last ten years because of economic problems.

There is much speculation in the literature as to whether young Kyrgyz men and women were ever allowed to choose their marriage partner or whether this is still the parents' business. In the Afghan Pamirs, even as recently as 25 years ago, both parties to a marriage were apparently not asked for their consent (it was probably quite a different matter unofficially, as we know from other conservative Islamic countries), but in the Soviet Murghâb the first step in many marriages was taken by the young people themselves because of the fact that both sexes spent their entire time at school together. However, we were told that in such cases it was normal to include the parents in arrangements. That is, the parents agree to the partner in marriage and take charge of arranging the dowry already described here.

In theory polygamy was allowed until the Soviet period, before being officially prohibited. However, most men could in practice only marry one woman for financial reasons. There were some instances of polygamous marriage even during Soviet times. Nowadays it is considered to be improper and out of date, although some men consider that it should still be allowed, in accordance with their cultural – and particularly their religious – interpretation of marriage. A polygamous marriage was undoubtedly considered respectable when the first wife was not able to have children. We do not know to what extent it was normal in the Pamirs for a replacement to be found within the family itself when a wife had died. We do know, however, that in the past a widow was obliged to marry a brother of her dead husband (the levirate custom), if he had any.

Dor and Naumann describe wedding ceremonies typical around 1975 in the

Afghan Pamirs. According to them the wedding ceremony, then as now, was conducted by an Islamic cleric (*mullah*), who asks the young couple whether they want to take the other to be their husband or wife (1978: 77). There are two witnesses to the wedding ceremony, as prescribed in Islamic law. After the official ceremony a banquet was held (and this is still done today), to show off the wealth of the families involved. There follows the bridal procession from the bride's *aûl* to that of her husband, the dowry and personal belongings going with her. We can assume that this was done ostentatiously, in order to show off the status of the families. However, it can no longer be described as a procession these days, as lorries have long since replaced the horses.

Traditionally a newly wedded woman had to fit into her parents-in-law's household, which sometimes meant she was subject to considerable restrictions. For example, she was hardly ever allowed to be seen in public with her husband and had to be subserviently respectful to her parents-in-law. A more relaxed relationship was only possible with her husband's brothers and sisters. Later on the situation would often improve for a young wife if a yurt was made available to the young couple. Recently this improvement has been reversed, because the lack of money means that new houses are seldom built and so the new family has to live in a very restricted space with the husband's parents.

In the literature there are various opinions on married life. These are on the Kyrgyz in general and not really on those clans who live in the Pamirs today. In spite of differing opinions there is general agreement on there being a wide degree of partnership in a marriage, although the women still carry the whole burden of the household and the upbringing of the children. This is a particular problem at a time of fuel shortages, since it is exclusively the women who are responsible for obtaining fuel.

Divorces are still carried out according to Islamic rites, or in earlier times at least by mutually agreed separation (see Lansdell 1885, I: 253). In the former case the dowry was used as compensation, in the second case the *kalym* had to be paid back.

Women age early in the climate of the high-lying valleys of the Pamirs. In spite of improved living conditions after 1950–60 under the Soviets, it was suitable to let women retire by 45 (men by 50). In former times most deaths occurred towards the end of the winter when colds and chills took their toll and the food situation dramatically worsened (e.g. there was hardly any milk). The descriptions in the literature of burying the dead within 24 hours must refer to the Islamic practice of burying a person who has died during the day by nightfall, and burying those who die in the night by the next sunset.

Even today the dead are still washed and wrapped in their shroud by a relative of the same sex. In former times they would be buried either in a small cemetery (*guristan*) or, if it happened at the summer camp, in the open countryside. Nowadays there are cemeteries near all the permanent settlements. The body is buried in a grave which is not filled with earth but covered, so that the dead person is not soiled by the earth (see Dor and Naumann 1978: 82).

Simple graves are given a surround of mudbricks. Important persons still have magnificent structures built on top of their graves, representing the miniaturised entrance to an ancient *madressa*, like the ones we are familiar with in Bukhara for example, with minarets at the sides.[14] Other structures are cube-shaped, with a dome (*gumba*) also made of mudbricks. Recent graves only have railings made of wood or iron. In the wilds of central Asia cemeteries like these – often set on a small rise – stand out starkly. Over the past few centuries Kyrgyz graves have often been the only relicts of Kyrgyz material culture in the Pamirs.

Gender

The relationship between the sexes amongst the Pamir Kyrgyz is certainly less problematical than in other Islamic societies, but although the literature mentions women's relative freedom there is no denying the fact that they carry out most of the daily chores. This also applies to physically more arduous work such as obtaining fuel and building the yurt.[15] Men predominantly spend their time dealing with the herds. The milking itself is taken over by the women, as are all the tasks to do with the processing of food. De Rocca's comment that Kyrgyz women have always played an important role because they did most of the work is therefore ambiguous (1896: 176). However, we go along with the author when he stresses that women's participation in decisions was a direct result of their responsibility for actually doing all the work.

As hunting has now steeply declined compared to what it was pre-Soviet times, the men's second and often very hard task has almost completely come to an end. Hunting used to involve the men in following animal trails for days on end, camping out in the open and then having to carry home the heavy kill on their backs for 10, 20 or more kilometres.

Dunmore states at the end of the nineteenth century that 'the Kirghiz treat their women very well and with more deference than most Mussulman tribes' (1893a, II: 118). The fact that for a time the Kara-Kyrgyz of the Alai were led by a woman in a war against the Russians (see Strong 1930: 114–115) suggests that traditionally women did indeed have a strong position in public affairs. De Rocca reports that in the nineteenth century women themselves took to arms if the camp was attacked (1896: 177). If we accept the view of Karutz, possibly the best authority on Kyrgyz society at the turn of the twentieth century, the strong position women had in his day was the result of rapid social change taking place, heralding the break-up of social norms which had previously been less favourable to women (1911: 114–116).

The Soviets' policy of support helped to further improve the position of women all over central Asia, even if this applies more to their recognition in the public domain than at home. However, the fact that a woman was allowed to be, for example, the leader of a kolkhoz, probably also helped to consolidate her position within the family. In comparison with the farmers in the oases of central Asia, Kyrgyz women were well placed for economic emancipation to take place (see Bacon 1966: 137, 171).

In recent years there has been a surprising change in the relatively new sphere of trade. Dor and Naumann report that trade was always a favourite occupation of the men in Afghan Wakhân (1978: 87), but in the Tajik Pamirs of the mid-1990s the explosive growth in private trade seems to have become almost exclusively a woman's business. The majority of the traders in the markets of Khorog and Murghâb town are women, and if the men do drive the battered old lorries, often used as the stall, the real business is actually done mainly by the women. For example, the men present had to ask their wives the price of the goods.

We know nothing about sexual freedom amongst the Kyrgyz of both sexes. Von Schultz stresses the strictly moral views of Pamir Kyrgyz women, who are known and respected for this far and wide (1910b: 250).

Kyrgyz entertainment

Dor and Naumann state that the favourite leisure-time occupation of Kyrgyz men is visiting other people. These visits serve the purpose of seeking advice, discussing problems or simply the exchange of pleasantries (1978: 87). As their horses made them much more mobile than the Pamiris, the Kyrgyz were able to visit more distant camps. One gets the impression that this is still the case, even if the vehicle which replaced the horse – the Russian motorbike with side-car, so widespread in the last decades of the Soviet Union – is becoming increasingly unfit for use.

The game of *buskashî* played by the Pamiris (see p. 121) is probably taken from the Kyrgyz game of *baîga*. The latter often used to be played (and still is, to a limited extent today) during the course of wedding celebrations. A slaughtered goat, or even a calf, is taken by a group of riders – in earlier times these were often large groups – to a predetermined place, the aim being to take possession of the dead animal from the other players, there being virtually no rules of the game. Krist observed a *baîga* event sometime after 1920, in which about 300 riders participated, and other sources mention up to 1,000 riders. Although they often rode full tilt down steep slopes during this chase after the dead goat, amazingly enough no one was ever seriously injured (1941: 117). However, other writers state that opponents were hit with a whip and fallen riders ended up under the horses' hooves (Breitenbach 1978: 108).

One thing is certain: the participants in a *baîga* had to be extremely skilled riders. For instance, in one case a yak calf weighing 50 kg had to be picked up by the riders at full gallop (Borchers 1931: 208–209). In earlier centuries living prisoners of war sometimes took the part now taken by the dead animal (see Breitenbach 1978: 108). Bearing this in mind it is interesting to note that in the twentieth century the Afghan Olympic Committee took up the cause of the *baîga* game and attempted to have it made into an authorised game with proper rules.

Only Olufsen mentions the so-called 'Attamascha', a 'game' in which a goat or sheep is tied to a post in the open. The participants came riding up one at a time and fired their gun at the animal as they rode past. Then the game was continued as a *baîga*. The successful marksman took the dead animal and rode off with it. If he was able to carry it to certain points without anyone getting it off him, then he was the winner (1900: 137). It is possible that this version of the *baîga* was only widespread in the Alai.

On our visits to Kyrgyz yurts and houses in the Murghâb we came across musical instruments much more rarely than we did in Pamiri households. We were only shown a tambourine and a plucked string instrument, similar to the *gitshak* of the Pamiris. Karutz mentions two instruments, which do not, however, originate from the Pamirs but from Western Turkestan: the *dutar*, a two-stringed guitar, and a reed flute. He explicitly states that the Kyrgyz had no tambourines or drums (1911: 196–212).[16]

Just as by and large there seem to be few musical instruments, little is written in the literature about music and nothing about dancing amongst the Pamir Kyrgyz. In earlier times they would instead drink heavily on festive occasions. In spite of asking several times, we were not once given the opportunity of meeting an experienced musician on our four or five visits to the Murghâb.

6

ISMAILIS AND SUNNIS

Islam and Islamic groups in the Pamirs

At the beginning of the eighth century the inhabitants of the Pamirs were confronted with Islam for the first time when they became involved in conflicts with Muslim military leaders advancing from the present-day Uzbek and Tajik western lowlands (see pp. 59–63). In view of the fact that many local princes had resisted the invaders over a long period of time, we can assume that it took centuries for Islam to spread throughout the valleys of the Pamirs.

It is interesting to note Olufsen's comments that Islam, in the form of the Ismaili Shia, only became the official religion in Garan and in the Wakhân towards the middle of the nineteenth century. However, he notes that in his day the lives of most normal people were hardly affected. He even says that 'in 1896, when the Vakhans were without a ruler, they declared themselves not to be Mussulmans' (1904: 209; 1911: 11). 'They asserted most pointedly that they did not say daily prayers ('*nâmas*') like the Mussulmans, but that they were only united with the direction of Providence through their altars with the holy lights and their sanctuaries' (1904: 199).

However, it is possible that the proximity to the Kafirs of present-day north-west Pakistan led to the Pamiris not professing their own religion whenever the Kafirs threatened the Wakhân on one of their frequent advances north. This may have actually been very easy to do, as Islam at that time was still substantially intermingled with elements of the Zoroastrian faith, particularly amongst simple farming families (see pp. 237–238). However, it may not be possible to generalise here, as many of the ruling class, the *sayyids*, considered themselves to be the descendants of the Islamic prophet Muhammad (see p. 148). The number of stories from Ishkashim depicting conflicts between the native people and the Unbelievers (the Kafirs) over previous centuries suggest that in the nineteenth century, if not earlier, Ishkashim and Garan at least had a large and devout Muslim population (Garan being situated between Ishkashim and Shugnân, which had clearly been Ismaili for centuries).

There is no information in the literature on whether followers of the Islamic Sunni faith used to live in the Ismaili valleys of today. On the other hand we do know that Ismailis made up the majority of the population in the past, certainly in the upper Wandsh and Darwâs regions, where the Sunnis have since made great gains. This was a result of compulsory conversion under Bukharan rule in the nineteenth century. For example, Sir Aurel Stein states that the population of Yasgulem was forced to convert to the Sunni faith (1933: 283).

There is a great deal of evidence that there were considerable differences between the Sunnis and the Shiites, and that these differences still exist. It may or may not be fortuitous that these differences run along ethnic or cultural borders, with the majority Shiite Pamiris on one side and the almost exclusively Sunni lowland Tajiks and Uzbeks on the other. For example, Grevemeyer quotes sources, although in a different context, in which the Ismailis are described by Sunnis in Badakhshan itself as 'shameful' (1982: 207, note 122). Biddulph even states that the Ismailis of the valleys in northern Pakistan were considered by the local Sunnis to be Kafirs (Unbelievers) (1880: 121). Even the majority of Shiites there regarded their Ismaili brothers in faith with a great deal of resentment (see Snoy 1975: 164).

Hence in Badakhshan too, and elsewhere, there must at times have been considerable pressure on the Ismailis from fellow Muslims, on the Afghan side at least. It is possible that in the western districts of Darwâs and Wandsh a conflict between Sunnis and Shiites might have arisen because the Ismailis who predominated here were being exploited by Sunni regional rulers, supported by the Emir of Bukhara (see Becker1968: 215). This would explain the positive reception some Pamiris gave the Russians when they moved into the Pamirs at the end of the nineteenth century. Evidently relations between Sunnis and Ismailis were at times so extremely tense that after the area of present-day GBAO had been handed over to Russia, as part of the Pamir Agreement of 1895, the Ismailis immediately turned to Tsar Nicholas II for protection against the persecution they were facing from the Sunni population.

Even now, 100 years on, one indication of the continuing antagonism between Ismailis and Sunnis was the 1992–3 dispute, within the 'Party of Islamic Re-birth' in Tajikistan, over the status of Ismailis within the community of the faithful.[1]

A short description of the differences between Sunnis and Shiites is appropriate at this point for those readers who do not have much knowledge of the various branches of Islam: although the Sunni branch of Islam easily predominates worldwide – around 90 per cent is the figure most frequently quoted – the majority in Iran and Iraq today are Shiites. There are large Shiite minorities in Afghanistan (the Hazara and Ismailis of Badakhshan) and also in Tajikistan (the majority of the Pamiris). Contrary to many accounts in the literature, the Shiites are not an Islamic 'sect' like, for example, the Mormons or the numerous American evangelical Christian organisations are sects. It is rather the case that the Shia faith represents an Islamic doctrine with fewer differences to the Sunni faith than exist between Christian Catholics and Protestants.

The main difference between the two branches of the faith is that the Sunnis only accord low significance to the role of the Prophet's family in Islamic leadership after the death of the Prophet Muhammad, whereas the Shiites *only* accept the role of the Prophet's family in the leadership (khalifate or imamate as the case may be) of the Islamic community. For this reason the imâms (see pp. 224–225) enjoy such great veneration today and the Ismailis – a subdivision of the Shiites – correspondingly venerate the Aga Khan as a direct descendant of the Prophet.[2]

Further differences exist over the role of the clerics, who are considered by the Shiites to be the interpreters of divine truth, whereas the Sunnis only acknowledge the clerics' teachings, and thus their religious authority, but they do not acknowledge that they make definitive decisions on divine truth. Other differences are only marginal, for example prayers or general rituals, and three of the five fundamental Muslim duties are identical (fasting, alms for the poor, pilgrimage to Mecca). With the fifth basic duty of every Muslim, the creed, the Shias add the words 'Ali is the wâlî of God and the heir of the prophet of God' to the Sunni words 'There is no God but God, and Muhammad is the Prophet of God'. Wâlî means 'deputy' or 'to be close to' in this context. Instead of five prayer sessions, the Ismailis only pray twice a day.

Irrespective of the continued conflicts between Sunnis and Shiites in the Pamirs, it may be assumed that amongst the autochtonous population at the time of the Russian occupation there were no longer any members of other religions apart from Islam. The exception may have been a few Jews, who according to our sources possibly worked as clockmakers in Khorog and as manufacturers or traders of jewellery in the Pamirs generally. The Jewish population, which is said to have been larger than the Christian one in central Asia in the tenth century (see Bacon 1966: 22), was later probably concentrated mainly in the towns of the Emirates/Khanates of Bukhara and Kokand. It is said that their language was a variant of Tajik Iranian, and this may explain their rise to prominence amongst the Samanids in particular. Some Jews, and a larger number of Christians, only re-entered the area of present-day GBAO with the Russian troops, only virtually to disappear once more when non-Tajik and non-Kyrgyz peoples emigrated after 1991.

The Ismaili faith

Even non-Sunni outsiders have invariably treated the Ismailis with a certain amount of suspicion. One reason for this was the evidently deliberate secrecy surrounding the religious beliefs and rites of the Ismailiyya,[3] which were guarded by a close circle of their own followers, in the manner of the Druzes. However, when in the mid-1990s a Western development expert spoke of a rebirth of old Ismaili traditions, including the tradition of assassins in the Pamir mountain range, this was a case of medieval prejudices emerging from the closet and having a field day. In his opinion 'militant Ismailis' in the Pamirs were attempting to revive the original traditions of the 'Ismaili Assassins': blind obedience to the point of self-sacrifice, the cult of 'the Old Man of the Mountain' and the 12-stage secret education, etc.

It would be easy to dismiss this talk as sheer nonsense. But in view of the lack of reliable information on social conditions filtering through to the West from central Asia today, even the wildest assertions might fall on fertile soil. Therefore the author wishes to add that in his own opinion it will be a long time before the Ismailiyya in the Pamirs complete the rebuilding of its theological principles, even amongst its most fervent followers, after 70 years of the Soviet dominion. The 'ideology' taught is indeed moving in the direction of a revival of deeply rooted and regionally shaped traditions. However, this strengthening of cultural identity – a positive step – is accompanied by the kind of modernisation of society, supported by the Aga Khan and the local institutions run by him, which can only be considered as Western and liberal in its religious elements. That is why it is absolutely absurd to start speaking of the Assassin tradition.

It is true that Ismaili 'Secret Teachings' are even mentioned in serious literature written by university teachers. But although it is said that the teachings of the Ismailis are generally kept concealed from people of other faiths, the main emphasis is on the fact that the Ismailiyya endeavours to fathom out hidden meanings in the writings of the Koran. Thus an Ismaili assumes that behind the 'external wording of the Koran' (*zâhir*) an 'inner meaning' (*bâtin*) is concealed, only known to the imâms and only passed on by them to the initiated (see Halm 1998: 141). The rulers in Egypt in the tenth and eleventh centuries, the Fatimid caliphs, who were at the same time the imâms of at least some Ismailis, insisted on their claim that their position was legitimised through having access to aspects of the inner meaning of the Koran. Belief in the caliphs and giving them their support was clearly linked to a promise of salvation for their followers. Further elements of Fatimid and Ismaili teachings referred to the creation of the world and its fate when it comes to an end (ibid.).

Fatimid Ismaili teachings were spread by missionaries called 'criers' or 'summoners' (*dâ'î*). It has already been mentioned (see pp. 60–62) that such *dâ'î* were active in early times in central Asia and persuaded the Samanid ruler Nasr ibn Ahmad Samanî to convert publicly to Ismailiyya.[4] As Badakhshan was then part of the Samanid empire, it is certainly possible that the foundations for the Ismailiyya in GBAO, and on the far side of the Afghan border, were laid at that time.

As already mentioned, the Ismailis belong to the Shiite branch of Islam. They are distinguished from the majority of Shiites – who are also called Twelver Shiites after the 12 legitimate Islamic leaders, the imâms, that include the Prophet Muhammad – by the fact that they recognise only seven legitimate leaders. After the death of Dja'far as-Sâdik in H 168 (AD 785/6), a group of his followers, the *nizârî*, held fast to the *imâmat* of his son Ismâ'il. Some of them maintained that Ismâ'il, as the seventh imâm, had not died and would reappear as the *mahdî*. Belief in a *mahdî* or 'Saviour' includes the idea that if ever hard times befall the Islamic community on earth, this Saviour will appear, will unite all Muslims and will make the world submit to true Islam. Other followers of the Shia recognized Ismâ'il's son Muhammad as their imâm (*Encyclopedia of Islam* IV: s.n. *Ismâ'îliyya*). Only the former are the members of the 'Sevener Shia', and they represent a minority out of some 20 million individuals amongst the present-day majority Shiites.

If we accept the statements in the *Encyclopaedia of Islam*, little is known about the Ismailiyya in the two centuries after its foundation, until the middle of the ninth century AD, 'when it appeared as a secret revolutionary organization carrying on intensive missionary efforts in many regions of the Muslim world' (IV: 198). An important Ismaili movement between the late ninth and twelfth centuries was that of the Fatimids, who came from North Africa to conquer Egypt and ruled the land until they were overthrown by Salah ed-Dîn. In Egypt at that time they assumed the title of caliph. During the last years of rule of the Fatimid Caliph al-Hakîm (AD 996–1021) extremist Ismailis in Cairo began to proclaim his divinity. Their leadership passed to a certain Hamza ibn 'Alî, who became the founder of the Druze religion of the Lebanon.

The work of the Iranian poet and philosopher Nâsîr-i Khusraw is of the greatest importance in the Pamir region. He was born about 1,000 years ago (1004–72) and was active as a Fatimid *dâ'î* in present-day GBAO in the mid eleventh century. The Pamiris considered him to be the founder of Ismailiyya in their region and a patron saint in the wider sense. Pictures of the celebrated poet can now be seen on walls in schools and offices, replacing those of Lenin or Karl Marx.

Towards the end of the rule of the Fatimid caliph al-Mustansir (1036–94) Ismaili policy in Iran was guided by Hassan as-Sabbâh, who later became known as 'The Old Man of the Mountain'. Under his leadership the famous fortress of Alamut was occupied from where generations of Ismaili leaders carried out an extremely controversial policy of violence against political opponents. This was also known as the 'Assassins'' movement, because its opponents were killed by young people sent on suicide missions.

Fantasies woven around Hassan as-Sabbâh, and his agents have spawned dozens of novels, and the English and French terms 'assassin' (meaning 'murderer') and 'assassinate' (to murder) were taken from the word 'Assassins'. This is the spine-chilling and exciting story which the development expert referred to on p. 223 attempts to transpose to the present. It is not clear even today whether the Assassins were acting as freedom fighters against what they saw as illegitimate political systems and dynasties in Iran, or whether it was a movement in which murder was only used for the purpose of blackmail and the extension of personal power of the 'Old Man of the Mountain'. It is most unlikely that any deeply religious Islamic movement was directed from Alamut, as pacts were repeatedly created with states involved in the Crusades.

If we accept the account in the *Encyclopaedia of Islam*, the Ismailiyya ended for the time being with the execution of the last 'Old Man of the Mountain', Imam Rukn ad-Dîn, after the capture of Alamut by the Mongols (AD 1256). Later lists of the imâms differ widely in their names, number and sequence. According to Shams ad-Dîn the lists divide, one line continuing with Kâsim Shâh, the other with Muhammad Shâh. From the mid-fifteenth century until the nineteenth century the imâms were usually affiliated with the Ni'mat Allâhî Sûfî order. In 1818 Hassan

'Alî Shâh Mahallatî has the title 'Aga Khan' bestowed on him by the Iranian Shah, a title thenceforward inherited by his descendants. In 1843 Hassan 'Alî Shâh moves to India, and Bombay becomes the permanent headquarters of the imamate.

The present Aga Khan, His Highness Prince Karîm Aga Khan, as he is addressed by his followers, succeeded his grandfather Sultân Muhammad Shâh in 1957. Today the imâm, educated in the West (a degree in Islamic history from Harvard University) and revered in GBAO because of his support after the crisis of 1992–3, has his headquarters in London. The most important Ismaili institutions, such as the Aga Khan Development Network and the Aga Khan Foundation are situated in London and in Geneva. The modernisation of Ismailiyya has been given further enormous impetus by Prince Karîm, with the result that the imamate is nowadays better known for its activities in the field of education, rather than in the publication of any religious statements.[5]

In order to complete the account of Ismaili history and the religious doctrine practised at the time of the Fatimids which I have briefly sketched out, it is necessary to refer to the explanations of Daftary (1998), Lewis (1940, 1967) and Hodgson (1955), and those in the *Encyclopaedia of Islam*.

Part of Ismaili doctrine is recorded in the *umm al-kitâb* (mother of [the] book[s]) dating from the tenth century, which has been handed down from Badakhshan. The Ismaili cosmology of the *dâ'î* al-Nasafî is important, as it influences symbolism in Pamiri culture. It is summarised as follows in the *Encyclopaedia of Islam*:

> In this cosmology God is described as absolutely beyond comprehension, beyond any attribute or name, beyond being and non-being. Through his divine Order or Volition (*amr*) be originated (*abda'*) the intellect (*'akl*). The *'akl* is the First Originated Being (*al-mubda' al-awwal*), . . . From the Intellect the Soul (*nafs*) proceeds through emanation. From the Soul proceed the seven spheres with their stars and move with its movement. Through the revolution of the spheres the single elements (*al-mufradât*) or natures, humidity, dryness, cold, and warmth, are mingled to form the composites (*al-murakkabât*), earth, water, air, and ether. As the composites mingle, the plants with the vegetative (*nâmiya*) soul develop. From them the animals with the sensitive (*hissiyya*) soul develop, and from the latter, man with the rational (*nâtika*) soul.
>
> (*Encyclopaedia of Islam*, IV: 203)

The shape of the roof on a traditional Pamiri house shows clearly how much the teachings on the elements have influenced everyday life (see pp. 170–171). Undoubtedly the ideas briefly portrayed here, going back to al-Nasafî, contain a number of elements which show a certain similarity to Sufism. Later, many years after Alamut, Nizârî doctrine in the Ismailiyya and central and southern Asiatic forms of Sufism showed many similarities. 'Ismâ'îlî ideas were often camouflaged in Sûfî forms of expression, especially in poetry' (*Encyclopaedia of Islam*, IV: 205). However, nowadays there is controversy, at least in GBAO, over whether the work of Nâsîr-i Khusraw, surely one of the most important poets of central Asia, was part of this tradition.

Ismaili functionaries in the Pamirs

As already mentioned, the Aga Khan is the head of the Ismaili Shia, with headquarters in Bombay (at present also in London). He is described as the imâm in accordance with Ismaili tradition. In the Sunni branch of Islam this term simply means prayer leader, but here it should probably be translated as 'religious leader'. However, this word means much more to a devout Ismaili. It means the caliph as a direct descendant of the Prophet and leader of the Islamic community, and also denotes a person who has direct access to God.

Although the term *baraka* is unknown today in GBAO and is not mentioned anywhere in the literature on the Pamirs (see Westermarck 1926, I: 35–261), it is useful to make a comparison here with the folk beliefs of the Maghrib and the Near East. A person sharing in this *baraka* is honoured by the people and all hope to receive a portion of the divine blessing. Thus the Aga Khan may be considered to be the most important bearer of this 'divine blessing', he is the vehicle through which it is passed on to believers. The idea heard occasionally in the Pamirs that the imâm himself personifies a divine being would be going too far, at least in the present-day understanding of the imamate, although the example of the Caliph al-Hakîm proves it to be historically accurate.

In the Pamir region the Aga Khan was represented by a small number of men called *pir* right up until the early Soviet period, and for even longer in the adjacent countries (*pir* approximately means 'the Elder'). They acted as religious leaders and also collected taxes for the imâm (Plate 6.1). Lentz equates *pir* with *ishan*, a title which is likewise occasionally used. The office was abolished under the 48th Aga Khan; that is, the grandfather of the present leader of the Ismailis.

Below the level of *pir* an active role was played by men referred to as *khalifa*, the term also used for the Prophet's successors at the head of the faithful. In spite of having this same name, they were in fact only lower-ranking religious functionaries. On the one hand they acted as the local tax collectors of a *pir*, and on the other they represented religious authority accessible to everyone. Although the *pir* chose them from the population at large, they enjoyed considerable standing. This was probably because they were the only individuals in the village acquainted with the background to the Ismaili religion, but it was also due to their often celebrated healing skills (see Lentz 1931: 181). It was likely that a *pir* received his training in Bombay, or was inducted into his duties by envoys of the Aga Khan, but a *khalifa* received instruction from the *pir* who was his superior. Most of the knowledge passed on in this way was probably not very profound in nature.

During the Soviet period this chain of instruction was interrupted and anything not handed down from father to son vanished over the sixty or so years between 1923–5 and circa 1985, the start of perestroika under Gorbachev. The office of *khalifa* was rarely practised at all, or if so, only secretly. By the 1930s the holy

Plate 6.1 Local leader from Ishkashim, end of nineteenth century (in Olufsen 1904, p. 67).

scriptures had had to be handed over to the authorities or hidden at great risk. As the office of *pir* no longer existed and all contact with the imamate had been severed, an official *khalifa* could no longer be appointed, with the result that the office could only be passed on informally in a few isolated cases from father to son.

Religion was most harshly suppressed in the years before the Second World War. It was said that in the Pamirs religious functionaries were arrested on Stalin's instructions as 'kulaks' and later murdered. The violent suppression of religion ceased after the war, but anti-religious policies continued throughout the 1960s and 1970s. Soviet anti-religious propaganda reached its height in Khorog in 1978, when a 'special seminar to train anti-Ismaili propagandists' was held (Bennigsen and Wimbush 1986: 123). Prior to this a number of pamphlets hostile to the Ismailiyya were published, one of them a paper called 'Modern Ismailism and its Reactionary Essence' (ibid.).

With the advent of perestroika – that is, some years before the collapse of the Soviet Union and Tajik independence – religious activity began to be tolerated once more. By the end of the 1980s, once it became clear that liberal attitudes to religion had for the most part turned into reality, the holy scriptures were taken out of their hiding places, and places of religious worship were restored. However, it is likely that the whereabouts of many of the books was forgotten after the death of their last owner.

The title of *khalifa* began to be used again. It was now given almost exclusively to the grandsons or great-grandsons of the last officially recognised bearers of the title. The new caliphs therefore only had minimal knowledge of the Ismaili religion. An Ismaili Centre and a branch of the Institute of Ismaili Studies, set up in 1995 in Khorog, were long overdue. Under the direction of an Ismaili Tajik Religious Education Committee, religious functionaries are once again being trained locally. At present there are a further thirty or so students from GBAO being instructed at the Institute of Ismaili Studies in London. The Ismaili Centre also sells religious documents and runs a youth programme.

In a number of villages during the last few years empty posts have been filled for the first time since Stalin was in power. For some caliph positions a new incumbent was found, with a surprisingly large number of young men being appointed. This change of generation will probably have an effect on the way religion is practised. Up until now the mostly older men were looked on primarily as spiritual leaders, whereas some of the younger bearers of office are also involved in youth and social work. This is likely to have a positive effect, because after 1991 the office of *khalifa* was the only one at a communal level which still commanded any vestige of authority.

It is still not clear what sort of relationship the Pamiris had in former times to the leaders of the Ismailiyya in Bombay. In the nineteenth century there were certainly direct links to the imamate in India, but these were stopped by the Soviets in 1923. The Pamir Ismailis' isolation was not just a result of the Soviets' aversion to any religious activity, it was more the case that since 1919 the British had attempted to influence the Ismaili community through the Aga Khan, who resided in British India. The initial aim was to win over the population of Badakhshan in favour of the British in the so-called Third Afghan War.

Efforts were later directed against the Bolsheviks as well, which turned out to be disastrous for the Ismailiyya in the Pamirs (see Kreutzmann 1996: 119). Numerous emissaries were sent to the Pamirs from Bombay, with the result that the Soviets started to suspect all the Ismailis of the Pamirs of making pacts with the enemy. The Pamiris became the main victims of the confrontation between the

Soviets and the British, and many *pirs* were arrested as spies of the British. As a result of British intervention the forwarding of taxes (tithes) paid up until then had to cease completely (ibid.). Moreover, many religious functionaries were forced to flee from the Pamirs to Pakistan.

During this short period of closer relations between the imamate in Bombay and the people of the Pamirs, religious structures were also reformed, at least in Afghan and Chinese Badakhshan. The influence of the *pirs* was reduced and any still existing mosques were replaced by meeting houses (*jamoât khôna*), in order to distinguish them from those of the Sunnis. In the Soviet part of the Pamirs the *pirs* were all relieved of their office in the years after 1923.

On the basis of various sources Kreutzmann has produced a map of the religious centres in GBAO shortly before the Soviet revolution. According to this map there was an Ismaili administrative centre in Khorog (there were similar ones in adjacent countries: Faizabad in Afghanistan, Chitral and also Gilgit in Pakistan [British India]). There were *pir*'s official headquarters in the present-day Tajik Pamirs in Basîd (Bartang valley), Porshnev near Khorog, Shakhdara, and in as many as five places in the Wakhân: Vrang, Nijigar, Shirgin, Zunk and Langar (Kreutzmann 1996: 121, pl. 14). These last five show the Wakhân's importance for the Ismailiyya and have to be regarded as evidence telling against the hypothesis mentioned earlier, according to which the area was penetrated at a late stage, or indeed not at all, by the Ismaili Shiites.

In the literature there are accounts of sometimes close relations between the Ismaili religious functionaries in the Pamirs and the imamate in Bombay, but an extremely one-sided picture also emerges. The poor were forced to pay tithes to their *pir*, and he in his turn had to send half of the income earned in that way to the Aga Khan in Bombay (see von Schultz 1916: 217). Even in the years of utter poverty after the mid-nineteenth century, tithes were levied on grain and a small contribution was levied on livestock.

There is barely a mention of the Ismaili imâm, for his part, having taken any interest in the people in the Pamirs.[6] One can only assume that the clerics' training was actually carried out from Bombay. However, demands for payment, instead of offers of support in their hour of greatest need, reflect badly on the Ismaili leadership of the time. The legendary wealth of the Aga Khan in the nineteenth century must also be judged against this background.

However, since Tajikistan became independent, the direction of the flow of tax revenue has clearly shifted. The Pamiris no longer pay religious taxes, but receive a large proportion of the emergency and development aid presently entering GBAO either directly, or through the imamate.

Ismailiyya in everyday life

The relationship between Ismaili popular belief and pre-Islamic religion is often cited in the literature. There is virtually no information on the primarily Islamic elements in the religion of everyday practice. The following comments, based on conversations with a number of caliphs after 1995, can only be regarded as shedding some basic light on the Ismailiyya in everyday life.

The Ismailis we interviewed stressed an important difference between themselves and the Sunnis: the fact that Ismailis had always had an imâm. They also seem to consider that the Sunnis lose out by not recognising one (compare our comments on the *baraka* idea, p. 227).

The Ismailiyya is based on the Koran. Ahadith (Sayings of the Prophet Muhammad) are recognised, but are considered of lesser importance than the Koran. The Ismailis do not have different schools of interpretation of the Koran (*madawâb*). In more recent times it has become especially important to have meeting rooms (*jamoât khôna*) instead of mosques. These rooms are used primarily for Islamic religious instruction and not for prayer. Men and women also socialise here.

Prayers may be said individually or communally in private houses. Lentz maintains that there was a mosque in Roshorve in the 1920s (1931: 157). Clearly this is a wrong use of the term, since all existing village mosques had already been specifically abolished by the second or third Aga Khan in the nineteenth century.

Before prayers ritual washing is carried out (*tahorât*). The special role in prayers played by Alî, the Prophet's son-in-law, has already been mentioned. In the Pamirs the Islamic creed (*shahada*) is supplemented by '*on 'Alian walî allah*' (this was translated to us as: 'Alî is the holiest of all men'). Prayers take place only twice a day, whereas the Sunnis pray five times a day: the first prayer (*namaz*) is said before sunrise and a further two prayers are said after sunset.

The circumcision of boys and the first prayer in the life of a child were mentioned on p. 158. Circumcision is obligatory, as it is with all Muslims.

The Pamiris main religious festival is Kurbam Baîram, as it is in Islam generally, though here it is called *id el-kurbôm*. Islamic believers also call it the festival of slaughter or *id el-fitr*, because each family slaughters an animal and consumes it afterwards. In the Pamirs the old custom still persists of throwing a live sheep off the roof of a house and then ritually slaughtering it, though we ourselves did not observe this. The meat is cooked in a large pot and is consumed by the family and its guests. According to Lentz, the custom was less cruel: the sheep was first ritually slaughtered on the roof and then thrown down to the ground (1931: 216).

Fasting (*rûza*) during the Islamic month of Ramadan is always carried out according to individual traditions. The Sunnis fast for exactly one month; in some countries this is done under considerable social pressure, or even state coercion. Devout Ismailis in the Pamirs were never – and are still not – put under this kind of pressure to fast. However, in the past pious men and women would fast for up to 40 days. Nowadays they often observe just three days of fasting. This is to help remind people of their religious prescriptions, but on the other hand will not render them unfit to work properly, as this is considered by many people to serve no useful purpose. During Ramadan visits to relatives are more frequent and a more substantial meal is eaten in the evenings. On the day the fast is broken (*ramadhân*) children are given sweets.

In contrast to the majority Shiites, especially in Iran and Iraq, not all the Ismaili Pamiris celebrate the Ashura festival (*oshûrâ*, traditionally known as *shadâ* or [*Shugnî*] *shidâ*), which serves as a reminder of the murder of the grandson of the Prophet Hassan by the Omayyads. We were told that on this occasion, in the past at least, certain especially pious men would not shave or bathe for ten days.

According to a *khalifa* we spoke to, the Naûrûz (Nawruz) or Spring festival no longer has any religious importance, unlike in Zoroastrian (and early Ismaili?) times. However, another religious dignitary stresses that certain rituals which are part of the Naûrûz could have some religious significance. On the whole, though, it tends to be a social event with public horse racing, competitions, and much music and dancing. On this day a *khalifa* is also supposed to say prayers for the dead. In Roshorve in the 1920s, Naûrûz was the most important festival on the calendar. Lentz states that because of the general poverty this festival was the only one celebrated with any extravance (1931: 215–216).

In the village the *khalifa* also acts as a healer. Although this does not necessarily have anything to do with his religious function, the role of healer certainly lends him more authority. He uses herbal remedies and also offers treatments which could be considered to be holistic or to involve magic, depending on one's individual point of view. One part of this magic involves written charms. One woman told us:

> A *khalifa* writes good things with his right hand and bad ones with the left. If you have toothache, for example, you go to a *khalifa*. He writes something down on a piece of paper, which you put in your mouth or on the tooth. The pain goes away. A *khalifa* can also write bad things, and this he does with his left hand. These pieces of paper are hidden in the house of the recipients of the message [i.e. the people one wants to harm].

In the past there were also written charms whose effect could be enhanced by the material on which they were written. One such material was bone:

> One woman had severe abdominal pain and was operated on every year. Again and again. One day a girl who has a special feel for these matters goes into her house and finds a human jaw bone at the entrance, or above the door, with evil words scratched into it. The woman's name has a 'Z' in it. Every year all those in her family with a Z in their name are afflicted by some misfortune. After the jaw bone had been removed from the house the woman no longer had to be operated on, nor did any other members of the family have any further misfortunes befall them.

Soviet harassment of religious functionaries, and also the excellent service provided by the Soviet health system, has nowadays led to the caliphs' role as healers (and as those who have influence on the powers of good and evil) being almost forgotten. However, there are young caliphs expert in traditional herbal medicine. Even during the Soviet period, herbal medicine was encouraged in GBAO and underwent widespread revival after the collapse of the Soviet Union.

There is a dearth of written information on Sufism (*tasawwuf*) and the role of dervishes in the Pamirs. However, a picture in the museum in Khorog, dated to around 1900 and also published by Gawrilyuk and Yurotshenko (1987), shows a group of dervishes at an unknown place in the Pamir region (Plate 6.2). The typical attributes of a dervish, such as pointed caps and begging bowls can be clearly seen (see Frembgen 1999: 50–53, 82–91). An old man on his travels, whom we met in Porshnev in 1995 (Plate 6.3), replied in answer to our question on where he came from and what he was doing: 'For decades I have been a disciple.' This remark clearly refers to the Sufi tradition of lifelong study. Although he wore a Shugnî cap on his head, it is possible that he was from another part of central Asia.

Some people interviewed recently deny that the famous poet and Ismaili envoy Nâsîr-i Khusraw was a Sufi. It is also said that Sayyid Jallâl al-Badakhshanî – whose grave lies on the Shakhdara not far from Tusyan, and was in the past frequently visited and venerated – was a pious man, but no Sufi. However, it is also said that the Ismailiyya and Sufism show certain similarities. One *khalifa* told us: 'We both take only the good things from Islam.' However, he pointed out one important difference: 'Sufis are ascetic, whereas Ismailis are not. That is why we are not Sufis.' If we agree with Daftary, who described the history of the Ismailiyya

Plate 6.2 Group of dervishes in an unknown place in the Pamirs, *c.* 1900 (Khorog Museum archives).

Plate 6.3 'For decades I have been a disciple' – an old man in the tradition of Sufism met in Porshnev (1995).

in detail (1998), there can be no doubt that it was primarily the Nizârî Ismailis who were most closely linked with Sufi mysticism and the art of poetry. For generations Nizârî imâms were considered to be the embodiment of Sufi masters.

The Sunnis in Gorno-Badakhstan

In the literature it only tends to be mentioned *en passant* that there has been a large Sunni minority in the area of present-day GBAO since at least the nineteenth century. It seems that describing local forms of the Sunni religion was not considered important, as the Ismaili tradition and pre-Islamic religious elements in the Pamirs were seen as more interesting to the reader. And so virtually nothing is known about the religious life of the Sunnis of Wandsh and Darwâs.

Literary sources on the Kyrgyz of the Murghâb mainly describe stereotypes. Like their relatives in the Tien-Shan range of mountains, they were considered to be non-devout Muslims, who had held on to many elements of their former shamanistic religion until at least the beginning of the twentieth century (see Machatschek 1921: 119; Olufsen 1897a: 335; Roskoschny 1890: 463; Capus 1890b: 515–516). As well as believing in the Islamic God, they also believed there were at least two other 'highest beings': a good one and an evil one. Moreover they believed that the earth was populated by countless spirits, amongst whom the spirits of the dead played an important role (see Roskoschny 1890: 463). Even now there remains a strong element of soothsaying, mainly based on interpreting entrails, or changes to bones when they are burnt. However, other residual elements of former shamanism, mentioned in some sources at the end of the nineteenth century, are no longer to be seen today.

However, this tolerant co-existence of the teachings of the Koran and traditionally handed-down religious ideas cannot have applied to all the Kyrgyz, as by the sixteenth century (see Shahrani 1979a: 47), and according to other sources until the mid-seventeenth century (Akiner 1983: 328), many large groups were already so influenced by Islam that wars waged, for example, against the 'heathen' Kalmucks, were on religious grounds.

The conflicts in the Murghâb between the Soviets and the Kyrgyz after 1923 have been described elsewhere. There was undoubtedly a religious element to these conflicts. For example the Basmatshi Uprising took place at that time, even though it may not have been exclusively for religious reasons. In the post-Soviet era the Sunni religion has developed into a significant focus for cultural life. If one looks at all the mosque building going on and the fact that even during hard times these often expensive buildings are financed by the people, then it can only be described as a religious revival. In almost every larger Kyrgyz village work had started on building a mosque by 1995 and was finished by 1998. However, if mosque attendance is taken as an indicator, it is clear that active religious belief is primarily restricted to the older men. The young people hardly ever go. Furthermore, it is generally the case that those who visit the mosque are not fanatical about religion. People are keen to exercise the freedoms which were missing for so long.

However, for a while it did seem as if the Sunni revival in the valleys of Wandsh and Yasgulem would become embroiled with religious fanaticism. In Yasgulem, from 1996 to 1998, an opposition group put pressure on the local population to prohibit music and dancing in public and also to prohibit men and women from socialising together in private. Since then the 'Islamic Opposition' in Yasgulem seems to have more or less broken up and the young men brandishing that perverse symbol of manhood, the Kalashnikov, have all gone home. It is to be hoped that cultural life has reverted to what it was previously.

Islamic opposition

The inhabitants of the Pamirs have always been anti-fundamentalist in attitude, apart from the few exceptions already mentioned in Wandsh (Yasgulem) with its Sunni majority. Shahin Bekhradnia states that after the fundamentalists seized power in Dushanbe many Pamiris at the time saw this as a reason for GBAO to secede (1994: 117). The Pamiris are, however, also aware of the fact that many Tajiks regard them with mistrust especially *because* of their religious and social liberalism. For example, at the beginning of the 1990s rumours abounded that the Pamiris slept with their sisters, mothers and all other kinswomen. Even without malicious rumours, it is possible that devout Sunnis might find it strange at least that in GBAO the members of a family (and their guests) all sleep in the same room, and in the cold winters traditionally in the same bed.

During our stays in GBAO from 1995 to 1998 there were, however, opposition groups near Khorog, in Wandsh and in Yasgulem who claimed to be 'Islamic'. Their political role will be dealt with elsewhere (see pp. 276–277). At this point I wish to pursue the question of the Islamic element. From conversations with representatives of various groups it became clear that these were mainly local 'Pro-Pamir' groups, opposed to the government in Dushanbe, who sometimes called themselves 'Islamic' solely for opportunistic reasons. This was certainly true of organisations found in the areas settled by Ismailis.

The first impression of the group in the Yasgulem valley, who were trying to teach the people Islamic ways, was that they were misusing Islam solely in order to further personal interests. Neither the leader of the group nor his armed followers had the slightest knowledge of the Koran. Although they were officially Sunnis, they neither knew the basic prayers, nor were they able to recite a passage from the Koran, let alone read it. If there really had been an Islamic opposition in Tajikistan in the past, or even if one existed now, it was obviously not to be found in the Pamirs.[7] However, it is striking that elsewhere in central Asia the fundamentalist followers of Islam are also noticeable for their absurd demands on human behaviour, rather than for their sound knowledge of religious texts.

Ancient religious traces and contemporary popular faith

The symbolism expressed in the roof rafters on a Pamiri house (the four elements) clearly has Shiite features, bearing in mind what has already been described. The positioning of the roof opening previously mentioned (see pp. 170–171), the role of the sun in relation to the calendar, the meaning of the Naûrûz festival, the jumping across fire, and a host of other rituals taken from traditional Pamiri culture also point to the influence of early, pre-Islamic ideas, at least until recent times.

The proven presence of Christian communities on the Silk Road in the fifth and sixth centuries, and of Manichaeans in the third century at the latest (Haussig 1983: 218ff.), is unlikely to be of importance in this context. It is also unlikely that Buddhism can be invoked as an influence in the above-mentioned rituals, since by the seventh century at the latest it had probably ceased to exist in the Pamir region, otherwise the traveller Hiouen-Thsang would have mentioned the presence of Buddhists (see Tomaschek 1877: 55). The role of the mainly town-dwelling Jews in central Asia can also be ignored, even if local sources occasionally mention their presence in Khorog.

Relicts of Zoroastrianism

Progress is much more likely if we look for connections to Zoroastrianism or the ancient Aryan Avesta religion. The Ismaili Abusaîd was the last to point to the close links between Aryan religious and philosophic outlooks and Ismaili Islam. For example, first of all the concept of God is the same in both religions: 'God is above notions of existence and non-existence. Therefore He is not seen, heard or perceived' (1997: 37–38). Second, 'during the first stage of creativity, God mastered the two origins of all creations, Minu – Spiritual world and Geti – Material world, that are closely associated. In Ismailism they were called Akl-e Kul (Universal Reason) and Nafs-e Kul (Universal Soul).' Third, 'the first eternal Ameshaspents in the Aryan religion (Surush, Mehr, Ardbon, Zamyod and Ozar) that were thought to be Angel-Protectors were materialized in the five columns of the Pamiri house. Under Islam they were renamed for the Five Holy Personalities H. Muhammad (S), H. Ali (A), H. Fotima, I. Hasan and I. Husein' (ibid.).

Abusaîd also sees similarities in the use of meeting houses instead of mosques: 'As long as the Aryan religion existed, it was forbidden to build a man-made house for worshipping. Thus during Ismailism Mosque construction and various cult facilities were not common among the people. Thus the Universe is the House of God and the Five Eternal Ameshaspents are present in every house' (ibid.).

The connection to Zoroastrianism becomes clearer if one considers the role played by the sun, and above all by fire, in Pamiri life, even until recently. Wood was the first traveller to draw attention to two facts: first, the people's repeated accounts of structures which were said to have been erected by fire-worshippers; second, the Pamiris' special customs relating to the use of fire. One of these was the repugnance with which a Pamiri blows out a light: 'A Wakhanî considers it bad luck to blow out a light by the breath, and will rather wave his hand for several minutes under the flame of his pine-slip, than resort to the sure, but to him disagreeable alternative' (1872: 218). Olufsen (1904: 205–206) and Reclus also mention this fear of contaminating fire with human breath. Moreover the latter cites a fire, or sun festival, during which large fires were lit (see p. 000).[8] He reports seeing sick people walking round a fire several times, or if they were able to, jumping over it three times (1881: 465–466). When small children fell ill, the mothers would jump over the fire with the child in their arms (von Schwarz 1900: 441).

The custom of 'fire flying' is no longer practised, or only as a child's game. According to Lentz, in the past twigs used to be lit in front of the house, and men and women would jump over the fire. Afterwards each person would throw an item of their personal belongings into the fire, while chanting: 'The evil spirits must go away! Our evil spirits into the fire' (1931: 218). Evidently jumping over the fire was in itself regarded as a cleansing act.

The parallels between the customs of the Pamiris and ancient elements of the Avesta religion are so close that some sources regard the Oxus valley as the cradle of the religion of Zoroaster (see Biddulph 1880: 108). Bekhradnia even poses the question as to whether Zoroaster might not actually have come from the Pamirs (1994: 109). Tomaschek also suggests that Zoroastrian belief was at its strongest in present-day Tajikistan, with the former area of Sogdiana as the actual centre of this belief (1877: 9). This would mean that it was not the Pamirs but western Tajikistan which was the cradle of the fire religion.

Ismaili popular faith

Other elements of more recent popular belief are probably also linked to Zoroastrianism. Shahin Bekhradnia refers to an old wedding ritual in the Pamirs, which could date back to a Zoroastrian tradition: 'When the groom is about to set off to bring his bride home, he first goes to the *zingak* or hearth fire, . . . and there he pays his respect by kissing the hearth and then touching his lips and chest with his finger' (1994: 118). He also says that the way in which the wedding is prepared and celebrated shows similarities to the *lork* ceremony among Iranian Zoroastrians.

Numerous places in Badakhshan have the word *mazâr* in their name. The most well known is surely Mazâr ash Sharîf, the old capital of Afghan Badakhshan. *Mazâr* played an important role in Pamiri popular belief until well into the Soviet era. Even today people sometimes visit such a place. According to Poliakov *mazâr* is a term used to denote any holy place. 'The term *mazar* . . . covers an enormous variety of structures, burial grounds, physical objects, trees, rocks, caves, springs, bodies of water, and simply places that people visit, but graveyards and graves have a particular significance' (1992: 99). In the Pamirs, a *mazâr*, or holy place, exists in practically every *kishlak*. Our Plate 6.4 shows a *mazâr* in the upper Wakhân, which bears a resemblance to the graves of Sunni holy men in North Africa or in the Near East.[9] In accordance with local tradition, the horns of a Marco Polo sheep are placed on top of the dome and to the left side of the front.

Plate 6.4 *Mazâr* or holy place in the upper Wakhân area (1998); note the huge horn of a Marco Polo sheep on the top of the cupola. This is typical of a *mazâr* in the Pamirs.

There is a different kind of *mazâr* near Tusyan on the Shakhdara river. It is a mud and stone structure without a roof, which was incorporated into a larger structure after 1991 and roofed over. At the centre of this *mazâr* is the grave of Sayyid Jallâl al-Badakhshanî, poet and leader of the Ismailis. There are other covered structures like this one, for example above Tusyan, or near Basîd in the Bartang valley. Another type of *mazâr*, for example that below the fortress of Namadgut in Ishkashim, is a structure in the form of a cuboid, likewise decorated with sheep and wild goat horns. One *mazâr* right next to the sinter terraces of Garm-Tshashma shows the close relationship between holy places and springs of water. Olufsen's description of this place where several small hot springs rise is the same as that seen by the visitor today: 'a small yard has been fenced about with a wooden paling . . . The altar consists only of some natural little caves in the rock beside the source – on shelves in these caves are placed a small copper lamp, a small earthenware lamp, and a round block stone' (1904: 30). An enscribed stone, possibly of importance in dating the site, was unfortunately taken back to Copenhagen by the expedition of that time, as Olufsen admits.

Typical of many of these places is the presence of a large, usually rounded stone, on which other smaller round stones are placed. Many of these places are under trees and near springs. Oil is sometimes poured over the stones and animal horns are almost always placed beside them.

The significance of these places is minimised today, although it is not only older people who can be seen touching the stones and then brushing their hand across their face and breast. There are definitely parallels here with the *baraka* concept referred to on p. 227. This becomes clear if we examine the past. According to Lentz, people traditionally went at least once a year to a *mazâr*, and some people even went every six months. Evidently this happened on particular days, as Lentz speaks of a *mazâr* processional festival. The women and girls dressed up for this occasion and took provisions with them. When they got to the *mazâr*, celebrations took place in separate groups of men and women, with music, singing, dancing and games (1931: 216–218; 1939: 71). Olufsen states that lamps were also lit and the people prayed in the direction of the altar or the stones, covering their faces with their hands as they did so (1904: 30).

The date on which a festival was to be celebrated was decided using a traditional calendar, and Lentz has devoted an entire monograph to this subject (1939). The year is divided into three-day and nine-day sections, which are counted by using the parts of the body, starting with the toenails. On the question of determining the date of the solstice ('sun at the knee'), Lentz quotes an informant, though the context is different:

> When the forty days of winter are past they start counting from the toenails upwards: three for the nails, three for the heel, three for the foot, three for the ankles, three for the shin, three for the back of the knee, three for the knee. When you have reached the knee, then it is time for our festival.
> (Lentz 1931: 217; 1939: 70).

Abusaîd considers that the *mazâr* was derived from the altars and fire temples of Zoroastrianism, and also retained a part of their ancient function. The addition of such items as the large stone, on which small round stones were laid ('stone altar'), and the horns of mountain goats and wild rams, perfectly preserved their former Aryan attributes (1997b: 102).

Quite possibly traditional animism may likewise be seen persisting in the context of the Iranian Avesta religion; many elements are also compatible with Jinn ideas in the Koran or belong to the same tradition as that found amongst other central Asian peoples. Olufsen mentions malevolent spirits from the Wakhân, who, like their relatives in North Africa and in the Sahara dwell in places with mystical associations: dark gorges, amongst clefts in the rocks, on old trees or near graves (1904: 200). One can readily envisage that in a region as well endowed with water as the Pamirs the folk imagination would also be likely to people rivers and lakes with spirits. This may be consistent with a belief in Nature as a living being. However, the belief in the *shaîtân*, the Devil, is definitely taken from the Koran. It is he who rules over legions of lesser, but equally evil, spirits.

Evidently the dead carry on living after they are buried, but in a different form. They have to be buried in a certain way, or else other members of the family will die, as a woman from Shugnân explained in 2003:

> The dead are wrapped in white sheets. A strip of cloth is tied round their head, so that the jaw does not drop open. If a member of the same family dies in the following year, then the strip might not have been tied tightly enough and the corpse might have eaten the sheet. They check on this by opening up the grave. It sometimes happens that the corpse is sitting up in the grave and the white cloth has gone through its mouth and body, because the strip of cloth had not been tied tightly enough. If it is now tied really tightly, then no-one else in the family will die.

Good and bad omens have always played an important role amongst the Pamiris. A whole range of customs have survived right up to the present day. In Wandsh the decision over who will have the honour of playing host at the next feast is not left to chance alone. Strength is the deciding factor here: the person who succeeds in breaking a mutton bone (Plate 6.5) has that honour; however, he also has to pay the cost of a sheep.

Olufsen states that it is a bad omen if a person steps across someone lying on the ground (1904: 206). Likewise something bad will happen if a young girl's right ear itches. Black cats crossing your path from the right bring bad luck. If you do something new on a Monday, for example undertake a journey, you will run into difficulties. If someone spills salt, this will lead to quarrels within the family. If you dream you are swimming, you will become ill.

However, something good will happen if a girl's left ear itches. If a girl's right eyebrow itches or hurts, a young man is thinking of her. If it is her left eyebrow, her mother is thinking of her. If there are bubbles in the bowl when tea is poured,

Plate 6.5 Older man from Yasgulem tries to break a sheep's leg bone in order to win the honour of welcoming guests to the next opulent meal (1998).

you should touch them and then touch your pocket or forehead with your fingers. This way you will receive money (later). If a star is very close to the moon – preferably a full moon – and you happen to see it, you can make one wish. If you come across a pregnant woman this will also bring good luck. Just as in Europe, it is believed that 'broken crocks bring good luck'. It is also lucky to put on your clothes back to front or inside out by mistake. Lastly, meeting a bride and bridegroom will bring you luck.

7

ECONOMY AND SOCIETY IN THE SOVIET SYSTEM

Public administration and Soviet development policy

Despite frequent earlier references, it is appropriate to devote this chapter entirely to development during the Soviet period. In this way one can demonstrate how the extensive and far-reaching negative effects on cultural life and personal ownership of land and property were offset by the enormous improvements in state services, in particular the welfare system. In comparison with the neighbouring countries on, or near, the southern border – Afghanistan, Pakistan and almost certainly India too – the Pamiris did extremely well under the Soviet Union, especially from the mid-1950s onwards. This is why, in spite of having been subjected to often violent change under Stalin, and suffering continued denial of political rights under the Soviet system, most people are united in their criticism of the changes which took place after Tajikistan became independent. If you ask anyone about the advantages and disadvantages of the old and new systems, the honest reply is almost always: 'We would like to have the Soviet Union back.' Although people do value democratic freedom, this does not help them cope with the actual physical hardships resulting from the present economic and political crisis.

Gorno-Badakhshan and the Soviet administration

In the years prior to the end of the Soviet Union there were 53 national regional units with varying legal status on Soviet territory. Tajikistan was one of the 15 republics of the Union. A republic of the Soviet Union, according to the Soviet view, was a state with its own government, which did not, however, have sovereign powers (see Brunnen 1988: 25). The principle of decentralisation of decisions only operated on a superficial level, because 'democratic centralism' was enshrined in the constitution of the Soviet Union. The absolutely binding nature of decisions made by the higher authorities in Moscow applied to every part republic, *de facto* since the founding of the Soviet Union and also *de jure* from 1977.

With regard to the autonomous oblasts (provinces), for example GBAO, the rule was that decisions taken by the regional Soviets could be overturned by the next level of authority immediately above; that is, by the executive committee of the

Communist Party of Tajikistan. The authority with the greatest power in decision-making was the Communist Party of the Soviet Union (CPSU) in Moscow. This was a centrally run, hierarchically arranged organisation, which had the power to abolish all constitutional rights of any government actually in power at any time. In the same way that the Party had absolute authority at every level over the governments of the republics and lower administrative units, the Party leadership had the right to impose decisions on the nominally independent parties in the Soviet republics.

From the early years of Stalin's rule, Russians dominated in all Party organisations, including those of the Asian republics. Only during the 1970s and 1980s, as in other central Asian Soviet republics, in Tajikistan the proportion of national functionaries holding elite positions increased (see Stringer 2003: 159). However, we will see that the national representatives of the Communist Party always successfully managed to fight for the material interests of their country. In the dying years of the Soviet Union the national members of the party organisation of Tajikistan became especially successful at this, managing wide-scale promotion of regional economic interests, in spite of informers within the party employed by Moscow. It should be mentioned here that in some central Asian states the practice of high-ranking national CPSU functionaries working for both sides even went as far as supporting and maintaining illegal underground parties during Stalin's time (see Hayit 1965: 55).

However, it is a well-known fact that national party functionaries in central Asia were constantly being watched, so that 'national egoism' could be denounced and prevented (Hayit 1965: 64–65). In the 1930s many national CPSU leaders were liquidated on Stalin's orders and replaced by cadres ostensibly loyal to the party line.[1] In the 1960s several attempts at fraud at a very high level were uncovered. The most prominent 'victims' were the first secretary of the Communist Party of Tajikistan in 1961 and the chairman of the council of ministers; that is, the two highest-ranking representatives of party and state authority in the republic. At the same time, however, other people who had been arrested under Stalin were rehabilitated.

The forerunner of present-day Tajikistan was the Soviet state created as an Autonomous Socialist Soviet Republic out of the former East Bukharan and Samarkand regions on 2 February 1925 as part of the republic of Uzbekistan. The country was separated from Uzbekistan, and granted independence by decree of the Central Executive Committee of the USSR in December 1929 (see Hayit 1956: 231–232), and, as such, admitted into the USSR.

Already at that time there was much criticism regarding the way in which Tajikistan had been divided. The sizeable areas settled by Tajiks around Samarkand and Bukhara were excluded from the new state, while the Eastern Pamirs, with their Kyrgyz majority, were included, although historically they had belonged not to Bukhara but to Kokand. Even today people in Tajikistan say that Stalin deliberately wanted to use this scheme to separate nationalities, in order to prevent national solidarity developing later on. The roots of present-day disputes between the neighbouring countries of Uzbekistan, Kyrgyzstan and Tajikistan indeed reflect the way the Soviet republics were originally created.

Tajikistan consists of several provinces (oblasts), the capital city area and other regions under government jurisdiction. Only GBAO has the status of autonomous oblast. In 1951 GBAO divided these autonomous oblasts into seven districts or rayons: Shugnân, Ishkashim, Roshtkala, Roshân, Bartang, Murghâb and Wandsh, and also the capital, Khorog. Subsequently the Darwâs rayon was separated from Wandsh, whereas Bartang was assimilated into Roshân, thus keeping the same number of districts. The most recent census of 1989 records a total of 47 nationalities in GBAO.

In view of the distinct ethnic identities of Pamiris and Kyrgyz, it is difficult to understand why GBAO was first made into a 'Special Region of the Pamir' in January 1925, and then later that year into an autonomous province (*avtonomnije oblasti*). In other cases such procedures were designed to enhance the status of ethnic minorities. This classification of their territory as an autonomous oblast gave the inhabitants the right to be represented in the Soviet of Nationalities.

Otherwise the term 'autonomous' was fairly meaningless under the Soviet system, except for the fact that an autonomous oblast could (in theory) decide independently on its official language (see Kolarz 1956: 33). As far as the choice of language used for teaching in schools is concerned, this right was never put into practice, as we have already seen.

A close look at the transition period from the political system under Lenin to that under Stalin illustrates the contradictions inherent in a system which, on the one hand, stresses the autonomy of a region, and on the other gives it no real rights. Lenin promoted a policy of ethnic rootedness (*korenisazija*), which in 1925 was still valid, at least on paper. However, by 1929 Stalin had decided that all ethnic, religious and cultural differences were to be reduced to the level of folklore and custom, in order to create a homogeneous Soviet people (*sowjetskij narod*). Ethnic minorities would continue to be allocated a certain role, but they would not be allowed to endanger the policy of centralism by making their own plans at a national level.

We do not know a great deal about local administration prior to the Second World War. Even under the early years of Stalin's rule there was, in general, little intervention in the administration of the settlements, which continued to be carried out by the *aksaqal* amongst the Kyrgyz and by similarly named village elders in Pamiri villages (see Hayit 1956: 103). They were responsible not only for internal organisation but also for levying taxes. Later, the villages were amalgamated into administrative units and village Soviets were introduced (*soveti qishloq*). The chairman of the village Soviet[2] virtually carried out the function of mayor.

Above the level of the villages (*kishlak*) there was the rayon, still in existence today, and usually translated into the term 'district'. These were formally responsible for the provision of regional health care and schools. In principle they should also have been responsible for providing the population with consumer goods, but in practice this duty was carried out by the sovkhozes (state-controlled farms). A Soviet had authority over a rayon and over a *kishlak*.

As the collectivisation of agriculture in GBAO began at the earliest in 1929, and in reality probably only in 1933, it was not until after the Second World War that there can be said to have been two concurrent administrative structures, or even, taking the party structure into account, a tripartite division of power. The originally small cooperative farms (kolkhoz) were first amalgamated into larger units and then, sometime in the early 1970s, the majority of these were turned into purely state-run farms. This created a strong economic unit with a mandate extending far beyond the actual work of a farm. The sovkhoz organised and maintained the entire infrastructure, ranging from water and energy supplies to running the nursery and primary schools. Democratically elected members of each Soviet were not able to make real decisions or carry out any administrative functions, because everything depended *de facto* on the leader of the sovkhoz and his budget. Amongst the people we interviewed, opinion was as follows: 'If the leader of the sovkhoz was a good man, the village in his area would flourish. If he was incompetent, or was just lining his own pockets, the Soviet was powerless to do anything about it.'

It is interesting to note that when we asked people about whether they themselves were allowed to become involved in political matters, they only ever mentioned the level of the sovkhoz, never that of village councillor. This confirms our picture of the insignificant role of the village Soviet. However, in the light of opinions expressed during interviews carried out in GBAO, we cannot share the general view that 'democratic centralism' permitted no individual participation. It was indeed impossible to openly attack a person in a position of political power, let alone the sovkhoz leader, as this would have had serious consequences, even in the years after Stalin. The leader of a sovkhoz was ultimately appointed by the party central committee in Dushanbe (formerly Stalinabad), and even the regional Soviets only had limited influence on who was appointed. Yet it was normal within working teams (brigades) to elect a foreman, who acted as the representative of the team.

Problems could be openly discussed within a brigade, and wishes openly expressed to the leadership to a greater or lesser extent, depending on the personality of the brigade leader. It was not really possible for a sovkhoz leader to ignore the criticisms and suggestions of his brigades for any length of time, as this would have quickly affected production and thus the planned targets. This was because the brigades could slow down production or even stop it completely, should they choose to do so. Sometimes large quantities of seed, harvest, or tools would suddenly go missing.

All this does not contradict legendary Pamiri honesty, emphasised particularly in Chapter 4. The assertion that 'Pamiris do not steal' is still widespread. In some places houses had no locks on their doors, or if they did have them, the house was left unlocked anyway when the occupants were out. Some people told us that you could serve yourself in some shops, and pay the shopkeeper when he came home in the evening. Helping oneself to sovkhoz products tended to be seen by some people as helping themselves from their own supplies and by others as a personal protest: it was not looked on as theft. Sometimes things would just turn up again later.[3]

Soviet development policy

The territory of present-day GBAO, like all of Badakhshan, had provided no substantial economic benefit in the past to any occupying power or empire. The value of the land lay in its function as a buffer zone or border area. Even the crushing taxes levied on farmers in the eighteenth and nineteenth centuries were used up by the cost of wars and holding court in the region itself. For the whole of the twentieth century and right up to the present day, this basic economic situation has not changed. However, during the Soviet period the Pamirs – on the border between two different social and economic systems – became strategically more important than ever in the triangle between China, Afghanistan and the Soviet Union itself. If the area of GBAO had generated no income up until the 1920s, neither had it been much of a financial drain, except for the upkeep of Russian troops. However, after GBAO became part of the Soviet Union, all this was to change radically when it was given political status as the 'southern window of the Soviet Union', in addition to its strategic function.

There were two reasons behind this. First, the aim was to demonstrate to the Pamiris, and to other central Asian peoples elsewhere, the 'unlimited' opportunities offered within the socialist system run by the Soviet Union. Second, the developed areas of GBAO (and Tajikistan) were to show the neighbouring poor peoples to the south in Afghanistan, India and Pakistan the superiority of the Soviet system in comparison to their own feudal and capitalist societies. The first aim succeeded until the break-up of the Soviet Union, though at enormous financial cost, mainly to the western Soviet Republics. Absolutely no one we interviewed complained about economic conditions in the last decades of the Soviet period. The second aim only floundered after the initial successes in the war against Afghanistan, which started in 1979, were almost entirely squandered.

Soviet propaganda, adopted, for example by the East German Klaus Hemmo in the book he wrote for GDR citizens, was seldom truer than when it pointed out the differences in living conditions on either side of the Pyandsh resulting from Soviet rule. Up until 1895, both sides of the river had at different times belonged to the same ruler and had been very similar:

> In der zur Tadschikischen Sozialistischen Sowjetrepublik gehörenden autonomen Hochgebirgsregion Badakhshan ist man gerade dabei, auch die letzten abgelegenen Siedlungen an das elektrische Stromnetz anzuschließen. Auf der anderen Seite der Gletscher aber bleibt es dunkel in den Hütten. In den Dörfern von Badakhshan [GBAO is meant here] gibt es schon lange keine Analphabeten mehr, jenseits der Berge [i.e.

> in Afghanistan] aber müssen die Hirten noch immer tagelang reiten, um einen 'Schriftgelehrten' zu finden, der ihnen einen Brief vorlesen oder schreiben kann.[4]
>
> (Hemmo 1970: 182–183)

A quick look across the Pyandsh in the years from 1995 to 2004 – disastrous years for the Pamiris of the former Soviet Union – immediately demonstrates the truth of Soviet propaganda in this matter. Even today, on the far side of the river, only some 100 metres from Soviet villages, conditions are quite medieval; indeed, material conditions are almost prehistoric. The houses have wooden shutters instead of windows. At night the rooms are dimly lit by petroleum lamps or wood-shavings. The houses shed almost no light onto the unmade streets. For a distance of 100 km in any direction there is not one single mechanical agricultural implement, and, apart from the automatic weapons (*kalashnikov*) of the mujahedin, not a single modern piece of equipment is to be seen.

In theory the development of present-day GBAO began when Russian troops moved in at the end of the nineteenth century. Virtually no investments were made during these early years, but for the people the dramatic reduction in taxes alone was a first step forward. In the early years of the Soviet Union, progress remained modest, in part because of the Basmatshi Uprising, which often prevented access between Osh and Khorog. However, in the years from 1926 to 1928, the Soviet Republic of Tajikistan received over 30 million roubles in aid out of the Soviet Union's budget (see Cleinow 1930: 119). Real economic improvement, and especially technological development, started very rapidly in GBAO at the end of the 1920s, eventually leading to a dramatic improvement in the standard of living. Development began in spectacular fashion with the introduction of air traffic. In 1929 an aeroplane landed for the first time on a temporary runway,[5] and in 1932, at a time when aeroplanes were still viewed as 'living gods' in Afghanistan (see Luknizki 1957: 302), there was already a proper airport in Khorog.

The first car probably reached Khorog via the high plateaux of the Pamirs in 1931. In 1932 construction was started on an asphalt road from Osh to Khorog, which was officially opened as 'The Stalin Road' in 1934. By 1940 a basic road network had been developed in the region with the completion of the westerly connection between Khorog and the capital Stalinabad (present-day Dushanbe). Because of the many constrictions in the river valley in GBAO, and the difficult passes on the route to Gharm, construction of this 525-km-long stretch of road was a much greater achievement than that of the 740-km stretch to Osh. However, within GBAO there were also regional differences in the state of development of the road network. As already mentioned, the construction of a road along the Bartang proved to be so difficult that it was still in progress here from the 1950s through to the 1970s. Just to make a comparison: even today on the equally densely populated Afghan side of the Pyandsh valley, entire villages and valley communities are connected almost exclusively by *owringi* (see pp. 184–185) to existing stretches of road which are anyway mostly unfit for vehicles.

There were ambitious plans to introduce scientific institutions into the Pamirs. The botanical gardens above Khorog – laid out in 1940 at a height of 2,320 m and well known even beyond the borders of GBAO – were, at the time, the second highest in the world after the gardens in Darjeeling in India. The construction of an observatory in 1932 on the Fedshenko glacier was another outstanding achievement by Soviet engineers and Pamiris. Its component parts, together with the scientists' supplies, added up to 3,000 loads, all of which had to be carried up on foot for dozens of kilometres (see Luknizki 1957: 283–94).

The Soviet Union's achievements in the region during the last 40 years of its existence are admirable, even if Tajikistan did remain the poorest country in the Soviet Union up until its collapse (see Grobe-Hagel 1992: 206–207) and GBAO, for its part, a 'disadvantaged' area within Tajikistan. One easily forgets what the region was like to start with, if one only looks at comparative figures for Ukraine or Belarus. An account of a meeting in Roshorve, the village which we have described as being perhaps the most isolated in the entire Soviet Union, is one good way of demonstrating the state of development in the Soviet Pamir region towards the end of the Soviet Union. After a car journey of 130 km taking 10 hours on an almost impassable road, during which time we nearly got stuck in a tributary of the Bartang, we were greeted by a group of people led by the *khalifa*, three doctors and a former professor of the university of Moscow. Our first discussions took place in the former cinema, where the old 16-mm film projector and hundreds of rolls of film still lay around. Films were already being shown here in the 1950s, the projectors having been carefully transported by donkey (see Mursajew 1956: 270). Ten to 15 years before our visit, German plays were being staged here in the original German.[6]

Collectivisation of agriculture and the economy of the state farms

Even if the changes in agricultural methods of production introduced by the Soviet system were not as far-reaching as is generally assumed, the situation in GBAO at the end of the 1980s, after 65 years of the Soviet Union, cannot really be compared with that of the early Soviet period. Essentially four areas are under consideration here: the organisation of production, the method of production, the area of agriculturally productive land, and agricultural products.

On pp. 103–122 the basis of traditional agriculture in the Pamirs was sketched out. The then newly introduced Soviet method of organising production was also referred to several times. After 1933 the main aim was to collectivise all the fragmented farms in order to employ more efficient methods of production. There were, of course, social reasons for this and there were also political reasons for the way it was distributed. However, it is not clear whether, in view of the small size of the landholdings – even amongst the better-off Pamiris – there were actually any dispossessions as a result of the kolkhoz movement. 'Kolkhoz' is an abbreviation for *kollektivnoe chozjajstvo* and means a collective economy; that is, cooperative production (see Kreutzmann 1996: 172). The farmers retained formal ownership of the land, but were forced to collectivise agriculturally productive land and also to work and use the infrastructure communally. Distribution of the proceeds was evaluated proportionally, according to the amount of land made available, any other means of production and individual performance. However, in practice, once any farmer in the Soviet Union had joined a kolkhoz he virtually surrendered all choice in deciding the methods of production.

It was only during the course of nationalisation of land and livestock in the early 1970s that farmers finally had their land compulsorily taken from them, leaving them only their gardens, usually of 800 to 1,200 square metres, which they were prohibited from selling. The now entirely state-run farms were called 'sovkhoz' after the *sovetskoe chozjajstvo*, (i.e. Soviet economy). The former farmers became *de facto* state employees when these Soviet farms were created, and were given a monthly wage for a certain amount of work, regardless of how much land they had formerly possessed. As a supplement, each member of a household might also be given equal amounts of potatoes, butter or other local products.[7]

As regards their work, farmers became mere labourers, as no one was given the job of running an entire farm but had to specialise in one (often a very narrow) kind of work. One farmer became a tractor driver, another was responsible for irrigation, a third became a cowhand, and the sons and daughters of the former farmers joined the sovkhozes as mechanics, economists, vets, soil experts or hydraulic engineers, once they had completed their training. The result was that when the Soviet economy ended and land was once more privatised, only the older men who had themselves been farmers many years previously were at all capable of running a farm properly.

In 1992, shortly after Tajik independence, there were 26 independent sovkhozes in GBAO. The government thought that the reintroduction of kolkhozes would be a way of counteracting privatisation, legal since 1993. We will discuss the fact that this led to a dead end on pp. 284–286.

Mechanisation of agriculture was linked to the amalgamation of landholdings. However, machines are not necessarily a prerequisite of more rationalised agricultural practices. Irrigation in particular, based as it is on gravity feed and with its intricate network of junctions and small channels, always remains labour intensive. As part of GBAO's role as window on the south, mechanisation served the political aim of demonstrating the efficiency of Soviet industry and agriculture. The result was that on the one hand modern combine harvesters were used (Plate 7.1), and on the other hand the number of agricultural labourers needed in a sovkhoz continued to drop, although in practice their numbers rose because of employment policies (see p. 263).

In effect, the Soviet Union was actually granting subsidies twice over to GBAO: first of all, work was subsidised by paying many more workers than were actually needed on a sovkhoz; second, the state provided collective farms with machinery which was not really needed, or was only needed in a more low-tech version. We know of no agricultural sovkhoz[8] which could show even a partially healthy

Plate 7.1 A modern combine of Soviet production on farmland near the Shakhdara river, *kishlak* of Tusyan (Soviet documentation from Khorog, about 1985).

balance sheet under these conditions. On the contrary, at the beginning of the 1990s the collective debt of all the sovkhozes was so high that privatisation of a collective farm as one entire unit was completely unthinkable.

Independent evaluation has shown that the sovkhozes, at least in GBAO, could never be economically sustainable at all. Even if they were amalgamated, the agriculturally productive land in GBAO was far too limited in size for economies of scale to work: the only economic way would be to run small farms. The number of workers, according to the locals we spoke to, was between twice and ten times as high as was necessary. The main problem lay not so much in actual agricultural practices but rather in the additional duties incumbent on the state-run farms. Within their catchment area they were responsible for the maintenance and expansion of almost the entire infrastructure, apart from the construction of trunk roads. That meant that it was not the rayon administration, but the respective sovkhoz that ran the nurseries and primary schools, supplied drinking water supply networks and, in some villages, even operated a district heating system. The sovkhoz was responsible for the maintenance of hospital wards, bridges and roads, etc., and in addition was responsible for supplying a range of goods in its own department stores. Also, the individual sovkhoz had yet more obligations going beyond those of its actual remit. For example, groceries were delivered free to state hospitals and to high schools, and, if there were any, to army bases situated on land belonging to the state farm.

It was only apparent to some of the functionaries (*apparatchiks*) that no profit could be made under such conditions. Loans taken out centrally – probably not even in Stalinabad but directly in Moscow – without which no wages could have been paid, were simply hushed up at the local level. Even in 1996 one senior functionary could not understand that sovkhozes would not have been viable without this external support, which according to insider estimates made up between 80 per cent and 90 per cent of the turnover.

In Ishkashim alone the area of agriculturally productive land during the Soviet period increased from 892 ha in 1905 to 3,293 ha in 1980. However, this impressive achievement did not keep up with population growth, because during this period the latter grew by a factor of 5.7, while arable land could only be increased by a factor of 3.7 (see Kreutzmann 1996: 175). In GBAO total cultivated land increased by a factor of 3.9 between 1926 and 1987; that is, from around 4,500 ha to almost 18,000 ha.[9] However, the productivity of the new land was very variable. With financial aid for costly drainage programmes some very good land came under the plough for the first time. On the other hand, some individual sovkhozes had almost no more land suitable for cultivation, with the result that very steep slopes or gravelly areas next to rivers were cultivated. Many of these latter areas were subject to flooding because of the high water table.

Another problem was that newly cultivated land at high altitude in the Gund or Shakhdara valleys only proved productive in good years; that is, when the weather was warm enough. In a cool year yields were extremely low. Since almost everywhere the best land was already being cultivated by traditional agriculture, the rate of increase in production remained by and large well below the rate of increase in new land brought into use.

Traditional agriculture in the Pamirs operated at a subsistence level. Surpluses were mainly used up for paying taxes, and, as many farmers were only able to harvest enough for essentials, taxes sometimes could only be raised by going without things. There was only limited barter of vegetables and cereals for animal products. Cultivation of cereals was easily the most important agricultural activity, and in the Pamirs this was invariably wheat for bread-making.

Soviet planners were correct in deciding to reduce the quantity of cereals and pulses grown and to increase cultivation of root vegetables, especially potatoes, instead. In theory this change should have produced enough food to feed around four times as many people, using the same amount of land. The earliest attempts to grow potatoes in 1925–6 failed, but from 1934/5 good results were achieved with imported seed potatoes (see Mursajew 1956: 263). However, it was only from the mid-1950s onwards that the potato gradually began to gain acceptance as an important basic food on a par with conventional crops. The same was true of other vegetables, which the Pamiris had previously only grown in small quantities. Most Pamiris considered that the sole way to secure sufficient supplies of food was to grow enough grain for bread, and they were reluctant to change their minds on this matter. In 1987, in spite of a big increase in arable land, only 3.7 per cent of the area under cultivation was put down to potatoes and only 0.5 per cent to other vegetables. This meant that they were far from being self-sufficient. This state of affairs was partly due to Pamiri tradition and partly to mistakes made in economic policy by Soviet planners, and once subsidies from Moscow ceased with Tajik independence the consequences were disastrous.

Let us now look briefly at production figures: from 1990 to 1993, according to various sources, only 10–20 per cent of the required supply of food was produced within GBAO itself. The most important local agricultural products were meat and milk. Very low priority was given to food-crop production. The area of land on which wheat was grown had remained virtually unchanged since 1926 in GBAO, with an overall growth rate of 12 per cent over 60 years, although, as already stated, the total area under cultivation had quadrupled. The 4,142 tonnes of wheat produced in 1989 only supplied around 20 per cent of the population's needs, and actually less if we include the amount fed to livestock.

The yield was extremely low, not just a result of the climate but also as a result of poor management of state-run farms and workers' lack of motivation (see p. 263). The average yield per hectare was 1.16 tonnes of grain, 1.06 tonnes of pulses and 16.9 tonnes of potatoes. Just as a comparison: an average yield in the European Community would be at least 6 tonnes of grain (that is, five times as much), and 120 tonnes of potatoes (at least seven times as much). People were aware of the low productivity, so to boost income there was a big increase in the cultivation of tobacco on state-run farms between 1970 and 1985, rising to 1,200 ha or 6.3 per cent of all arable land. For this purpose, mainly good land was taken out of food production.

Soviet planners were also aware of low yields in the Pamirs. For this reason there was a significant shift towards livestock breeding within the economy of GBAO in the years after the Second World War. From 1925 to 1988 the number of cattle in the Pamirs increased by 270 per cent and that of sheep by 260 per cent. In 1988, the year in which a survey was carried out, there were 74,500 cattle and 346,500 sheep and goats in GBAO. In the last years before 1988 there has been a particularly large increase in the numbers of privately kept livestock.

At first sight, the Pamirs, with their vast grazing lands, appear suited to extensive livestock farming. This has turned out to be wrong on two counts. First, it was impossible for the sovkhozes to sell the animals profitably because of the remoteness of the region. For example, according to Belkina, in the 1960s yaks from the Murghâb had lost 35 per cent of their weight by the time they arrived at Osh in the Ferghâna valley. That meant a net loss of 100 to 150 kg per animal (1966: 225). This fact alone made livestock farming largely unprofitable, although such figures were certainly much better than equivalent figures for arable farming. This relatively positive economic situation – one could also call it an economic situation with a smaller deficit – was the result of the fact that the livestock-based sovkhozes were able to achieve a higher yield per worker with lower running costs.

The main problem with livestock farming was, however, the fact that it was not possible to keep large numbers of cattle and sheep in such a harsh climate without providing extensive additional fodder. Large quantities of animal fodder were brought into the Murghâb at high additional cost for this purpose[10] – for example, concentrated feed made from cotton seed. After Tajikistan became independent, the extensive sowing of barley and legumes, especially alfalfa, for animal fodder on arable land, even in GBAO itself, turned out to be an absolute disaster for its population. In 1987 6,900 ha or 38.3 per cent of all cultivated land was used for such perennial fodder plants, most of this being valuable irrigated land. Apart from the high cost involved in the production of this fodder, it also led to the above-mentioned low production rates of basic, locally produced, foods.

To summarise the agricultural situation at the time of independence: (1) in view of the increase in the population, the large-scale expansion of agriculturally productive land still proved to be insufficient; (2) some of the additional land was unproductive; (3) in spite of the change from grain to root vegetables, in itself a sensible measure, the Soviets did not manage to achieve a large enough increase in basic food production; (4) once they had made the wrong decision to concentrate on livestock breeding, this led to most of the irrigated land being put down to fodder crops. Consequently no provisions were made that allowed the population to grow enough food for human consumption. In addition, this concentration on livestock and provision of fodder meant that without external aid it was impossible to start producing more food.

Social infrastructure in Soviet times

In the literature Tajikistan is repeatedly referred to in a disparaging way as a Third World country within the Soviet Union. Some authors seem to have lost all sense of proportion in the matter. There is, for example, no point in making the comparison that in Tajikistan in 1987 there were 'only' 27.2 doctors per 1,000 inhabitants, whereas in the Soviet Union as a whole this figure was 46.3 (see Grobe-Hagel 1992: 206), when, viewed from the economic angle, there was no way in which even these 27.2 doctors could be sensibly employed. After all, in GBAO itself even the tiniest hamlet of a few dozen inhabitants almost always had its own doctor.

The following synopsis is intended to give a general impression of the social infrastructure towards the end of the Soviet period. This should explain why so many people continue to regard the old system in a favourable light, in spite of its shortcomings. When interviewed, most people praise the health and education systems in particular.

An international report from 1993 summarises the health system inherited from the Soviet Union as follows:

(1) the health status of the population in GBAO is better than that of most middle-income countries in the world;
(2) the health system is accessible to everyone, with facilities located in even the most remote settlements and there are no economic barriers to access;
(3) it is equitable in its treatment of groups of people who, in many other systems, are often disadvantaged, such as women, the poor, those living outside major towns, etc.;
(4) there are large numbers of well-trained professional staff, both doctors and nurses;

(5) there are 15 hospital beds per thousand population, a higher ratio than in almost any country in the world;
(6) there is a higher ratio of doctors and nurses to population than for almost all middle-income countries, etc.

The use of herbal medicines was very much a part of the local tradition, and herbal medicines are widely used. Only public health measures such as clean water supply systems and adequate sanitation systems have been largely ignored, and there was little emphasis on health education.

Some figures are available from 1989 to 1991 that record the state of health of the population relatively objectively. For example, the infant mortality rate was about 30/1,000 and the maternal mortality rate about 81/100,000. These figures are much lower than the average in developing countries.[11] Specific services are also recorded: for instance, every birth was preceded by 16 to 17 antenatal visits to the doctor, with the delivery being carried out in hospital by a doctor or midwife. The staff in one clinic made 1,053 home visits during one month in a single village of 200 families. In the whole of GBAO in 1987 there were 24 hospitals with 2,070 beds, 124 medical and surgical centres, and 24 gynaecological, prenatal and early child-care clinics.[12]

The extent of the Soviet Union's achievement in the field of health care is summarised by stating that the health system was accessible to everyone, with facilities located in even the most remote settlements. Most illnesses were treated without charge by doctors in the villages themselves. More complicated cases were referred to hospitals in the rayon centres, and the most serious cases were referred to the hospital in Khorog, where there were specialists in almost every field, ranging from orthopaedic specialists to cardiologists. Treatment there was virtually free, a fact that is all too often forgotten when wages under the Soviet system are discussed.

The same report also goes into details on the education system towards the end of the Soviet period. According to this report, the vast majority of the school-age population of GBAO, probably at least 90–95 per cent, had nine years of schooling; 70–75 per cent had eleven. Prior to the civil war in 1992/3, approximately 12 per cent of school-leavers went on to university every year; 78 per cent of teachers took five-year university diplomas, another 13 per cent took courses after grade 11 in colleges of education, lasting two and a half years. The curricula were academically as demanding as in Western countries, probably more so in mathematics and the sciences. Teachers' professional behaviour was acceptable and the teaching style was friendly. The teacher–pupil ratio was far more favourable than any Western countries would ever be willing to support, with 10 to 15 children per class as the norm. The education system in GBAO was remarkably standard and fair, without urban–rural and male–female disparities and without the corruption in the examination and promotion systems which in general bedevilled the Tajik education system.

There were some negative aspects to the education system which did not in practice affect the way schools were run, but are difficult to understand from a present-day perspective. The basic teaching load in GBAO was only 14 hours per week and so teachers' salaries were correspondingly low (although they had a secure, if simple, lifestyle until 1991). On the whole they were well motivated, as there was usually another member of the household working in a sovkhoz. In some schools the number of ancillary staff (e.g. such as cooks and nurses) was equal to, and in some cases even greater than the number of teaching staff.

Today we would disapprove of the way history and social sciences were taught, on the grounds of the narrow ideological content. It is interesting to note that the syllabus was often so detached from real issues that after even a few years after leaving school the pupils had no idea what capitalism was, or knew anything about the West. On the other hand, factual knowledge was excellent in all subjects. Geography teachers, for example, could go into great detail on the general and physical geography of England and Germany, although they had never been to either country.

The teaching of foreign languages was certainly a problem. As well as Tajik and Russian, German was compulsory in four out of seven rayons, English in two, and French in one, usually depending on the availability of subject specialists. No language teachers in the Pamirs had experience of study abroad with native speakers, as the political and financial state of Soviet universities made this impossible.[13] This meant that the level of competence in the foreign language was very low.

The people we interviewed showed no consensus on the relationship of the mother tongue to the Russian language in Soviet schools. Some people complained about Russian being taught right from the first grade, although children in this year in fact had to learn Tajik as well. In addition most of them had only spoken Shugnî, Wakhî or another Pamiri language before going to school. But at least the pupils were allowed to use their national language – that is, Tajik – during lessons, right up until the time they left school, because Tajikistan was a titular nation within the Soviet Union (see Brunner 1988: 37–38).

In retrospect it transpired that having to learn Russian had a positive effect on the school-leavers' later prospects. It allowed them to benefit from a range of training and job opportunities which would otherwise have remained closed to them. It is already noticeable that the recent downgrading of the teaching of Russian in present-day independent Tajikistan has tended to restrict an individual's employment prospects and has had a generally negative effect on the country's economy.

The education system's infrastructure was good or very good. In 1990 or thereabouts, the rayon of Ishkashim alone had 44 schools for 6,300 pupils, with 800 trained teachers (Kreutzmann 1996: 181). In GBAO there were altogether around 300 schools (1991), of which 88 in smaller villages taught only grade 1–4. Schools in larger villages taught grades 1–9 and there were 153 high schools or *makhtab miane* teaching all 11 grades. In principle, a settlement of 100 households or more was eligible to have a high school. The target of having a primary school in every village was achieved in all but the smallest hamlets. Boarding schools were set up in Khorog, the main towns in the rayon, and also in some sovkhoz centres for the children from these hamlets, and for older pupils. The largest boarding schools were in Murghâb town, where most shepherds' children were accommodated. Pupils received free board and lodging and their every need was catered for. All school books and educational materials were free. The parents or pupils only paid a 'voluntary' contribution occasionally, if there was some special activity in school, or if it was for a 'good cause'.

Under such favourable conditions the drop-out rate was virtually nil (0.1 per cent). Even when the children had to travel a few kilometres further away to the high school after the fourth grade, there was no problem, as under the Soviet system transport was provided free of charge.

At the end of the 1940s the first nursery schools were set up in GBAO. There is conflicting information on the level of provision in those early years. Some people pointed out that the sovkhozes were obliged to find places for workers' children, while others point out that the demand for nursery places was not that high, as most families had relatives who looked after pre-school children. The figure of 'only' 2,100 children in nursery schools in the whole of GBAO in 1993 therefore probably also applies to the number of places available in the latter years of the Soviet period.

Virtually any town or village of respectable size had a public library during the socialist period. The collected works of Lenin, Marx and Engels, which can be clearly seen on Plate 7.2, were compulsory. They were hardly ever read, and formed only a small part of the collection of books available, which ranged from classic Russian literature to standard works on central Asia and Tajikistan, including books on history, nature and Tajik literature. Even expensive picture books were made available to all libraries up until about 1990. An examination of library index cards shows that in any town or village many younger people were regular customers, as well as other age groups. Well-known novels were, and still are, especially popular, in addition to Tajik literature and even poetry. Stocks of these books – valuable contributions to the cultural heritage – have generally not been replenished since the beginning of the 1990s.

Youth clubs and old people's or senior citizens' day clubs were a part of the social infrastructure. Every town or village of any size had a youth centre and at least one room available for elderly people. Here courses were provided, and films were shown once a week, in remote places once a month; sometimes there were special celebrations, and even plays were staged. Youth clubs organised sport and leisure activities. You could travel by bus to the museum or theatre in Khorog. In many villages both young and old could take music lessons, so there were numerous traditional and modern groups in GBAO. In remote Roshorve (Bartang), up to a dozen different bands were counted.

One of the state's duties was to run food stores. In 1980 the rayon of Ishkashim had a minimum of 33 retail outlets, plus ten food stores (see Kreutzmann 1996:

Plate 7.2 Village library in Tusyan (rayon of Shakhdara). It has received no new books since 1990/1 but is still frequented by the villagers (1996).

179). In 1987 there were altogether 222 shops in GBAO, 198 of which were outside of Khorog. Everyday goods were on sale here, but also allocated luxury items such as television sets or even motorcycles. While certain items were always in plentiful supply and shortages were virtually unknown (e.g. in towns, flour, sugar, pasta, potatoes), the supply of 'luxury' goods was always chaotic under the Soviet system. For months on end radios or TVs were unavailable, then whole lorries full would arrive in Khorog and the items would be distributed to every single village shop. In spite of the shortage of luxury goods, in GBAO it was still possible to be allocated a new car; but an extremely long wait was to be expected. Surprisingly enough no one complained of corruption when items were distributed, though we did hear some complaints that this was the case in Khatlon in south-west Tajikistan.

Energy supply was an important part of the infrastructure, and we have already referred to present-day problems many times. During the Soviet period coal was used at first, later being supplemented by hydroelectric power. Electricity was also used for heating during that time. The electrically heated public baths (*hamom*) in Khorog were probably the only ones of their kind in the Soviet Union (see Satulowski 1964: 232). All rented accommodation in Khorog was electrically heated, while in the villages all households were allocated subsidised coal.

The electricity supply was not always reliable and could not be guaranteed 24 hours a day, although in Khorog and along the main roads it was reasonably good. From the 1970s onwards, diesel generators were installed in remote villages, although in some places this only happened at the end of the 1980s. In Roshorve, where a 150 kW generator was installed in 1991, the electricity supply only lasted 12 months because in 1992/3 the plant had to be shut down due to shortages of spare parts and fuel.

Some people interviewed criticised the (public) housing supply. In Khorog, as in all rayon centres, for each five-year plan (between 1965 and 1985), the state built around 30,000 to 40,000 square metres of accommodation (i.e. about 600 flats per annum). This was much less than was needed, even though each family was only allocated about 50–60 square metres. On the other hand, the state supplied almost free accommodation to its employees and workers, as well as electricity, running water and, in Khorog at least, a toilet and heating. After 1992/3 no more state flats were built and those begun in the Soviet period were never finished.

In villages the state built accommodation only if there were factories employing workers who were from outside the village. In such cases simple but permanent dwellings, divided into flats, were made available. This was also the case in many villages in the Murghâb, where the supply of accommodation served the main purpose of attracting Kyrgyz families to settle permanently within the area covered by the infrastructure. These villages had the greatest shortage of accommodation and for this reason two or three families would live under one roof. It was almost impossible to obtain building land before 1985, as it was under strict governmental control. The building of houses on arable land or on land suitable for irrigation, or on gardens, etc., was prohibited. Mass construction of new houses only began with the arrival of perestroika.

Employment, income and individual prosperity

In 1987 industrial production in GBAO had increased in value by a factor of 71.8, compared with the figures for 1940. Production of building materials had increased 42.4-fold, that of light industry 600-fold, and processed food 12.7-fold, each of these sectors having started from an extremely low base line. In 1987, industry employed 2,658 people, most of these in Khorog, where there was a flourishing textile and shoe industry. In fact, most of this industrial development only started in the 1970s and 1980s.

In GBAO in 1987, 20 per cent of the total population, that is 43,965 people, were employed in the state sector,[14] the sovkhozes alone employing 40.7 per cent; that is, 11.8 per cent of the total population. The state sector of industry employed 6 per cent of the workforce, the commercial sector and public transport employed 6.2 per cent, the construction industry 5.8 per cent and the communications sector 1.9 per cent. The education service employed 3.6 per cent of the workforce and the health service 1.3 per cent.

The statistics on Tajikistan are used by some authors to try and prove how disadvantaged the country is compared with other republics in the Soviet Union, but this is not very meaningful when applied to society in GBAO, because it does not take into account the high level of education – and with it the averagely higher salaries. So the comment: 'the social indicators of development are high but income levels are very low' is only partially true.

Because of the Pamiris' fundamentally liberal attitude towards women, the percentage of women in the workforce was much higher in GBAO in the last decades of the Soviet Union than the 38 per cent figure for Tajikistan as a whole (compared to 52 per cent for the Soviet Union in general). In 1985, 54.3 per cent of all workers and employees in GBAO were women. This meant that individual incomes were probably slightly higher than the national average for rural areas: compared to the national average, 18 per cent more women had an income, and had an almost 10 per cent higher employment rate. This resulted in a family income in GBAO that could have been also 10 per cent or more above the national average.

In 1987 the average monthly salary of workers and employees in GBAO was approximately 152 roubles. The industrial average was 145 roubles, in agriculture 112 roubles, in the transport sector 179 roubles, in the construction industry 182 roubles, and for qualified jobs in technology and education it was 221 roubles. Managers of large concerns, senior administrators and directors of sovkhozes earned top salaries, typically 300 to 350 roubles.

It is difficult to estimate the purchasing power of the average monthly income.[15] Buying a car over the long term was not impossible in a two-income household, and the majority of households fell into that category. By the end of the Soviet era, around one-third of all households in the lower valleys of GBAO owned a serviceable car. Since then the figure has dropped to less than 5 per cent.

One possible indicator of buying power is the price of flour. In the late 1980s this was 0.20 to 0.26 roubles per kg, with a 500 g loaf costing 0.25 roubles. Butter cost 3.50 roubles per kilogram. An average monthly income would therefore buy 585 to 760 kg of flour. If we work on the assumption that at the same time the monthly wage of a similar employee in Europe would buy up to 5,000 kg of flour, then the income appears low. However, if we take into account that the running cost of a flat was at most 15 roubles, which included water, electricity and heating, that transport to work was free and that sovkhoz workers (in fact almost 41 per cent of state employees) were given free rations of potatoes, wheat, vegetables and animal products in addition to their wage, then the disposable monthly income could add up to a considerable amount. If you also take into account that a flight to Moscow only cost 30 roubles, then even a lowly employee could make his wages go quite far. Actually it would be more appropriate to make such comparisons not with Europe but with Afghanistan, India, Pakistan and possibly Iran.

Past holiday destinations, mentioned by many people interviewed, are an indicator of income and the standard of living in general. Although not commonplace, it was possible for an engineer, or even a teacher, to fly occasionally on holiday with his family to Georgia to a resort on the Black Sea. One man in Roshorve, which today is completely isolated, told us about study holidays which had taken him to other countries in central Asia and as far as eastern Siberia. Such trips were of course only possible because the flights were highly subsidised. This kind of subsidy, which even included board and lodging at the holiday destination, must be seen as part of the socialist benefit system. The sweeping statement that only party functionaries enjoyed these benefits is completely false.

According to the way it is assessed, state social services in the Pamirs provided between 50 and 70 per cent of gross earnings. In Germany the state provides perhaps 10–20 per cent of these services; in the USA it is 5 per cent. The figures on wages referred to above would therefore nominally have to be almost doubled, in order to take into account the value of these social benefits.

Domestic appliances, and especially electronic goods, were generally expensive in the Soviet Union. Even a simple radio cost 20–30 per cent of one month's income and people allegedly had to work for up to six months to afford a television. However, in 1993 some 50 per cent of all households did have a television (the villages without electricity have been statistically included), and this is a clear indication that a TV was far from being an unaffordable luxury.

The supply of food and clothing also has to be taken into account when assessing the standard of living. There was no lack of basic foods, but sometimes there were delays. As people knew that the supply lorry might not appear for days, they usually bought up stocks of flour, sugar, tea or paraffin.

However, it is true that some foods were in short supply during the Soviet period. The high consumption of bread – in 1987 in Tajikistan generally it was 173 kg per head, compared with only 132 kg per head in the rest of the Soviet Union – is offset by the marked lack of vitamin-rich food. If the consumption of fruit as a national average was already 'below the clinical norm' (see Grobe-Hagel 1992: 206), in the Pamirs it was so low that children had to be given vitamin supplements with their normal free school dinners. There was little chance of obtaining vitamin-rich foods, as the shops had none apart from dried fruit. They did stock meat and milk products, but milk in particular was not freely available on a regular basis, as the sovkhozes were obliged to supply nurseries, schools and hospitals in the first instance.

On the other hand there was no shortage of clothing, as this was made locally. It is true that the quality of clothes readily available in the shops was sometimes very poor, but those who worked in a sovkhoz – in rural areas this was at least one member of each family – could obtain good winter clothing and, above all, excellent shoes.

Soviet society, family and gender

Socialist Islamic society

The Soviet regime made a sustained and massive effort to eradicate religious belief and to substitute 'scientific atheism' and communism for Islam. However, the Ismaili-Islamic beliefs were so deeply rooted amongst the Pamiris that even Soviet anti-religious propaganda completely failed to make them give up their religious traditions. We have already seen that persecution under Stalin had brought public religious life almost entirely to a halt, but in the villages religious ceremonies such as marriages continued to be carried out quite openly. Most people had their marriages registered officially, in accordance with the regulations, but there was also an unwritten rule that the marriage would simultaneously be celebrated according to Islamic rites. Another example is the continued acceptance of figures of religious authority. The *khalifa* was latterly no longer appointed by the imamate, but had simply inherited his office because all contact to the imamate had been officially prohibited. The holders of this office did, however, enjoy the same standing as if they had been directly appointed by the Aga Khan.

Evidently these religious practices were tolerated by the national political leadership. Svat Soucek does, however, draw attention to the contradictions inherent in Soviet policy on this matter. On the one hand, religion was being officially suppressed in Soviet Turkestan, and on the other some members of the Islamic religious hierarchy were retained and indeed even given the protection of official status (2000: 230).

In Tajikistan during the last decades of the Soviet Union the excessive advocacy of national concerns *vis-à-vis* the party machine in Moscow would almost certainly include cultural traditions. The political leaders in GBAO – apart from a few Russians these were mainly Pamiris and some Sunni Kyrgyz – therefore had no reason to interpret the official religious policy narrowly. With this in mind, one might well be justified in interpreting the anti-religious propaganda in Khorog in 1978, referred to on pp. 228–229, as a show of toeing the party line, the better to pursue their own true political agenda.

Although some people interviewed reacted with annoyance when the conversation turned to mismanagement in the sovkhozes, they never criticised the behaviour of Soviet functionaries in matters of religious policy, and they always stressed the importance of religion to the Pamiris. Occasional reports that high-ranking employees and party functionaries frequently lost their jobs because they were too active in religious matters must refer to the 1950s and 1960s.

'We chose Tajikistan', 'there was always a Tajik way' and 'we did it our way': these comments describe the attitude of the national political leadership of Tajikistan, as related to us by a former member of the central committee of the CPSU. Although there must have been dedicated communists on this committee, Tajik members were so much of one mind when it came to protecting the interests of their own country that a sort of 'double book-keeping' was practised, in spite of Russian informers. This mostly affected economic production data, which were evidently deliberate forgeries, thus artificially increasing the level of subsidy needed by the republic.

From the start of official perestroika, looking after national interests also included promoting religion and getting rid of any restrictive rules and regulations. However, it is likely that restrictions on religious activity imposed by Moscow were already being ignored from the 1970s onwards, with the tacit agreement of the political leadership of Tajikistan. Unfortunately we have no eyewitness reports on the matter. This made it possible for at least some of the *khalifas* in GBAO to be employed in respectable state positions, which would have been completely unthinkable if official regulations had been followed.

In Tajikistan this kind of contradiction between official Soviet ideology and actual practice was also evident in other spheres of activity. Poliakov mentions the private sector, which officially did not exist, and which had started to expand by the beginning of the 1980s, and he also mentions the illegal sale of land (1992: 49). Much of this illegal activity was justified by reference to tradition: 'public opinion is shaped through the *mahalla*, which condones any actions by its adepts as long as they do not violate traditional norms' (ibid.). As far as Tajikistan and especially GBAO are concerned, there is a need to modify the wide-spread notion, expressed in many Western publications, of a homogeneous Soviet system exerting control over every aspect of life. In the post-Stalin era, at least, the Soviet Union's view on its citizens' social responsibilities were distinctly less prescriptive, and alternatives more readily accepted, than has generally been believed.

The Soviet system and Pamiri traditions

Retrospectively at least, the people we interviewed regarded the Soviet economic system positively. If we are to believe what they say, the contemporary Soviet political and social system was largely accepted. As well as the material improvements already mentioned, the fact that even under 'democratic centralism' a certain amount of participation was possible at a local level, and the *de facto* tolerance of religious practices, there were other reasons which came into play. The introduction of the Soviet system, especially the kolkhoz and sovkhoz economy, had fewer consequences in the Pamirs than in the western republics of the Soviet Union because of the Pamiris' cultural traditions. They had, for example, been accustomed to collective work over many generations. In this context, the people we interviewed repeatedly referred to the *amtabaq*, a system in which small groups of people within a neighbourhood cooperated closely in all kinds of work. This ranged from agriculture to house building and raising livestock. For this reason, the introduction of the team, or to use Soviet terminology, the *brigada* ('brigade'), was nothing new.

What was completely missing under the system of collective agriculture was a system of incentives. Collective work had previously served the purpose of maximising production. Gradually, however, as wages were no longer paid according to output but solely for going through the motions of doing the job, and sometimes merely for attendance, individual productivity declined ever more steeply. Overmanning in many of the sovkhozes proved to be extremely damaging to productivity, leading to the absurd situation exemplified in one place in Roshân of employing more than 130 workers on about 30 hectares of land. In situations like this, many workers could only feign doing something useful, but in reality made no contribution to production. Such idleness led to low motivation amongst those who still had to work. The result was that the yield per unit of land dropped dramatically, and in cases where more capital had been invested, especially in fertiliser and machinery, the yield still did not increase.

It was a different matter in the case of privately owned land. There was not much land in this category, but early marriage made it possible for some to exceed the upper limit of 0.15 ha per household (the upper limit was in practice seldom more than 0.1 ha),[16] thus making enough land available to earn additional income. They mainly grew products that were in short supply or were too expensive in the shops, such as vegetables and fruit, and by growing fodder crops contributed indirectly to the supply of meat. Although the Pamiris are renowned for their remarkable honesty, they do admit that many people helped themselves to seed and fertiliser from the collective farms for use in their own gardens.

In addition to the cooperative work mentioned (on pp. 107–108), the Pamiris also had a long tradition of working voluntarily for the local community (now called *subbotnik*) in their own village on community buildings, road and path maintenance, or construction and maintenance of irrigation systems. The Soviet system did not change either the content or the organisation of this work. Moreover, in contrast to work done in the sovkhozes one cannot say there were inadequate incentive systems, because the *subbotnik*'s work really did benefit everyone.

The collectivisation of agriculture must be viewed as a more complex issue. Initially the introduction of kolkhozes in their original form did not involve any great change to traditional practices: for example, the Pamiris already looked after the herds communally and shared out produce. People probably did not criticise the amalgamation of small fields at first either, as the harvest was still being shared out according to the amount of work done by each ndividual, and also because large quantities of seed and fertiliser were freely available, something that no private farmer could ever have afforded.

It was only the subsequent dispossession of land, the result of turning kolkhozes into sovkhozes (i.e. from communal to state-run farms), that may have led to discontent, if not to outright public dissent. However, the people we interviewed showed no consensus on the opinions held by their grandparents' generation. Some said that the Pamiris had previously owned so little land that they would definitely have received more when sovkhoz products were shared out amongst the workers. Others stressed that many farmers had anyhow only come into possession of land at the beginning of the twentieth century and that was the reason why dispossession was such a shock for them. In any case, it is unlikely that the introduction of the sovkhoz system caused a great deal of discussion, as this only took place at the beginning of the 1970s, and the members of the kolkhoz had lost control over their own land long before then.

From a present-day perspective, the years between 1938 and 1950 were indeed difficult for many farmers, mainly because of the years of terror under Stalin, but especially because of the Second World War. By 1942 the supply of food and essentials had broken down, though fortunately dependence on supplies from outside the region was not as great then as it was later. In the 1950s, things improved so much because of guaranteed employment on the state farms that almost everyone who had lost land to the state was now much better off than they had been previously as a smallholder.

It is not at all clear why the Soviets made this last move from kolkhoz to sovkhoz, as up until then members of the kolkhoz had taken no part in any decisions on methods of production. Kreutzmann assumes that it was primarily aimed at increasing productivity. Reduction in the labour force on the very limited arable land available was intended to free human resources for employment in the non-agrarian sector (1996: 177). In the following years hundreds of job opportunities in industry were indeed created, the younger generation taking them up eagerly because the wages were better and the work was easier.

However, even two decades after agricultural collectivisation, if several members of one family of a sovkhoz worker moved to Khorog to work in industry, that still left more people employed in the sovkhozes than ever had been in the kolkhozes. Outside of Khorog, at least one person per household continued to work in agriculture, so that there was almost no change in the figure of 100 per cent of households involved in that sector.[17] This situation remained constant until the demise of the Soviet Union, and at village meetings in GBAO in the mid-1990s there was unanimous agreement that each and every family should be given land from the former sovkhozes.

Up until now one of the least clearly answered questions on the Soviet system concerns the ideological framework: were people in GBAO dedicated Soviets during the socialist period, in view of the fact that at least latterly there was no apparent opposition? Did they just cooperate with it, but without personally supporting the system, or was there some secret opposition to the system? The large number of Soviet monuments still in existence in 2003 indicate that today at least there are no militant anti-socialists (see Plate 7.3).

On the other hand, from 1995 to 1998 probably only a small minority of hardliners still extolled the benefits of the Soviet sovkhoz system, denying that it could only function because of generous subsidies. We heard the same comments again and again: 'we accepted the system because it provided us with a good income and benefits', and 'we would have been just as happy under a system with a different name, if the outcome had been the same'. An economist at the university of Khorog made this important comment when describing the basic attitude of the Pamiris to social justice: 'We were not interested in the ideological principles of the economic and political system. What was important was that everyone profited from it in equal measure.' Thus, if social justice could only be achieved under the Soviet system, then the Pamiris would always remain dedicated Soviets. We consider that the positive attitude of much of the population towards the old Soviet Union will become increasingly strengthened as a result of the social differences now emerging in GBAO.

The Pamiris regard the Soviet occupation of Afghanistan as a very difficult period in their recent history. Afghan Wakhân was the only part of the country which Soviet troops managed to keep completely under their control (see Kreutzmann 1996: 154). In contrast, the occupying forces had almost no control over the Afghan regions of Ishkashim and Shugnân. Afghan Badakhshan was the heartland of the Tajik mujahedin leader Ahmed Shah Massud – the 'Lion of

Plate 7.3 Karl Marx, Friedrich Engels and Vladimir Illich (Lenin) – the 'founding fathers' of socialism and communism – on a painted board in a rayon centre (1998).

the Pandshir Valley' – who organised by far the most successful campaign of resistance against Soviet troops during the conflict (see de Ponfilly 1988).

The Pamiris were, naturally enough, also sympathetic towards the Badakhshanis – some of whom were Ismailis – living on the other side of the river which formed the border, and we can assume that news of the Afghan war, the destruction it caused and the sufferings of civilians, reached Soviet GBAO. It is a fact that this made people hostile to Soviet policy on Afghanistan and led to close surveillance by the KGB and the armed forces, who had stationed countless guards and checkpoints in every village along the border and the surrounding area. This is how one man summarised the situation at the time: 'We did not know whether it was Afghanistan or GBAO that was actually being occupied.' However, the war also brought many benefits to GBAO, as additional money was pumped into the region on the 'carrot-and-stick' principle, with the aim of reconciling the Pamiris with the situation. Moreover, people living along the border had been used to restrictions even before the Soviet invasion of Afghanistan. The armed forces kept the border very strictly under their control, and as many villages were situated directly by the Pyandsh, people had been forced as long ago as the 1920s to live with a constant army presence.

Gender issues

In Soviet GBAO, there were significantly fewer barriers to the participation of women in all sectors of society than in other southern countries and even in Tajikistan as a whole. They enjoyed equality with men in almost every sphere of life. Women and girls were almost certainly required by the party or government institutions to participate in meetings and public demonstrations. The Soviet state also tried to provide every possible help to women who were willing to hold political or management positions. From pre-natal care to day nurseries, from nursery schools to school meals, from the 'Young Pioneers' (the children's organisation of CPSU) to the *komsomol* (the youth organisation of the CPSU), absolutely everything was done to provide women with the best support. Bearing this in mind, Shirin Akiner is of course correct in saying that 'the manipulation of gender politics was also used as a means of undermining the old order' (1996: 6). But why is this given a negative undertone? Earlier Russian policy, which had abolished slavery, torture and political murder in the state of Bukhara, was also manipulative, designed to bring an end to the old order. But who could object to that?

The Soviet policy on women was not, however, quite so revolutionary in the Pamirs as it may have seemed in Bukhara and Samarkand. Although in GBAO women were able to profit from their guaranteed absolute legal equality with men during the socialist period, they were also favoured by traditional customs and religious law. This meant that they enjoyed a much higher status than in neighbouring regions. Up until the mid-nineteenth century the position of women had not been good in every sphere, but well before the Soviet era some, possibly important, improvements in their position had already taken place. Soviet policy was one of sustaining these trends and building on them in a consistent way. One change was to simplify the divorce system, which hitherto had caused problems, by giving women the same rights as men. The result was that the old order did start to crumble, as exemplified by the fact that during the last few decades of the Soviet period men from educated families usually did their share of the housework. However, in more traditional families housework continued to be regarded as women's work.

It can of course be assumed that today women in GBAO would not have achieved equality with men in most matters without Soviet legislation and political support. However, comparisons with the western part of Tajikistan show that this process would not have been completed so smoothly in the absence of a favourable cultural background or the Ismaili religion, and it is possible that achievements would have been less long-lasting. In the Pamirs, at any rate, there was no need for the spectacular public burning of veils that was carried out in Uzbekistan in March 1927 at the climax of the women's campaign for equality.[18]

Undoubtedly the Soviet period did not just bring positive developments. Hayit points out some of the negative side-effects of agricultural collectivisation on women and girls. As men did not at first earn enough to feed a family, women were also obliged to undertake farm work in the kolkhozes. He says that children also had to work in the fields up until 1950/60, having to be taken out of school for that purpose. Furthermore, this farm work forced women to neglect their own families and households (1956: 287). These general comments on the situation in central Asia are also likely to have been true in GBAO. However, it is also true that women had been traditionally employed in agriculture, and we know that their work was not restricted to certain hours, at least not over the last few decades. The position was, rather, that certain tasks had to be fulfilled, and it was left to the brigades to decide internally on the hours individuals worked. The impressive number of children starting school is at variance with Hayit's comment that children did as a rule have to work on the state farms.

The women certainly benefited from no longer having to help out on their men's land, but from earning their own wages in the kolkhoz (sovkhoz). Although the wages were sometimes lower, because some jobs paid less well, especially those done by women, many of them had 'clean' jobs which additionally offered better pay – for example, in the sovkhoz administration (e.g. as bookkeepers) or in the service sector in the state farms and nursery schools.

Education is undoubtedly a showpiece in the Soviet policy of equality. In 1988, a total of 45,093 children were attending an educational institution in GBAO, and 49.3 per cent of these were girls: 49 per cent in primary education (grade 1–8), and 50.8 per cent in secondary education. However, it should be noted that in areas with a Sunni population (Darwâs and Wandsh rayons) girls' access to education was limited after leaving primary school. On the other hand, we can conclude from this that more than 50.8 per cent of the pupils were Ismaili-Shiite girls. All schools were mixed, both at primary and secondary level.

Although these figures dating from the latter years of the Soviet period are undoubtedly the result of the introduction of compulsory education, the Pamiris did not regard sending girls to school as a fundamental attack on the old order. In the early literature on the Pamirs, the first comment made on education states that whenever there was a teacher (*mullah*) in a village, both boys and girls were sent to school (Olufsen 1904: 139).

In employment there was also at least formal equality. We have already seen that in 1985 54.3 per cent of all workers and employees in GBAO were women. Of specialists with a higher education 34.2 per cent were women, and 29 per cent of all schoolteachers were women. They represented 14.3 per cent of engineers in industry and the construction sector, 15 per cent of senior management in industry, 50 per cent of all factory supervisors, 15.4 per cent of departmental heads in administration, (only) 3.6 per cent of agricultural engineers, but 54.4 per cent of all technicians, 28.3 per cent of craftsmen and 42.9 per cent of so called engineer-economists. In the construction sector, in which women are usually not employed, 20 per cent of all engineers, 20 per cent of technicians, 30 per cent of engineer-economists and 33 per cent of economist-statisticians were also women. In addition, 50–63 per cent of all doctors were women (1984–93).

Although the pay was the same for men and women doing the same job, women's income was on average lower than men's as they were employed in jobs officially classified as light. Under the Soviet system this included doctors and teachers, while jobs in the construction industry and mining – jobs seen by Western society as requiring lower qualifications – commanded the highest wages. As an example: in the 1980s, health workers were paid on average 127 roubles, those in education 132 roubles, but those in the transport sector 187, and in construction 198 roubles. Only 4 per cent of employees in the transport sector were women, 6 per cent in construction, but 73 per cent in the health service and 43 per cent in education. By way of compensation, women were given three years' paid maternity leave and additional time off on full pay for bringing up children. Moreover, the retirement age for women was 50 years, whereas it was 55 for men.

There are no comments in official reports on how much individual freedom was enjoyed by women and girls. On the one hand women could be found employed as mayoresses, directors of state-run enterprises and building-site managers. On the other hand, they still bore the main responsibility for the household and bringing up the children, resulting from the still-prevailing relationship between the sexes. The former gave them more scope, but the latter, in its turn, restricted them, mainly for practical reasons. We can conclude from this that women, even in good jobs, had less time for themselves than men, the latter undoubtedly making less contribution than women to running the home and looking after the children, even in progressive families.

In contrast to all other Asian cultures beyond the Soviet borders, Pamiri women enjoyed extensive individual, economic and political rights. Although these were enshrined in the constitution, they were also for the most part accepted by society, which was not the case in other cultures. For example, a woman could leave the house at any time to go on an errand, to attend a cultural event or to take part in festivities. However, there were (officially) very strict moral codes relating to dress and appearances in public. Unmarried women managed to bend these rules more easily than married women. Moreover, as regards the amount of freedom given to married women, Pamiri society is possibly the most liberal of any country calling itself Islamic.

Girls enjoyed a large degree of freedom as well, even though their lives were generally more restricted than those of boys. The changes would certainly not have been as great without the Soviet system. The Soviet children's organisation, the 'Young Pioneers', and the youth organisation, *komsomol*, supported young people of both sexes and treated them identically. They organised a range of leisure activities – for example, youth camps, sports events, *subbotnik* activities and many more besides. Apparently many young people got to know each other in this way, which eventually led to marriage.

The predominantly positive portrait of the Soviet period which has emerged during the course of this chapter must be qualified on two counts. First, the many social achievements in education, in employment, in material wealth, in relation to gender issues, etc., only really came into effect after the Second World War, and in some cases only during the 30 years before the break-up of the Soviet Union. Second, the population was concurrently almost completely excluded from political decision-making right up until the end of this period.

Yet we do not have the right to emphasise only the negative aspects of Soviet policies and at the same time belittle the positive achievements, as has so often been done in the West since the collapse of the Soviet system. What matters today is how the people themselves regard their past and their present, now that they have the right to freedom of opinion. Not surprisingly, however, they still tend to regard the past more positively than the present, in view of current day-to-day problems and a still uncertain future.

8

THE ECONOMIC COLLAPSE

The end of the Soviet Union and the civil war in Tajikistan

In the mid-1980s the Soviet leader, Gorbachev, introduced reforms which allowed open discussion of the weaknesses in the system for the first time in the history of the Soviet Union. These reforms – designed to safeguard the old system – became widely known as 'glasnost' (openness, transparency) and 'perestroika' (reconstruction, restructuring). In 1988 a political process was set in train which ultimately was to cast doubt on the whole Soviet system and the USSR itself. The call for autonomy was first heard in the Baltic states, and was taken up by almost all the other republics in 1990.

One Soviet republic after the other declared sovereignty, although initially they did not all want independence under international law. In August 1991 the failed attempt at a putsch by the old guard based in Moscow marked the last stage in the dissolution process of the Soviet Union. Those central Asian republics which had wanted (limited) independence were now so afraid of a reversion to totalitarianism as a result of this failed putsch that they decided to complete the process immediately. Almost all of the republics agreed to break away from the Soviet Union, and thus the Union in its current form ceased to exist. At the last session of the People's Congress of the Soviet Union on 5 September 1991, the executive committee of the Union was formally dissolved and the Soviet Union became legally defunct. In December 1991 Ukraine became the last country in the former Soviet Union to break away from the old system, which by then no longer had any legal status (see Götz and Halbach 1993: 11).

Tajik independence and civil war

In August 1990, Tajikistan followed the general trend by declaring sovereignty. On 9 September 1991 they declared independence on the authority of the Supreme Soviet. In breaking away from the Soviet Union they were only accepting the inevitable, as initially there had been no intention of making a complete break. Traditionally, Tajik leadership had always been closely linked to the central organisation in Moscow and to the Soviet Union. Every member of the political leadership was well aware that the Tajik entity was a product par excellence of the Soviet era, and had little historical tradition of its own. Tajikistan had no external pole of attraction or point of support (except Russia); no country fully shared its culture, religion, or language. Only a coherent project for a confederative union guaranteed by the Kremlin could save Dushanbe from the threat of territorial reorganisation of the region (see Hammer 1998: 48). Moreover, there were financial considerations to be taken into account, as an end to the subsidies from Moscow would lead to total economic collapse. It is likely that right from the start the Russian government rejected on economic grounds the idea that Tajikistan might join them, although for a time it was pursued as an alternative to independence.[1] And so, in spite of these reservations, they had no choice but to declare independence.

This political realism on the part of the Tajik communist leadership is not at variance with the country's nationalistic tendencies. These had always been directed towards drawing maximum benefit from membership of the Soviet Union and never towards achieving national sovereignty or separation from the Soviet Union. However, the trend was towards greater independence. The national Communist Party leadership, for example, when put under pressure by its own ranks, unhesitatingly enhanced the status of the national language, Tajik, in relation to Russian, establishing Tajik legally as the only state and official language in 1989. Russian, which had been dominant up until then, became the language of 'communication between the nations' (see Götz and Halbach 1993: 222).

Informal parties began to emerge in the years after 1988, as a result of perestoika. The Communist Party leadership in Tajikistan had at first resisted this new development, resulting in Gorbachev having to impose it from above. At first, these parties were not well organised and only exercised opposition to the still-dominant Communist Party at a local level. It was only in February 1991 that the opposition managed to create substantial political pressure by using mass demonstrations (unknown up until then), which the regime immediately suppressed. The attempted putsch in Moscow in August 1991 was a radical turning point. The Tajik party leader and president, Makhkamov, had compromised his position within the party, even with the moderates, by supporting the rebels and had to resign after mass protests. After the failed putsch he could no longer rely on the loyalty of Russian troops stationed in Tajikistan, and ultimately this caused the downfall of the old regime (see Trutanow 1994: 187).

His successor was parliamentary president Aslonow, who took the radical step of dissolving the Communist Party of Tajikistan, in line with the other former Soviet republics, whereupon the parliament, still led by the dominant Communist Party, removed him from office and legalised the former Communist Party under the new name of Socialist Party. The new parliamentary president was Rahmon Nabiyev, deposed by Gorbachev in 1985 because he represented the old regime, which was unwilling to introduce reforms. Nabiyev was installed as president in November 1991 after a controversial election (see Götz and Halbach 1993: 222).

His share of the votes was 57 per cent, while his opponent, Khudanazarov, a Pamiri, got 30 per cent (see Rubin 1993/4: 77).

Nabiyev came from Leninabad (today Khodjand). In Soviet Tajikistan it was functionaries from this region who had traditionally held power in the party and state leadership. The literature on this subject generally stresses that rule was based on clan membership and that this system remained unchanged, in spite of the long period of Soviet rule in Tajikistan. The increasing protests of the opposition and countermeasures by the government already foreshadowed the later divisions of the civil war. Other clans from the Kulyab region, who were partly armed, gave their support to Nabiyev and his clan parliamentary party,[2] while the opposition counted on the support of clans from present-day Khatlon (Kurgan-Tebe), the Gharm valley, and the Pamiris in GBAO.[3] The Islamic Renaissance Party (IRP) played an important role here, especially amongst the clans from the Gharm valley and in the area around the town of Kurgan-Tebe in Khatlon oblast.

The IRP had been founded as the party representing Islamic interests during the Soviet period and has independent offshoots in all central Asian states, although it is not legalised in all of them. The IRP is a moderate Islamic party, prepared to form coalitions with other parties, even if they are non-religious (see Rashid 2002: 129–150). In the run-up to, and during, the Tajik civil war, the IRP formed the strongest opposition, although by the 2001 elections its share of the vote had declined to less than 10 per cent. Its leader, Said Abdallah Nuri, is generally seen as a moderate and a critical observer of the present system. However, some of his former military commanders have now secured influential positions within the government of Tajikistan (ibid.: 182).

Nabiyev attempted to push through an authoritarian presidential system, which resulted in increased opposition pressure on the old regime. Every action taken by the president led to protests amongst the different opposition groups, for example the arrest of the mayor of Dushanbe on 6 March 1992 and the dismissal from office of the minister of the interior (who came from GBAO) on 25 March 1992. For two months there were daily demonstrations in front of government buildings in Dushanbe by about 5,000 people, mainly young, but also elders (*aksaqal*), the representatives of traditional sources of authority. Many of the participants were Pamiris living in the capital. The opposition, still heterogeneous and mainly consisting of Islamic and nationalistic forces, forced the government to accept some representation in May 1992 by means of these mass demonstrations. Ultimately, the deciding factor here was the defection of the national guard, who had joined the demonstrators and provided them with arms. Nabiyev could no longer suppress opposition with his police force alone.

However, those clans from the north and from Kulyab who supported the president opposed participation by the opposition in government and began to set up their own armed forces. They threatened independence for Khodjand and the Kulyab if the Islamic Renaissance Party were not removed from government (see Rashid 2002: 137). In May 1992 the two groups clashed for the first time in the Kulyab and near Kurgan-Tebe (Khatlon oblast), although the various political aims were only of secondary importance. In reality it was mainly a struggle for regional and state power between clan members of the two factions. During these clashes entire villages were razed to the ground and the population murdered (see Trutanow 1994: 191).

Russian troops took control of strategically important positions, without actually taking a direct part in the conflict,[4] but by the end of 1992 around 200,000 Russian civilians had left the country. At the beginning of September 1992 Nabiyev was deposed from power and the opposition formed its own government, which was dominated by members of the Islamic Renaissance Party.[5] Akbarshah Iskandarov, the Pamiri chairman of the Supreme Soviet, became acting president (Rubin 1993/4: 79). The new government, which relied on clans from Khatlon, Gharm and GBAO, was attacked, for its part, by troops of the Nabiyev clan and its supporters from the Kulyab. The fighting increased in intensity, especially in Khatlon oblast and later on in Dushanbe and in the gateway to the Gharm valley (see Götz and Halbach 1993: 222–223). In some regions of Khatlon whole tracts of land were destroyed, the people fleeing to Dushanbe and Islamic activists fleeing to Afghanistan.

Against the backdrop of these events, the Tajik parliament, still in existence and still with a communist majority, elected as its new president Emomali Rakhmanov in October 1992.[6] Rakhmanov had previously been Communist Party leader in the Kulyab. The interim president, Iskandarov, who had not acknowledged the elections, was able to hang on to power until 6 December, when he and his government were driven out by Kulyabi forces, who for the first time took control of the capital Dushanbe.

Rakhmanov threw away any chances of reconciliation by filling all ministerial posts with people from his own clan, and in spite of the later peace process these people still dominate the country today. After a short interlude of only three months, during which time the opposition was in government, power then shifted from the Khodjand clans to their former bondsmen in the Kulyab on Rakhmanov's establishment in office. In Dushanbe in the ensuing days and weeks, those in opposition and indeed all inhabitants considered by the perpetrators – mainly Kulyabi militia – to belong to the opposition, were murdered in their thousands. Having an official stamp in your identity card showing you were from Khatlon (Kurgan-Tebe) or GBAO was enough reason to be shot, along with your entire family. Whole villages in Khatlon and at the gateway to the Gharm valley were systematically destroyed by Kulyabi troops, armed by the Russians.

The weakened opposition was not able to topple Rakhmanov in spite of putting up strong resistance, and although the latter reorganised the Tajik army, he in his turn was not able to crush Islamic and nationalist resistance. Open warfare turned into a guerrilla war, with Islamic forces from Gharm, Kurgan-Tebe and Afghanistan continually attacking newly formed government troops and militia from the Kulyab (see Rashid 2002: 138–139).

Under the leadership of Said Abdallah Nuri, the opposition[7] moved its headquarters abroad, with a base in Moscow from where they organised resistance.

In 1995 the largest opposition groups jointly founded the United Tajik Opposition. Deadlock was reached, with the government controlling some regions and the opposition others. Gharm and (*de facto*) GBAO, remained independent during this period.

When the Taliban took power in Kabul in 1996, thus creating the possibility that Islamic fundamentalists would advance towards Tajikistan, both government and moderate Islamic opposition realised that agreement had to be reached. There was also considerable pressure from abroad, especially from Russia and Uzbekistan, who wanted to put a stop to any process of Islamification. Additionally there was pressure from Iran, which had supported the fight against the Taliban, and from the Tajik warlords in Afghanistan, Rabbani and Shah Massud, who needed a secure back-up area in order to continue their struggle against the Taliban (see Rashid 2002: 139–140).

In 1997 a peace process was negotiated with the help of the UN. However, this was only concluded during the course of parliamentary elections in 2000, because some opposition groups had at first boycotted the peace agreement as they had initially been excluded from negotiations. The troops belonging to opposition groups taking part in the agreement were integrated into the Tajik armed forces and the parties supporting them were officially recognised. Elections were held, during which Rakhmanov's ex-communists, now called the People's Democratic Party, obtained 64.5 per cent of the votes after rigging the election, whereas the Islamic Renaissance Party obtained only 7.5 per cent. However, the latter accepted the contentious election results in order not to endanger the peace process. We can assume party leaders realised that the vast majority of the population in Tajikistan wished to avoid religiously motivated political tensions. Their courageous recognition of the facts is remarkable.

The results of the civil war of 1992/3 and of the seven unstable years that followed were disastrous. The number of dead alone stood at between 50,000 to 100,000. Many more were injured, women and girls raped, and countless children traumatised. A quarter of a million people fled to Afghanistan, Pakistan, Iran or to other countries in the Confederation of Independent States (CIS). About half a million people, mainly from rural areas in Khatlon, became homeless. The infrastructure in entire districts was completely destroyed (see Bliss 2003). The economy of Tajikistan, already weakened by the withdrawal of subsidies from the Soviet Union, now collapsed completely. Russia took the remaining currency and a share of those industrial resources which had been mortgaged for the purchase of weapons and munitions. Drug smuggling became firmly established as a consequence of the civil war. It was based in Afghanistan, with supplies then passing through Tajikistan and onward to Russia and Western Europe.

The CIS border troops currently stationed along the border of the Pyandsh with Afghanistan are likewise a result of the civil war. They were imposed on Tajikistan mainly by Russia and Uzbekistan. Russian troops are stationed here today, as well as Kazak, Uzbek and Kyrgyz troops. The whole Pamir region between the Kyrgyz and Afghan borders is controlled by these Russian border guards.[8] This greatly affects Tajikistan's sovereignty, as the border troops do not just patrol all access routes into the Pamirs in the legitimate search for drugs and weapons but also obstruct all private and commercial traffic in a completely arbitrary way.

However, border troops are now an important part of the economy, as the soldiers are relatively well paid. Up until 1996 the sovkhozes had to provide free food to the border troops, but since privatisation the situation has been reversed, with the troops now spending their money in local markets. Increasingly, Tajik mercenaries are replacing Russian other ranks, thus also providing work and income. The downside is that until 1998 there were repeated clashes along the border (in 1993 alone there were 90 incidents involving the military), and since then there have been repeated instances in which innocents bystanders on the Tajik side have been killed by nervous soldiers.[9]

The Pamiris in the civil war

The role of GBAO and the Pamiris in the civil war has not been reappraised up until now, and is anyway described in contradictory terms even by those involved. Some people stress the active involvement of the Pamiris in any opposition to the old regime, but others see the population of GBAO simply as the victim of events over which they had no control. The people we interviewed said that when political groups started to form at the beginning of 1992, the government immediately identified them with the people from Gharm and thus with the Islamic opposition. Branded as enemies of the Kulyabis and the Khodjand faction, hundreds of Pamiris in Dushanbe and other towns were murdered. Thousands fled to GBAO, where a fluctuating number of 30,000 to over 50,000 refugees placed additional strain on the already difficult supply situation. However, according to the people we interviewed, the Pamiris had split away from the Gharm clans, and had withdrawn entirely from the conflict at the time when most of the latter started forming an Islamic opposition and entering into coalitions with fundamentalist groups.

A regional party had in fact been founded in the Pamirs: the Lal-i Badakhshan (Ruby of Badakhshan) party, which had already declared independence for GBAO on 9 December 1991. This party was formed in 1989 when Tajik nationalism was on the rise, with the specific aim of representing the interests of the Pamiris, most of whom did not feel themselves to be Tajik (see Trutanow 1994: 193). This declaration of independence cannot really be distinguished from similar declarations in other parts of the country, but the government in Dushanbe considered it to be a hostile move. From December 1992 until September 1993, the government imposed a blockade on GBAO, cutting it off from all supplies, even though very few Pamiris actually took part in the armed struggle against the government. In 1992 only 30 per cent of normal supplies actually reached the Pamirs.

One result of the blockade was an increase in efforts to gain independence, but it also led to famine in the winter of 1992/3, and for the first time ever it drew GBAO to the attention of countries involved in development policies (see Chapter

Plate 8.1 Armed opposition forces (GBAO in origin) controlling the entrance to the Wandsh valley (1997).

9). Old ties to Russia were discussed in Khorog and by referring to the Pamir Agreement of 1895 a reminder was given that the Pamiris had become 'subjects of the Russian Tsars for 100 years to come' (Trutanow 1994: 193). However, the reaction from Moscow was muted.

And so in March 1993 a settlement was made with the Rakhmanov government in Dushanbe. The Pamiris retracted their declaration of independence and Dushanbe declared itself willing to call off any military intervention in the Pamirs. Moreover, some armed opposition groups living in the Pamirs (Plate 8.1) were unofficially tolerated, although they were to come partly under the control of Russian border guards, and action against them was suspended. Even as late as 1998, remnants of armed opposition groups were to be found in Khorog, though they did not actively intervene in the fighting in the west of Tajikistan.

There were only a few instances of conflicts between opposition forces and border troops between 1993 and 1998. Although many Pamiris almost certainly supported the Islamic Renaissance Party, hardly any of them supported the more extreme position of the opposition leader, Majnûn. In the winter of 1994/5, during a clash between Majnûn followers and border troops not far from Khorog, with five dead on each side and one innocent civilian victim, they expressly demanded that Majnûn leave Khorog and GBAO (see Emadi 1998: 15–16).

Economic collapse

It would be difficult to understand the humanitarian disaster in GBAO without knowing something about the background at national level. This is why we intend to examine the reasons for the collapse of the entire Tajik national economy and then briefly describe the consequences. There were essentially two reasons for Tajikistan's economic collapse, both mutually dependent and reinforcing the other. First, after Tajik independence, its people became *de jure* foreigners in Russia (as did the members of all the other states that replaced the Soviet Union) (see Kaiser 2000: 148), even though Russia continued to look on the other former Soviet republics as 'neighbours abroad' and as regions in which they had a large stake. The reverse also applied, with Russians becoming foreigners in the new republics if they did not want to take up citizenship, or were not allowed to. Obstacles placed in their way made citizenship difficult to obtain; for example, one had to provide proof of competence in the national language. By 1996 this had led to around 300,000 Russians leaving Tajikistan (see Akiner 1996: 18), and of these 200,000 alone left during the civil war of 1992/3.

All existing agreements were automatically annulled at the time of independence under international law and on the dissolution of the Soviet Union, and agreements were only honoured if they had been specifically endorsed or had been replaced by newer agreements, for example the CIS treaty. The agreement on where Russian troops were to be stationed in Tajikistan formed part of this treaty. The continuation of subsidies to the Tajik state budget did not, however, form part of it, so that Tajikistan was suddenly cut off from its previous source of finance, which across all sectors had accounted for, on average, between 50 per cent and 80 per cent of the GDP.[10] For this reason alone, from 1989 to 1992 the GNP fell from US$ 2,340 to US$ 1,250 per head of population (a drop of 53.4 per cent on the 1989 figure), or from 47 per cent of the Soviet Union average, to only 34 per cent (see Götz and Halbach 1993: 228–229). On the other hand it was true that after the collapse of the Soviet Union, GNP also fell sharply in Russia and the rich former Soviet states of the West.

Today, people in Tajikistan are reluctant to discuss the consequences of the emigration of the Tajik Russians to Russia. At present the Russian population consists mainly of pensioners and lowly labourers trying to make a living. Amongst the first to emigrate were some of the most highly trained specialists in the country, who immediately found new employment in Russia. It was impossible at first to find Tajiks to fill their specialised jobs in industry, administration and the utilities. The far-reaching consequences of this brain drain must have caused many problems in, for example, the energy industry and regional administration. The exodus of these better-off Russians had a huge effect on retail consumption in the towns, leading to a drastic drop in commercial demand, but this fact is hardly ever acknowledged in economic analyses. There are no figures available on this subject for GBAO, but the fact that we now regard the economic role of the border troops as so important must mean that the former, much larger, Russian population had played an important part in the economy as customers and guarantors of production.

It is only in the last few years that the consequences of Tajiks becoming foreigners in the Russian Republic (RR) have become dramatically clear. It is (still) possible to travel to Russia on a Tajik passport without a visa, but taking up employment there is still prohibited. Hundreds of thousands of Tajiks and thousands of Pamiris still continue, as they always have done, to look for work (illegally) in the RR.

Two new studies in Khatlon oblast have shown how difficult and economically unviable this is (see Bliss 2003). At least half of the income earned is consumed by bribes, necessary for entry into Russia, necessary as part of the daily routine, and also in order to send currency home. In addition, most illegal work is done on an informal basis, for example on building sites, and is usually badly paid. This leads to serious problems, especially in GBAO, whose population, and therefore economy, ought to benefit from these migrant workers. This is in addition to the fact that every year several hundred Tajiks become the victims of violent crime in Russia. In 2002/3 some two dozen men from Shugnân and Roshân alone are said to have been killed in the Moscow area.

The second factor responsible for economic collapse in Tajikistan is the civil war, with the continuing insecurity it caused in many parts of the country, even after 1993. The consequences have already been briefly summarised in the previous paragraph. Additionally, the presence of refugees in Gharm, Khatlon and also in GBAO continued to cause problems until the end of the 1990s. The shattered infrastructure is still in the process of being rebuilt in the western part of Khatlon oblast. In Dushanbe and near Kurgan-Tebe numerous businesses have not been able to re-start production after the war, and in rural areas in the south of Khatlon oblast the entire irrigation and drainage systems have collapsed, a legacy of the war that has lasted into the twenty-first century.[11]

A third reason for the present economic problems must also be mentioned: although it has not yet been closely investigated, it is likely that in Tajikistan (and in some neighbouring Soviet Union republics), an economic crisis was already underway in the second half of the 1980s. At the very least the economy had stagnated, resulting in the beginnings of an exodus of Russians from the region.[12] After years of stagnation, industrial production in 1987 fell by 1.7 per cent, although it rose again by 12.2 per cent in 1988. The real downward trend began in 1989 with a 1 per cent fall. This trend accelerated, so that in 1991 it was –9 per cent and in the first half of 1992 alone it was –15 per cent (over 1992 as a whole it was around –30 per cent).

There might have been several reasons for stagnation in the Tajik economy in the 1980s: first, the rapid rise in population in the previous few decades (see Deutsches Institut 1993: 40), and the lack of new jobs to match this rise; then there was the war in Afghanistan and the arms race, which continued to drain the wealth of the Soviet Union; and last, the restricted base on which the Tajik economy was founded was beginning to create problems, as it relied entirely on cotton growing and aluminium production. Moreover, 80–90 per cent of trade was with countries of the Soviet Union and for decades this had resulted in a deficit for Tajikistan. It is also possible that the enormous debts of the sovkhozes were already beginning to act as a brake on investment.

The consequences of economic collapse are still being felt today: the majority of the population in Tajikistan lives at or below the poverty line. Depending on how it is measured, between 60 per cent and 95 per cent of the population are still considered to be poor. According to one survey, 60 per cent of the population consider themselves in that category. Over 95 per cent of the population live below the 'minimum consumption basket' (World Bank), four out of five are 'poor' or worse, a third are 'very poor' or worse, and nearly 20 per cent are 'extremely poor' (below US$1 per capita per day; see Falkingham 2000: iv).

In 2002, the total level of economic output was still only 43 per cent of that in 1991. There was a sharp drop in employment from almost 70 per cent in the early 1990s to only 55 per cent in 2000. Tajikistan dropped down to 116th place out of 174 nations on the Human Development Index (HDI) (Bliss 2003; Tajikistan 2002; UNDP 2004; World Bank 2000a; World Bank 2004). If the figures for education and health did not have such a high rating on the HDI, the country would become, according to income, one of the 30 poorest countries on earth.

In order to understand what effect the economic crisis was having on individuals, one must be aware that after independence wages and pensions continued to be paid in roubles at the old rates. Although these were low, people could still live a reasonably decent life, as the cost of living was also low. When the civil war started, most payment stopped, only recommencing in 1995 following the currency reform, at a rate which was at most 10 per cent of the old amount. If this were converted into dollars, pensioners would get about US$3 per month and social security for the poor would be less than US$1.6 per month. A teacher would get between US$8–10 and agricultural workers on state farms less than US$2 per month.[13] Wages have barely increased since then, although prices continue to rise. In 1992/3 a disaster was only averted because many families still had enough supplies in stock from the good years of the Soviet era. After the destruction caused by the civil war of 1993–4, conditions were so bad that some of the population did not have enough to eat and there were reports of children being sold.[14]

If people in the heart of Tajikistan felt as though they were falling into an abyss during the civil war and the ensuing years, one can imagine the effect on the Pamiris and Kyrgyz living in isolation in the Pamir valleys. The one remaining positive aspect of life in GBAO was the fact that the oblast itself was spared the destruction of the civil war, even though many people had lost their relatives as a result of the killings in and around Dushanbe.

Even in the years before the civil war, there were signs of a deteriorating economic situation in GBAO, similar to the one in the western oblasts. The situation in the sovkhozes was symptomatic of this. Although workers received full wages up to and including 1991, already by the end of the 1980s the lack of spare parts, fertiliser and imported seed was being felt, resulting in a slight fall in yields.

However, as there were still large stockpiles of fuel and spare parts, the damaging mismanagement at first went unnoticed. In fact, private households acted no differently to professional business men. From mid-1991 onwards the political events in Dushanbe had begun to unsettle everyone, but no one had had any inkling of the impending disaster and therefore everyone continued to use up their existing savings (e.g. by building houses – see p. 290), and then lost any unused savings anyway through inflation.

In fact spiralling inflation should have warned of the impending economic crisis much sooner. In mid-1991 a kg of wheat still cost 0.31 roubles. By the summer of 1992 the price had risen to 6 roubles, although this upward trend was disguised in GBAO, as sovkhoz workers were still receiving their allocation of farm produce. In June 1993, when the disaster finally struck, the small amount of wheat available in state-run shops officially cost 37 roubles per kg, but 130 roubles on the open market. In GBAO prices were even higher and by September 1 kg of flour had already risen to between 250 to 400 roubles. It was only by the end of 1992 that people in GBAO started to realise the gravity of the problem, and even then everyone believed that it was just a temporary crisis.

Many people still thought this until as late as 1995, when by the fourth year of the crisis the extent of the economic collapse slowly became evident to the bulk of the population. By then, the aid programme organised by the Aga Khan Foundation had been in operation for some time and was the main factor in enabling people to remain in GBAO and in averting an exodus with concomitant disastrous consequences. Later, many people asked why the Pamiris had not left the region in 1993, but at that point the civil war was still raging and hundreds of thousands of people had been displaced. Where could the people from GBAO have gone, when a quarter of the country had already been destroyed and reconstruction was still unthinkably far off?

In GBAO after 1993 there was almost no public sector money left to invest in business, let alone in the maintenance of the infrastructure. By 1995 the budget deficit stood at 95 per cent compared to 1991. Unemployment had reached a level of 70–80 per cent. Agriculture, still almost entirely state run, was no longer able to guarantee even the previous level of 20 per cent self-sufficiency without outside help. Supplies of fuel for vehicles and heating from outside sources had reached a figure representing 1–2 per cent of the base value, without taking into account the aid programme run by the Aga Khan Foundation. People were suffering from the cold, and at least throughout the winter of 1992/3 and all of 1993 they did not have enough to eat. There were almost no vehicles on the roads, and schools closed for the whole winter as there was neither means of heating nor shoes for the children.

The effect of the crisis on individuals only becomes clear when one considers conditions in rural households. In the summer of 1995, and in 1996 and 1997 also, we came across almost empty houses. In the villages some households were entirely without food, or maybe just had enough potatoes to last one week. More than 90 per cent of all families in GBAO relied heavily, or even totally, on humanitarian aid. After several years of this economic crisis most people's reserves of clothing, shoes and general household goods had run out.

One could of course say that in Africa an average family in the Sahel zone is no better off today than the people in GBAO during and after the economic crisis, and so why all the lamenting? This comparison is inappropriate on two counts. First, even in Africa there is usually enough food, except of course in crisis situations. Second, GBAO is a country which materially and from the point of view of education and employment was well on its way towards catching up with Europe. Everyone was literate and employed in skilled or very skilled jobs. For at least 30 years they had received regular, rising wages and basic supplies had been extremely good. However, the real difference with the situation in Africa is that people in GBAO had not developed a strategy for coping with emergencies of this kind, and no experience in how to go about extricating themselves from a crisis.

Employment, income and diet

With the collapse of industry in Khorog, people faced job losses for the first time in the more recent history of GBAO: 1,200 mainly female employees lost their jobs in the textile industry here and a further 600 employees in other industries. From 1992/3 the remaining industries, sometimes only operating part-time like the transport sovkhoz of Khorog, only paid 50 per cent of an employee's wages (if they were lucky), and the remaining 50 per cent was settled by bank remittance. However, the credit was never properly honoured and from 1994 onwards no wages were paid at all.

There were no job losses in the numerous health, welfare and education institutions or in administration, but wages simply ceased to be paid, probably also from 1992. Employees now had to work without any remuneration until mid-1995. However, this did not cause any additional hardship, as one member of almost every family worked in a sovkhoz, and this person was given enough coupons for the whole family to spend in the sovkhoz shop. The rations allocated on the sovkhoz coupons (*talons*) were less than generous: for example 20 kg of pototoes and 15 kg of flour per person (for a half or whole year's work!). However, it is important to make clear that even if wages had been paid, it would not have changed the situation very much, as inflation meant that an average monthly wage could now only buy a few kilos of wheat flour.[15]

Once wage payments had ceased, then apart from the system of *talons*, there was virtually no other means of payment until the introduction of the Tajik rouble (TJR) in mid-1995. The lack of money meant that very few goods were brought into GBAO, and so the markets were practically empty, even though the road to Osh in Kyrgyzstan in fact remained open. The only place that could always boast a modest supply of goods was the Murghâb, where by 1994 the Kyrgyz population had found a way of making money by selling meat to Kyrgyzstan.

The food situation in GBAO in 1993 was extremely serious, indeed much worse than in the rest of Tajikistan where there was extensive damage caused by the civil war. Taking 400 g of wheat flour per person per day as an absolute minimum requirement, then the total amount of flour required in GBAO for a population of 213,000 would be 32,000 metric tonnes per year or 43,000 tonnes of wheat equivalent. Only 3,500 tonnes came out of local production, 2,100 tonnes from central government. From 1993 until 1995, various donors under the umbrella of the AKF and the WFP provided between 18,000 and 20,000 tonnes of wheat flour as food aid per year. Nevertheless, that still left a shortfall of 6,700 tonnes for 1995. The donor organisations worked on the basis of providing only 1,200 kcal per person per day in 1995, which left an energy shortfall of 1,000 kcal per person per day. A survey carried out in 1996 showed clearly that a general deficit of micronutrients existed (iron, iodine, vitamins A, B, C, D, and minerals) resulting in diet-related health problems such as goitre, rickets and anaemia.

How did the people manage to feed themselves? First, there was the emergency aid programme, described in the next chapter, which gave support to all households independently of their income based on the size of the household, and which formed by far the most important contribution to basic supplies from 1993 until 1998. Those who had money or coupons from the sovkhozes, could buy a limited amount of additional food in the shops run by state farms. This provided between 15 and 20 per cent of basic supplies. It was thanks to widespread membership of the sovkhozes that in rural areas a relatively large number of people had access to their products. Food was also available on the open market, but supplies were extremely limited and prices exorbitant. Some groups received extra support in the form of special rations provided by the sovkhozes (e.g. a children's home in Khorog, hospitals and some of the boarding schools), but in 1995/6 these supplies ceased.

In the villages, increasing use was made of private gardens as subsistence production became ever more important. Unfortunately, seed, fertiliser and – most of all – experience were in short supply. The other problem was that private gardens in GBAO are only between 300 to 700 square metres per household, which is much smaller than the average in Tajikistan (1,000 square metres). All the same, we worked out that up to 50 per cent of a family's food deficit could be made up in this way, provided they grew the most suitable combination of potatoes and vegetables. In the villages they also kept some livestock, thus providing livestock products, but lack of fodder limited the number.

In larger towns and villages, where many people had no private garden, every square metre of land was used, creating even the tiniest of vegetable gardens. Some of the men went so far as to sow barley and grow potatoes in the town park of Khorog. They even removed the stone slabs from the courtyards of some of the blocks of flats to create vegetable gardens. These temporary solutions remained widespread until 1997/8.

Although no one spoke of social differences, there were of course some groups of people who fared better and some who fared worse in obtaining their share of food. However, there were no protection rackets or nepotism, as the oblast government no longer had control of resources and emergency aid was being distributed equally to the population by the AKF and the PRDP/MSDSP. Even many years later the recipients of the aid voiced no complaints about actually receiving their share.

The most disadvantaged families were those in Khorog and in large villages and towns, who had no land of their own and no access to sovkhoz rations. Those people who were given nothing by their relatives in the villages, or had none, had to live on the food aid alone and on the few extras made possible by their meagre wage (which was only paid at first). Those people who were best-off lived in villages, especially those in the lower-lying villages with more agricultural land. Here the private gardens were larger, the yield per unit of land was greater and the sovkhozes were able to distribute much more than those in the high-lying valleys. For many town families, the situation only improved when the market in Khorog was up and running again and a substantial number of people had access to a regular income through employment with the numerous aid organisations.

From 1993 to 1995/6 the daily menu was extremely monotonous, even for the average village family. It consisted mainly of pieces of bread soaked in a liquid resembling water rather than tea, and there was also potato soup. In the summer they added herbs to the soup, and ate any fruits available. Meat was virtually unobtainable in Khorog and was only rarely available in the villages. One of the worst problems was that food could not be preserved for the winter, as sugar, salt and vinegar were almost entirely unobtainable on the market. Many Kyrgyz were slightly better off, even though they had initially suffered the most when state supplies of grain and vegetables came to an end in 1992 because they had no means of growing their own supply. Once aid started they were in a better position than the Pamiris as they had more livestock and animal products per head.

One particular problem mentioned by many people we interviewed was the babies' and small children's diet. Milk powder was completely unavailable before international aid arrived, and breast-feeding, often by anaemic mothers, was only supplemented by an indigestible flour-and-water mixture or mashed potatoes. When asked if there were any positive aspects to the economic crisis, the first thing mentioned was always help given by neighbours. Whoever had milk in the house would share it with the neighbours' children, and it was said that many families gave away more than they kept. The people we interviewed said that hospitality was as generous as ever: if you arrived at mealtimes, you would automatically be served whatever food was in the house. All they did was add some more water to the soup and serve smaller portion of potatoes all round.

Agriculture, industry and trade

However improbable it may seem to outside observers, the management in most of the sovkhozes initially made no changes to their method of planning as a result of the economic crisis of 1992/3. This applied to the proportion of land put down to fodder plants, grain and vegetables, and other products, as well as to production targets and processing of the harvest. In 1993, the entire produce of any sovkhoz was still handed over to the state, which then had it shared out between various recipients, including hospitals and schools. Workers could buy their food from state-run shops, which were also supplied in this way, and a further share of the produce was given to the CIS border troops. The sovkhozes received nothing in return from the state. Because of the lack of income (Moscow had stopped paying wages by 1991) the sovkhozes were unable to pay their workers. In lieu of pay they were given a small amount of 'wage substitute' food coupons, for use in the local shops or state-run farm stores, referred to on pp. 257–258. However, the sovkhozes were unable to buy spare parts and fuel, import seed, or buy the simple fertiliser needed for agricultural production.

As a consequence, from 1992 to 1994 the arable area under sovkhoz management fell by 15 per cent and total crop production fell by 10 per cent annually (more specifically, within three years, potato production fell by 25 per cent, vegetables by 48 per cent, and fruit by 38 per cent). During this period 39 per cent less fodder was produced, and the total number of cattle in the sovkhozes decreased by 22.7 per cent. Production covered a family's basic needs for only two months of the year. It is important to bear in mind here that between 1989 and 1992 production had already decreased by 72 per cent of the benchmark figures for 1989, and that these figures themselves reflected the already very low yield per hectare of Soviet times (see p. 253). The overall picture was indeed very gloomy.

There were two further problems which management on the state farms had not considered and which were to seriously affect future development. First, the irrigation channels were no longer looked after properly, with the result that some main channels became completely blocked by landslip and thus entire tracts of irrigated land were lost to cultivation. This loss of arable land was usually blamed on lack of fuel, but the rehabilitation work – mainly done by hand – carried out by the PRDP on these particular channels after 1995, proves that it would have been easy to keep the channels unblocked. The sovkhoz management evidently lacked the flexibility needed to adapt properly to the new situation.

The second problem was one over which management had no influence: replacing machinery and equipment. If they had had the financial means to buy spare parts at an early stage, many tractors and lorries would certainly have remained serviceable for much longer. Previously, almost all machinery and equipment had been purchased with subsidies from Moscow and there was now no way of finding the money to replace them, with the result that over successive years more and more equipment broke down and was not replaced. This meant that an increasing proportion of the work had to be done manually instead of mechanically, outlying fields could no longer be cultivated, transport became increasingly restricted and the harvest could no longer be processed.

At first people had no idea how to carry out the work manually, having been used to machinery; that is, how to employ traditional technology, which in any case had almost died out. For example, ploughing now had to be carried out by oxen instead of tractors, but in some villages oxen had not been used for ploughing for at least 30 years. Although ox-ploughs had been widely distributed in all the rayons by 1995, there were not enough suitable draught oxen, and if there were any, they were completed untrained. In 1995 and subsequent years we had many opportunities to observe driving and ploughing with oxen, and could clearly see how difficult it was for a tractor driver, or maybe even a book-keeper from a state-run farm, to suddenly have to start using an ox-plough.

The managers of the sovkhozes were faced with the same problem of how to cut, thresh and clean the corn by hand, which at first led to almost ludicrous situations. Although it was quickly accepted that combine harvesters now had to be replaced by sickles, and that where formerly one combine harvester covered 5 hectares per day it now took 75 man-days to cover the same amount of land, they could at first find no solution to the threshing problem, apart from driving the few serviceable tractors round and round in circles over the ears of wheat, thereby using up the last drops of fuel to be had. If they had cast their eyes across the Pyandsh to Afghanistan they would have seen how to do the threshing with oxen. In fact this method was gradually introduced in GBAO, first in individual households and later in the sovkhozes (see Plate 4.12).

Just as ill-advised was the idea of using large wind machines to separate the wheat from the chaff, thereby using up valuable fuel which should have been kept for more important things. Much of the harvest went to waste, because the grain was left lying around for weeks on end until a wind machine became available, even during the months of greatest hardship throughout the winter of 1992/3. During our first visit to GBAO in 1995 we noticed that they were gradually rediscovering the method used in Afghanistan, which was winnowing by hand assisted only by the wind! It was very obvious that some of the managers of the sovkhozes were ashamed of having to demonstrate this archaic technology to us Western visitors, while Soviet combine harvesters lay around rusting.

The decline in fruit production cannot be blamed on the economic crisis. Before 1938 the harvest is said to have been 40,000 tonnes annually (apricots, apples, mulberries, grapes for raisin production, etc.), while by the beginning of the 1990s it had dropped to only 5,000 tonnes. The blame lies mainly with the political planners, who decided to slash the number of orchards in order to replace them mainly with fodder crops (alfalfa). Another reason for this decline can be found nearer home: the people did not bother looking after the fruit trees, and the sovkhozes no longer knew how to look after them. This is an aspect of agriculture in the Pamirs which has great potential, but which has been neglected as a result of errors made by Soviet planners.

However, in 1995 some managers realised for the first time that the absence of subsidies from Moscow was not just going to be a temporary misfortune but a permanent state of affairs. Although they were subjected to harsh criticism from the oblast administration for doing so, they started refusing to deliver their produce to state-run institutions and instead distributed some of it directly to their workers, in lieu of wages, rather than giving them *talons*. Furthermore, they finally started taking some of the produce to the market, where it was bartered in exchange for fuel, spare parts and other urgent necessities. One state-run farm in the Murghâb, which had been renamed a kolkhoz in 1994 or 1995 for psychological reasons, continued delivering 6 tonnes of meat to the administrative authorities for the sake of appearances, but meanwhile would directly sell 200 tonnes to Kyrgyzstan.

During the economic crisis, livestock kept mainly for export became increasingly useful, as the Pamiris could now fall back on this supply of meat and meat products. However, as we have already seen, too much arable land was taken up for fodder crops and therefore could not be used directly to produce food (see pp. 253–254). Between 1992 and 1995 the number of cattle dropped accordingly by 12.5 per cent from 76,400 to 66,900. The number of sheep and goats, which had already dropped considerably in 1991 and 1992, dropped even more steeply. Between 1991and 1995, the numbers fell by a good 29.5 per cent from 241,000 to 170,000. This trend seems to be continuing today, although these small ruminants are still the most important capital reserve.

However much of a disaster this was for individual families, the reduction in livestock numbers brought environmental benefits, as overgrazing on much of the land decreased. In all, there was a clear fall in the use of livestock. Between 1991 and 1993 milk production in the sovkhozes declined by about 50 per cent because of the shortage of imported concentrated feed. As a result of this, the sovkhozes were no longer able to fulfil their obligations to supply dairy and meat products to local health and welfare institutions.

Although much of the previously mechanised work could now be done by hand, there was still a shortage of implements, new arable land, water, fertiliser and seed. One observer who analysed the state of agriculture in 1993 told us: 'I would have to rate most of the wheat and potato fields that I saw on state farms as among the poorest example of crop production practices that I have ever seen.' We saw with our own eyes freshly harvested potatoes which were so tiny that over a hundred were needed to make up a kilo. And there were no means of producing seed or fertiliser locally. By 1993 the future of state-run agriculture in GBAO looked very bleak indeed and a further drastic fall in production seemed inevitable.

The year 1992 was the *annus horribilis* for industry as well. Production came to a complete standstill in almost all the factories, mainly because there was no energy supply and no more raw materials were being delivered. Locally there would still have been a demand for many goods, particularly building materials, clothing and shoes. We have already described the consequences on employment: for example, the largest textile concern alone sacked 1,175 workers, one building materials factory sacked 100 employees, one food processing plant likewise 100 workers, and so on. The population of Khorog, and also the inhabitants of nearby villages within a range of 20 to 30 kilometres, were the most seriously affected by job losses.

By 1993 trade had also completely collapsed: on the market in Khorog in that year there were apparently only two or three stalls selling a few potatoes, noodles and flour. Clothes, shoes and all household goods disappeared from the shops, even though the shop assistants, in true Soviet style, absurdly insisted on manning their posts with nothing to sell until 1995 (Plate 8.2).

Plate 8.2 Almost empty government store in Khorog (1995).

Social infrastructure and services

By the end of 1993 the education system in GBAO was close to collapse. Although most teachers were still carrying out their jobs, by the second half of that year school supplies had almost run out. Even if parents had had the money, no textbooks, exercise books or pens were to be had on the market. By November it had become clear that schools would have to close for the next few months, as there was no means of heating them in winter. If parents and teachers did not themselves manage to carry out repairs to the school buildings, then they simply remained in a state of disrepair. At that time they could not help themselves to equipment and spares from sovkhoz buildings, as these were only dismantled later, and no international aid had yet arrived.

The supply of shoes in 1992/3 was, surprisingly enough, still good enough for teaching not to be disrupted for lack of children's shoes, although the situation deteriorated from 1994 until 1996/7. Several years later, when investigating the whereabouts of the almost 20 per cent of children not attending school, we were inevitably told it was because they had no shoes. The shortage of shoes became so serious that even in winter many children had to come to school in socks and plastic sandals. During one visit we made to the school in Rang-kul in November 1996, more than half of the pupils were not wearing proper shoes, although the temperature in the classroom was below 5°C. In 1996/7 a survey on day-to-day problems which we carried out in 12 villages showed that the shortage of clothes and shoes was then considered even more pressing than the lack of basic food.

It must be stressed that by the middle or end of 1993 all teachers still in school – and in some schools none of them had left – worked almost entirely without pay. It was only later, during the land reform of 1995/6, that they were given access to land which they could cultivate and use to live off. The currency reform in May 1995 did nothing to change teachers' poor position, as salaries were only between 2.6 and 4 US dollars, and as late as 1998 an average teacher's salary was still only 6.5 US dollars. Even in 2003 they only received 23 to 38 TJS, depending on the type of school; that is, from 7 to 12 US dollars at most. Even the Tajik Poverty Reduction Strategy Paper openly admits that such a low income only just covers 20 per cent of basic needs (Tajikistan 2002: 22). Incidentally, prices today, especially food prices, are lower than they were in 1993/4, the period when salaries were at their lowest.

In 1992/3, with a few exceptions (some institutions in district centres), the entire nursery and pre-school education system, which had previously been so successful, was shut down. This was not because staff had left their jobs but because there was no more food for the children and no means of heating the buildings.

Bearing these events in mind, it is astonishing that the University of Khorog opened its doors in 1992, and at least from 1995 onwards was able to run successful courses. The pessimists, who in 1993 had pointed out how isolated it was from the outside academic community and predicted that it would just become a superior kind of senior high school, were soon to be proved wrong.

The fundamental problems in the health system caused by the economic crisis were very similar to those in the education system. The problems can be divided into three groups: upkeep and maintenance of each institution; the supply of medicines and medical equipment, including spare parts; and staffing. In the winter of 1992/3 most of the available fuel was given to the hospitals, which also took delivery of the first external relief supplies. However, outlying health posts in the villages had to be closed in winter. The doctors always referred more serious cases to any hospital which was still open and in less serious cases treated their patients at home.

Apart from a few essential medicines, virtually no medication or equipment reached GBAO until the end of 1993,[16] when Médecins Sans Frontières (MSF) started the first deliveries of aid. In 1994 there was still a shortage of medicines and vaccine for children.[17] In 1998 most village health posts were still very poorly equipped, although the doctors and nurses we interviewed complained more about the poor condition of the buildings and the lack of heating.

Staff in the health sector were no better off financially than those in the education sector; on the contrary, salaries were even lower than those of teachers, with a doctor earning about 30 per cent less than a high-school teacher. In fact, the differences in earnings have not changed in Tajikistan even today (2003). While teachers at least get 23 to 38 TJS, a nurse's salary is just 7 TJS and a doctor's 8.5 TJS per month (between 2.3 and 2.8 US dollars). And yet people in the health system acted in the same way as their counterparts in education: it was a matter of honour to go to work every day, in order to keep a 'normal' health system running, and in the first five years of the economic crisis fewer than 20 per cent of the staff abandoned their posts.

State-run housing projects stopped altogether in 1992. Many almost-finished buildings were never completed, in spite of the housing shortage, which was exacerbated in the winter of 1992/3 by the arrival of many tens of thousands of refugees. The only building projects to be completed were those carried out by individual families in which use was made of local building materials (wood, mud, sand, stone, etc.). As the full extent of the economic crisis had not yet dawned on them, some families used up all their savings on these building projects.

In 1992/3 only a fraction of the quantity of fuel that had previously been supplied reached GBAO. Admittedly the hydroelectric power supply in the Pamirs developed by the Soviets had never worked properly, but in the 1980s even the most remote villages had some sort of power supply. However, because of the shortage of spare parts, breakdowns in the system became ever more frequent and there were numerous power cuts. In order to maintain the power supply to Khorog city, many villages which had been on mains power were now cut off for the whole winter. As a consequence of the shortage of electricity, particularly for cooking and heating, local forests came under pressure. In the winter of 1992/3, roughly 25 per cent of the trees around the villages and 5 per cent of all the trees and bushes in GBAO were cut down (see pp. 176–178). Probably the first project people organised in reaction to the crisis was small-scale local reafforestation, which began in 1993 around the villages, though even today the reforested area is still only a fraction of what is actually required.

Maintenance of the physical infrastructure became a major problem. From 1992/3, asphalted and, more especially, unmetalled roads continued to deteriorate and many bridges became almost impassable (see Plates 1.2 and 1.3). Without the collective help of the local community, access to many villages would have become virtually impossible. Public transport was brought to a standstill. People had to walk 10 or 20 km a day in order to reach their office or place of work, and if they wanted to visit members of their families in other villages or settle administrative problems in the capital of the oblast, a walk of two to three days was not uncommon. Several times we interviewed people walking along the road who were making, or intended to make, a 120- or even 160-km journey on foot.

There has been no law enforcement in GBAO since 1992/3, as the police, like everyone else, had no fuel for their vehicles. However, public security was never under threat and in the villages it was still possible to go around the streets at night safely. The information we were given on the situation in Khorog is contradictory. We could never agree that armed groups in some of the villages served the interests of public security, as this directly contradicts the Pamiris, often proudly expressed view that they do not need a police force at all because they have traditionally always been law-abiding.

It was an enormous social achievement to look after and integrate all the refugees from the civil war from the winter of 1992/3 onwards, in spite of all the problems already mentioned. The supply situation had deteriorated further with the arrival of between 30,000 to 55,000 refugees in GBAO at the beginning of 1993 (these numbers varying according to the source),[18] but the refugees who originally came from GBAO were still integrated into their former villages, and if they wanted to settle they were later given the same amount of land as the resident population. Refugees from elsewhere were accommodated in schools and other public buildings until their return home. There are many accounts of how the local population always shared its meagre resources with the refugees.

Socio-cultural effects

In our first work on GBAO in the period 1995 to 1998 we concentrated on investigating the influences of the economic crisis on the norms and values of the Pamiris, under the heading of socio-cultural effects. In addition to this we now intend to deal briefly with the questions of skills, cooperation within society and political participation.

Right from the start, a 'return to old traditions' was stressed in discussions on the socio-cultural consequences of the crisis in the Pamirs. Up until the end of the Soviet Union, Tajikistan was considered to be the least 'Russified' of the part-republics. Even before the dissolution of the Soviet Union the subject of cultural identity was being openly discussed using such titles as 'Islamic values' and 'the Iranian roots of Tajik culture'. Highlighted in these discussions as symbols of independence going back a thousand years were names such as Abdul-Hassan Rudakî and Abdul-Kasim Firdaûsî, and most especially that of the Samanid king, Ismaîl Somonî, the 'founder of the Tajik state'. Both Islamists and laypeople all over the country considered a return to the old customs ('priorité aux bonnes moeurs') to be a desirable goal (see Bertrand 1992: 213).

Even in the years before the crisis, the question of the Pamiris' origins was the subject of intense discussion. They discussed their Aryan origins and searched for clues on any cultural elements inherited from the Aryans still to be found in present-day culture (see Abusaîd 1997b). They also emphasised their own language, which was what actually distinguished them from other Tajiks, as did their Ismaili faith amongst Shiites. Although strict believers in Islam tended to be found in the Gharm valley and in Khatlon oblast, with a scattering in Wandsh, it was surprising how much the Pamiris stressed their own religiosity, contrasting their beliefs to those of other strict Muslims, whose beliefs the Pamiris considered to be contentious. Apparently it was even subtly implied that other Muslims did not follow Islamic moral principles as closely as did the Pamiris. The old Sunni prejudices against the Shiites were also revived and deliberately and self-confidently reversed (see pp. 222 and 236): it was claimed that during the economic crisis, Ismailis, but not Sunnis, were the ones best able to uphold traditional values.

In 1995 we started noticing disparities between life in the villages, where morals and traditional customs were upheld and in fact reinforced, and the situation in Khorog. On the few occasions when people we interviewed did actually admit that there was some consumption of drugs, occasional criminality or prostitution in GBAO (although in fact this does happen), they said it only happened in Khorog. Some of the people we interviewed also gave us the impression that although they considered drug taking to be immoral, they did not consider drug smuggling to be a criminal activity. At any rate, when people stated that no criminal activity went on in the villages, this also included villages where drug dealers were known to be operating.

Some people told us about the regrettable emergence of begging in Khorog and some of the villages. We got the impression that begging was seen as reprehensible because it discredited all those involved: the beggars themselves, because they were doing something just not done in GBAO (up until then), and both those who gave to them and those who gave them nothing since helping needy neighbours should have been a matter of course. Seen from this perspective, it appeared to be a failure of communal responsibility in the village that some families had been forced into begging.

However, everyone interviewed agreed that in general there was still great solidarity amongst the people, and that this was now even stronger than in Soviet times. Examples were given of households in which the occupants had ended up in serious difficulties as a result of helping neighbours because they themselves were so poor. Thousands of refugees were known to have been taken in by private households, even if they were only distantly related, or not at all related. By the end of 1993, a total of 5,746 refugees had found permanent homes in this way.

One example of the spread of cooperation at village level and amongst neighbours are the *tabaq* (*amtabaq*), already referred to in Chapter 4, which after 1992/3 were apparently formed much more frequently and given much higher status than in previous times. Whereas previously people might have just shared the same store room, a much higher level of cooperation and responsibility was required of these now-frequent communal groups in order to be able to share an ox-plough. When private land management was introduced it became ever more important to maintain these ox-ploughs, which along with labour, soil and irrigation constituted the most important investment capital.

Communal projects in a village or amongst neighbours – already referred to in connection with the Soviet period – became increasingly important during the course of the economic crisis. The amount of private communal work undertaken was now probably lower, as from 1992 to 1995/6 fewer houses were built than previously, and house building had been the most frequent reason for neighbours to engage in such communal projects. On the other hand, there was an increase in the importance of the *subbotnik*, whereby 'voluntary' work was carried out under pressure from the village community and for that reason not always popular. A cynic might describe all activities in GBAO after 1992/3 as voluntary work, in view of the almost symbolic nature of wage payments; but here we mean supplementary tasks, which had already existed in Soviet times – for example, road cleaning and maintenance, construction of community buildings, repair of paths and irrigation channels, and so on. By 1995 this kind of work had almost completely replaced state-run maintenance of the infrastructure, having been given a boost by development projects.

GBAO is not just some Third World region, as it enjoys a standard of education comparable to that in Europe. During the Soviet period in Tajikistan the Pamiris had always been considered to be the cultural intelligentsia (see Rubin 1993/4: 76). After 1992/3 this proved to be to their advantage when it came to development of the country; but it also proved to be a substantial hindrance. We have already described the difficulties experienced by former intellectuals and first-time farmers in ploughing by traditional methods (see Kreutzmann 2002: 43). Later we will show that even today in the Pamirs no professional irrigation technology is used (see pp. 315–316). Although there were specialists in many fields, there were practically no trained craftsmen such as blacksmiths and carpenters in the villages. And although some women in Khorog were able to sew shoes by machine, no one in the Pamirs had ever learnt how to actually make shoes out of a cowhide. The most widespread skill in existence was the use of herbal remedies, based on medicinal plants gathered in the mountains.

After 1995, in Roshorve as in other villages, we could observe the gradual revival of long-lost skills, sometimes through trial and error but also by applying knowledge gained from books, reconstructing old implements or learning from Afghans still competent in traditional technology. The *khalifa* of Roshorve, his opposite number in Basîd, and some other men showed us shoes, for example, which they themselves had sewn out of very amateurishly tanned leather (Plate 8.3).

There were frequent attempts to make electricity generators and water wheels, with the aim of harnessing water power or raising water (Plate 8.4). However, most attempts failed. Although with the aid of water from a stream, a small generator, a few lengths of wire and some light bulbs, one could generate a few hundred watts of electricity, which would be just about enough for five or six light bulbs, most of these home-made contraptions did not last. Probably the most successful of these installations, ones situated on the Bartang, were regularly washed away by the river after only a few weeks.

Open discussions on the political past began by 1995 or even earlier. At the time it was not possible to say how an economy based on private enterprise would work in comparison with the Soviet system, as a new system of this kind was not yet in place, and all that was happening was crisis management. By 1995 not much land had yet been privatised, and so no one was in a position to compare output from state-run farms with that of privately run farms. However, increased yield per hectare on privately managed land and occasional surpluses were often the only positive achievement mentioned in reports where the present system was compared with the Soviet one. In 2003, every time both systems were compared, the old Soviet system came out better than the 'capitalist economy' of the present day. However, although some people did point out the lack of political freedom in the past, others said emphatically that if they had known what was to follow the Soviet Union they would have been much less critical of the old system at the time.

Plate 8.3 The old *khalifa* from Roshorve shows two pairs of boots that he made himself after the complete collapse of the supply systems (1997).

Plate 8.4 Near a government-owned tenement in Khorog some people built a water wheel on the Gund river to replace the collapsed urban water supply system (1996).

In GBAO, just as in other former Soviet republics, the former leader of the Communist Party of the Soviet Union, Gorbachev, was blamed for the collapse of the Soviet Union. 'He is the one who should be made responsible for the disaster. His policy of glasnost and perestroika confused the people and led to a breakdown in discipline, etc.' In the same context they referred to the period under Leonid Brezhnev as a time without any hardship or problems.

In 1995 and 1996, and sometimes even after the start of privatisation in 1997–8, we continued to be amazed at the attitude of certain former Soviet functionaries (sovkhoz and party leaders and oblast government officials), who, in spite of the civil war and the dissolution of the Soviet Union, still regarded the crisis as an 'industrial accident' and not as a completely new, irreversible situation. They were the ones who fiercely resisted privatisation of land and the dissolution of the sovkhozes (see pp. 301–311). Clearly they did not understand that state-run concerns had previously been viable only because they were heavily subsidised. 'Who is supposed to supply the hospitals with food in future?' and 'where are people supposed to find work?' were frequently repeated questions. Might it be that even the elite regional leaders of the Soviet system had been kept in the dark over the financial structure of the economy?

Some of the older men made interesting remarks. They thought that the crisis was God's way of punishing them for men's mistakes: 'He punished them because they had lived peacefully for 70 years without needing God, and therefore had forgotten Him.' People had even ended up throwing bread away, into the bin, or onto the streets. That was why God was punishing the people.

In GBAO in the first few years after 1991 nothing much changed in the political system. Widespread participation in the political process only became common with the arrival of reconstruction aid from the mid-1990s onwards. Oblast and rayon administrative authorities continued in office, working in more or less close cooperation with the elected councils. These still bore the name of 'Soviet' and were still the place where old-style functionaries had a seat. However, people expected little or nothing of the administrative authorities or of the councils, as their complete lack of financial means was plain for all to see. The administrative authorities also lacked authority because they had only restricted powers to act. The real decisions were made in the villages by the local authorities, which initially included the old establishment (that is primarily sovkhoz managers). They were joined in ever-greater numbers by traditional sources of authority such as the *khalifa* and also by respected experts, amongst whom were many young people, for example engineers who were able to keep the irrigation system working or economists who were able to give good advice on land management.

9

INTERNATIONAL DEVELOPMENT AID

On the basis of the level of support from Western donors per head of population, GBAO is today the most favoured oblast in Tajikistan.[1] There are three historic reasons for this. First, of all the oblasts, GBAO suffered the most from the effects of the war of 1992/3, although there was no actual war damage. Second, with the exception of the city of Dushanbe, it was the administrative region in Tajikistan least capable of producing its own food. Third, GBAO was completely cut off from the rest of Tajikistan after the road to Gharm had been destroyed, and it would not have survived without outside aid.

During the civil war in 1993, the government in Dushanbe allocated GBAO less than 10 per cent of the amount of food required. In 1994 it supplied less than 25 per cent, based on a theoretical amount calculated according to the type of product (basic food, fuel, spare parts, etc.). Until the middle of 1995, national government in fact only provided 3 per cent of the wheat-flour requirement and less than 2 per cent of the cooking oil, although in 1994 and 1995 the region was still only producing 20 per cent of its own food. This resulted in a shortfall of more than 75 per cent, which could only be made good by external aid.

The level of national support given today is almost as low as it was in the first few years after the civil war. The government in Dushanbe has certainly not begun to consider that GBAO should be given priority in the distribution of national resources. It is likely that traditional enmities between Sunnis and Shiite Ismailis (see pp. 221–223) are the cause of this state of affairs, because even after the peace agreement of 1997/8 mutually hostile attitudes persist. However, it is also a well-known fact that successful intervention of foreign donor organisations relieves a national government of its own responsibilities. In the case of Tajikistan, it is definitely worth questioning the attitude of the government in office to development.

Today, production of food has reached a record level of 80 per cent self-sufficiency, which is a radical improvement on the situation of 1992/3.[2] In 1997 it was still being stated unequivocally that the upper limit for self-sufficiency in GBAO would be 40 per cent. The current percentage rate realistically sets a limit which can only be increased in very small stages. In years of drought, self-sufficiency may even drop to below 80 per cent. This means that GBAO will continue to rely on external aid if it does not succeed in developing any other sectors apart from agriculture. However, these would have to be economically important enough to not only compensate for the underproduction of food but also to ensure that the standard of living of the population rises above mere subsistence level in the medium term.

The Humanitarian Assistance Programme of the Aga Khan Foundation[3]

The organisation of the programme

According to Kreutzmann, famine in the Pamirs was officially acknowledged for the first time in January 1993 (1996: 185). However, by September and October 1992 AKF workers had already arrived in GBAO, at the request of the imamate, to assess the needs of the population and to work out what kind of aid programme would be required. Initially only 48,000 people were classified as especially needy; this was because all the consequences of the civil war had not yet become evident, in particular the effects of people fleeing their homes, and the fact that GBAO had been completely cut off from supplies in Dushanbe. However, it soon became clear that the entire population of 242,000 – at that time including up to 55,000 refugees – was in immediate or imminent need of aid.

With the support of international donors such as US-AID, the EC, the Swiss government and other organisations, US3 million were made available in January 1993 and in March the first humanitarian assistance was sent to GBAO (see AKDI 1994/5: 3). In 1993 a total of 1,500 tonnes of wheat was sent. The Pamiris founded an aid organisation, the Pamir Relief Programme, with logistical help from the AKF, and in September 1993 this was registered as an NGO (non-governmental organisation) called the Pamir Relief and Development Programme (PRDP).[4] The donors assigned two international experts to coordinate emergency aid for the PRDP.

In 1994 the PRDP was given additional support through the World Food Programme and with funds from TACIS (the EU emergency aid programme for Asia). As a result of the increase in funds, in 1994 the population of GBAO was provided with around 11,375 tonnes of wheat flour, 1,135 tonnes of butterfat, 870 tonnes of powdered milk, 200 tonnes of rice, 40 tonnes of tea and 105 tonnes of soap. In the same year, the agricultural support programme for GBAO began with the aim of increasing production of cereals, fruit and vegetables in the Pamir region. Other aims were to improve livestock farming and to find other sources of employment and income.[5] A secondary aim was to support private production, but in 1994 this played only a minor part (see pp. 306–311). In 1996 the amount of humanitarian aid had reached its highest level of 22,000 tonnes of wheat flour and grain. In 1997, as local production was now increasing, this dropped to 19,500 tonnes. In 2001 only 4,000 tonnes were necessary, as by then 90 per cent of agricultural land in GBAO was in private hands.

In 1995 Germany became one of the most important donor countries. It took part in the Humanitarian Assistance Programme (HAP) until 2003 and contributed the largest amount of support to the agricultural programmes of the PRDP. In the six years up until 2000, almost DM22 million (in 2004 about US$14 million were donated through the German GTZ. After the USA, Germany is the second largest donor to the AFK programme in GBAO. A follow-up programme is still in operation and has been extended to the Gharm valley and to projects in Kyrgyzstan and Afghanistan. In May 1995, the author and a colleague carried out an assessment of the project for the German GTZ, and from 1996 to 1998 introduced the first measures to monitor and evaluate its impact (M&E).

Other donors, some of whom continue to support the current measures, are various Ismaili communities throughout the world, the World Bank (Tajikistan Social Investment Fund) and governmental and non-governmental organisations from Norway, the Netherlands (NOVIB) and Canada (CIDA). In the first years about 80 per cent of the aid was used for humanitarian support, 10 per cent for agricultural development and 10 per cent for health, education and infrastructure projects, and also the promotion of community projects at village level.

In Osh (Ferghâna valley, Kyrgyzstan), a base was set up for the organisation of the Humanitarian Assistance Programme. For supplies to GBAO, Osh is the end of the railway line linking Western Europe, via the old Soviet network, to central Asia. It was here that aid arrived, which was then either delivered by the donor nations and organisations themselves, or bought on the open market as cheaply as possible with the funds made available. The donors offered aid in different ways: the USA in particular sent its own agricultural surpluses (especially wheat flour and soya oil), while EU countries sent money and also sent stockpiled food surpluses (e.g. butterfat from Germany).

The 750-km-long stretch of road from Osh across the Alai passes and the Pamir highlands, including passes of up to 4,655 m, had to be covered by lorry. In central Asia lorries are traditionally fairly small, and although they are sturdy and do the job well they only take a small load. For 1,000 tonnes of wheat flour about 200 lorries were needed; that is, 2,275 trips were needed just to deliver supplies for the whole of 1994. In addition, hundreds of lorries were needed for the rest of the food supplies and also for emergency heating fuel supplies for the Murghâb. We estimated that in order to carry out the entire HAP, up to 5,000 lorry loads had to be transported annually between Osh and the Pamirs between 1995 and 1998. The problems encountered on the road between Osh and Khorog have already been referred to. When it snowed, the lorries would often be stuck on the passes for days on end. As many as ten road checks were carried out by the Kyrgyz police and the CIS border troops, thus wasting a great deal of time. The logistical achievements of the PRDP in providing a smooth delivery service, without costly extra storage being required en route, are therefore all the more admirable.

In Khorog, the supplies were sent directly to the rayon centres and from there to the distribution points, without being reloaded or stored. Supplying the villages on the main road network was quite easy. Local PRDP workers took delivery of the humanitarian assistance and distributed it according to the lists of villages (Plate 9.1). In principle this system also worked in winter, but, as is already known, many villages in the Western Pamirs can only be reached using tracks which in winter are impassable for months on end. Between 1993 and 1998 there were additional problems (some of which still exist today): bridges became impassable, tracks were blocked by mudslides, rock fall or landslides, or, as was the case in the Bartang valley, were undermined by the river and collapsed. In these instances, the main HAP had to be supplemented by emergency measures to rebuild the infrastructure (Plate 9.2). If our information is correct, between 1995 and 2003 more than a hundred bridges of varying sizes were repaired from PRDP funds. It is not known how many times damaged roads had to be repaired.

We benefited from one of these unrecorded operations in June 2003, when we were held up between Basîd and Shadûd on the way back from Roshorve, where a part of the road had fallen into the river. The men had been working for several hours trying to widen the track on the side next to the slope, and making only slow progress, when by chance a Caterpillar arrived on the other side. It was actually supposed to be levelling a piece of ground near Basîd for the MSDSP. Even with the aid of the Caterpillar it took a further two hours until the track had been widened by just 3 metres. The nearest Caterpillar otherwise available would have been in Roshan, and if this one had not fortuitously arrived we would have had to leave our Jeep and walk the last 60 km to the main road; furthermore, the whole of the upper Bartang valley, where there are approximately twenty villages, would have remained closed to vehicles for days.

It was often impossible to bring the humanitarian assistance to remote settlements in the Bartang valley or into the side valleys of the Gund or the Shakhdara, even with the best will in the world. Those receiving the aid simply had to fetch their allocation of sacks and tins by donkey, or if they had none, then carry them home on their backs. In one case we gave a lift to a man who intended to carry a 50 kg sack of wheat flour for 14 km back to his village.

The content of the humanitarian assistance

The humanitarian assistance was vital for the local people right into the late 1990s. Many families would not have had enough money to emigrate from their remote valleys, and in any case the refugees from GBAO would probably not have been allowed to enter Kyrgyzstan even if they had somehow been able to get through the Murghâb. In spite of the aid, most people lived at subsistence level, especially if they were not able to grow garden produce. The most severely affected were the people who lived in the high-lying valleys where it was almost impossible to grow any produce, and where there was not enough livestock because of the shortage of fodder.

The situation in 1997 in Jelondî in the uppermost Gund valley (3,500 m) might have been extreme, but it was not the exception. Formerly the village had been a supplies station with a large workshop, and had also run a sanatorium based on

Plate 9.1 Food aid store in the Gund valley. In the first phase of the PRDP/MSDSP, support was mainly focused on food aid that was supplied to all inhabitants of GBAO. Later, food aid was complemented by reconstruction and development aid (1998).

Plate 9.2 In 1997 and later, rehabilitation of infrastructure became more important so as to ensure basic communication (2003).

its hot springs. No wages had been paid since 1993 and there was no other source of income. In November in Jelondî we found virtually no heating fuel, apart from some peat. There was no longer any electricity, as the villages had been cut off in winter, and for several years it had also been impossible to replace broken window panes and roof tiles. Unfortunately, most of the 48 families were not living in relatively well-insulated mud houses but in barrack-like, state-owned rented accommodation.

As the potato harvest had almost completely failed that summer, and the wheat crop had had to be harvested unripe and fed to the livestock at the onset of the cold weather, for days the people had only had bread to eat. Even tea had run out and in its place people were using herbs they had gathered. There had been no sugar for weeks. If the children, at least, had not been receiving modest amounts of supplementary rations through special aid programmes they too would have had nothing but bread to eat for weeks at a time.

In order to get an impression of PRDP food aid, the individual rations from 1993 to 1997 are given here: between August 1993 and November 1994 each person, depending on the rayon, received between 70 and 86 kg of wheat flour, 5.6 to 6.6 kg of cooking oil and 4.1 to 5.8 kg of powdered milk. In the following 13 months to December 1995, rations were slightly increased to between 92 to 105 kg of wheat flour, 2.3 to 2.6 kg of oil, 3.8 to 4.2 kg of powdered milk and 120 to 140 g of tea. In 1996 each person received 83 to 94 kg of wheat flour, 3.2 to 3.3 kg of lentils for the first time, 2.6 to 2.7 kg of oil, 13.6 to 14 kg of rice, 3.7 kg of sugar, 190 to 350 g of tea and 2.3 to 2.4 kg of powdered milk. In the eight months from January to August 1997, 56 to 63 kg of wheatflour, 9.2 to 6 kg of lentils, 1.9 to 2.6 kg of oil, 2.9 to 3.1 kg of sugar, and, for the first time, 4.2 to 4.6 kg of dried beans were handed out (see Bliss and Mamadsaid 1998a). Until 1997 these rations made up 90 per cent or more of the food supply for about a third of all households (with the exception of school supplies through the WFP). It is easy to work out how much each person received per day during that period.

The food situation only improved markedly in 1998 when the amount of wheat grown was doubled and the quantity of potatoes grown was trebled, even though the amount of aid per head was reduced slightly that year to about 60 kg.

Several donors carried out surveys on the state of the population's diet between 1996 and 2000. The first results were not encouraging. Although basic needs were largely met up until 1996/7, 3.5 per cent of the child population under 5 years of age was suffering from acute malnutrition and more than 40 per cent from chronic malnutrition. Anaemia among young mothers in the Pamirs, already evident before the crisis of 1992/3, had continued to increase.

Distribution of micronutrients was increased as a result of the initial findings of these surveys. However, it soon became obvious that external aid alone would not radically improve the situation, unless the people altered their dietary habits. Changes in agricultural practice – already mentioned – in favour of growing more fruit and especially more vegetables, were also essential if this were to happen, as was the actual consumption of fruit and vegetables.[6] Third, increased availability of sugar, salt and vinegar on the market from 1998 onwards, after an absence of several years, made it possible once more to preserve fruit and vegetables for the winter.

For the last ten-year period, an overall figure for the amount of food aid donated is still pending. Up until 2000, approximately US$112 million of emergency and development aid had been donated to the population of GBAO through the AKF. The value of the donated food alone exceeds that supplied by central government in Dushanbe by a factor of 19. By now up to two hundred people have worked for the PRDP/MSDSP locally in GBAO. Hundreds of volunteers in offices and in the villages have ensured a generally smooth distribution process. It cannot be repeated often enough that up until 2003 not a single person had complained to the author about irregularities in the distribution of aid.

Other sectors of humanitarian assistance and other donors

Even though the PRDP/MSDSP was, and indeed still is, easily the largest and most important aid programme in GBAO, the contribution of other organisations should not be overlooked. For example MSF France has been involved in the health sector since 1993/4, supplying the central hospital in Khorog and numerous local health centres with medicines and vaccine, as well as essential surgical instruments, up until 1998. Since 1994, the WFP has supplied about 50,000 schoolchildren with food (wheat flour, cooking oil and sugar), which was distributed by the IFRC.

After its first endeavours at delivering emergency aid, the AKF was forced to adapt its programme to suit the worsening conditions in the Pamirs during the course of 1993 and subsequently. Although they had initially only planned a food security programme, over the following months it became clear that almost the entire social infrastructure was in danger of collapse if no external support was forthcoming. The first emergency programme for schools in 1994 provided 4,000 square metres of glass to repair at least some of the windows in school buildings. Each of the approximately 50,000 schoolchildren in GBAO was given a pen and five exercise books, and 46,600 pairs of shoes and more than 19,000 items of clothing were distributed to pupils so that they would not have to stay at home during the spring and autumn because they had no shoes. (In the coldest months from December to February schools had to close anyway because there was no means of heating them.) Similar programmes were carried out from 1996 to 1998. The AKF also started to distribute new school textbooks, probably in 1997. Although these few thousand new textbooks represented a great step forward they were still only a drop in the ocean, and as late as 1998 most lessons were still being taught from Soviet textbooks.

In subsequent years other donors took part in programmes to refurbish schools and keep them running. Heating in winter is still a problem, solved in some villages by parents giving some of their meagre supply of fuel to their children to take to school with them. All the same, schools now have their own small budget, which enables them to buy at least some fuel for the winter.

The programme staff

The positive side of the transformation process in GBAO can be seen in the local people employed by the Aga Khan institutions. Almost all the employees – from managers to drivers – of the old PRDP and the subsequent MSDSP had received their training during the Soviet period. Some of the management had held top jobs under the old system, which meant that they knew virtually nothing about the kind of modern project management needed during such an emergency, the kind based on flexibility and personal responsibility. However, in an astonishingly short time, and with the support of only a few foreign consultants, an independent organisation has been built up which since 1995 has only occasionally required specialist help from outside. The only areas where external consultants are still employed today are those such as project monitoring, and also community participation and community-based self-organisation – neither of which formed part of the Soviet tradition.

One of the main reasons for the staff's rapid adaptation to the requirements of their task was the fact that the educated elite in GBAO had an explicit role in development. A second reason is the fact that the majority of employees are Ismailis and that the project is directly supported by the imamate, which is strongly motivating for the individual employee. A third reason is that although salaries are not high compared with those offered by other donors, they do guarantee some security for the families of employees. Fourth, one has to acknowledge that the former training of cadres in the Soviet Union did have its positive side. For example, it is well-known that planning was important at all levels in the organisation of the social system and that under the Soviet system improvisation skills were essential, even in good years.

Fifth, a reminder here of how proud the Pamiris are of their reputation for honesty. As we have already seen, this virtue was still alive and well during the crisis and was to play an important role in ensuring that valuable food was distributed fairly, whereas in other countries the distribution process would have invited extensive abuse of the system. We accompanied the PRDP/MSDSP for four years, and in all the villages we visited not once did anyone ever complain about misappropriation of aid.

However, the staff had one weakness, and this should be mentioned: initially there was little enthusiasm for letting the general population take any part in decision-making because in Soviet times there had been so little public participation. During the first phase of emergency aid this did not pose a problem as almost everyone agreed on what needed to be done first. Later on it became clear that supplies of aid would have been distributed differently if more of the population had been involved. The project team could also have been relieved of many tasks if participation at village level had been organised sooner and if it had been possible to decentralise the project earlier.

Agricultural development

The agricultural situation in GBAO at the beginning of the PRDP may be summarised as follows: from as far back as the end of the 1980s, cultivation of the 18,200 hectares of arable land available had been becoming steadily more extensive because of the lack of inputs in the form of fertiliser, irrigation, etc. In 1993/4 around 15,500 ha were still being irrigated. Wheat and potato yields fell because of a shortage of suitable seed or seed potatoes, whilst for years a large proportion of the agricultural land had been used to grow animal fodder rather than food. The shortage of spare parts meant that use of machinery increasingly had to be replaced by manual work, the irrigation system fell into disrepair and workers' motivation dropped sharply as they were not paid.

Target private land management

As a result of these circumstances, in 1993 the management of certain sovkhozes decided to allow the agricultural workers themselves to elect their brigade leaders, instead of leaving this to management as had been the case up until then. Moreover, land was to be leased to farmers, who would cultivate it independently and give some of the harvest as rent to the sovkhozes.[7] In 1994/5, this idea was taken up by the PRDP, whose objective was to support individual farmers only, not the sovkhozes. In 1993, however, a mere 83 hectares of land had been let, rising to 190 hectares in 1994 but representing only about 1 per cent of the available land. By 1995 the area of land that was more or less independently cultivated by farmers had risen to 491 ha. Independent cultivation of land might also include traditional cultivation by an *amtabaq*; that is, a group of neighbours working together. This kind of communal responsibility suited many farmers who had initially had grave doubts over assuming individual responsibility for the land. There were, for example, small groups of three people sharing two or three hectares, but there was also a larger group of 17 people, farming about 20 ha together.

However, in 1995 the whole concept of private land management started to fall into disrepute, following the disastrous harvest that year, because of the terms and conditions of the lease. When the farmers took over the fields they had had no idea of how much work was really involved and clearly had no idea either of how much yield to expect. In any case, they had accepted tenancy contracts which in any country under the rule of law would be described as 'immoral'. The sovkhoz did not demand a certain percentage of the harvest, but a fixed amount based on a norm set in Soviet times. In the first two cases of such tenancy agreements, one in Namadgut (Ishkashim) and one in Tusyan (Shakhdara), this amounted to 100 per cent of the norm, as it was expected that the farmers would actually produce more than the sovkhoz. In reality, the levy fixed under the tenancy agreement ended up being *de facto* 130 per cent of the actual harvest, as the norm set in GBAO during the Soviet period had not been achieved for a number of years.[8] On later investigation it turned out that the sovkhoz management itself had not regarded this norm as achievable.

With the support of the PRDP, the agreements were renegotiated in 1995 and it was decided that 30 per cent of the actual yield should go to the sovkhoz and 70 per cent to the farmers. On the basis of these now acceptable tenancy contracts, input arrangements were now made between the farmers and the PRDP. These did not fundamentally change until the end of the 1990s, although land-use agreements have been altered since then. Those farmers who had concluded a tenancy contract were allowed certain inputs from the project in the form of a loan (improved seeds, fertiliser, and sometimes fuel for tractors). The amount of input was calculated on the basis of the exact amount of land being farmed. Distribution was at first arranged through PRDP workers locally, but since 1996/7 through the farmers themselves who had to form user associations at village level.

The equivalent of the inputs had to be paid back in kind after the harvest (e.g. seed potatoes). In order to partially recoup marketing costs, and to prepare the farmers for the pressures of the financial market, 10 per cent of the value of the inputs was added to the repayment. Farmers who had concluded a favourable contract with their sovkhoz were allowed to use their tractors – if they were still working – at no cost, if they provided their own fuel, but others had to pay extra for this (also in kind). This system of inputs was to be replaced as quickly as possible by sales paid for in money. However, it turned out that most of the farmers were unable to grow enough to have surpluses for the market where they could have sold some of their produce, and therefore they received no cash payments. This meant that the PRDP/MSDSP had to continue with the system of repayment in kind for much longer than planned.

In 1995 another problem emerged which brought private land management further into disrepute. When land had first been allocated in Tusyan and Namadgut, it turned out that the sovkhozes had leased only the worst land to the farmers. Most of the fields were stony, some of them lay outside the village (Tusyan), and the water supply was not always adequate. If this sort of policy had continued it would have put off any farmer from taking the risk of going private. For that reason, fundamental changes in the tenancy system were worked out in negotiations with the oblast government of GBAO, with the aim of establishing a policy of essentially private land management. These changes were based on an older Tajik Land Reform Law from 1992, which had made private land management possible in principle.[9] It was only then that the so-called Agricultural Reform Programme of the PRDP became worthy of its name.

The Agricultural Reform Programme

The Agricultural Reform Programme (ARP) of the AKF and the PRDP had the aim of laying the long-term foundations for self-sufficiency in food production for the population of GBAO. Detailed aims were as follows:

1. To produce enough food, especially from privately run farms.
2. After an initial period, the farms were to produce their own seed, or buy locally produced seed from other farmers.
3. Livestock farming and grazing arrangements were to be incorporated more effectively into the farm's activities.
4. Conditions for marketing agricultural products were to be improved.
5. Democratic self-help organisations were to be created at village level.

In order to achieve these results, the AKF itself formulated four agricultural policy aims, which were to overhaul completely the land use system in its present form, and which would then be taken over by the PRDP:

1 To put decisions in the hands of the farmers.
2 To support the dilution of the sovkhoz system.
3 To rationalise land allocations.
4 To increase yields through the use of better agricultural technologies.

A timetable was agreed with the government of GBAO, with the interim aim of privatising 2,330 ha of land. The distribution of larger areas of land to farmers carried out in 1996 set into motion a cycle of improvement, expected by neither government nor sovkhozes, nor by the PRDP. (By the end of 1996 this was at least 1,400 ha, plus 377 ha of new land and 246 ha of leased land under the old terms and conditions 70 per cent: 30 per cent.) For the first time, farmers were given good land and were able to use the inputs from the PRDP efficiently, which then led to a clear rise in yields. Yields on sovkhoz land, deliberately left unimproved, dropped further for lack of inputs, emphasising the divide. In 1997, this in turn led to a further 1,220 to 1,460 ha of land being allocated to farmers and a further 246 ha being leased.

By the end of 1997 and the beginning of 1998, the sovkhozes had collapsed completely and any land they still owned was released for distribution. The PRDP policy was supported by the oblast government, whose members either actively supported privatisation after initial hesitation or were simply unable to halt this trend, in spite of some individuals' opposition. The president of the oblast was considered to be the strongest advocate of private agriculture. In addition, the rayon leaders, some of whom had previously rejected privatisation (e.g. in Ishkashim), came out in favour of change and even the dissolution of the sovkhozes. Even the managers of some state-run farms advocated privatisation, in view of the completely untenable state of their businesses.

By the end of 1998 approximately 7,000 more hectares had been handed over to farmers, making up a total of 10,500 ha under private management at that point. In the following years, with the exception of 1,500 ha, all agricultural land in GBAO, including new land, was distributed to farmers. In 2000, farmers took possession of roughly 16,500 ha. As there were around 19,000 ha of agricultural land actually in use in the Pamirs at that time (i.e. including land newly reclaimed with the support of the PRDP/MSDSP), this meant that 92.1 per cent of the land was then in private hands.

The term 'private' must be explained more fully in this context. In general, 'private land management' is what people refer to today in GBAO, rather than 'private land use', in order to emphasise that farmers were not given ownership of the land they now use, but only a kind of long-term lease. Even in 2004 the question remained open as to what exactly constitutes private land management. A high-level negotiation process is currently taking place in Dushanbe, with the participation of the World Bank, and this will probably continue for several years.

At the present time one can assume that, in GBAO at least, a kind of inheritable agricultural tenancy has evolved on former sovkhoz land. Farmers have the right to continuity of use of land allocated to them and rights of use may be handed down to heirs, but the land may not be handed over to a third party and may definitely not be sold. At the moment the farmers' only obligation is payment of a small amount of tax. The rules on this in GBAO are very different to those in other oblasts – for example, Khatlon where a farmer may be obliged to grow cotton on 90 per cent of 'his' land.

All the farmers we spoke to[10] had been unsure of the legal position until the end of the 1990s. Many of them worried that the government might reclaim the land. In other regions of Tajikistan this is a real and present threat, as even the World Bank has not yet succeeded in actually privatising the land, in spite of the investment of large sums of money into numerous projects. Many 'private' farmers (*dekhan*) in Khatlon[11] are now giving up because they are being economically stifled by contradictory regulations, prohibitive charges for water and electricity and being forced to grow certain crops (usually cotton).

In GBAO, however, the situation is fundamentally different because almost all sovkhozes here were dissolved.[12] This gives the new landowners a large degree of peace of mind, even though Land Reform Law No. 544 still makes it possible for land to be confiscated by the state under certain circumstances (where there are governmental needs, unsatisfactory efforts by the farmer, etc.; see Bliss 2004). One basic problem in the development of the country is the fact that land cannot be treated as bank and financial security, so that private farmers have no legal means of obtaining loans and advance finance using their land as surety (mortgage).

Land distribution

In GBAO the distribution of land from 1996 to 1998 through village community groups was, on the whole, carried out in an exemplary way, although it was not entirely without surprises. In Tusyan (Roshtkala) we observed the process in 1995/6: in the spring of 1996 all the land belonging to the sovkhoz – which was dissolved soon afterwards – was distributed amongst the families in the village, with everyone being given the same amount: 0.06 ha. Distribution of this land was carried out in spite of the results of a democratic vote, which by a small majority had voted in favour of *retaining* the sovkhoz: 148 men and women had voted for distribution, but 153 had voted against. On the basis of the vote, the final decision was taken by the president of the oblast himself, who came out in favour of distribution of the land as the sovkhoz of Tusyan was clearly in such a state of economic collapse that it was no longer salvageable.

As well as the land, the remaining assets of the sovkhoz were shared out amongst the 345 families in the village: around 100 tonnes of seed, 150 cattle and around 1,000 small ruminants. All the buildings remained in state hands until 1998 and were then sold, if they had not gone to ruin by then. The machinery was pooled; that is, handed over to the village for anyone's use. In practice, the former drivers took charge of the few remaining serviceable tractors and lorries, although they did not actually become their property.[13] If a farmer needed to use a particular implement he was required to provide the driver with enough fuel for the job to be done. Until 1998 this fuel was virtually only obtainable through the MSDSP input credit system, but subsequently it became available in small quantities on the open market. The driver was paid by work done on a reciprocal basis or by agricultural produce.

During the first year of private cultivation of the land, the former sovkhoz management attempted to persuade the farmers of Tusyan to hand over 10 per cent of the harvest to them, 'as they were still in office'. Our M&E team and other MSDSP workers told the farmers that it would be foolish to do so. However, people in Tusyan only began to be convinced of the advantages of private agriculture in the summer of 1996 after the harvest had been brought in. The wheat harvest per head of population came to about 55 kg, which was the first time such a large amount had been harvested. The Humanitarian Assistance Programme supplemented this amount by about 60 per cent. When we last questioned them on the matter in 1998, all of the people who had voted against privatisation at the beginning of 1996 were now in favour.

The members of each sovkhoz distributed the land in the way they thought fit. On the recommendation of the PRDP a committee of experienced men was usually formed (only occasionally did a woman take part), men who knew what types of soil were to be found on the sovkhoz land and what condition they were in. A *khalifa* was usually on the committee and also one or two *aksaqal* with personal authority (e.g. a veteran of the Second World War).

Where there was only one type of land use, and all the land was of the same quality, distribution was easy. Based on the number of people in the household, each family was given a plot of land situated as near as possible to their house. However, as there were usually at least three categories of land use – good arable land, irrigated land of poorer quality for animal fodder, and horticultural land or orchards – each family ended up being given at least three plots. Frequently there were different types of soil, meaning that individual families would have been at a disadvantage if they had only been given a plot of marginal land. For that reason arable land was subdivided, where appropriate, into classes I to III, and each family was given a portion of land from each class. Although it would have been simple, they did not allocate poorer land in larger shares to make up for poor quality, as they felt that unfairness might creep in. And so in many instances the fields were divided into ever-smaller units, which was not a problem in the medium term, as there was still a severe shortage of machinery, but would need a solution in the long term.

In practice there was still some unfairness, despite the efforts of the committee, and some individual farmers ended up getting only marginal land, notwithstanding the care taken in the distribution process. Such instances were, however, the exception, and on the whole there were few complaints. In practice it was smaller matters which posed more of a problem. In some villages, land was distributed so late in the year that it was too late to sow or plant anything. Many families did not have enough manpower to cultivate the land without machinery. In several places agricultural inputs arrived too late. In 1996 and 1997, the project was simply unable to cope with giving suitable advice on agricultural matters to the large number of first-time farmers. This meant that although improved seed was available, the correct methods were not always used, and follow-up care was either lacking or carried out wrongly. Subsequently, though, the problems encountered over these first two years were largely overcome.

The real problems of land distribution were of a more fundamental nature. One basic hindrance to agriculture was the small size of the fields distributed, which, depending on the region, worked out at between 0.3 and just under 1 hectare per family, averaging 0.5 ha (this is still the case today). In the first few years, most people wanted to grow cereal for bread, but on 0.5 ha this meant a maximum yield of 1 tonne of wheat, and even if yields increased dramatically this was far too little for an average family of seven or eight to live on. It was only in subsequent years that more potatoes and vegetables than wheat were grown, thus markedly improving the rate of self-sufficiency.

Many of the new landowners were not really experienced farmers, but teachers, doctors, sovkhoz administrators, etc. It had, however, been decided that everyone should be treated equally when the land was distributed, and that therefore all families living in the village at that time should have their share of land. Households without an able-bodied man, or those families whose members held other time-consuming jobs, were naturally not able to make the best use of their land.

There is also the fundamental question of whether it is part of a teacher's or doctor's job to earn his living as a farmer after carrying out a full day's work in his own profession.[14] However, there are examples from Kyrgyzstan which show that if land is only distributed to the families of former sovkhoz workers this results in a minority of households in a village becoming completely excluded and marginalised. For this reason, GBAO's policy of equal treatment is in principle correct,[15] although some questions have still not been answered: why should a teacher, for example, not be allowed to sub-let his land and increase his salary by the rent generated in this way? The teacher would then be able to concentrate on his job more effectively, and also larger units of land would be created, which could be cultivated more efficiently and profitably, especially when machinery once more becomes available.

It is a fact that land in GBAO and Tajikistan has not yet been totally privatised, which makes selling the land impossible. This situation is sometimes criticised in the West, but it offers effective protection of the base on which the people's long-term security is built, as in emergency situations too many families are prone to be duped by con-men and speculators.

Agricultural extension activities

The regular supply of most agricultural inputs through the PRDP since 1995 must be viewed as an extraordinary logistical achievement. Moreover, it has not yet proved possible to adapt simple solutions from other countries to suit agricultural practices in the Pamirs, therefore trials and tests have to be carried out in order to ascertain which new varieties can or cannot be grown. The first step taken was detailed stocktaking of these inputs in order to find out what was needed. The PRDP decided to sort out the most pressing requirements first of all, and to put on hold the matter of fuel and maintenance of machinery. In 1995 and in the following years, the most urgent needs were to provide the farmers with improved seed and a minimum of fertiliser, after five years of shortages.

In the first two years, most of the seed was imported, but the logistics for local production were also worked out. However, tests had to be carried out in order to establish which varieties would grow at heights ranging between 1,700 m in Darwâs and over 3,300 m in Javshangoz. The experiences of a previous AKF project in the high-lying valleys of north Pakistan were called upon and a qualified international agrarian consultant accompanied each series of the PRDP tests on site. These were very time-consuming, as a total of 16 different kinds of potatoes had to be trialled in 1996 and 1997 in order finally to identify the two most suitable varieties. Seed potatoes were then produced in two ways. First, land was rented by the project in the Alai,[16] where workers were paid to produce seed potatoes. Second, the production of seed potatoes was encouraged by the input system itself. By paying off their debts in kind (i.e. in seed), local seed suited to the climate was produced at minimal costs.

The PRDP did not use fields of its own for seed trials in the Pamirs. Instead, it carried out trials with individual farmers, who acted as advice centres for other farmers in a village. This type of agrarian research and guidance had previously been successfully carried out in Pakistan. The advantage is obvious: by giving detailed guidance to a few farmers only a small number of staff are required to train them to disseminate the information, so that they can then instruct the bulk of farmers. In this way the project even has some spare capacity, so that the staff's additional expertise can be called on in special cases – for example, plant protection.

From 1997 onwards, organising competitions with prizes at rayon level became one means of increasing production. With the additional incentive of winning 50 or 100 US dollars, or free inputs, the harvest increased to 3 tonnes of wheat per hectare in some of the fields in high-lying Roshorve in 1997, after a long-running average of only 1 tonne. In Porshnev in 1997 we saw the first potatoes being harvested in a field used in the competition. Until then they had harvested between 9 and 12 tonnes per hectare, but now the women were digging up this amount from only 1,000 square metres – admittedly using new seed potatoes for the first time. There were shouts of amazement and disbelief at each potato they dug up, many of which weighed more than 500 g (see Plate 4.8).

Altogether, the supply of inputs in GBAO helped increase the average yield of wheat from 0.9 to 1.77 tonnes/ha and that of potatoes from 8–9 tonnes/ha to 16.7 t/ha between 1995 and 1997. Per unit of land the yield had, therefore, been almost doubled. There are no comparative figures for vegetables, but in 1997 the average yield was 22.3 tonnes per hectare. However, it was years before many of the farmers became convinced of the need to grow large quantities of vegetables.

Today, probably 50 per cent of agricultural surpluses are due to this change in attitude, and the ample supplies which we saw on the market in Khorog during our last visit in June and September 2004 are testament to this successful change of heart.

In conclusion, some figures on the level of inputs supplied through the PRDP: in 1996 a total of 200 tonnes of seeds and seed potatoes were supplied, and also more than 630 tonnes of various fertilisers. As it was too late to use some of the fertiliser in the 1996 growing season, 'only' 450 tonnes were supplied in 1997, but also 540 tonnes of seed and seed potatoes. This meant that the farmers were supplied with only 4 tonnes of fuel in 1996, but 60 tonnes in 1997. Conditions of transport for agricultural inputs as well as for other goods need to be borne in mind at this point: for all the inputs in 1997 at least 200 lorries were needed. The farmers had to carry these inputs home or out to the fields themselves, in the same way as they had done with the humanitarian assistance, in some cases for kilometres at a time on their backs.

The number of partners making input contracts with the PRDP stood at 4,800 in 1997 and rose to more than 9,600 by 1998. As this number was set to increase further, they decided to found Village Organisations (VO) in 1998, which would be responsible for distribution and repayment of inputs. These VO were created as a local NGO, and were to act as an associate of the PRDP/MSDSP, representing hundreds of farmers (see pp. 318–320).

Land reclamation and construction of irrigation channels

A land reclamation component to the PRDP project was planned early on, consisting of building new irrigation channels, which were to increase the level of self-sufficiency by a horizontal development of the land, running in tandem with its vertical development. In 1994/5 the creation of new agricultural land was given priority, as no one in the PRDP or amongst the international donors expected the speedy privatisation of sovkhoz land. It was thought that farmers could be given their own land sooner if it did not involve having to take land away from the state-run farms.

The land reclamation component was carried out in two phases.[17] In the first phase, operating until 2000, the construction of 32 new channels with a total length of 220 km was planned. Five projects of this kind were to be carried out in Darwâs, two in Wandsh, 11 in Roshân, three in Shugnân, nine in Roshtkala and two in Ishkashim. Twenty-five of these projects were started in 1995 with groups of local volunteers comprising people interested in the new land (Plate 9.3). The PRDP gave working parties technical help and materials, and they also sometimes contributed to their food. They supplied about 27 tonnes of cement, more than 15 tonnes of explosives, 18 tonnes of fuel, hundreds of metres of pipe and 7.5 tonnes of wheat flour. In 1996 almost 110 km of channels were completed using these materials. In the same year, about 100 km of existing, damaged channels were

Plate 9.3 Volunteers from Roshorve (Bartang) digging a 3-km trench on an extremely difficult slope in order to build a new water supply canal (1997).

repaired as part of a food-for-work programme. The channel-building programme was to provide an additional 325 ha of new land in 1997, and more than 600 ha in 1998.

Altogether, around 4,000 hectares of potential new land were identified in GBAO, but only a small proportion of this could be developed easily. This meant that the channels built in 1996 only resulted in 215 ha being developed. Although an additional 40 km of channels were completed in 1997, only about 130 ha of land were actually developed. Repairing existing channels proved to be much more successful: in 1997 64 km of restored channels enabled 281 ha of land to be recovered, and in 1998 this increased to 880 ha of land from approximately 120 km of channels.

As the channel-building programme did not completely reach its targets, a second phase was introduced, with 67 projects planned altogether, totalling 875 km of channel and about 3,300 ha of new land by 2002. The target figures were again not reached, mainly because the largest of the projects, the channel in Roshorve (Bartang) which was to irrigate up to 1,000 ha of new land had still not been completed by mid-2003.

This channel may be used as an example to explain the difficulties of constructing irrigation channels. As already mentioned in Chapter 4 (pp. 125–129), even in modern agriculture the irrigation system is based on gravity; that is, the water has to start from an elevated position and run downhill to the fields using the natural gradient. Glacial streams are suitable sources of water, usually running right through the alluvial fan on which the cultivated land is to be found. However, the streams are often too small and periodically dry up, so that streams in neighbouring valleys have to be drawn on as well.

In the case of Roshorve, where the agricultural land lies on a high plateau (3,000–3,150 m), the only possible intake for a new channel was a very fast-flowing stream about 3 kilometres away, which channelled the melt waters of the Pic Revolutija into the Bartang. However, almost the entire stretch between the high plateau of Roshorve and this stream consists of steep scree slopes or rock faces. In order to build an irrigation channel providing more than 10,000 cubic metres of water per day, a channel had to be dug along the slope and blasted out with explosives, which turned out to be extremely difficult. Instead of the estimated two years of construction it has already taken seven years. The work was supposed to be finished by the end of 2003 and the water was to start flowing in 2004. By June 2003 the work had at least made enough progress for some of the pipes to have already been delivered.

At least twenty men were always at work on the site, often in two or three shifts a day and sometimes with the additional help of a Caterpillar. They worked for at least six months of the year. Hundreds of metres of channel had to be blasted out of the rocks with dynamite. The 3- to 4-metre-wide channel line was situated about 800 m above the valley floor, and working up there was extremely dangerous. To the left was a slope or rock face, to the right a very steep scree slope descended for half a kilometre, with a final vertical drop in the rock face of several hundred metres. In spite of all the care taken by the Pamiris and all their experience in the mountains, two people have already fallen to their death during construction work. Clearly a high price will have been paid for this channel by the time it is finally finished.

Only the first stage of land reclamation has been completed once the principal channels have been laid. At this stage, arable land is not usually yet ready for cultivation. First of all it must be levelled, stones must be removed and if necessary it must be terraced. Very little terracing has been carried out up until now, but even simple bulldozing and levelling pose a problem because of the shortage of heavy plant. Finally the actual irrigation system has to be laid; that is, the delivery channels, branching off from the principal channel. Until now, little importance has been accorded to how these smaller channels are laid.

From a present-day point of view, some shortcomings do show up in the conception and implementation of the new land programme. On the one hand, the basic premise that new land was absolutely necessary to encourage privatisation turned out to be false. In reality almost all sovkhoz land was privatised at the same time as the first channel-building programme started. On the other hand, the estimates were right in stating that the amount of land already in use would be inadequate to ensure self-sufficiency however much production was increased, and that therefore more land would have to be developed. However, it became clear that repairing existing channels produced much speedier results, with almost as much new land being developed in the first few years using this method as by building new channels. What they did not realise at all was that more effective use of existing water resources would have been the most efficient way of increasing the amount of new land in use.

Our investigations in 2003 for the most part confirmed the conclusions we had come to between 1995 and 1998 that most farmers in GBAO still do not have sufficient knowledge of irrigation systems, in spite of the long-standing tradition of irrigation in the Pamirs. That is why in some regions an estimated 50–70 per cent of the water is wasted because the channels were not laid properly, are damaged, or the farmers do not even possess the basic technological skills required to extract water from a channel and irrigate fields.

In Roshorve, the place where lives were sacrificed and so much time and effort were invested into its hopefully now completed irrigation channel, they could eventually only irrigate about 110 to 130 ha of the 300 ha available 'because there was not enough water'. However, one glance at the network of delivery channels shows that they made every mistake that it is possible to make in an irrigation system: no consistent differentiation between principal channels and delivery channels, poor foundations to the channels, no use of insulating material, no offtake regulators attached, etc.

As a consequence, water leaks out of the channels everywhere and drains away unused underground. Here in Roshorve, and in other places in GBAO, faults in the irrigation system are continued on the fields and in the checks. Many fields are not levelled. Instead of laying irrigation furrows horizontally one above the other, following the contour lines, these furrows often run directly downhill from the delivery channel. The result is that the water does not stay on the fields but flows off immediately, without being put to any use. In the process huge quantities of topsoil are washed off the fields. If our estimates of more than 50 per cent water loss are correct, the amount of arable land in Roshorve could have been doubled without building any new channels if the water management system had been better. More support for the irrigation system in GBAO would certainly be a useful contribution to further agricultural development (see pp. 340–341).

Other economic and welfare activities

Even after 2000, the MSDSP contributed to the maintenance of much of the transport infrastructure. They repaired 26 bridges or stretches of road, in many cases ensuring access to entire valleys. The World Bank is now heavily involved in such projects and the oblast government also receives funds for the maintenance of the infrastructure. Yet the general condition of the roads and bridges is no better today than in 1993, as there are no funds available for basic reconstruction of asphalted roads or even for building new ones. This is particularly true of the main roads to Dushanbe via Gharm and Kulyab, which are in a very poor condition.

Individual food-for-work projects were set up from 1996 to 1998 and in the years afterwards. These involved groups of village workers being given food and building materials in exchange for renovating and refurbishing public buildings such as schools and hospitals and other parts of the local infrastructure. The building or repair of irrigation channels was also included, with each worker being given 0.5 kg of wheat flour per day. In 1996 around 7.5 tonnes of flour were supplied, rising in 1997 to almost 18 tonnes and in 1998 to more than 110 tonnes. From 1997 each person received 1.5 kg of flour per day.[18] Typical projects included the renovation of the small hospital of Vîr in Shugnân, the renovation of numerous schools and village health posts, the repair of roads and bridges, the repair of electrical power-lines, and afforestation.

Food-for-work only makes sense as long as there is no flour to be bought on the market. Once this is no longer the case, it is better for everyone if work is remunerated with money. For this reason the PRDP early on deliberately supported the monetisation of wheat-flour supplies, which was a courageous step, even though the costs, unfortunately, are not always shared by the WFP.

Many other social infrastructure projects set up by the MSDSP were continued, though not as food-for-work schemes: between 2000 and 2003, 91 medical centres, 48 schools and 89 drinking water or sewage treatment plants were built or renovated.

In 1997 the first small-scale hydroelectric project was set up, with the aim of improving power supplies. By 2002, 24 of these only moderately successful small-scale projects had been set up, supplying a total of just 1,900 kW. The main reason for the limited success of these micro-hydroelectric power plants is the problem of the water supply. Many of the streams are only seasonal, and in winter especially the flow of water drops sharply at a time when demand for electricity is at its highest. The huge variation in the supply of water has also led to some parts of the system being damaged when the streams are in spate.

The social consequences of building micro-hydroelectric power plants had not been considered at all. In 1997/8, the notability of two villages, who were utterly obsessed with the principle of equality, levied a charge on all households in order to pay the contribution required from the village. All households had to take part and pay their share. Those who had no money had to pay with food from their small supply of humanitarian assistance. This was one of the few instances in which the Pamiris' otherwise praiseworthy principle of equality was put to wrong purpose.

The so-called 'Pamir Private Power Project', negotiated in July 2002, should make a much greater contribution to improving electricity supplies in GBAO. The IFC, together with AKFED and IDA, is financing the operation and management of existing electricity production, and also transmission and distribution systems in the Pamirs. IFC financing will also be used to complete the construction of Pamir I, a partially completed, but operational hydroelectric power station, presently producing 14 MW and with a design capacity of 28 MW (World Bank 2003: 12). The aim of the project is to privatise electricity supplies in the Pamirs, and to increase capacity in order to meet the needs of the population. The success of this project will depend on whether an impoverished population can be given enough support to be able to afford at least a basic supply of electricity. The existing Tajik welfare system is totally inadequate in this respect (see Bliss 2003).

Last, here is a list of supporting measures taken by the AKDN, which made a significant contribution to the economic reconstruction work of the MSDSP:

1 The Education Reform Programme, which is involved in working with primary teachers, and with secondary language teachers, supporting curriculum enrichment, developing a health education curriculum, increasing community involvement in education, renovating school infrastructure, and promoting key education institutions.
2 The Health Reform Programme, which is involved in rationalising pharmaceutical policy and management, reproductive health and post-natal survival, support to hospitals, and health sector reforms.
3 A programme for promoting integrated rural development in Tajikistan, which covers the same measures taken by the MSDSP on agricultural reform in GBAO, but which also supports the development of small enterprises and the promotion of community organisations and associations for economic development.

(see AKDN 2003a)

Communal development

In 1997, GBAO was composed of the seven rayons already referred to and the capital, Khorog, 44 sub-districts (*jamoat*), 302 villages and a total of nearly 500 hamlets.[19] Heading the oblast government was the president of the oblast and a group of senior officials, who could be described as secretary of state, or out of courtesy as 'minister'. Khorog had a mayor, but the rayons were administered by a district officer, likewise called president (also called *raîs*, or chief), and each sub-district by a sub-district officer. District administration in GBAO, as in the whole of Tajikistan, is called *hukumât*, the elected council *majlis*. Below the level of sub-district there are villages (*kishlak*) and in the rayon centres so-called *mahallas*, subsectors or wards. However, since 1991 there has been virtually no state-run administration at this level.

From 1992/3, although still officially in office, these Tajik administrative institutions were almost entirely without funds, and therefore could not function properly. Once the PRDP/MSDSP started implementing the Agricultural Reform Programme in addition to the HAP, and ran numerous infrastructure projects on its own, the administrative institutions became mere bystanders, although the PRDP/MSDSP still valued a close exchange of information with state authorities.[20] On the other hand, as already described, the number of tasks carried out by the PRDP/MSDSP had increased so greatly that it was no longer possible to cover all the work done in the villages with existing or affordable staff. The lack of decision-makers, and thus partners in the project, became noticeable at village level – for example, when preparations were being made towards taking independent decisions and passing resolutions.

For that reason, in 1997/8 village self-help organisations (Village Organisations, VO) were set up, which were to take over general village administrative tasks as well as project tasks. With the guidance of the MSDSP, village chiefs (*raîs kishlak*) were elected for the first time by the population, whereas previously they had been chosen by the government and were therefore largely ignored by the people. These elections were carried out informally and were largely accepted by political leaders. The only instance in which tensions surfaced was in Wandsh in 1997 because the rayon chief did not accept the elections and wanted to install former functionaries instead. However, by 1998 there were democratically elected village chiefs here in Wandsh as well. At first most of those elected were teachers, but subsequently successful farmers were often elected.

As well as a chief and often a deputy, most villages elected a small group of people to form a kind of village council, whose work was not formally regulated and therefore was carried out on an informal basis. The MSDSP also formed groups of farmers at village or hamlet level, also *de jure* informally, who were to organise the distribution of inputs supplied by the project. These groups elected a chairman to represent the farmers' interests to the project.

The representatives of the village councils and farmers' groups in the villages we visited in 1997/8 were finding it difficult to differentiate between the functions of these two organisations. That is evidently the reason why they were later amalgamated into one unified structure and given the name of Village Organisation (VO), which is the only way they are now referred to by the MSDSP. On our last visit in June 2003 there were more than 450 such VOs and there was already a plan to amalgamate the VOs at *jamoat* and rayon level with their own committees so that certain issues would only have to be negotiated with representatives at that level. At present, the VOs have about 55,000 members, 49 per cent of whom are women. It is assumed that over 90 per cent of all rural households are represented in the VOs.

The VOs are not just grass-roots organisations set up by the project, but are village councils which discuss public development schemes in a village, plan and make decisions on them and oversee their execution. Subjects considered include the running of schools and health centres, maintenance of roads and bridges, running and maintenance of youth clubs, food and agriculture, energy supply, afforestation, finance and credit, activities to promote the VO itself, etc. The quality of the work done by each of these relatively new VOs is, however, very variable.

For the present, the VOs as community planning councils continue to be entirely informal in character: that is, they are bodies convened *ad hoc* to discuss specific projects and so far do not have any foundation in the Tajik community constitutional framework. It may be noted, however, that comparable structures are set up in the context of development aid almost everywhere in the world and are often very successful. Problems might occur if legal structures were ever set up below the *jamoat* (sub-districts) at village level. Although the VOs are to a great extent legitimised by their wide membership and public elections, their relationship to any official mayor and village council created in the future will have to be clarified. Two parallel structures at village level should certainly be avoided.

The question of the parallel structure of project and state bodies must also be posed in relation to the constitutional *jamoats*, rayons and indeed the oblast administration. Since 1992 the policy-making and advisory functions of the GBAO government have been almost totally lost. Although the PRDP/MSDSP stressed the aim of encouraging the government to resume taking responsibility for the various policy sectors right from the start, this has proved difficult to put into practice. After all, until 2000 and in some sectors even now, development aid and not the government has provided practically all the funds and resources arriving in GBAO. A certain degree of frustration has clearly surfaced amongst government civil servants; however, this is not restricted to GBAO. The complaints most often heard are to do with government employees' poor working conditions, lack of incentives and also legislation which has not addressed political and economic realities (see Breu and Hurni 2003: 59).

Although only a registered NGO, an organisation such as the PRDP/MSDSP combined material aid with political ideas, which were then successfully implemented, one example being the Agriculture Reform Programme. Sometimes great pressure was exerted in order to carry out the reforms, as was the case when aid was given only to private individual farmers not to the sovkhozes. In this particular case it was clearly legitimate, as state-run farms were not economically viable – indeed, they were at the core of the problem of under-production of food in GBAO. However, Tajikistan's sovereignty and administration might well be affected by the implementation of other possible policies (e.g. an unrestricted and total privatisation of land). How far a development aid organisation should be allowed to go in implementing its own policies therefore has to be carefully considered. It is time to let state administration, and above all political organisations (oblast assembly and rayon assemblies), participate more in decision-making, in the way that the local population participates in the VOs.

The programme's impact on agriculture, productivity and diet

It is interesting to speculate on whether land reform would have been carried out in GBAO without the intervention of the PRDP/MSDSP. In Khatlon oblast this has still not really been implemented. The number of private farmers (*dekhan farmers*) in most of the rayons there can be counted on the fingers of two hands, and in Beshkent, for example, there is not a single one (see Bliss 2003). However, cotton is grown in Khatlon and cotton production is a profitable business, even though most of the sovkhozes in Khatlon are heavily in debt. This is one case where privatisation has not been necessary and that is the reason why it has not yet been carried out, despite pressure from Western donors. (The negative consequences for the population are described in Bliss 2004 and 2005.)

It is more fruitful to make a comparison with the Gharm area, which resembles GBAO structurally in many respects, although Gharm has more arable land in relation to the size of the population. The sovkhozes here have been bankrupt, without exception, for many years. Agricultural yields here are low and the fields and vegetable gardens seem to be in very poor order and not used efficiently.[21] Despite this fact, privatisation of land has only just started. As in GBAO, action of this kind is only being taken thanks to the intervention of the MSDSP, which for some time has been trying to extend the kind of work done in the Pamirs to the neighbouring Gharm valley.

These two examples show clearly that it is highly unlikely there would have been such large-scale, or indeed any, privatisation of agricultural land in GBAO from 1995 onwards without the involvement of the AKF, the PRDP/MSDSP and international donors. If agriculture had not been so comprehensively supported by inputs, the increase in production already referred to would never have been achieved and the level of self-sufficiency would have remained on the whole the same as in the years from 1993 to 1995. Today it is impossible to tell whether the government in Dushanbe would have provided the Pamirs with more inputs than they did if there had been no intervention by the PRDP. However, the fact remains that their contribution would have been much less than that actually made by the PRDP. We know, for example, that as a result of agricultural practices in Khatlon and Khodjand – the oblasts closest to the government – supplies there were almost entirely discontinued in 1993.

The World Bank arranged to carry out an external assessment of the success of the MSDSP's agricultural programme. Their 'Poverty Assessment 2000' makes clear that 'In contrast to the process throughout most of the country, nearly all land in GBAO was distributed to individual families during the period 1995 to 1999. With support for input provision . . . this agriculturally disadvantaged region has moved from being 15 percent self-sufficient in wheat in 1995 to a projected 80 percent self-sufficiency in 1999' (2000a: 61).

A new study shows some differentiation in the figures on the drop in the food deficit. According to this study, there was a 65 per cent drop in the food deficit in 1997, which then dropped to 40 per cent in 1998 and to only 22 per cent in 1999. The droughts of 2000 and 2001 throughout Tajikistan caused the figure to rise to 32 per cent and 31 per cent respectively (see Breu and Hurni 2003: 20). It will only be possible to keep the deficit at a level of 30 per cent if the population of GBAO does not continue to rise.

The World Bank emphasises the conditions necessary for success: 'The support from the donors was conditional on individualized, private farm management' (World Bank 2000a: 61). This model is being transferred by the AKF into the Karategin region in Gharm oblast. In comparison, the increase in the rate of production on privately managed farms in other regions of the country can be regarded as negligible. Although the World Bank supports the privatisation of sovkhozes across the whole country, in practice this takes place so slowly and with the state creating so many obstacles that at present one cannot speak of privately managed agriculture in Tajikistan, except in GBAO and Gharm (see Bliss 2003; World Bank 2000a, 2004).

One may therefore conclude that without the intervention of the PRDP and the international donor community, it might have been possible to increase agricultural production slightly, but the fourfold increase in production between 1993 and 1998 is almost entirely due to the work of the PRDP/MSDSP. Without humanitarian assistance, by 1994 or 1995 at the latest there would have been a food supply crisis in the Pamirs.

In Khorog and in the lower valleys of the Gund, the Shakhdara and the Pyandsh the situation today is relatively stable with only some of the population still dependent on humanitarian aid. However, in other areas of GBAO the food situation is still not as satisfactory as it should be. The people in high-lying valleys continue to suffer from shortages of vitamin-rich food. During our visits in 2003 to Javshangoz (3,350 m) and Sejd (2,850 m), for example, we found that production had dropped in the last few years due to weather conditions, and livestock numbers had also fallen. Those few families with migrant workers have a low, but secure income, but most families still live a hand-to-mouth existence, relying on humanitarian assistance. The fact that they still need micronutrients proves that they will continue to rely on external support for the foreseeable future.

One reason that the food situation is not entirely satisfactory is to be found in the people's traditional attitude to food. We have repeatedly stated that the Pamiris consider it more important to grow wheat than potatoes and other vegetables because 'first of all there must be bread on the table'. One thing we began to notice in 1998 is that the Pamiris' excessive hospitality is often at the expense of the weakest members of their own family. When they say they have 'plenty of fruit', this does not automatically mean that every member of the household gets enough vitamins. Fruit can be sold, or might be used for guests. We noted at the time that 'the sugar from the HAP, which was distributed only for the benefit of children, has become a major resource for feeding guests'. It is true that people take turns to be guests, and someone might be a guest one day and a host the next day, but the fact is that most of these guests are men. As a rule, women and children profit much less from these extra meals with their good-quality, nourishing ingredients.

Impact on industry, business and trade

The PRDP/MSDSP's main objective is to support self-sufficiency in agricultural produce at local level. Setting up community organisations, contributing to maintenance and expansion of the transport infrastructure, and even supporting the education and health sectors, contribute indirectly to this plan as their aim is to stabilise rural regions and prevent a wholesale exodus of the local population. Most of the additional activities since 1997/8 – enhancing women's participation, poultry projects, orchards, bee-keeping, vegetable projects, etc. – also aim to increase income in the agricultural sector. Support of micro-enterprises in the villages – for example, setting up workshops or small businesses to process animal or vegetable products – is also closely linked to the agricultural objectives of the PRDP/MSDSP.

On the other hand, they never directly planned to influence industry, trade or commerce as such, even though other AKDN organisations and outside donors have been involved to some extent, with only moderate success up to date. Direct support of industry and manufacturing proved to be very difficult for several reasons. First, the population completely lacked any experience in running private businesses. Second, after the collapse of the Soviet Union, the traditional market for GBAO products crumbled. Third, Khorog has never been a suitable location for industrial production because of its isolated position (550 km from Dushanbe and 750 km from Osh, and as yet without any permanently open border with China and Afghanistan). This is all the more relevant when raw materials for a product are not obtainable locally. In Soviet times most industrial production was based on imported raw materials, which means that it has only been possible to revive a few of the old factories in Khorog. Only one business, the gemstone polishing factory in Porshnev, has been able to continue production with some of its former employees, since its raw materials, for example lapis lazuli from Shakhdara, originate within GBAO.[22] The building materials industry could probably be revived in the future, and a small cement works might even be profitable.

After 1992/3, reliable running of the Khorog and Pamir I power stations depended on the supply of spare parts and equipment organised by the AKDN (up until 1998 valued at around US$275,000).[23] Without this support, electricity supplies would have collapsed completely by 1995. Less successful were efforts to develop a primary energy source in the Pamirs in the form of brown coal or hard coal, supported by AKFED amongst others. Some of the coal deposits in the Murghâb proved to be too small and of poor quality. Larger deposits in the mountainous area between GBAO and Gharm have not yet been exploited. The costs of extraction would make the coal so expensive that no one in GBAO could afford it. However, the Tajik government needs to work out how to solve the existing energy crisis in GBAO in the medium term. Perhaps subsidised coal extraction would offer a cheaper solution than wholesale environmental damage in the highlands.

Indirectly at least, the PRDP/MSDSP and other development organisations have had a positive effect on trade and commerce in Khorog and other places. Agricultural surpluses play a large part in this, as do certain inputs (e.g. vegetable seeds), a proportion of which had to be repaid in cash, thus breaking the cycle of an economy based on payment in kind. From 1995 to 1998, PRDP/MSDSP employees' salaries were probably higher than those of all employees in public administration in GBAO. That is the most likely reason for the steady increase in the supply of goods on the market (*basar*) in Khorog after 1995 (Plate 9.4). Other reasons might be the effects of monetising wheat flour, the work carried out by hauliers and lorry drivers, who clearly brought in small quantities of other goods to sell on the market at the same time as bringing humanitarian aid into GBAO, the fleet of vehicles belonging to the PRDP/MSDSP and the other organisations giving employment to mechanics, the maintenance of aid organisation buildings and, last, a certain amount of personal consumption by the aid organisations' foreign workers.

Plate 9.4 Small-scale food sales and petty trade at the *basar* of Khorog were the first flimsy signs of an economic recovery (1997).

The privatisation of sovkhoz land and subsequent dissolution of state-run farms had some unexpected effects. Although GBAO's public transport system had completely collapsed between 1993 and 1995, by the end of 1996 the first buses were already back on the roads. Vehicles taken from the sovkhozes and somehow 'privatised' were repaired and kept in working condition by privately run small businesses for the purpose of transporting people and goods. In spite of repeated queries, we never found out how these vehicles had come into the possession of their owners at that time. What is certain is that they were not bought. Although fares were high in relation to the income of the passengers, they were in absolute terms much lower than would have been conceivable had the vehicles been bought for their real value. And so the mysterious handover of these machines was in everybody's interests, owner and passenger alike.

Society in transition and the 'new thinking'

Values in transition

In our first report on GBAO in 1995, in which we examined the possibility of German involvement in AKF projects, we had already stated that the population of the Pamirs continued to uphold many Soviet ideals. We said that voluntary community work (*subbotnik*), communal work (*amtabaq*, brigades) and, above all, the social element in development objectives formed a widespread and highly valued tradition which should be respected in any future projects. The greatest regard of all should be accorded to the overriding principle on which land distribution is based, namely that everyone in the village is to have an equal share of land and water. Development organisations in GBAO should therefore not regard land, soil and water as goods to be traded freely on an open market, and development aid in particular should take absolutely no part in supporting the commercialisation of land and water. The mistakes made during the transformation process in the GDR, under pressure from West German interest groups, should be held up as an example of bad practice.

In the eight years up to 2003 this assessment has proved to be correct, even if implementation of these ideas was not (mainly) due to the author's recommendations. The traditional social values of the Pamiris, which the Soviet Union maintained under a different name, are more than ever highly valued today. The people we interviewed reject sweeping criticism of the Soviet Union and the Soviet system, even though they increasingly accept that its disastrous economic policies were in part responsible for its collapse.

For reasons we have already given, people criticise two recent trends: first, towards a private economy; second, the emergence of social differences. Many people state that although cooperation at the village level still persists, in agriculture it is actually declining. Although there are many new local groups they are faced with a majority of farmers who prefer to farm on their own, rather than amalgamating the fields and cultivating them together with other farmers. This individualistic attitude is understandable, as farmers have owned their fields for only a few years and many of them remember that the amalgamation of fields 60 years ago was the first step towards collectivisation of the economy.

A man's wish to farm his own little plot of land together with his family should therefore not be criticised, even by neighbours who might prefer cooperation. However, there is a regrettable trend towards wanting to market agricultural produce and livestock on an individual basis. In 1998 we came across one case in which 40 sheep sold that year were taken, at great personal cost, by almost the same number of individual families, to the market in Khorog and sold there. Even today, hundreds of farmers bring one sack of potatoes or onions to the market individually, thereby needlessly expending a great deal of time and money on transport. The MSDSP has recognised this problem and given advice on 'marketing' for some years, with varying degrees of success, as we found out in 2003 in Javshangoz.

This isolated village, situated at a height of 3,350 m, must be one of the poorest in GBAO. Since 1998 the levels of livestock have dropped dramatically and one can imagine that the people there are in desperate need of every *Somonî*. However, they actually take no personal responsibility for selling their animals on the market in Khorog. Instead of sharing a hired lorry they wait for traders to turn up. On the few occasions that this happens they have to accept the prices offered, which are at least a third lower than those in Khorog. When we asked them why they did not actively do anything about the situation themselves, they told us it was because of a bad experience they had had some years previously when they had taken some of their animals to Khorog but had not succeeded in selling them. Instead of making them increase their efforts to cooperate, this incident made them give up even trying.

If willingness to participate in *subbotnik* activities is likewise declining today, this is certainly a result of the food-for-work programme. People have simply got used to being given food for 'voluntary' work. The WFP practice – carried out in many other countries – of giving food as wages, undermines self-help projects in GBAO.[24] The PRDP/MSDSP handed out food for a quite different purpose: the flour was simply to provide food for workers on building sites. However, the decline of the *subbotnik* only affects the public domain. A decline in willingness to help neighbours has been reported from only a few villages, where people say that it is not the result of ill will but is due to the fact that farmers have less time in summer. Therefore we do not agree with Breu and Hurni when they state that 'weak and sometimes conflicting norms, values and social rules' put (already) substantial constraints on development (2003: 52).

The second point, that of increasing divergency within a previously very homogeneous society, tends to be a topic people reflect on privately. This subject is not much discussed in public. Although, or perhaps *because*, the population insisted on absolute equality in the distribution of food after 1993, some social differences are beginning to emerge. The most favoured are always villagers with good land and easy access to the markets. People who backed cooperation with the PRDP from the start and were persuaded to grow new varieties of cereals and vegetables are now doing well. We recently visited a farmer whose family owned 1 hectare of land, who had a harvest of 11 tonnes of potatoes and 500 kg of tomatoes to take to the market, naturally using his own transport. The gross earnings of 3,850 TJS for the potatoes and 500 TJS for the tomatoes worked out at the equivalent of US$1,380 in 2003. Those who managed to get hold of a vehicle from former sovkhoz stocks are also making reasonable profits. Families with successful migrant workers also do well. In one village not far from Khorog in 2003, the first four cars since 1989 were bought with money earned by migrant workers. However, migrant work is no general guarantee of above average family income.[25]

It is not known how many people profit from drug smuggling in GBAO. The number is most probably larger than might be expected, in spite of the Pamiris well-known high moral standards.

One relatively new issue in GBAO is the level of participation of the local population in, for example, Village Organisations. We have stated elsewhere that during Soviet times opinions could be voiced relatively freely within the brigades. On the other hand, in the Pamirs there is no tradition of public discussions in which everyone takes part, including younger people, women and girls, workers as well as management. In fact, only 15 years ago it would have been extremely risky to voice one's opinion publicly, in spite of glasnost and perestroika. This had the effect of restricting the degree of real public participation in the first few years after

1992/3. Initially the old functionaries would speak at meetings, more recently they were replaced by the elected representatives of the village, the *khalifa* or the *raîs kishlak*. Hardly anyone else took part in the debates, which usually concluded with a declaration of agreement from all present. On occasion it was found out later that dissenting opinions had in fact been voiced, or positive suggestions made, but these were not, however, made public.

Gender issues

The role of women in GBAO has changed quite considerably over the last ten years. Some changes are for the better – for example, the HAP has made women economically less dependent on men – but there are other less positive aspects to the changes and in reality it is clear that negative aspects predominate (see Breu and Hurni 2003: 46). Women must be seen as the main losers in the radical changes which took place after 1991. This is, however, not readily admitted in GBAO, as the Pamiris are proud of the equality enjoyed by their women.

At any rate, women's role in politics has been drastically reduced. Although in 1997 women still held relatively high positions in the oblast administration (49 of 139 employees), with five deputy departmental heads and one deputy to the president, in Soviet times there had been 11 female deputy departmental heads and at least one departmental head. The CPSU, represented by its organisation in GBAO and Khorog, has now been dissolved and the approximately 20 per cent of female managerial posts, amongst them the position of party secretary in Khorog,[26] have therefore disappeared and will not be replaced. The managerial positions in the mass organisations, 35 of which alone were filled by women, have also gone.

In 1997 there were only three female representatives in the oblast assembly, which had a total of 70 members, whereas in Soviet times it was 13 out of 80. By 1997 there was only one rayon chairwoman and two deputy chairwomen (out of seven), whereas latterly under the Soviet Union there had been two chairwomen and four deputy chairwomen. At that time the mayor of Khorog was also female. In Soviet times, 12 of the 39 *jamoats* were headed by women, whereas today the figure is five out of 44. In the rayon assemblies in 1997 women held 16 out of the total of 267 seats, whereas previously it had been 49 out of 350 seats.

In 1997, as far as is known, there was not a single woman holding the top position in a village. Only a few elected village or *mahalla* committees had female members. In Darwâs, project employees even had to insist that women be invited to meetings on village issues; otherwise they would never have appeared at official village meetings or would have had to sit out of the way at the back.

Many women have also been deprived of important positions in areas other than politics, but here they have not been ousted by men as they have been from political committees. The positions they held as leading engineers or business managers simply disappeared with the collapse of industry. Of course the decline in top female functionaries does not necessarily mean that women's role in society has become more restricted, but one surely needs to reflect on the situation after hearing a retired rayon chairwoman stating: 'I have to work in the fields and in the house and nobody helps me.'

Economic problems have apparently led women to retire voluntarily from politics in order to find the time to look after their children. Obviously men do not have the same problem, as no cases are known of men leaving office for family reasons.

Within its own sphere of influence the PRDP/MSDSP has at least always tried to include women as equal partners. However, more could have been done as far as their own staff is concerned. Some women we interviewed said that the project had made a great contribution to their support. During the course of several discussions with, for example, the woman vice-president of the oblast, we had asked about the effect of various policies on women and pointed out the negative trends in the sphere of politics. In reply we were told: 'Forget the question of political representation. If you enable women to say "now we know what to cook tomorrow for our children" this is the best you can do for them.'

The humanitarian assistance undoubtedly makes an important contribution to fulfilling practical gender needs, but that alone does not promote strategic gender needs. Even a woman in Afghanistan, locked up at home or forced to stumble across the street in her *burka* (the bulky robe covering the whole body, including the head and face), has probably got enough food to feed her children. It is therefore important to keep, or create afresh, a structural foundation for women's participation in public life and the decision-making process. The situation of Pamiri women has improved so much in the last 100 years, and is so advanced compared with the countries bordering on the south, that the ambition of all those taking part in development in GBAO should be to retain the standards set during the latter years of the Soviet Union, or where necessary reintroduce them.

A summary of external development assistance

The AKF and its international partners have now achieved almost all of their goals to ensure a reliable food supply and to support agricultural production. By 2000, grain production had increased almost fourfold to around 21,000 tonnes, and potato production to 23,000 tonnes. Vegetable production has reached 6,700 tonnes, almost a fourfold increase on the 1993 level, and grain or grain equivalent production is now 125 kg per head of population, which achieves between 75 per cent and 80 per cent of the FAO guideline on the minimum level of locally produced food. Altogether, the level of self-sufficiency has risen from below 20 per cent to around 85 per cent. These final results are probably an international record, even though the original level was artificially low because of mistakes and mismanagement in the sovkhoz system.

There are many conditions under which external aid can be successful, but in this case, a unique combination of factors came into play, which is the reason why PRDP/MSDSP projects in the Pamirs cannot simply be replicated elsewhere. The conditions for success were as follows:

1 The commitment and absolute honesty of local people involved in the distribution of food; this led to the speedy delivery of equal quantities of aid to all individuals, without any initial conditions being imposed on it.
2 The insistence on privatising agriculture, until now only implemented in GBAO, where over 90 per cent of the land is being privately managed; this created the conditions for increasing production per unit of land.
3 The integrated agricultural programme which combined advice, the supply of fertiliser and seed, and the local production of seed; this was a practical way of promoting increased production on private land.
4 Combining the increase in production with an emphasis on high yield and more nutritious varieties of cereals and vegetables.

With regard to the last point, there should have been a more intensive advisory programme, with, in some cases, the project insisting on a more rapid change in production methods. There was too much discussion over the distribution of micronutrients. They should have instead insisted more widely on distributing vegetable seeds and how best to use them. They should also have tested the strategy of actively advising farmers not to grow wheat.

One weak spot in the HAP was that it took too long to differentiate between the varying degrees of neediness amongst the population. Although right from the start more aid was distributed in some rayons than in others, the differences were generally slight and were based solely on regional and not individual criteria. This led to better-off regions, with better soils, receiving aid for longer than was absolutely necessary ('necessary' is of course a relative term here), whereas villages in which the population was not thriving, even with the minimum allocation of aid, received too little.

Even within one village, the concept of treating all people more or less equally led de facto to preferential treatment of the better off. In numerous cases it was the local decision-makers who bear most of the responsibility for this state of affairs, as they continued to insist on equal treatment for all. Smaller families with less manpower were unable to take advantage of land distribution and inputs to the same extent as those who had ample manpower. It would therefore have been legitimate to allocate them a larger share of humanitarian assistance than the other families.

In ten years of external aid in GBAO it has not proved possible to revive the economy in general, but this was in fact never a key aim of the PRDP/MSDSP. There have been tentative attempts made by other organisations, but everyone we spoke to in Khorog or Dushanbe in 2003 had to admit that they had not yet come up with any convincing proposals on how to achieve this aim. It is clear that completely new ideas must be formulated, which should also provide an answer to the question as to whether it will ever be possible to sustain such a large population entirely from local resources in a region like the Pamirs.

10

DEVELOPMENT CONSTRAINTS AND PROSPECTS

We have now demonstrated, particularly in the last three chapters, the way in which Gorno-Badakhshan has progressed from a very low level of development at the beginning of the twentieth century – one comparable to that of bordering Afghan territories – to a relatively secure standard of living, even judged by modern standards. This was a consequence of the Soviet reconstruction programme, mainly since the 1950s. There is no point criticising the fact that the level of income in GBAO was lower in 1990 than in the rest of Tajikistan, and was here much lower than in Russia for instance, as other criteria have to be taken into account. We entirely agree with Hafizullah Emadi's statement:

> In the Soviet era Gorno-Badakhshan received Soviet support in education, health care, housing and other amenities of life, similar to that received throughout the rest of the Soviet Union. The people of Badakhshan are indebted to Lenin's socialism for transforming their primordial economy and enhancing their standard of living.
>
> (Emadi 1998: 21)

The author points out, however, that this development was no guarantee of sustainability, but rather that it led GBAO into a position of dependency. Although this dependency certainly existed, our comments on recent trends in Chapter 9 have already made clear that options for positive economic change without external assistance are indeed very limited, for reasons which will be elaborated on. This situation has remained the same over the last few decades. For that reason it is not justified to criticise the Soviet development programme in the Tajik Pamirs on the grounds that it lacked sustainability, where in any case there was only limited scope for improving the level of sustainability. On the contrary, it should be recognised that for a variety of reasons the Soviet economy was willing to subsidise GBAO heavily, indeed sometimes at the expense of other regions (for example Ukraine). We have already stated that this was not merely for humanitarian reasons but also, maybe even primarily, for political reasons. Comparisons with other regions of the Soviet Union of less strategic importance, for example parts of northern Mongolia or Turkmenistan, show, however, that the Soviet system aimed to achieve a uniform standard of living even when there were no pressing strategic reasons. The political leadership in Dushanbe also widely used illegal stratagems to help subsidise the Tajik economy (see pp. 244 and 272).

At least since the 1960s the vast majority of Pamiris have paid tribute to Soviet endeavours and have proved to be loyal Soviet citizens. One reason is because many features of the Soviet system criticised by the West, such as the collective economy and the individual's duties and responsibilities to society, were perfectly compatible with the traditional values and customs of the Pamiris. According to many people we interviewed the lack of formal political freedom – so highly valued by the West – and even the lack of the right to free speech, were considered unimportant once their material wants were securely provided for.

Most people in GBAO still heavily criticise the changes introduced under Gorbachev, which – in conjunction with general economic trends – finally led to the collapse of the Soviet Union. Even though increasing numbers of people know that it is unrealistic to expect a return to the Soviet system, there is so far, with the exception of some young people, very little enthusiasm for the capitalist system. After all, the blame for the collapse of the Soviet Union is not attributed to structural problems – many of which are surely exaggerated by the West – but on the completely directionless policies of the Soviet leadership under Gorbachev.

The experiences of the last decade confirm that a capitalist economy in no way automatically leads to the regeneration of a marginal area such as the Pamirs, and this is a viewpoint that has to be taken into account in any discussions on development prospects in GBAO. It is not the Soviet system that has failed in the Pamirs but the attempt to keep an economic 'desert' artificially in flower. A stronger emphasis on sustainability in the economy would have reduced, but certainly not have entirely eliminated, the need for subsidies. Assessment of development potential and constraints demonstrates that even under a capitalist system the Pamiris can only survive in their homeland with external support.

The development potential and constraints of the Pamir region

The Pamirs consist of arable land, grazing land and woodland or scrub. There has never been much of the latter. In addition, as a result of the shortage of fuel, the natural vegetation has been cut down in large quantities over the last ten years. The two most important traditional sources of wood, *artsha* and *tersgen*, have been almost entirely destroyed in areas accessible to people.

Some of the grazing land has been damaged by overgrazing due to excessive livestock levels and the discontinuation of concentrated feed imports between 1993 and 1995. Reduction of livestock numbers, coupled with environmentally suitable grazing regimes managed by the Kyrgyz in the Murghâb, has prevented further deterioration, or at least slowed the process down considerably. Against this background it would appear that increases in livestock numbers are precluded for ecological reasons, and consequently, in the long term, for economic reasons.

Until now there has been virtually no resumption in the processing and marketing of animal products such as wool and skins. However, it must be said in all honesty that the amount of wool produced in the Pamirs is insufficient to supply even the needs of the local population, and that the skins are often of poor quality because of the conditions under which the animals live. It would be unrealistic to expect the creation of any more than a few dozen jobs if leather processing were to be resumed.

At present the total area of old and newly developed land in agricultural use covers between 19,000 and 20,000 hectares, so that its full potential has not yet been realised. However, there are only around 2,000 hectares of potential additional land to be reclaimed, and to do this would be costly. Other potential land, especially the so-called *dasht* zones (plains or 'desert'), is mainly at a high altitude and remote from settlements; thus bringing a water supply to this land would be extremely costly. Large-scale levelling and terracing would be necessary in almost all instances. There would also be the added expense of constructing distribution channels. Although there are more than 5,000 hectares of *dasht* zones in GBAO, financial considerations will almost certainly prevent their development.

As far as minerals and organic raw materials are concerned, the first surveys after 1993 painted a gloomy picture. There is coal, but it is of poor quality (Murghâb), or almost inaccessible (Darwâs/Gharm). Mining of the known lapis lazuli deposits above the Shakhdara might succeed on a limited scale, but access would first have to be restored at great cost and effort. Marble in the area of Wandsh rayon is high grade and relatively easy to quarry, but it is 250 km away from Dushanbe and can only be transported over passes which are closed for six months of the year. For that reason it cannot be seen as a resource suitable for export. Suggestions such as ruby mining (for the precious stone 'Tusyanit'), or gold washing, are based on recollections of earlier times rather than on the evidence of geological feasibility studies.

Water power is the main resource in the Pamirs with future potential. The two medium-sized hydroelectric power stations, Khorog and Pamir I, only use a fraction of their existing potential, which has been estimated at between 1,000 and 4,000 megawatts (MW) according to different sources (see Breu and Hurni 2003). Even without building dams it may be possible in many places to use larger rivers such as the Pyandsh or the Bartang, as well as dozens of other streams, to generate power. However, many things have to be taken into consideration here. The high investment costs would have to be provided by external sources, which might be difficult in view of the current insolvency of local and regional customers (e.g. Afghan Badakhshan). Inaccessibility is the main stumbling block to the realisation of what is probably the largest economically viable individual project, the exploitation of Lake Sares on the upper Bartang, which could provide 100–200 MW of electricity relatively easily.

Furthermore, international agreement would also be needed for exploitation of the Pyandsh, and this would in its turn depend on stability in Afghanistan. It is certainly worth investigating the possibility of generating power in the Pamirs for western Tajikistan, and even for Uzbekistan, via the central Asian grid. However, it will require great effort on the part of Tajikistan to restore the existing facilities and ensure they run reliably by 2007. In the present climate, new investments of the order of several hundred million US dollars are almost out of the question.

One of GBAO's most important resources is its people. A similarly high level of education is nowhere else to be found in the whole of greater south-central Asia and the northern part of south Asia. However, at present there is a danger that people will not keep up with technical developments and will even forget what they have learnt, as they have no opportunity to apply their skills. Thousands of engineers, mechanics, economists and specialists are currently unemployed, or work in jobs for which they are not trained (usually in agriculture). In Tajikistan today it is normally difficult to secure the services of a good builder, electrician or plumber, because those who trained for these jobs have not worked in their field for ten years or more. Moreover, modern technological developments require the introduction of completely new qualifications, and this has not yet happened.

AKDN has supported the University of Khorog both materially and spiritually particularly since the imam's visit to GBAO in 1995 (Emadi 1998: 20–21). This is a way to sustain and improve the Pamiris' high standard of education. The 'University of Central Asia' project, focusing on modern communication technology and continuing education and run by the AKDN, is another excellent way of contributing to improvements in education (AKDN 2002), but by 2003 this university still only comprised the establishment founded in Khorog. Even if they ever succeed in establishing a globally unique concentration of departments studying subjects based on 'Sustainable Development of Economies and Societies in Mountain Regions', it will be a long time before the population in GBAO feel any of the direct economic benefits which may arise.

Another important resource is the population's enthusiastic attitude towards development, without which reconstruction would have been much less successful. Much that would be difficult elsewhere – for example, the responsible involvement of such a large number of people in the distribution of aid, or easy access to loans – is facilitated in the Pamirs by the fact that there has been little or no corruption so far, even amongst the police force. On the other hand, a certain lack of flexibility when issues need to be resolved and an unwillingness to take risks are noticeable, but hardly surprising in view of circumstances in the Soviet era. Such factors hinder widespread development. Individuals also lack the experience necessary for self-employment. If former sovkhoz workers have not made good farmers for lack of previous experience, how can the second generation of state farm workers become businessmen?

Other assets are their continued willingness to do things for themselves and to cooperate at a local level, without which reconstruction work would have proceeded much more slowly. Such values must be fostered and maintained in future, in spite of the spread of private enterprise. Even if renewed collectivisation cannot be recommended, it is a matter of urgency that the Pamiris' fundamental willingness to cooperate be channelled into improved agriculture and marketing for the common good. The new structure of landownership based on smallholdings should not be interfered with, but farmers would have to be persuaded that ten adjacent farmers should not each put down one small field to potatoes, one to wheat and one to alfalfa, and then irrigate, harvest and process the produce individually, but should cooperate in order to increase yields and income.

The relative equality of society must be regarded as another asset to development. This equality continues to be seen as a factor which has indeed been known to impede justice in issues relating to the definition of obligations, but – far more importantly – is increasing equality of opportunity and also the frequency with which opportunity is in fact grasped. The worst thing the donor community could do now would be to encourage social differentiation, which is unfortunately the case at present in western Tajikistan and in other countries formerly part of the Soviet Union. Any donor who currently wishes to make loans or other forms of support dependent on owning a minimum amount of land or on other proof of assets would be well advised not to get involved.

The gender situation in GBAO inherited from the Soviet Union (see pp. 267–269) also offers many advantages for future development in comparison with conditions in neighbouring countries to the south (Plate 10.1). With the support of external aid, society and its political leaders should do everything to sustain such advantages over the long term.

Until recently, the widespread absence of the state in GBAO has both promoted and inhibited development. In spite of all the efforts made by the international

Plate 10.1 Younger women and men at a festival near Khorog (1997). Their appearance shows the increasing availability of 'modern' clothes.

donor community – led by the AKF – towards averting a humanitarian disaster in the Pamirs, long-term sustainable development will not be possible without the guidance and support of the state. If we compare the situation in GBAO with that in other parts of Tajikistan, the large contribution made by donors has hitherto undoubtedly had a positive effect. Land would not have been distributed so extensively, and the level of participation in society, as manifested by the Village Organisations, would have remained much lower.

Once the situation has improved, the state must resume its responsibilities. On the one hand central government will need to provide GBAO with a large enough budget to maintain and improve administration and infrastructure, and on the other hand oblast government and the elected oblast assembly must in future take responsibility for development planning and play a leading role in the coordination of donors in GBAO. In order to fulfil these requirements, institutional and management advice to the government, administrative authorities and assemblies is probably more urgently needed today than, say, building individual bridges or implementing village poultry projects.

One of the government's most pressing tasks is to solve the energy supply crisis, which is probably the greatest problem faced by the population today – even greater than the food and clothing problem. Another important task is to maintain the existing infrastructure, which is the cornerstone of any economic development alongside human resources.

GBAO has no direct influence over the Tajik social security system, in which the current allowance is rapidly dwindling to nothing. In the national PRSP they for once openly admit that the 4.4 million TJS estimated for the 2001 budget is so little 'that even when people are paid this allowance, they are still considered poor' (Tajikistan 2002: 20). A marked increase in the budget for social allowances could, however, be used as an instrument of social equality, which would especially benefit populations in disadvantaged regions like GBAO.

GBAO's policies likewise have no effect on the present-day politically and geographically peripheral location of the Pamirs. The great distances to Dushanbe and Osh, and the absence of a hinterland to the east (China) and to the south (Afghanistan), constitute impediments to progress which only changes in foreign policy can overcome in the long term.

Finally, the extreme climatic conditions in the Pamir region must be taken into consideration. Any form of development will have to take account of this fact, as working against climatic conditions would involve wasting resources. For example, there is absolutely no point in carrying out experimental agriculture in the Murghâb, as was unsuccessfully done in Soviet times. Likewise it must be accepted that some regions of the Pamirs are always cut off in winter. Constructing roads passable all year round would tie up too much capital needed elsewhere.

Induced development constraints: drugs and border troops

Two further obstacles to development will now be added to those listed above, covering issues which are as contradictory as they are interesting. They are contradictory because although they bring money into the region they also have a harmful effect. The first one is drug trafficking, which probably goes back as far as the Soviet occupation of Afghanistan but has increased dramatically since 1992. Drug trafficking is of great financial interest, especially in view of the low entry-level price for opium and heroin in Afghanistan. In 1998 a kilogram of opium could still be had for US$30 in Afghan Badakhshan, but by 2000, after the intervention of the Taliban, this had risen to US$700 per kilo. Now the prices are going down again, as the area of land on which opium poppies are grown has increased more than ninefold: from 8,000 hectares in 2001 to 74,000 ha in 2002 and is continuing to increase.[1] Heroin is said to be available for US$500 a kilogram, and even cheaper from the Afghan border. And there is a vast supply of opium and heroin on the Afghan side of the border: the 2001 harvest of 185 tonnes of opium had already increased to 3,400 tonnes by the following year (see Kleveman 2002: 15). Unlike the Taliban, the Northern Alliance has never attempted to stem the growth in opium cultivation in the last two years in which it has been in power. The government under Karzai, which depends on the support of the Northern Alliance warlords, is therefore unwilling to control opium cultivation. Since 2002 the state has virtually given up fighting the drug trade in Afghanistan (see Bröckers 2002: 230–233).

Bearing in mind the huge profits to be made in heroin on its route via Tajikistan and Russia to Western Europe, it is easy to understand why some individual Pamiris have joined in with the drug smuggling carried on by some of the foreign troops stationed in GBAO: between the Afghan border and Osh or Dushanbe the price increases to US$2,000, and by the time it gets to Moscow it has risen to between US$5,000 and 10,000. Based on these figures, one consignment of 100 kilos confiscated by customs in GBAO in mid-2003 made the smugglers a net profit of US$150,000 just on the road between Pyandsh and Osh, at a cost price of less than US$50,000 and a sale price of 200,000. Bribes can easily be paid with such high profit margins.

Since 1998 Tajikistan has been the main trade centre for Afghan heroin on its way to Russia and Europe (see Rashid 2002: 143). Tajiks and Pamiris are involved in its trade and transport purely to make money. At no time has drug trafficking in the Pamirs been used widely to finance weapons, as was erroneously claimed in a report in *Le Monde* ('Le Pamir entre deux feux' of 12 August 1993).

There is some dispute over the possible effects on Tajikistan and GBAO of an increase in cheap supplies of opium and heroin coming in from Afghanistan. Observers in Khorog assume that heroin consumption in the city itself is declining again, although there are still as many as 500 mainly juvenile drug users. The involvement of young men in the criminal drug trade seems to be more of a problem for the local authorities. And the volume of drugs being transported through

Tajikistan is generally increasing. According to the 'Times of Central Asia' of 18 June 2003, in the first five months of 2002 approximately 1.8 tonnes of drugs, including 1.25 tonnes of heroin, were confiscated by the authorities, which here also includes the Russian border guards. In 2003 within the same time span this had already risen to 4.7 tonnes, 3.16 tonnes of which were heroin alone. It is not known, however, how much of it was confiscated in GBAO. There are in fact some observers who claim that there has been a slight drop in the volume of drugs being transported through GBAO. According to these observers, in the last two years the Kulyab in the west has become established as the new drug route to Dushanbe and Russia.

One of the duties of the Russian border guards (i.e. the CIS troops; see Plate 10.2) is to prevent drug trafficking across the borders of the countries involved. Custom controls are usually extremely thorough. On the road from Khorog to Osh at least five checkpoints have to be passed, and two or three between GBAO and Gharm. We often saw lorries being searched thoroughly, but the question arises as to what purpose these searches serve. Do they really find drugs or do these controls perhaps serve the dual purpose of making money, whether in the form of bribes, if drugs are found, or the drugs themselves, a proportion of which can be confiscated and sold? Whatever the case may be, it is the Russian officers who make the decisions and not the ordinary soldiers, who at best can hope to make a small amount of cash out of it. As the authorities are aware of these facts, the CSS (Committee for State Security) – still known locally as the KGB – is said to carry out very strict internal controls.

However, it is doubtful whether the CSS really has its officers under control, as was stated in an interview in 2002 (Kleveman 2002: 15). In another interview in the same year, an Afghan trader stated that drug trafficking is extremely easy:

> 'You bring the stuff by donkey or jeep to commanding officers near the border, for instance near Khorog.' He went on to say that they then get in radio contact with their accomplices on the Tajik side, Russian border guard officers, and arrange a time and a safe place for handing over the goods. Sometimes there are problems with young Russian officers, who are still overzealous and not open to bribes, but that soon sorts itself out after a few weeks on duty.
>
> (Kleveman 2002: 18)

According to this report, the border guard officers not only tolerate drug smuggling but are themselves actively involved in it. Rashid states that the border guards are notoriously corrupt and that even some senior officers have been involved in drug smuggling (2002: 287).

The authorities in Khorog admit that they are indeed having trouble guarding the border. Apart from a few vehicles, for which there is virtually no fuel, some guns and a few old radio sets, Tajik customs are almost powerless against the smugglers. The only effective weapon used against them is insider information

Plate 10.2 CIS troops ('Russian border guards') with light tanks near their headquarters in Khorog (most probably early 1990s).

occasionally given to the Tajik police. For example, it was reported that in mid-2003, as a result of an insider tip-off, they succeeded in apprehending an otherwise completely innocent-looking women who was being used as a mule to carry more than 100 kilos of heroin.

One can only speculate on the economic effects of Pamiris being involved in drug smuggling. What is certain is that the small number of new cars, some of them from the West, which had started to appear in Khorog during the economic crisis from 1995 to 1998, are almost certainly financed through drugs. One also cannot imagine that the young men buying large quantities of imported alcohol in the *basar* in Khorog – the only people to do so apart from foreign experts – earned their dollars by working in the fields. However, it is doubtful whether in GBAO large quantities of 'dirty drug money' are being invested for the benefit of the region.

Quite apart from their likely involvement in drug smuggling, Russian border guards play an ambivalent role in GBAO. Although from 1995 onwards they successfully prevented infiltration of Afghan forces into GBAO during the civil war, with losses sustained at times on their own side, such a large presence can no longer be justified. As far back as 1996 the German press had pointed out that border incidents, reported occasionally from Khorog, had not necessarily actually taken place.[2] An intense exchange of fire in 1995 lasting several hours, during which heavy artillery was fired over our heads in the direction of Afghanistan, transpired that very same day to have been 'training under realistic conditions'. The following day the Western press reported heavy fighting at the border. Clearly such incidents were stage-managed in order to justify the continued presence in Tajikistan of CIS peace-keeping troops and Russian border guards.

Today this kind of justification is no longer necessary, as more than half of all border guards are Tajik mercenaries, as already referred to elsewhere, or even, as Rashid writes, army conscripts (2002: 287). Russian officers' and soldiers' salaries are 50 per cent higher than those paid to Tajiks. In the light of these facts, we need to weigh up the economic benefits to be derived from the continued presence of border guards in GBAO. We have already referred to the purchasing power of the troops. Some of the money is certainly spent directly in the local markets in Khorog, Ishkashim, Roshân or Kala-i Khumb. In addition, these local markets now profit from bulk buying by troops to supply their daily needs, since now that the sovkhozes have been dissolved the armed forces are no longer able to obtain the free supplies available between 1993 and 1996. Lastly, it is likely that the border guards – at least until mid-2004 – provided paid employment to a certain number of civilians from GBAO.[3]

Since then the replacement of Russian troops by Tajik forces has been carried out, and this will have a significant impact on the economic situation of the whole Murghâb area, leaving approximately 500 to 750 persons without income. As a consequence, and mainly in Murghâb town, at least some former well-to-do households will fall back into poverty thus increasing the number of vulnerable households in the area. The troop withdrawal will also have a negative impact on the local market (dramatic drop of local purchasing power) and on the supply of necessary goods such as diesel or petrol, coal, spare parts and all articles which formerly were bartered by the Russians against local products and services.

The latter has already exhausted the range of positive factors. Traders from Khorog told us that controls on the main roads to Osh and Dushanbe, formerly by Russians, now by Tajiks, are having a very damaging effect on the flow of goods. They informed us that money is often demanded in order to pass through the checkpoints and that this process is repeated at each checkpoint. This considerably increases the price of the goods. It is also claimed that returning migrant workers have had part of their savings taken from them as a result of corruption at the checkpoints. There is repeated confirmation of disruption to trade, and even the political authorities regard it as a problem, but no independent sources have yet been found to corroborate the other accusations. What is certain is that these controls increase the time taken to travel from Osh to Khorog on average by several hours. It should be obvious to the authorities that the practice of carrying out such controls is likely to discourage any potential tourists.

Development prospects and conclusions

GBAO's future success is linked to external aid, which will allow it to make better use of its potential than has been done over the last few years. This will still apply to arable and livestock farming, and to a limited extent to commerce, trade and industry. One thing needs to be made clear to all those involved and to be built into all strategic planning: even if the prognosis is optimistic and all known resources are utilised, the region will not be able to provide its population with the economic standard achieved during Soviet times by the end of the 1980s. It is possible that the entire food-based economy will operate at a subsistence level, with agriculture remaining at the level of development typical of a low-income country, where surpluses supplying the market are possible only on a limited scale, if at all.

One feasibility study shows that agricultural produce could be increased in one of three ways: (1) an increase in agricultural land to the level referred to above; (2) vertical land development (i.e. improvement in irrigation, agricultural technology and farm management); and (3) choice of the best plant varieties for production. An increase of around 10–15 per cent is possible in the first instance and in the second not more than 50 per cent, following the large increase in production after 1997. The latter is, however, a very optimistic figure.

A further increase in the amount of vegetables and other nutritious food grown would also boost productivity per unit of land. However, it must be realised that export of agricultural produce is almost impossible in view of the distance to potential markets. Furthermore, a great deal of unprofitable marginal land used in GBAO should be taken out of production. Some of the newly cultivated land is already showing signs of erosion damage and therefore no increase in yield can be expected. On the contrary, it is likely that in the medium and long term yield here will drop.

Let us now look in detail at some ideas which have been put forward repeatedly as showing development potential. In GBAO, as also elsewhere, it is not true that growing medicinal plants would increase the value of agricultural production. The competition in this area is far too great and medicinal plants are already being grown and harvested mechanically at low cost on a large scale in other countries. The supposed advantage of the existence of a processing plant in Khorog proves spurious on closer inspection. Even in Soviet times this plant was considered to be primitive and out of date. Processing facilities were restricted to preserving fruits, leaves and seeds rather than extracting plant essences, and that would, of course, preclude access to any markets.

Any discussion on developing new land must take into account the fact that irrigation channels have already been laid on the most accessible land. Any new channel would probably only irrigate poorer quality land at a higher cost per unit of land than on previously developed land. In some areas soil quality could probably be improved by terracing and removing stones, but it is doubtful whether it would be worth the investment.

Improved management of fruit trees is already under way in some local projects, but there is unlikely to be a market for fruit. Much of the increase in productivity resulting from better methods of cultivation and new orchards must be directed towards providing the local population with fruit; there is, however, a shortage of suitable land for this purpose. Anything else would be completely irresponsible in view of the continued vitamin and mineral deficiency amongst women and children.

Several years ago we drew attention to the need for improved water management in order to maintain the present high level of production on developed land even during droughts. Fundamental improvements are needed in the construction of principal and delivery channels. The existing channels urgently need to be stabilised and offtake regulators with simple valves need to be installed. If it is not generally possible to level the land, then horizontal irrigation furrows should at least be made along the contour lines, and if needs be a field should be divided into individual squares with mud walls around them to retain the water. Where irrigation systems already exist there is not much scope for irrigating additional fields or improving the yield by increasing the volume of water used on the fields, as the PRDP/MSDSP have already done this very successfully during the first few years of the project.

What other alternatives to agriculture might there be? Temporary migration to work in other regions where there is a demand is a possibility, or permanent resettlement in areas with more opportunities (see Herbers 2001: 21). However, at present there is no demand for a workforce in other oblasts of Tajikistan. Even in Khatlon real unemployment[4] is at a very high level, and privatisation of the sovkhozes will not result in land being distributed amongst families, but rather – if it happens at all – in the creation of larger units. That is why respondents to a survey in Kurgan-Tebe (Khatlon) and in Gharm estimated that 70 per cent of the town's adult males worked in Russia or in the Islamic Republic of Iran (see Gomart 2003: 68). If there is any point in emigrating from GBAO, then it only makes sense to go abroad to countries with a much higher GDP.

In the last five years an astonishingly large number of people have actually migrated to such countries in search of work. However, they are not from the problem areas of GBAO (i.e. the villages in high-lying valleys) but from the better-off areas, since these are the only families who can afford the expensive journey. The main destination of migrant workers is Russia, with the highest concentration in Moscow and the surrounding area. We have already described the living and working conditions of the migrant workers elsewhere, and explained the limits to migration. There would only be widespread improvement, with concomitant greater benefits to the economy, if migration were managed properly in future and, above all, if Russia made it legal. Examples from Khatlon show that if migrant workers are successfully (i.e. legally) integrated into the Russian labour market this can certainly provide other members of the family at home with an acceptable standard of living.

Plans made by the government in Dushanbe to resettle the inhabitants of marginal areas have not yet proved practicable. On the contrary, all resettlement plans are at present discredited in view of what happened to refugees from Dasht in the Shakhdara valley when they were resettled in Beshkent in Khatlon. About 170 families were settled in Beshkent II in tumble-down huts almost in the middle of a salt marsh, after their village in the Pamirs had been destroyed by a landslide. They have no agricultural resources nor any alternative sources of income, in spite of all the promises made to them, and survive almost exclusively on humanitarian aid. If they had enough money they would have all returned to the Pamirs long ago. Every future offer of resettlement will therefore be viewed with suspicion and in many cases will not be entertained at all,[5] even though there are some areas, especially in Khatlon, where several thousand families could live if they were each allocated a small amount of land. However, such plans are ruled out at present as land is not supposed to be parcelled out in small units.

There is much to be said for the idea that a return to peace in Afghanistan and an ideological liberalisation in China might restore the Pamirs – the region of the first and the second, still-continuing 'Great Game' – to its important position as the main crossing point on the central Asian routes from east to west and from north to south.[6] This is an opportune moment to bring in the development of tourism. The 'official' opening of the border in 2001 was the first step taken in the process of opening borders, liberating GBAO from its role as a terminus, and transforming it instead into an important stopping-off place on the central Asian road network. The second step would be the actual opening of the already built border crossing point to China, but a bilateral border agreement has not yet been drawn up. An extension of the Karakorum Highway could then be considered, and also a section going west into the Pamirs and on to Osh in Kyrgyzstan (see Kreutzmann 2002: 43). Opening the border to Afghanistan for general traffic and trade would initially only create a small amount of additional traffic, but closer links between GBAO and Afghanistan in the medium to long term would certainly provide many opportunities. The impact of the new border checkpoint between Tajikistan and China so far does not have a major impact on the local economy as transit is still on a low level and the border has recently (September 2004) again been closed for unknown reasons. A trade volume of some US$45,000 as reported for 2004 does not constitute a major stimulation of the local economy. A high percentage of the sales constitutes a pure replacement by Chinese goods of those which were formerly purchased from Osh in Kyrgyzstan.

On the question of tourism, planners are backing the development of biodiversity and wildlife in the Pamirs. The 'neglect of existing laws and the inadequacy of nature conservation systems' are, however, affecting its potential (Breu and Hurni 2003: 58). Unfortunately, the way in which some central Asian countries are increasingly isolating themselves is also counterproductive to tourism. Many potential tourists are likely to be put off by being required to have at least three visas, whereas previously there was a joint one for Kazakhstan, Uzbekistan, Kyrgyzstan and Tajikistan. The Tajik government also has to clarify the current contradictory situation in which it aims to promote tourism and yet only allows Westerners to enter the country if they have an invitation, setting up extra hurdles for GBAO in the form of expensive additional visas. So far there is only limited infrastructure for small-scale, outdoor-based group tourism. Only recently, transport facilities, accommodation, and tour organisation for ecotourism has been established by a project supported by the French NGO ACTED. The natural environment and culture of the Pamiris and neighbouring Afghans nevertheless offer many opportunities for tourist development. The people of GBAO in particular would easily adapt to the demands of modern sporting and cultural holidays and ecotourism, because of the high level of development they achieved during the Soviet period.

Last, many Pamiris will still be forced to earn some of their income as migrant workers, under the difficult and often inhumane conditions which we have already described. Supporting them is one of the tasks of the policy dialogue which the international organisations and the bilateral donor organisations have to carry out with the target countries, especially Russia.

GLOSSARY

[*Tajik (either Pamiri or Tajik) = taj.; Russian = rus.; Arabic = arab.; Kyrgyz = kg.]. According to the usage of the words by various authors using different transcription systems we also cannot present a consistent system for transcription.*

afiun	opium (taj.)
ahadith	Sayings of the Prophet Muhammad (arab.)
aîrân	heated and fermented milk (kg.)
akhavdsh-mikh	iron borers (taj.)
akhikht	trough for the preparation of bread (taj.)
aksaqal/aqsaqal	Village elder in both taj. and kg. villages
ambur	tong (taj.)
amir (amîr)	traditional political leader (taj., arab.)
amtabaq	neighbourhood group in which people work together (taj.)
apparat	administration (of a state farm) (rus.)
apparatchiks	members of a (sovkhoz) administration (rus.)
arbab	traditional local leader (taj.)
arôs	bride (taj., arab.)
arra	saw (taj.)
arúsa al-qamh	'bride of the wheat'; netting made from wheat ears to induce divine blessing (baraka) (arab.)
arzen	millet
art	col (kg.)
artsha	juniper (taj., kg.)
aryk	irrigation channel (kg.)
ashkhana	kitchen of the yurt; also partition walls or curtains (kg.)
aûl	camp, village (kg.)
'awam	humble folk, lower classes (taj.)
bâbâ	familiar name for grandfather (taj.)
baîga	see 'buskashî' (kg., taj.)
baqla	horse bean (taj.)
baraka	divine blessing
bartang	narrow in profile (taj.)

basar	market (taj.)
beg	traditional honorary title (taj.)
bîğûr	upper millstone (taj.)
brigada	working team (rus.)
brigadier	foreman, forewoman in the sovkhoz (rus.)
buskashî	competition played on horseback with dead goat/sheep (taj., kg.)
butshkighîdj	transverse beam over the entrance of the living room decorated with carvings and often brightly painted (taj.)
chidgor	traditional unit of land (taj.)
chôna/khôna	house (taj.)
chupân	coat (taj.)
daf	drum (Farsî)
dâlis	entrance hall of the house (taj.)
dâm	skin bellows (taj.)
damullah	local Sunni religious leader (Darwâs); cf. 'mulloh' (taj.)
dârga	tambourine
darya	stream, river (taj.)
dasht	plain, also desert (taj.)
dast seftz	band made out of glass discs (taj.)
dâya	midwife (arab.)
dekhan	'private' (farmer) (taj.)
dîn	religion (arab.)
doira	percussion instrument
dosrand	plane (taj.)
dostarkhan	tablecloth (kg.)
dsham	grain measure, 12 dsham = one por (taj.)
dumba'	fat-tailed sheep (kg.)
dutar/dutâr/dutor	two-stringed guitar (kg.)
fanûs	petroleum lamp (taj., arab.)
garmoshka	accordeon (rus.)
gidora	disc (taj.)
gitshak	tambourine (taj.)
glasnost	transparency, openness (rus.)
goruh	kinship group (taj.)
gozkhoz	state farm (cf. 'sovkhoz') (rus.)
guibosi	a type of polo; also called 'buskashî' or 'ram brawl' (taj.)
gulistan	garden (taj.)
gupsar	float (taj.)
guristan	cemetery (taj., kg.)
guzdon bog	full-bellied jug with a handle (taj.)
hakim, hakem	traditional political leader, doctor (taj., arab.)
hasitan	wooden pillar, also named 'Muhammad' and sometimes referred to as the 'king's arrow' (taj.)

hukumât	government (taj.)
imâm	person leading Muslim prayer; head of mosque
intelligentsia	'brain workers' in the Soviet system (teachers, doctors, etc.) (rus.)
jaktaî	summer tunic of thin material (taj.)
jamoat	sub-district (taj.)
jamoât khôna	Ismaili meeting house
jenû'b	south
jirâb	tights (taj.)
kafir/kafîr	nonbeliever (taj., arab.)
kala	castle (taj.)
kalym/kalîm/ kaling/kaleng	dowry (kg.)
kamar	leather belt (taj.)
kamitsh	large cooking and stirring spoon
kara	black (kg.)
kasi, kazi	judges responsible for trying petty crimes (taj.)
keîmak	cream (kg.)
kepka	hat (rus.)
kerege	lattice frame of the yurt (kg.)
khalat	caftan, coat (taj., kg.)
khalifa	religious functionary of the Ismailis (taj., arab.)
khan/khon	traditional ruler (taj., kg.)
khadurdsh	water mill (taj.)
khawass	Pamiri aristocracy (taj.)
khazonî	winter seed (taj.)
Kheek	low-grade social group (taj.)
khodjagî	privacy, 'private farmers' (taj.)
khon, khan	old honorary title (taj.)
khona	term for any building (taj.)
khonâ sûr	male circumcision (taj.)
Khuja	social group (religious leaders) (taj.)
kijik	ibex (kg.)
kishlak	village (rus.)
kitsûr	traditional oven for breadmaking (taj.)
koleb	hammer (taj.)
kolkhoz	cooperative farm in the Soviet system (rus.)
komsomol	youth organisation during the Soviet period (rus.)
konda	clan leader/s (taj.)
konda	'trunk', kinship group (taj.)
kuknar	poppy (taj.)
kulak	wealthier educated people, enemies of the Soviet system (rus.)
kumys	fermented horse milk (kg.)

kurga	forge, workshop of a blacksmith (taj.)
kurgân	hill, castle (Turkish)
kurût	dried, salted, non-perishable cheese (kg.)
kutshkar	*Ovis polii* (kg.)
kyryar	mutual help within kinship group (taj.)
la'l	type of ruby (taj.)
langar	rest house (taj.)
ljadshuar	lazurite (taj.)
lup-undr	traditional unit of land (taj.)
madawâb	schools of interpretation of the Koran
madrassa	religious school (taj., arab.)
mahalla	subsector, ward (e.g. in municipality of Khorog); informal (?) association of village elders (taj., arab.)
mahalli	village level (taj.)
mahr	bride price; money to be paid to the father (arab.)
maîdan	place, plaza (arab.)
majlis	elected village council (taj.)
maktab	school (taj.)
marǧûn	coral (arab.)
marvorâ	beads
mashrik	east (arab.)
mazâr	holy place (taj.)
mingbashi	regional governor (taj., kg.)
mir	mountain (taj.)
mir/mîr	local/regional political leader (taj.)
mirdah	local administrator (taj.)
mirea	man responsible for the management of irrigation (Afghan Wakhân)
mirob	man responsible for the water distribution (taj.)
mirza	honorary title for educated men, scribes (taj.)
mojuk	lentils
mullah/mulloh	religious functionary of the Sunni Muslims (Iranian)
musa	leather stockings/boots (taj.)
nagora	percussion instrument (taj.)
naï	flute
namaz/namoz/ nâmas	prayer (taj.)
nisba	family tree document; family tree (arab.)
nokar (pl. nûkaran)	military entourage of political leaders (taj.)
non/nôn/nân	bread (taj.)
nugulmaî	dish (taj.)
oblast	autonomous region (rus.)
owakh	frame ornamented with carvings on the terraces of older houses (taj.)

owring (pl. owringi)	footpath along slopes and cliffs (taj.)
padishah	king (of Afghanistan) (taj.)
parnom	ice shoes (taj.)
parzist	bracelet made from silver or base metal (taj.)
paski-tîn	the part of the living room with the stove (tîn or kitsûr) set into a hole in the raised floor
pekh	traditional shoes (taj.)
pela	bowl for tea (taj.)
perestroika	transformation, conversation, reorganisation (of the Soviet system) (rus.)
pik	mountain (rus.)
pikht	flour from dried mulberries
pioneers	children's organisation during the Soviet period (rus.)
pir	mountain, summit (taj.)
pir	religious leader (taj.)
pirân	woollen underskirt (taj.)
piruzâ	fragments of coral (taj.)
pitshka	type iron oven (rus.)
pjandsh	five, five (rivers) (taj.)
plov/palaw	'Pilav', rice dish (taj.)
plug	wooden plough (taj.)
por	measure for about 15 kg of wheat grains (taj.)
primak	husband living in his wife's household (taj.)
pyrk	stringed kernels of apricots (taj.)
qazi/qasi	judge (taj.)
qûm/qaûm/qoum	lineage (taj.)
qurût	dried cheese (taj., kg.)
rabâb, rabôb	stringed instrument (taj.)
rafak	see 'owring'
randa	pick (taj.)
rayis/raîs	chief, headman, president (taj.)
rayon	district (rus.)
Roshtkala	red castle (taj.)
Roshan	'the bright (place)', district in GBAO
ruband	embroidered veil for marriage ceremony (taj.)
rubob	music instrument (taj.)
rûza	religious fasting (taj.)
salat	prayer (arab.)
salla	turban (taj.)
samin	grain and land measure (taj.)
sandûq	wooden case/box (taj., arab.)
sayyid/sayyed	religious dignitaries, descendants of the Prophet Muhammad (arab.)
sekund	winnowing fork (taj.)

Sha-ana/shaná	high-grade social group (taj.)
shah/shoh	(local) political leader (taj.)
shahada	Islamic/Ismaili creed (arab.)
shaîtân	devil (arab.)
shakh	horn (taj.)
shargo	elevating mechanism to raise or lower the paddles of a water mill (taj.)
shir	milk (kg.)
shkâf	small fitted closet or closed rack (taj.)
shljapa/shlap	hat (rus.)
shnak	cradle (taj.)
shurpa/shurpó	soup (kg., taj.)
sidôn	granary (taj.)
sigandor-phaî/ zigandor-phaî	spade with long handle, the blade made out of wood or metal (taj.)
sindôn	anvil (taj.)
siptak	woven satchel (taj.)
sitar/sitor	guitar (taj.)
Somonî	Tajik currency unit
sotih/sotikh	unit of square measure = 100 square metres (rus.)
sovkhoz	state farm in the Soviet system (rus.)
sû	water (kg.)
subbotnik	'voluntary' labour during the Soviet period; self-help group, self-help work (rus.)
tabaq/amtabaq	plate, 'co-operative group' ('people who eat from the same plate'); subsector of a village, subdivision of a mahalla (taj., arab.)
tahorât	religious washing before prayer (taj.)
tandûr	oven for bread (taj.)
tarsuk	float made of inflated goatskins (taj.)
tash	stone (taj., kg.)
tersgen	a shrub used as fuel wood (kg., taj.)
teyzak	dried dung cake (kg., taj.)
tîğûr	lower mill-stone (taj.)
tirdôn	powder horn (taj.)
tog	coin pendant (taj.)
tokhm	'seed', kinship group in Wakhân (taj.)
toki/tokin/toqi/sket	embroidered cap of the Pamiris (taj.)
tsamak	false coral beads (taj.)
tshalak	hand spindle (taj.)
tshang	cymbal (taj.)
tshangak	hook (taj.)
tshapâr	snowshoe (taj.)
tsharkh	spinning wheel (taj.)

tshashma	spring (taj.)
tsheb	(wooden) eating spoon (taj.)
tshebbitz	small (wooden) spoon (taj.)
tshîd	living room (taj.)
tshirtshoî	tea with butter, milk and bread (taj.)
tshoî	tea (taj.)
tshor khôna	hood opening of the yurt (kg.)
tshor khôna	roof dome of the traditional Pamiri house (taj.)
tshorsî-ga	part of the main living hall of a house where guests are entertained (taj.)
thsukht	wooden frame for transport (taj.)
tsoothwm	see 'tersgen' (taj.)
tündük	dome or vault which forms a yurt's roof-opening (kg.)
tursuk	small float made out of inflated goatskin (taj.)
tût	mulberry (arab., taj.)
tutu	felt covers (kg.)
ûl	bent poles for the ceiling of the yurt (kg.)
ustô	man doing the circumcision of boys (taj.)
waltsh parra	mounds between ditches for planting potatoes and vegetables in (taj.)
wazir/wazîr	minister (taj., arab.)
wez	irrigation ditch (taj.)
wirth	irrigation canal (taj.)
yurta	yurt, felt-house of Kyrgyz nomads (kg.)
zaghir	flax (taj.)
zakât	alms, religious tax (arab.)
zamin-e shahi	private land belonging to a pir (taj.)
zekund	winnowing fork (taj.)
zer-phaî	wooden spade with a very long handle for irrigation work (taj.)
zirf/zirw	hand sickle (taj.)

NOTES

1 INTRODUCTION

1 In newer sources in Tajik: Viloyati Mukhtori Kuhistoni Badakhshon.

2 There are different views as to the reasons the Soviet authority supported Tajikistan, and especially GBAO, so massively. Some point to the use it afforded propaganda in presenting the southern border regions of the Soviet Union in a favourable light to Afghanistan and Pakistan within the 'Systems Race'. Naturally the population had to be won for the Soviet Union in the long run. Bordering on Xinjiang Province of China, the Wakhân Corridor and the Afghan region of Badakhshan, GBAO also had clear strategic importance to the Soviet Union, particularly after the invasion of Afghanistan. However, there are hints that the nationalist(!) Tajik leadership may have succeeded in going behind the backs of the central government in Moscow in order to procure unjustified material advantages for their land. The indication contradicting this argument, that Tajikistan and GBAO had not been particularly advanced at all but merely represented the economic and socio-political status quo within the Soviet Union, will be examined in Chapter 7.

3 A local term such as 'Property of the Mir' could of course have been a misunderstanding by those not familiar with the language of a geographic designation (like the somewhat ubiquitous mountain in Africa called 'I don't know'). As the word Pamir does, however, also appear in works by Iranian-speaking authors, a parallel to the typical misunderstandings in study and exploration is in this case untenable.

2 GENERAL FEATURES OF GORNO-BADAKHSHAN

1 However, the high-mountain character is soon felt, particularly when breathing becomes difficult with the smallest movement. Even the Pamiris suffer from this despite their apparently more robust build. They are said to use the term *tunk* for difficulties in breathing (see Yule 1872a: 470).

2 Lately also under the name Qullai Ismoili Somoni (see CIA World Factbook 2002 – Tajikistan).

3 The gorges are probably the result of a more recent rise of the entire mountain range and are not entirely due to water erosion (see von Klebelsberg 1914: 58).

4 Today there are two villages of the same name: the older Ishkashim of the classic travel literature lies in Afghanistan south of the Pyandsh. In Soviet times, a Tajik Ishkashim was founded as capital of the district of the same name several kilometres north on the right bank of the Pyandsh.

5 An exception is the Markansu, which has its estuary in the Kashgar on the other side of the Chinese border and loses itself in the Tarim Basin.

6 The peculiarity that a river has several names along its course possibly finds its roots in the direction of settlement, which went from downstream to upstream. When the population came to a tributary it was obviously unclear which of the two arms was the actual source river, so both were given new names (see Renner 1975: 52).
7 In 1997 we got stuck once ourselves around 5 p.m. at a tributary of the Bartang 30 km below Roshorve, although we had already crossed it several times before in the morning without problem. The tributary, some 30 m wide, had a depth of about 35 cm in the morning and around 55 cm in the afternoon.
8 Renner's report (1975: 177), according to which –63°C was measured in Bulun-kul, could not be confirmed by the rayon administration.
9 Even now, the mountains on both sides of the Pyandsh rise an amazing 6 cm each year (cf. St. George 1975: 126). This is due to pressure exerted by the Indian subcontinent as it squeezes under the central Asian plate. This is also most probably the source of the frequent earthquakes.
10 Stone (1992: 269) shows a figure with epicentres of earthquakes in central Asia verifying that GBAO is a land of high risk.
11 Agachanjanz (1980: 43) gives new numbers for the water flow at the beginning of the 1960s. At that time, 49 cubic metres of water per second flowed into Lake Sares and slightly more than 47 cubic metres per second flowed out of it, which would cause a constant enlargement of the lake.
12 On the fauna of the Pamir cf., among others, Dor and Naumann (1978: 33–37), Geiger (1887: 57–62), Machatschek (1921: 104–107) and von Schulz (1916: 211–213).
13 A rough overview for resources of minerals and raw materials in Tajikistan is provided by Stone in his figure 7.7 (1992: 273).
14 Not mentioned in the publication, but offered for sale or as a present to the author on two occasions by informants. In both cases the examples were very small, perhaps 0.2 carats.
15 Olufsen reports having found some gold himself ('traces of gold in the river sand' – 1904: 48).
16 In practice the people used even this term mostly for foreigners, whereas they usually described themselves according to their local origin (regional or valley community), for example as Shugnî or Ishkashîmî.
17 Possible activities in mining or trade with China were not considered. They are not, however, realistic options at this time.
18 Sources for 1940, 1959, 1970 and 1986 are the oblast administration (1998); for around 1920: von Schultz (1916: 6); for 1926 and 1956: *Encyclopaedia of Islam*, 'Badakhshân' entry for 1929: Lentz (1933a: 18).
19 Sources are censuses by the Russian commanders of Pamirskij Post.

3 HISTORY OF THE PAMIRS

1 Even the very comprehensive study of the Pamirs by Gawrilyuk und Yurochenko (1987) only starts with Marco Polo.
2 See map facing p. 48 of Zelinsky (1965).
3 Le Coq's remark also confirms our initial comments on the difficulty of crossing the Pamirs. In 1913 an avalanche buried an entire caravan of 36 people on the Terek pass (1928: 19).
4 For this reason all accounts and sketchmaps showing a route along the right bank of the Pyandsh are definitely inaccurate (e.g. Shahrani 1979a: 23).
5 According to Litvinsky's (1984: 14) plan of the site there is a kurgân on the right bank of the Pyandsh between Langar and Ishkashim in the Wakhân, a site (Kunti-Mush) on the upper Shakhdara in Shugnân, one in (Kal'ta-Tur) not far from Lake Sares, still in

Roshân, and several others in the high-lying valleys of the Murghâb (Kojujbel', Baljand-Kiik, Rang-kul, Jashil'-kul).

6 We should be cautious when using local statements, but in other cases it can be proved that until the break-up of the Soviet Union regional cultural treasures were not left in local museums and archives but were taken to Moscow and St Petersburg.

7 Freed from Seleucid rule by Diodotus, the Greek governor of Bactria, around 250 BC.

8 'Treasure hunting' was widespread over the whole of central Asia, and also in other former Soviet areas, in spite of strict conservation laws, and is also reported from Shugnân. Many sites were plundered before Soviet scientists were able to carry out proper archaeological investigations. Hoards of gold and silver often continue to be destroyed (melted down), as the thieves are primarily interested in their material value.

9 The Parthians had only recently taken over Roman weapons and military technology, which evidently gave them superiority over the Chinese. It is interesting to think that quasi 'Roman' legions marched through the Eastern Pamirs at that time.

10 Known by Herodotus as the Issedons, the Yüe-chi are an Indo-European people, horsemen of the steppes, credited with having invented the stirrup (see Baumer 1996: 44).

11 The reference here is primarily to the interminable, covert rivalry, sometimes erupting into open hostilities, between the principal Arab tribes (Azd, Qais, Bakr or Rabîa) for supremacy in the Eastern Omayyad empire.

12 At this point there is nothing to be gained from discussing whether the Tajiks should be described as an ethnic group, in the strict sense of the word, or as a cultural group or community.

13 This was also a typical situation in Europe in the Middle Ages, when a French territorial ruler could be at the same time a German imperial nobleman.

14 Strictly speaking the present-day Tajik part of the Wakhân district belonged to the Khanate of Kokand until the Russian occupation in 1875/6.

15 From the comprehensive literature on the subject it is worth mentioning the following: Hopkirk ([1990] 1992), Alder (1963), Coates and Coates (1951), Hayit (1971), von Hellwald ([1875] 1880), Krausse (1899), Pierce (1960), Saray (1982).

16 When discussing Russian and British interests here, it is worth noting that the areas under discussion have been settled since time immemorial and had their own sovereignty. For that reason mutual expansion did not primarily mean damaging the other side, but it meant violation of the local population and of the occupied states. Lord Curzon, who was the official Viceroy in India at the turn of the twentieth century, acknowledged quite openly: 'Afghanistan, Transcaspia and Persia are for me only figures on a chess board, used in the game of world domination' (quotation from Kreutzmann 1997: 169). Power is the only driving force here, and not the hypocritical reasons for colonisation so often given elsewhere, such as attempts to bring civilisation, missionary work or peace-keeping.

17 It is not clear from the sources whether this is a document of any significance in terms of international law or a mere exchange of notes.

18 Unfortunately I did not myself have access to Elias's rare book: *Confidential Report on a Mission to Chinese Turkistan and Badakhshan in 1886–6* (Calcutta 1886).

19 The Briton Younghusband's contribution is still the subject of contention (see Verrier 1991). His book – which might have shed light on the matter: *Confidential Report of a Mission to the Northern Frontier of Kashmir* (Calcutta 1890) – was not available from any library during research on this book. In his book: *The Heart of a Continent* (1896) Younghusband leaves the reader in the dark about his own contribution.

20 According to records in circulation in Khorog, there must have been invasions in previous years, which were, however, not considered as occupation.

21 The Afghan invasions are depicted vividly according to the oral tradition and local historical records.

22 Evidently women, girls and boys continued to be abducted by local Bukharan warlords even after 1895.
23 As part of the so-called 'Nomads' Khanate of Alai'.
24 Kreutzmann points out how arbitrary the borders were, as they divided settlements and exploited people, as ethnic minorities, for political ends (1997: 177). 'Tajikistan' was created in this way, with Dushanbe as its capital (formerly Stalinabad), but the traditional centres of Tajik culture – Bukhara and Samarkand – remained in Uzbekistan.
25 Even Herodotus mistakenly has both rivers flowing into one, which he called the Araxes.
26 Severtzov's study (1890) discusses in great detail the question of which place names mentioned in accounts from ancient times and the Middle Ages could refer to areas identifiable today. It would be too much to go into this in detail here.
27 There are various written forms in the literature, such as Hien-Thsang, Xuanzang, Hiuen-sang, etc.
28 See the English edition: *Xuanzang. A Buddhist Pilgrim on the Silk Road* (Boulder 1996).
29 Agachanjanz assumes, in his work 'Der Pamir im Buch des Marco Polo', that he was in the Pamirs for the first time in 1273 (1972: 54).
30 Compare Aurel Stein (1932: 7–20).
31 The most comprehensive description of the journeys of Wood and his British and Russian successors must be that of Paquier (1876), in which he discusses Marco Polo and other earlier travellers at great length.

4 ETHNOLOGY OF THE PAMIRIS

1 Olufsen gives the term 'Vakhé', just as the population of the Ishkashim region is called 'Ishkashimé' and that of Garan, 'Garané' (1904: 59).
2 Von Hellwald assumes that, in eastern Turkestan, the Persian-speaking population was only designated as 'Tajik' starting in the thirteenth century ([1875] 1880: 261).
3 According to Schurmann the word 'Tajik' is derived from the Arabic *tai* or *tâzî*, plus the Middle Persian suffix -k. Originally it meant a non-Muslim Arab. Later, in the form Tâzik, it came to mean a non-Arab Muslim in general (1962: 73, note 81).
4 The in-depth studies of Russian scientists on the languages of the Pamir (to cite a few: Salemann 1895; Tumanovi' 1903; Adrejev 1904, 1927, 1928; Zarubin 1924, 1926, 1927, 1930; Bartold 1925, 1927; Mallickij 1925) have been taken into consideration by Lentz (1933a).
5 In this case it is truly Modern Persian that is meant, not the rather different Tajik. The religious texts of the Ismailis are written in this language.
6 It cannot be ruled out that Olufsen did not differentiate between Shugnî and Tajik, so that Shugnî was truly introduced in lessons only under the Soviets and before that Persian or Tajik was used. Hjuler, who accompanied Olufsen on the second expedition, writes that 'Shugne and Vakhe are not and never were literary languages' (1912: 3).
7 Even the ruby mining in Garan was definitely done on an artisanal scale. Its importance is, at least since the existence of accurate records starting in the nineteenth century, marginal in any case.
8 Unlike wasteland, good grazing ground belongs to a village, even if it lies 100 km away near another village.
9 Although, proverbially, one cannot argue with taste, though melons are available at the higher altitudes, they do not have much taste.
10 The calculations were based on *Desjatines* of 1.09 hectares, which explains the odd numbers.
11 We found practically the same technique in the 1980s in the oases of the Egyptian Western Desert (see Bliss 1989).

12 'Every time there stands near the villages along the streams these small mills. Each clan has its own mill . . . The mills are built of wood and measure about 2.50 × 2.50 × 2.70 m. The wheel lies horizontally and powers two millstones against each other. A conical woollen sack hung above them contains the grain; an independent device and a groove are responsible for adding grain.'
13 See also de Grancy (1974: 72–73, and fig. 33).
14 What is probably meant is a leather sack which may be found among many central Asian peoples.
15 Based on Russian sources, Hayit reports that until 1917, 327,000 soldiers and more than 1.2 millon Russian farmers were settled in Turkestan, thus causing over 30.3 million *Desjatines* of land to be redistributed (1956: 23).
16 According to other sources, already in 1929.
17 There are great similarities with the irrigation system in the north Pakistani Hunza region (see Snoy 1975: 90–93).
18 This is a phenomenon that can also be observed in other parts of central Asia as well as in the north Pakistani Hunza region (see Snoy 1975: 81–81).
19 As in the Arabic-Islamic world, they were used for the ritual washing before prayer and to wash the hands before and after the meal. One jug, shown to us in the Wandsh valley, together with a basin to catch the washing water, is almost identical to similar examples that we recorded in Egypt at the beginning of the 1980s (Bliss 1994: 70, fig. 31).
20 We found no mention of men as potters in the literature. One informant's vague memories that men had previously also made pottery was not confirmed by third persons.
21 Von Schultz's indication that there was only a 'dürftige Holzkultur' (1916: 218) may, in any case, refer to the agricultural implements: among others the wooden plough and the yokes.
22 We came upon a similar exception in the Egyptian Oasis of Farafra, where, contrary to the surrounding oases, primarily men spun (see Bliss 1983).
23 A civil servant in Germany around 1910 earned between 60 and 120 German Marks. If the inhabitants of the Bartang really made, in 30 days (0.5 to 0.75 Marks per day), 15 to 22.25 Marks net, then gold prospecting certainly had a much greater importance than is mentioned in the literature.
24 Cf. Burns (1835, II: 215–216), Capus (1890a: xiii), Lullies (1887: 10), Michell (1889: 504–505), Wood (1872: 243–244).
25 The grain tax is confirmed, among others, by one of the earliest reports on Wakhân, penned by the so-called Mirza from British India (see Montgomery 1871: 157).
26 The term comes from the Arabic *sayyid* (*sayyed*) and designates a person who can trace his ancestry back to the family of the Islamic prophet Muhammad.
27 For example, in the author's 2003 study in Tajik Khatlon oblast, more than half of the inhabitants classed as poor earned in fact only half the income necessary to be considered 'poor' according to the national standards (see Bliss 2003).
28 An oft-mentioned negative memory of the Soviet era among our interview partners in Dashte Lutsh in Darwâs contrasted with the much-praised later concessions.
29 In north Pakistani Hunza – also settled by Shiites (though not a majority of Ismailis) – it is on the contrary a duty for the 'betrayed' husband to catch his unfaithful wife and her lover *in flagrante delicto* and kill them (see Snoy 1975: 139).
30 The author was frequently able to observe this fact in Egypt in the 1980s.
31 Von Schultz gives a list and short description of the most important castles of the Pamir region (1914: 62–64).
32 According to Le Coq such constructions are diffused as far as to Turfan, Chinese Turkestan (1926: 80).
33 Bows of this kind are also known from the north Pakistani region of Hunza.

34 For this, there was and is only insufficient methods of protection, such as rubbing the skin with tallow or other materials.
35 Olufsen says that 'the trinkets of the women are few and primitive. Earrings of silver are highly prized, as are also rings for the fingers' (1904: 70).
36 Almost all travellers tell of these paths, among which are Forsyth (1877), Cobbold (1900), Olufsen (1900, 1904), von Schultz (1914, 1916), Stein (1916, 1928, 1933), Borchers *et al.* (1929), Rickmers (1930), Lentz (1931), Coates and Coates (1951), Mursajew (1956), Stanjukowitsch (1961), Satulowski (1964).
37 On the other side of the Pyandsh, these *owringi* serve even today as the only means of reaching many villages lying along the river. See also the situation in north Pakistani Hunza, where such paths, called there *rafik*, were and are still common (d'Orléans 1906: 219–222, 230).
38 Such constructs, as well as some construction steps, are well illustrated in Kussmaul (1972: 57).
39 'In the time of times there was – [or] was not – a king, king Behram. Alkais was [his] Vizier. Another vizier was Bachtek. He sent them out to trade. On the way, they found something. Within were the riches of the world. They divided [it] among themselves . . .'

5 THE KYRGYZ OF THE MURGHÂB

1 Apart from Kyrgyz there are also many immigrant Pamiris who found work here in the Murghâb during Soviet times. Prior to that there were no non-Kyrgyz permanent residents in the entire Murghâb, except in Pamirskij Post (Murghâb town). Settlements such as Jelondî on the upper Gund and villages further north and north-east such as Bulun-kul or Sassyk-kul, which have an important Pamiri population, were artificially created by the Soviets without ever having been traditional settlements.
2 Lansdell says, however, that the term 'Kergis' or 'Kirgis' was probably first used in 569 during the reign of the Byzantian emperor Justinian II (1885, I: 231). According to Dor and Naumann (1978: 40), Krader (1962: 59) and Shahrani (1979a: 47), the Kyrgyz were mentioned even earlier, under the name of Kein-kuen, and going back as far as the Han period (206 BC to AD 220).
3 Cf. Gordon (1876: 221), Dubeux and Valmont (1848: 116), Olufsen (1904: 91) and Kreutzmann (1995: 162–163).
4 These measurements agree with those of Andrews, who quotes a height difference of 500 metres for migrations in the Little Pamirs (1997: 112).
5 In the very cold winter of 1995/6 large numbers of yaks also died when the temperature remained below –50°C at night for several weeks (down to –56°C).
6 Roskoschny gives a good description of how to make and use *kumys* (1890, II: 464–467).
7 The work of Dor and Naumann (1978: 57–66) and Andrews (1997) provides a good description, the latter illustrating every part of the yurt in detail. Van Leeuwen *et al.* (1994), Krist (1941) and Karutz (1911) give shorter accounts.
8 For *khalat* or *chalat* there is also the term *tshapan* (see von Schwartz 1900: 258).
9 We only once saw an old saddle which had obviously 'survived' the Soviet period: on both sides of the saddle cloth, which was also made of leather, the previous owner had had 200 large silver coins worked into it, mainly silver Russian roubles, which even 80 or 90 years ago must have given the saddle a value of several thousand dollars at present-day prices.
10 See the photo in Michaud and Michaud (1972: 463).
11 In rural parts of Egypt, or in Morocco and Tunisia to some extent, 'modern' positions were filled in a different way. Until well into the 1980s the traditional authorities in these countries sent their sons and nephews into the elected district councils, where they basically followed the instructions of the older generation.

12 However, still in early 2004 about 70 per cent of the whole population of the Murghâb was officially registered on the list for humanitarian assistance (see Kraudzun 2004: 14). According to the MSDSP survey from 2002, over 56 per cent of the population are in the poorest quartile, in Wandsh only 7 per cent (2004: 5).
13 Thus marriage between relatives of the first to fifth degree – counting from the father – is (or was) forbidden (Dor and Naumann 1978: 73–74). This does not correspond with Islamic marriage guidelines, which do allow parallel cousins to marry. Likewise there were restrictions to be observed with regard to adoptive parents, step-parents and their relatives.
14 Cf. Sommer (1842: 73), von Hellwald ([1875] 1880: 39), Lansdell (1885, I: 237) and Capus (1890b: 516, 1890c: 539).
15 Our Plate 5.3 showing a man taking part in building a yurt is thus, to a certain extent, a 'modern' exception. According to many accounts the men usually enjoy taking their ease on the saddle cloths while the women build the yurts on their own, even in bad weather (see von Schultz 1910b: 252).
16 It remains a matter of speculation whether the Kara-Kyrgyz also used shaman drums and thus whether individual drums might have survived into the present day.

6 ISMAILIS AND SUNNIS

1 See Kreutzmann (1996: 187); confirmed in conversations with leading Pamiris from the time of the civil war.
2 For some brief information on this, refer to the relevant entries in the *Encyclopaedia of Islam* (1960–95).
3 While the faith itself is supposed to be called 'Ismailiyya', to accord with the Arab term, the followers of this religion are called 'Ismailis'.
4 Samanid rule lasted altogether from 874 to 999.
5 It is only worth mentioning the ongoing project of the Aga Khan University of Central Asia, with a campus in Tajikistan (Khorog), Kyrgyzstan (Naryn) and Kazakhstan (Tekeli) (AKDN 2002).
6 Only Rickmers briefly mentions that the Ismaili leader looks after his 'far-off children' (1930: 287).
7 Followers of the national 'Islamic Rebirth Party' party, founded in 1990, or its Tajik offshoot Hizb-i Nahzat-i Islâmî did, however, seek refuge in Khorog during the civil war and in the ensuing years. There must be doubt over whether the party had much influence in GBAO itself because of its ideology, and not just because of its close ties to the Pamiris in the civil war, as Brown claims (1998: 88). The other large Islamic party, the Hizb ut-Tahrir al-Islâmî – active in central Asia and with offshoots in Tajikistan as well – is extremely anti-Shiite (see Rashid 2002: 160) and for that fundamental reason no ally of the Pamiris. This party would drive all Shiite Muslims out of central Asia according to various statements it has made.
8 It is almost certain that the sun festival was Naûrûz. Coates and Coates mention in this context that the new year festival coincides with the rituals we know from ancient Iran at the time of the Sassanids (1951: 193).
9 There is no intention here of comparing a *mazâr* with a *marabout* (Tunisia), a *kubbit ash-shikh* (Egypt) or a *wâlî* (Palestine). However, it would be interesting to look for parallels with the concept of the *baraka* (see p. 227) which, as is known, can be passed on at a sacred place like this.

7 ECONOMY AND SOCIETY IN THE SOVIET SYSTEM

1 With only moderate success, as the up-and-coming young elite was just as nationalistic in outlook (see Hambly 1975: 251).

2 A Soviet is a *de jure* council elected by members of the next level down. The chairman of the Soviet holds a *de jure* administrative function as councillor or mayor. At rayon and oblast level there was also a party organisation with a secretary who was higher-ranking than the leaders of the Soviets concerned.
3 Unlike in the cotton-growing areas in western Tajikistan, where according to Elizabeth Gomard 'stealing of harvests was widespread' (2003: 79).
4 'In the Autonomous Highland Region of Badakhshan, which is part of the Soviet Socialist Republic of Tajikistan, the last remaining remote settlements are in the process of being connected to the mains electricity supply. On the other side of the glaciers, however, the huts remain in darkness. In the villages of Badakhshan illiteracy has long since been stamped out, but on the other side of the mountains the shepherds have to ride for days, in order to find a "scribe" who can write or read out a letter for them.'
5 As the altitude of the runway had been underestimated, the plane was evidently unable to take off again until a proper runway had been built, which would have taken two to three months (Strong 1930: 24).
6 Pander mentions the theatre in Khorog, which regularly went on tour round the villages. One of the plays they staged was Schiller's *Kabale und Liebe* (1982: 338–339).
7 That is, every member of the family of a sovkhoz worker received a given amount of the produce, regardless of whether one or more persons worked for the sovkhoz.
8 It is possible that one or more livestock sovkhozes in the Murghâb showed a healthy balance sheet.
9 If no other references are given, the dates in Chapters 7 to 11 have been ascertained by the author himself, mainly based on regional and local authority statistics in GBAO.
10 In Soviet central Asia the main way of keeping livestock (see Leeuwen *et al.* 1994: 71).
11 In 1996, the mortality rate per thousand for children under five was 85 in India, 123 in Pakistan, and over 200 in Afghanistan.
12 This contradicts considerably the general data provided by Stringer (2003: 157–158) for Soviet central Asia.
13 There was a regular pool of language teachers from East Germany, but only in institutions in Moscow. The advantage with East German teachers was that they did not need to be paid in convertible currency. This fact, and to a lesser extent the fact that some of the population were of German descent, at least partly explain the prominence given to teaching German in central Asian schools in the past.
14 Up until 2003 we were not able to find out how many people were working privately. The number was probably extremely low and would have been concentrated mainly in trade and possibly the building of private houses.
15 According to Grobe-Hagel, average wages in 1987 in Tajikistan were 165.9 roubles per month, while the rate in the whole of the Soviet Union was 216.1 roubles (1992: 206). As this included the large workforce in the sovkhozes, where the earnings were about 110 roubles, the average income of qualified staff was much higher. In GBAO there was a higher number of white-collar workers than average because of the higher standard of education.
16 See Poliakov, who cites this figure as being standard for central Asia in general (1992: 28–29).
17 We assume that the sovkhoz management employed extra workers as part of the strategy of looking after regional interests. As these supernumeraries had their wages paid centrally, for thousands of Pamiris it was a good way of finding additional income.
18 March 8, 1927, was the climax of a campaign during which around 90,000 women in Uzbekistan responded to the call to burn their veils (see Gorzka 1990: 89).

8 THE ECONOMIC COLLAPSE

1 The personal opinion of a former member of the central committee of the Tajik Communist Party.
2 In the 1970s Kulyabi clans were already becoming established as bondsmen of the Leninabad faction who ruled the party (see Rubin 1993/4: 75).
3 Clearly the GBAO faction had already been deprived of power by the new Communist Party leadership, which was loyal to Gorbachev, after having been deliberately encouraged at the start of the Soviet invasion of Afghanistan (see Rubin 1993/4: 75).
4 However, most Western commentators agree that Russian troops provided the Kulyab faction with weapons, munitions and fuel during the civil war.
5 Some of their supporters may have been devout Muslims (see Asadullajew *et al.* 1998: 32–33). However, the opposition was motivated less by ideological reasons than by the fact that, as representatives of disadvantaged parts of the country, labels such as 'Democracy', 'Islam' or 'National Renaissance' would help them get a share of the power.
6 The office of president was abolished and replaced by that of parliamentary chairman, which was now the highest executive post.
7 Particularly the Islamic Renaissance Party, which formed flexible alliances with the Popular Front 'Rastokhes' (renaissance), the Democratic Party of Tajikistan, and Lal-i Badakhshân, the most important Ismaili party in GBAO.
8 In late 2004, the withdrawal of the Russian border guards started along the entire border to China and Afghanistan, leaving only some observation posts in strategically important localities.
9 The general public, surprisingly enough, is not aware that CIS border troops killed many more civilians during the course of legitimate, or simulated, defensive action against attacks by Afghanistan. With our own eyes we witnessed heavy weapons being arbitrarily fired across into Afghanistan in 1995, without any attack having first come from that direction. Murderous armed attacks of this kind were obviously designed to deceive the general public and legitimise the presence of border troops.
10 The Tajik Poverty Reduction Strategy Paper of June 2002 quotes 40 per cent budget allocations from Moscow (p. 10).
11 Usually the shortcomings are blamed on a failure to maintain the system. It must, however, be remembered that at the end of 1992 the Kulyab militia destroyed many of the pumping stations in Shartuz and near Kurgan-Tebe.
12 Occasionally, the emigration of Russians is confused with the exodus of Germans from central Asia into the then Federal Republic of Germany. In the 1980s, this exodus was organised at great financial expense by the Conservative German government in mutual agreement with Moscow.
13 After the currency reform, salaries, pensions and rates of welfare benefits had, if anything, less buying power. This is based on prices for local products that are about 50 per cent of the European rate, and about 40 per cent for food products. For the last few years many families have, for the first time, had to pay rent, and also charges for water, electricity and other services.
14 Apparently 11- to 12-year-old girls were actually sold into prostitution: 'a family would consider it a big luck if the family can get a bag of flour or other food staff in exchange for a girl' (Bruker 1997).
15 In Tajikistan in 1993, the monthly minimum wage was doubled on three occasions: on 1 January from 1,000 to 2,000 roubles, on 1 May to 4,000 and on 1 October to 8,000 roubles (see IMF 1994). However, even if you were actually paid, your money had much less buying power than previously. Whereas in 1991 a monthly salary would buy 484 kg of wheat flour, by the end of 1993 this had dropped to just 62 kg, which was no longer enough to feed a family. In GBAO this wage 'adjustment' was apparently never carried out.

16 In 1993 each person was allocated exactly 1.7 US dollars for health services under GBAO's budget.
17 In the Tajik Poverty Reduction Strategy Paper it is openly admitted that even in 2000, 21 per cent of children under 1–2 years had never been vaccinated (Tajikistan 2002: 23).
18 The majority of the refugees were Pamiris who had lived in Dushanbe before the civil war; only a small number originally came from Gharm or Khatlon.

9 INTERNATIONAL DEVELOPMENT AID

1 GBAO is still the worst-off region in Tajikistan though, followed by Khatlon (see Falkingham 2000: 18). In 2000, 39.1 per cent of the people of GBAO belonged to the poorest quintile of the population (in Khatlon 'only' 26.8 per cent). According to a MSDSP survey, in 2002 this poorest quintile had a total average annual income of 137 TJS (2004: 5): 97.5 per cent of the sample households from the survey lived on less than 1 US dollar per day (i.e. they lived under the poverty line [standard used by the WB]).
2 However, according to a MSDSP survey from 2002, 87 per cent of the households from the sample did not grow enough staples to cover basic needs (2004: 5).
3 The AKF was inaugurated in 1967 by the incumbent Aga Khan, with the aim of supporting a search for solutions in social development problems. The main target groups were Ismailis. Later it was recognised that this aim would not be achieved if it were only directed towards one social group in a region, and since then regional projects have been carried out regardless of the population's religious affiliations. The AKF has offices in Bangladesh, India, Pakistan, Tajikistan, Tanzania and Uganda. The Foundation's chief supporters are Ismaili groups in Great Britain, Canada and the USA. The AKF is part of the Aga Khan Development Network (AKDN), which is under the control of the imamate, and implements its social development projects.
4 The PRDP had its name changed to Mountain Societies Development and Support Programme (MSDSP) 1997/8, because its field of activity was extended to the Gharm valley and other neighbouring areas.
5 In 2002, 19 per cent of the male population and 41 per cent of the women still consider themselves unemployed (MSDSP 2004: 6). Only 27 per cent of the men and 17 per cent of the women have off-farm jobs.
6 In 1997 about 50 per cent of the vegetables produced were sold. Although this seems like overproduction, in reality they were often selling off food needed by their own families.
7 According to Elizabeth Gomart, leasing of sovkhoz land in Tajikistan seems to have been going on previously (2003: 73–74).
8 Gomart gives an example from Roshtkala, where a levy of 1.5 tonnes per hectare was imposed, although the harvest was only expected to be 0.8 tonnes (2003: 74).
9 Law No. 544 of 5 March 1992 was first put into practice on a wide scale in GBAO. In other places, people in influential government circles successfully blocked its implementation.
10 In 1998 we visited around 30 villages, concentrating on 12 so-called 'reference' villages (Tusyan, Roshorve, Vîr, Dashte Lutsh, Namadgut, Bunaî, Konakurgan, Jelondî, Javshangoz, Shidz, Sejd and Jomdsh).
11 A study carried out in the summer of 2003 in five rayons in Khatlon showed that there were only 30 private farmers out of around 58,560 households (Bliss 2003).
12 Dissolution carried out here was more or less final and irreversible, as the entire assets, including the buildings, were sold off or distributed. In Khatlon, on the other hand, the sovkhozes still possess over 95 per cent of their land and farm it themselves.
13 This is, however, not always the case. We subsequently met many people who

considered the lorries and even buses from former sovkhozes to be their own property. They confirmed that in many cases they had paid nothing for them.

14 Of all households, 84 per cent have kitchen gardens and 72 per cent have some other type of 'private' land received during the privatization process of the 1990s (see MSDSP 2004: 6).

15 The Pamiris' desire for equality even went so far as allocation of land to refugees from Dushanbe, for example, even if they had previously not lived in GBAO (see Herbers 2001: 20).

16 The Soviet Union's curious demarcation of the borders of 'independent Tajikistan' in the 1920s had led to the creation of numerous small, and in some cases tiny, enclaves on Kyrgyz territory. Large-scale seed production was carried out for the PRDP in one of these enclaves in the Alai.

17 This component was supported internationally, for example through the German GTZ and especially by the World Bank. Since 1997, the latter has supported the construction of 32 channels with a total length of 107 km, as part of the TASIF (see World Bank 2000b: 7).

18 I would like to comment here that the WFP did not come to any agreements with the lead donor, the MSDSP, and for its part 'paid' 3 kg of flour per day as food-for-work.

19 In a more recent report, Breu and Hurni mention 45 *jamoats* and 386 villages (2003: 46).

20 From about 2000 there is a discernible trend in the opposite direction: administration is gradually being given funding again and has begun resuming its duties.

21 In September 2003 we went on a short reconnaissance trip to Gharm with the purpose of comparing development there with that in GBAO.

22 The total value of industrial production in 1996 is estimated at not more than US$2,000.

23 In 1998, US$850,000 had already been earmarked for other projects.

24 Unfortunately, because of the way in which their projects are organised, the WFP's tempting offers repeatedly succeed in discouraging local people's own initiative. This includes projects run by other donors, who hitherto have only promoted self-help.

25 See Bliss (2003) on Khatlon oblast.

26 That is, the highest representative of the CPSU in Khorog.

10 DEVELOPMENT CONSTRAINTS AND PROSPECTS

1 The USA, an ally of the Northern Alliance, bears a large share of the responsibility because of its support for the warlords in northern Afghanistan. The latter are responsible for most of the opium poppy cultivation.

2 Dorothea Razumovsky, 'Inszenierte Kämpfe?' ('Staged fights?'), an article in the newspaper *Frankfurter Allgemeine Zeitung* (27 March 1996).

3 When this book was written in 2003/04, the economic consequences of the withdrawal of the Russian border guards in late 2004 were difficult to foresee: a substantial dismissal of civil staff with loss of income for hundreds of families and a considerable reduction of purchases of local and imported goods on the markets are most probable.

4 In theory many people are still employed by the sovkhozes, but they are only paid 1–3 dollars per month.

5 Of the 1,100 families who originally expressed interest in resettlement (also mentioned by Herbers) in a survey carried out in 1999, most no longer do so (Herbers 2001: 21). Any evaluation of such a survey must bear in mind that older people in particular are unlikely to actually want to be resettled, as they will remember previous forced resettlements.

6 There is a lack of information whether the Sino-Soviet territorial dispute in the Pamir region has definitely been settled. In 1969, the Chinese government specified that Russian forces had illegally occupied more than 20,000 square kilometres of 'Chinese territory' to the west of the Sari-kul range (Garver 1981: 107, 116–117, and map I).

SELECT BIBLIOGRAPHY

Abaeva, T. G. (1964): *Ocherki istorij Badakhshana* (Outline of the History of Badakhshan). Tashkent.

Abusaîd, Schochumorow (1997a): Pamir – The Land of Aryans, in Schochumorow Abusaîd (ed.) *Pamir – Strana Ariew* (Pamir – Land of Aryans). Duschanbe, 30–56.

Abusaîd, Schochumorow (1997b): Aryan Religion – Harmony of Two Worlds, in Schochumorow Abusaîd (ed.) *Pamir – Strana Ariew*. Duschanbe, 95–115.

ACTED (Agency for Technical Cooperation and Development) (2003): *Mission Report on the Impact of Different Activities of the Pamir High Mountains Integrated Project (PHIP)*. Hamburg (by Tobias Kraudzun).

Adamec (n.d.): *Gazetteer of Afghanistan*, Vol. 1 *Badakhshan* (reprint). Vienna.

Agachanjanz, Okmir E. (1972): Der Pamir im Buch des Marco Polo, in *A. Petermann's Mittheilungen aus Justus Perthes' Geographischer Anstalt* 116, 53–57.

Agachanjanz, Okmir E. (1980): *Auf dem Pamir*. Moskau.

Agachanjanz, Okmir E. (1985): Ein ökologischer Ansatz zur Höhenstufengliederung des Pamir-Alai, in *A. Petermann's Mittheilungen aus Justus Perthes' Geographischer Anstalt* 129, 17–23.

AKDI (Aga-Khan Development Institutions) (1994/5): *Development Network Bulletin* 15.

AKDN (Aga Khan Development Network) (2002): *University of Central Asia. An International Initiative for Education and Development in Central Asia*. Geneva.

AKDN (Aga Khan Development Network) (2003a): *Mountain Societies Development AKDN Support Programme* (Integrated rural development in Tajikistan; Health reform programme; Education reform programme). Dushanbe.

AKDN (Aga Khan Development Network) (2003b): *AKDN Country Strategy for Tajikistan*. Dushanbe.

Akademia Nauk Tadshikskoj SSR (1968): *Atlas Tadshikskoj Sowetskoj Sotzialistitsheskoj Respublikij*. Dushanbe and Moskwa.

Akiner, Shirin (1983): *Islamic Peoples of the Soviet Union*. London.

Akiner, Shirin (1996): *Central Asia: Conflict or Stability and Development*. Minority Rights Group International Report No. 6. London.

Akiner, Shirin (1997): *Political and Economic Trends in Central Asia*. London.

Albaum, L. I. and Brentjes, B. (1972): *Wächter des Goldes. Zur Geschichte und Kultur mittelasiatischer Völker vor dem Islam*. Berlin.

Albaum, L. I. and Brentjes, B. (1978): *Herren der Steppe. Zur Geschichte und Kultur mittelasiatischer Völker in islamischer Zeit*. Berlin.

Alder, Garry John (1963): *British India's Northern Frontier 1865–95*. London.

Allworth, Edward (1967): *Central Asia. A Century of Russian Rule*. New York.
Andreev, M. S. (1953, 1958): *Tadzhiki doliny Khuf* (The Tajiks of the Khûf valley), 2 vols, Stalinabad.
Andrews, Peter Alford (1997): *Nomad Tent Types in the Middle East*. Part I: Framed Tents. Vol. 1: Text, Vol. 2: Illustrations. Wiesbaden.
Anon. (1865): The Sia-Posh Kafirs, in *The Church Missionary* XV, 85–87.
Anwar Khan, Mohammed (1963): *England, Russia and Central Asia 1857–1878*. Peshawar.
Asadullajew, Ischandar *et al.* (1998): Tadschikistan Spezial. *WOSTOK* 5.
Asian Development Bank (ADB) (2000): *Women in Tajikistan*. Country Briefing Paper (by Jane Falkingham).
Asian Development Bank (ADB) (2002): *Economic Assessment Tajikistan*. Dushanbe.
Asian Development Bank (ADB) (n.d.): *Environment Profile of Tajikistan*. Dushanbe.
Atabaki, Touraj and O'Kane, John (eds) (1998) *Post-Soviet Central Asia*. London.
Atkins, M. (1989): *The Subtlest Battle: Islam in Soviet Tajikistan*. Philadelphia (Foreign Policy Research Institute).
Atkinson, Thomas William (1860): *Travels in the Regions of the Upper and Lower Amur*. New York.
Atkinson, Thomas William and Middendorf, A. Th. von (1864): *Reisen in den Steppen und Hochgebirgen Sibiriens und der angrenzenden Länder Central-Asiens*. Leipzig.
Attar, Ali (1997): Nowruz, das Frühlings- und Neujahrsfest der iranischen Völker, in *Der Arabische Almanach* 7, 3–11.
Bacon, Elizabeth (1966): *Central Asia under Russian Rule*. Ithaca.
Badenkov, Yuri (1998): Mountain Tajikistan: A Model of Conflictory Development, in Irmtraut Stellrecht (ed.) *Karakorum – Hindukush – Himalaya: Dynamics of Change. Pakistan–German Research Project*. Scientific Studies 4(II). Köln, 187–206.
Bakhramov, Z. (1957): Zemel'nye otnosheniya v Shugnane v kontse XIX – nachale XX (Land conditions in Shugnân at the end of the XIX and beginning of the XX Century), in *Ocherki po istorij Tadzhikistana* 1. Stalinabad, 47–85.
Baumer, Christoph (1996): *Geisterstädte der Südlichen Seidenstraße*. Stuttgart and Zürich.
Becker, Seymour (1968): *Russia's Protectorates in Central Asia: Bukhara and Khiva, 1865–1924*. Cambridge.
Behm, E. (1879): Das Quellgebiet des Oxus (with topographic map), in *Petermann's Mittheilungen aus Justus Perthes' Geographischer Anstalt* 25, 9–11, pl. I.
Bekhradnia, Shahin (1994): The Tajik Case for a Zoroastrian Identity, in *Religion, State and Society* Vol. 22(1), S. 109–121.
Belkina, M. (1966): In the Pamirs, in *Central Asian Review* 14, 221–231.
Bennigsen, Alexandre (1987): Afghanistan and the Muslims of the USSR, in Rosanne Klass (ed.) *Afghanistan. The Great Game Revisited*. New York, 287–299.
Bennigsen, Alexandre and Wimbush, S. Enders (1986): *Muslims of the Soviet Empire. A Guide*. Indianapolis.
Berg, Gabrielle van den (1998): Religious Poetry in Tajik Badakhshan, in *ISIM Newsletter* 1, 21.
Bernatzik, Hugo (1939): Tadschiks, in *Die Grosse Völkerkunde* Bd. 2. Leipzig, S. 47–52.
Bertrand, André (1992): Naissance d'une opinion publique au Tadjikistan, in Catherine Poujol (ed.) *Asie Centrale: Aux Confins des Empires, réveil et tumulte*. Paris, 205–215.
Biddulph, J. (1880): *Tribes of The Hindoo Koosh*. Calcutta.
Blacker, L. V. S. (1917): From India to Russia in 1914, in *Geographical Journal* 50(6), 399–418.

Bliss, Frank (1983): *Die Oasen Bahriya und Farâfra. Bestimmungsfaktoren und Folgen des sozialen und wirtschaftlichen Wandels in zwei Oasengesellschaften der Westlichen Wüste Ägyptens*. Bonn.

Bliss, Frank (1989): *Wirtschaftlicher und sozialer Wandel im 'Neuen Tal' Ägyptens. Über die Auswirkungen ägyptischer Regionalentwicklungspolitik in den Oasen der Westlichen Wüste*. Bonn.

Bliss, Frank (1994): Küche und Gastrecht in den Oasen der Westlichen Wüste Ägyptens, in *Archiv für Völkerkunde* 48, 45–83.

Bliss, Frank (1995): *Sozio-ökonomisches Gutachten 'Ernährungssicherung in Gorno-Badachschan, Tadschikistan'*. Remagen (for German Technical Cooperation).

Bliss, Frank (2000): *Die Praxis der deutschen Entwicklungszusammenarbeit*. Bonn.

Bliss, Frank (2003): Power Rehabilitation Project (ADB Loan 1817–TAJ). *Socio-Economic Report Vol. II: Socio-Economic Survey and Benchmark Study on Five Rayons in Khatlon Oblast*. Dushanbe.

Bliss, Frank (2004): *Socio-Economic Development in Khatlon (Tajikistan). Impact Review of ACTED Development Activities*. Dushanbe (with support of Luise Zagst).

Bliss Frank and Mamadsaid, Mamadsaidov (1998a): *Socio-economic Change in Gorno-Badakhshan. A Monitoring Report of the MSDSP 1997–1998*. Khorog.

Bliss Frank and Mamadsaid, Mamadsaidov (1998b): *Socio-economic Change in Gorno-Badakhshan. 12 Case Studies*. Khorog.

Bliss, Frank *et al.* (1997a): *Socio-economic Change in Gorno Badakhshan*. A Monitoring Report of the Pamir Relief and Development Programme. Khorog.

Bliss, Frank *et al.* (1997b): Case Study Tusyan. Annex 1 to *Socio-economic Change in Gorno Badakhshan*. A Monitoring Report of the Pamir Relief and Development Programme. Khorog.

Bliss, Frank (2005) Tajikistan needs policy change, in *Development and Cooperation* 32(2), 72–74.

Bobrinskij (Bobrinykoj), A. A. (1902): Sekta Izmail'ja (The Ismaili Sect). *Etnograficheskoe Obozrenie* 2(1).

Bobrinskij (Bobrinykoj), A. A. (1908): *Gortsy verkhov'ev Pjandzha* (Mountaineers of the Upper Pyandsh). Moscow.

Boivin, Michel (2003): *La Rénovation du Shî'isme Ismaélien en Inde et au Pakistan*. London.

Bonvalot, Gabriel (1889): *Du Caucase aux Indes à travers le Pamir*. Paris.

Bonvalot, Gabriel (1890): Voyage dans l'Asie Centrale, in *Bulletin de la Société de Géographie* 11, 469–498.

Borchers, Philipp (1931): *Berge und Gletscher im Pamir*. Stuttgart.

Borchers, Philipp *et al.* (1929): Bergfahrten im Pamir, in *Zeitschrift des Deutschen und Österreichischen Alpenvereins* 60, 64–142.

Bower, H. (1895): A Trip to Turkestan, in *Geographical Journal* 5(3), 240–257.

Breitenbach, Markus (1978): *Im Land der wilden Reiter*. Wien.

Brentjes, Burchard (1977): *Mittelasien*. Leipzig.

Brentjes, Burchard (1983): *Völkerschicksale am Hindukusch*. Leipzig.

Breu, T. and Hurni, H. (2003): *The Tajik Pamirs: Challenges of Sustainable Development in an Isolated Mountain Region*. Berne (Centre for Development and Environment).

Bröckers, Mathias (2002): *Verschwörungen, Verschwörungstheorien und die Geheimnisse des 11.9*. Frankfurt.

Brown, Bess A. (1998): The Civil War in Tajikistan, 1992–1993, in Mohammad Reza Djalili *et al.* (eds) *Tajikistan: The Trials of Independence*. New York, 86–96.

Broxup, Marie (1983): The Basmachi, in *Central Asian Survey* 2(1), 57–81.
Bruker, Natalia (1997) Prostitution – The Profession of Poverty and War, in *Asia-Plus Bulletin* 20.
Brunner, Georg (1988): Die Rechtslage der Minderheiten nach sowjetischem Verfassungsrecht, in Georg Brunner and Allan Kagedan (eds) *Die Minderheiten in der Sowjetunion und das Völkerrecht*. Köln, 23–56.
Brunnhofer, H. (1893): *Die Urgeschichte der Arier in Vorder- und Centralasien*, 3 vols. Leipzig.
Buckley, M. (ed.) (1997): *Post-Soviet Women: From the Baltic to Central Asia*. Cambridge.
Buddruss, Geog (1989): Review of Isidor Levin (ed.): *Märchen vom Dach der Welt. Überlieferungen der Pamir-Völker* (Köln 1986), in *Zeitschrift der Deutschen Morgenländischen Gesellschaft* 139(2), 449–454.
Burnes, Alexander (1835): *Reise nach und in Bokhara*, 2 vols. Weimar, (Engl. edition: *Travels into Bokhara*. London 1835.)
Capus, Guillaume (1889): Le Kafiristan et les Kafirs-Siahpouches, in *Revue Scientifiques* XVII, 1–8; XVIII, 237–241; XIX, 424–432.
Capus, Guillaume (1890a): *Le toit du monde (Pamir)*. Paris.
Capus, Guillaume (1890b): Pamir et Tchitral, in *Bulletin de la Société de Géographie* 11, 499–533.
Capus, Guillaume (1890c): Les Kirghizes du Pamir, in *Association française pour l'Avancement des Sciences, Compte rendus de la 19e session*, 533–540.
Capus, Guillaume (1893): Observations et notes météorologiques sur l'Asie Centrale et notamment les Pamirs, in *Bulletin de la Société de Géographie de Paris*, 316–338.
Castagné, J. (1925): *Les Basmatchis*. Paris.
Centlivres, Pierre and Centlivres-Demont, Micheline (1998): Tajikistan and Afghanistan: The Ethnic Groups on Either Side of the Border, in Mohammad Reza Djalili *et al.* (eds) *Tajikistan. The Trials of Independence*. Richmond, 3– 13.
Chalfin, N. A. (1975): *Rossija i Bucharskij emirat na zapadnom Pamire* (Russia and the Emirate Bukhara in the Western Pamir). Moskwa.
Champdor, Albert (1957): *Tamerlan*. Paris.
Cleinow, Georg (1929): Die Grundlagen der Nationalitätenpolitik in Russisch-Zentralasien, in *Osteuropa* Jg. 4, Heft 9, 559–573.
Cleinow, Georg (1930): Die neue Bundesrepublik Tadschikistan, in *Osteuropa* Jg.5, Heft 2, 116–120.
Coates, W. P. and Coates, Zelda K. (1951): *Soviets in Central Asia*. London.
Cobbold, Ralph W. (1900): *Innermost Asia*. London.
Craig, Robert W. (1977): *Storm and Sorrow in the High Pamirs*. Seattle.
Cumberland, Charles Sperling (1895): *Sport on the Pamirs and Turkistan Steppes*. London.
Cummings, Sally N. (2003): *Oil, Transition and Security in Central Asia*. London and New York.
Curzon, George N. (1889): *Russia in Central Asia*. London (reprint 1967).
Curzon, George N. (1896): The Pamir and the Sources of the Oxus, in *Geographical Journal* VIII (7, 8, 9) (reprint Nendeln 1978).
Daftary, Ferhad (1998): *A Short History of the Ismailis. Traditions of a Muslim Community*. Edinburgh.
Dauvergne, Henri (1892): Exploration dans l'Asie Centrale, in *Bulletin de la Société de Géographie* 13, 5–40.

Debelak, Julius (1875): Die Central-Asiatische Frage, in *Österreichische Militärzeitschrift*, 117–148.

Deutsche Wakhan-Expedition 1964 (n.d.): *Erfahrungen. Erlebnisse. Berichte.*

Deutsches Institut für Entwicklungspolitik (1993): Die zentralasiatischen GUS-Republiken Kirgistan, Usbekistan, Turkmenistan, Tadschikistan. *Berichte und Gutachten* 6. Berlin (by Irina Deutschland).

Djalili, Mohammad Reza *et al.* (eds) (1998): *Tajikistan. The Trials of Independence.* Richmond.

Djen-Hua, Hu and Dor, Rémy (1992): Littératures orales: un art de vivre, in Catherine Poujol (ed.) *Asie centrale. Aux confins des Empires, réveil et tumulte.* Paris, 125–131.

Dodikhodoyev, R. Kh. (1975): *Pamirskaya mikrotoponomiya.* Duschanbe.

Dor, Rémy (1975): *Contribution à l'étude des Kirghiz du Pamir Afghan* (= Cahiers Turcica 1). Paris.

Dor, Rémy (1976): Note sur le Yak au Pamir. Le Yak. Son rôle dans la vie matérielle et culturelle des éleveurs d'Asie Centrale. *Ethnozootechnie* No. 15. Paris, 126–132.

Dor, Rémy and Naumann, Clas M. (1978): *Die Kirghisen des afghanischen Pamir.* Graz.

Dubeux, M. and Valmont, M. V. (1848): *Tartarie, Beloutchistan, Boutan et Népal.* L'Univers Illustré. Histoire et description de tous les peuples. Paris.

Dubin, Lois Sherr (1997): *Alle Perlen dieser Welt*: Köln. (Engl. edition: *The History of Beads. From 30,000 B.C. to the Present.* New York, 1987.)

Dudoignon, Stéphane A. (1998): Political Parties and Forces in Tajikistan, 1989–1993, in Mohammad Reza Djalili *et al.* (eds) *Tajikistan. The Trials of Independence.* Richmond, 52–85.

Dunmore, Earl of (= C. A. Murray) (1893a): *The Pamirs*, 2 vols. London.

Dunmore, Earl of (= C. A. Murray) (1893b): Journeying in the Pamirs and Central Asia, in *Geographical Journal* 2(5), 385–402.

Durand, Algernon (1974 reprint): *The Making of a Frontier.* Graz.

Durrieux, A. and Fauvelle, R. (1901): *Samarkand la bien gardée.* Paris.

Economist Intelligence Unit (1994): *Country Report. Georgia, Armenia, Azerbaijan, Kazakhstan, Central Asian Republics.* London.

Eisener, Reinhard (1991): Auf den Spuren des tadschikischen Nationalismus, in *Ethnozität und Gesellschaft.* Occasional Papers 30. Berlin.

Elphinstone, Mont-Stuart (1815): *An Account of the Kingdom of Cabul.* London.

Emadi, Hafizullah (1998): Politics of Transformation and Ismailis in Gorno-Badakhshan, Tajikistan, in *Internationales Asienforum* 29(1–2), 5–22.

Encyclopedia of Islam (1960–95): s.n. Badakhshân; s.n. Ismâ'îliyya; s.n. Shughnân. Leiden.

Etherton, P. T. (1911): *Across the Roof of the World.* London.

Faiz Bakhsh, Múnshi (1872): see Yule (1872a).

Falkingham, Jane (2000): *A Profile of Poverty in Tajikistan.* London (Centre for Analysis of Social Exclusion, CASE paper 39).

Fedtschenko, A. (1872): Reise in Kokan und zum Nordende des Pamir, 1871, in *A. Petermann's Mittheilungen aus Justus Perthes' Geographischer Anstalt* 18, 161–168.

Von Ficker, H. (1914): Die Pamirexpedition des Deutschen und Österreichischen Alpenvereins 1913, in *Zeitschrift der Gesellschaft für Erdkunde zu Berlin*, 355–364.

Von Ficker, H. (1919): *Untersuchungen über die meteorologischen Verhältnisse der Parmirgebiete.* Wien.

Von Ficker, H. (ed.) (1929): *Die Alai-(Pamir) Expedition 1928.* Aus der Arbeit der Notgemeinschaft der deutschen Wissenschaft Heft 10. Berlin.

Von Ficker, H. and Rickmers, Willi Rickmer (1932): *Wissenschaftliche Ergebnisse der Alai-Pamir Expedition 1928*, 3 vols and maps. Berlin.

Figes, Orlando (2001): *Die Tragödie eines Volkes. Die Epoche der russischen Revolution 1891 bis 1924*. München. (Engl. edition: *A People's Tragedy. The Russian Revolution 1891–1924*, London 1996.)

Filchner, Wilhelm (1903): *Ein Ritt über den Pamir*. Berlin.

Filchner, Wilhelm (1950): *Ein Forscherleben*. Wiesbaden.

Finsterwalder, Richard (1929): Das Expeditionsgebiet im Pamir. Zu den Bild- und Kartenbeilagen der Alai-Pamir-Expedition 1928, in *Zeitschrift des Deutschen und Österreichischen Alpenvereins* 60, 143–160.

Fleming, Peter (1998): *Tartaren-Nachrichten*. Reinbek. (Engl. edition: *News from Tartary. A Journey from Peking to Kashmir*. London 1936.)

Forsyth, T. D. (1875): *Report on a Mission to Yarkand in 1873*. Calcutta.

Forsyth, T. D. (1877): Ost-Turkestan und das Pamir-Plateau nach den Forschungen der Britischen Gesandtschaft unter Sir T.D. Forsyth 1873 und 1874, in *A. Petermann's Mittheilungen aus Justus Perthes' Geographischer Anstalt* Ergänzungsheft 52. (Engl. edition: *Report on a Mission to Yarkund in 1873*. Calcutta 1875.)

Frembgen, Jürgen (1999): *Kleidung und Ausrüstung islamischer Gottessucher. Ein Beitrag zur materiellen Kultur des Derwischtums*. Studies in Oriental Religions Vol. 45. Wiesbaden.

Gabain, Annemarie von (1979): *Einführung in die Zentralasienkunde*. Darmstadt.

Gablenz, C. A. (1937): *D-Anoy bezwingt den Pamir*. Oldenburg.

Galwan, Rassul (1924): *Servant of Sahibs* (2nd edn). New York.

Garrone, Patrick (1999): Baksylyk: A Muslim Declination of Shamanism, in *ISIM Newsletter* 4, 15 (International Institute for the Study of Islam in the Modern World, Leiden).

Garver, John W. (1981): The Sino-Soviet Territorial Dispute in the Pamir Mountains Region, in *The China Quarterly* 85, 107–118.

Gauthiot, R. (1916): Notes sur le Yazgoulami, dialecte iranien des confins du Pamir, in *Journal Asiatique* 11(7), 239–270.

Gawrilyuk, Aleksandr and Yurotshenko, Wiktor (1987): *Pamir*. Moskwa.

Geiger, Wilhelm (1887): *Die Pamirgebiete. Eine geographische Monographie*. Wien (= Geographische Abhandlungen II, 1).

Geiger, Wilhelm (1898): Die Pamir-Dialekte, in Wilhelm Geiger and Ernst Kuhn *Grundriss der Iranischen Philologie* I(2), 287–344.

Goeje, M. J. de (1886): Mémoire sur les Carmathes du Bahraïn et les Fatimides. *Mémoires d'histoire et de géographie orientales* I. Leiden.

Goes, Benedict (Bento) de: see Wessels (1924).

Gomart, Elizabeth (2003): Between Civil War and Land Reform: Among the Poorest of the Poor in Tajikistan, in Nora Dudwick *et al.* (ed.) *When Things Fall Apart. Qualitative Studies of Poverty in the Former Soviet Union*. Washington, 57–93.

Gordon, T. E. (1876): *The Roof of the World*. Edinburgh.

Gorzka, Gabriele (1990): Frauen zwischen Islam und Sowjetmacht, in Kristine Von Soden (ed.) *Lust und Last. Sowjetische Frauen von Alexandra Kollontai bis heute*. Berlin, 84–95.

Götz, Roland and Halbach, Uwe (1993): *Politisches Lexikon GUS* (2nd edn). München.

Government of the Republic Tajikistan (2002): *Poverty Reduction Strategy Paper*. Dushanbe.

De Grancy, R. Senarclens (1974): Siedlungsbild und Hausformen der Ortschaft Wark im Wakhan, in Gratzl (ed.) *Hindukusch* (2nd edn), S. 61–75.

De Grancy, Roger S. and Kostka, Robert (1978): *Großer Pamir. Österreichisches Forschungsunternehmen 1975 in den Wakhan-Pamir/Afghanistan*. Graz.

Gratzl, Karl (1973): Materielle und geistige Struktur einer Siedlung am Oberlauf des Amu Darya. Dokumentation der Ortschaft Wark im Wakhan (NO-Afghanistan). Teil I, in *Ethnologische Zeitschrift* (Zürich), 54–83.

Gratzl, Karl (ed.) (1974): *Hindukusch. Österreichische Forschungsexpedition in den Wakhan* 1970 (2nd edn). Graz.

Grevemeyer, Jan-Heeren (1982): *Herrschaft, Raub und Gegenseitigkeit: Die politische Geschichte Badakhshans 1500–1883*. Wiesbaden.

Grierson, George Abraham (1920): *Ishkashimi, Zebaki and Yazghulami*. London (Prize Publication Fund Vol. 5).

Grjunberg, A. L. and Steblin-Kamenskij, I. M. (1976): *Skazki Narodov Pamira* (Narratives of the People of the Pamirs). Moskwa.

Grobe-Hagel, Karl (1992): *Rußlands Dritte Welt. Nationalitätenkonflikte und das Ende der Sowjetunion*. Frankfurt.

Grötzbach, Erwin (1964): Kulturgeographische Beobachtungen in Farkhâr-Tal (Afghanischer Hindukusch), in *Die Erde* 95(4), 279–300.

Grousset, René (1952): *Les empires des steppes*. Paris.

Halle, Fannina W. (1938): *Frauen des Ostens. Vom Matriarchat zu den Fliegerinnen von Baku*. Zürich.

Halm, Heinz (1998): Die Vielfalt des religiösen Lebens zur Fatimidenzeit, in Wilfried Seipel (ed.) *Schätze der Khalifen. Islamische Kunst zur Fatimidenzeit*. Wien, 141–143.

Hambly, Garvin (1975): *Zentralasien* (2nd edn). Frankfurt (= Fischer Weltgeschichte 16).

Hammer, Michel (1998): Perestroika as seen by some Tajik Historians, in Mohammad Reza Djalili *et al.* (eds): *Tajikistan. The Trials of Independence*. Richmond, 45–51.

Haussig, Hans Wilhelm (1983): Die *Geschichte Zentralasiens und der Seidenstraße in vorislamischer Zeit*. Darmstadt.

Haussig, Hans Wilhelm (1988): *Die Geschichte Zentralasiens und der Seidenstraße in islamischer Zeit*. Darmstadt.

Hayit, Baymirza (1956): *Turkestan im 20. Jahrhundert*. Darmstadt.

Hayit, Baymirza (1962): *Sowjetrussische Orientpolitik am Beispiel Turkestans*. Köln.

Hayit, Baymirza (1965): *Sowjetrussischer Kolonialismus und Imperialismus in Turkestan*. Oosterhout.

Hayit, Baymirza (1971): *Turkestan zwischen Russland und China*. Amsterdam.

Hayit, Baymirza (1997): *Berichte und Forschungen über Turkestan*. Köln.

Hayward, G. W. *et al.* (1871): Ost-Turkestan und seine Grenzgebirge, in *A. Petermann's Mittheilungen aus Justus Perthes' Geographischer Anstalt* 17, 257–273.

Hedin, Sven (1897): Forschungen über die physische Geographie des Hochlandes von Pamir im Frühjahr 1894, in: *Zeitschrift der Gesellschaft für Erdkunde zu Berlin* 29(4), 289–346.

Hedin, Sven (1900): Die geographisch-wissenschaftlichen Ergebnisse meiner Reisen in Zentralasien. 1894–1897. *A. Petermann's Mittheilungen aus Justus Perthes' Geographischer Anstalt Ergänzungsheft* 131.

Hedin, Sven (1919): *Durch Asiens Wüsten*, 2 vols. Leipzig.

Heine, Peter (2001): *Terror in Allahs Namen. Extremistische Kräfte im Islam*. Freiburg.

Hellwald, Friedrich von (1874): *The Russians in Central Asia*. London.

Hellwald, Friedrich von ([1875] 1880): *Centralasien. Landschaften und Völker in Kaschgar, Turkestan, Kaschmir und Tibet*. Leipzig.

Hemmo, Klaus (1970): *Abseits von den großen Straßen. Begegnungen zwischen Eismeer und Pamir*. Leipzig.

Herbers, Hiltrud (2001): Transformation im tadschikischen Pamir. Vom Proletariat zum Bauerntum, in *Geographische Rundschau* 53(12), 16–22. (Modified Engl. version in *Central Asian Survey* 20(3), 367–381.)

Herrlich, Albert (1938): *Land des Lichtes*. München.

Hetmanek, Allen (1990): The Political Face of Islam in Tajikistan: A Review of Muriel Atkin's *The Subtlest Battle*, in *Central Asian Survey* 9(3), 99–111.

Hiouen-Thsang (1857): *Mémoires sur les contrées occidentales, traduits du sanscrit en chinois, en l'an 648, par Hiouen-Thsang et du chinois en français par M. Stanislas Julien*. Paris, 2 vols.

Hjuler, A. (1912): *The Languages Spoken in the Western Pamir (Shugnan and Vakhan)*. The Second Danish Pamir Expedition. Copenhagen.

Hodgson, M. G. S. (1955): *The Order of Assassins*. The Hague.

Holzwarth, Wolfgang (1980): Segmentation und Staatsbildung in Afghanistan: Traditionelle sozio-politische Organisation in Badakhshan, Wakhan und Shegnan, in Kurt Greussing and Jan-Heeren Grevemeyer (eds) *Revolution in Iran und Afghanistan*. Frankfurt, 177–235.

Holzwarth, Wolfgang (1990): *Vom Fürstentum zur afghanischen Provinz. Badakhshan 1880–1935*. Berlin.

Hopkirk, Peter (1980): *Foreign Devils on the Silk Road*. Oxford.

Hopkirk, Peter ([1990] 1992): *The Great Game: On Secret Service in High Asia*. New York.

Hopkirk, Peter (1996): *Östlich von Konstantinopel. Kaiser Wilhelms Heiliger Krieg um die Macht im Osten*. München.

Hue, Fernand (1885): *Les Russes et les Anglais dans l'Afghanistan*. Paris.

Huttenbacki, Robert A. (1975): The 'Great Game' in the Pamirs and the Hindu-Kush: The British Conquest of Hunza and Nagar, in *Modern Asian Studies* 9, 1–29.

International Development Association/International Monetary Fund (IDA/IMF) (2002): *Joint Staff Assessment of the Poverty Reduction Strategy Paper (Tajikistan)*. Washington.

International Finance Corporation (IFC) (2004): *Business Environment in Tajikistan as Seen by Small and Medium Businesses*. Dushanbe.

International Monetary Fund (IMF) (1994): Tajikistan. *IMF Economic Review* 14. Washington.

El-Isztachri (al-Istakhrî) (1845): *Das Buch der Länder* (translation A. D. Mordtmann). Hamburg.

Ivanoff, Dr (1884a): Letter on the Russian Pamir Expedition of 1883, presented in *Proceedings of the Royal Geographical Society* VI, 138–142.

Ivanoff, Dr (1884b): Expédition russe au Pamir. Lettre du Dr. Ivanoff, in *Comptes rendu des séances de la Société de Géographie* 6, 163–166.

Iwanow, D. (1885): Orographischer Charakter des Pamir, in *A. Petermann's Mittheilungen aus Justus Perthes' Geographischer Anstalt* 31, 123–128.

James, Lawrence (reprint 1999): *Raj: The Making and Unmaking of British India*. London.

Janata, Alfred (1975): Beitrag zur Völkerkunde Afghanistans, in *Archiv für Völkerkunde* 29.

Jettmar, Karl (1975): *Die Religionen des Hindukush. Die Religionen der Menschheit* 4, 1. Stuttgart.

Jettmar, Karl *et al.* (1966): *Geschichte Mittelasiens*. Leiden and Köln.
Jochelson, Waldemar ([1928] 1970): *Peoples of Asiatic Russia*. New York.
Joyce, T. A. (1912): Notes on the Physical Anthropology of Chinese Turkestan and the Pamirs, in *Journal of the Royal Anthropological Institute of Great Britain* 42, 450–484.
Kaiser, Markus (2000): Translokale Zivilgesellschaft im postsowjetischen Vergesellschaftungsraum, in Manfred Glagow *et al.* (eds) *Russland auf dem Weg zur Zivilgesellschaft?* Münster, 143–160.
Karl, Uta (1972): Sie nannten mich Rotstrumpf. Als erste Europäerin am Dach der Welt, in *Westermanns Monatshefte* 11, 187–196.
Karutz, R. (1911): *Unter Kirgisen und Turkmenen*. Leipzig.
Karutz, R. (1925): *Die Völker Nord- und Mittelasiens*. Stuttgart.
Klass, Rosanne (1997): The Great Game Revisited, in Rosanne Klass (ed.) *Afghanistan: The Great Game Revisited*. New York, 1–29.
Klebelsberg, R. von (1914): Die Pamir-Expedition des Deutschen und Österreichischen Alpenvereins vom geologischen Standpunkt, in *Zeitschrift des Deutschen und Österreichischen Alpenvereins* 45, 52–60.
Kleveman, Lutz (2002): Opium für die ganze Welt, in *Die Zeit* 48, 15–18.
Klimburg, Max (1966): *Afghanistan. Das Land im historischen Spannungsfeld Mittelasiens*. Wien.
Klöden, G. A.von (1880): Das Hochland Pamir und der Lauf des Oxos, in *Aus allen Welttheilen* XI, 147–152, 180–185, 193–196.
Knight, E. F. (1893): *Where Three Empires Meet* (3rd edn). London (reprint Taipei 1971).
Kohn, Albin (1880): Aus dem Berichte der Ferghana-Expedition über die Wüste Pamir, in *Zeitschrift für Wissenschaftliche Geographie* 1, 21–27.
Kolarz, Walter (1956): *Die Nationalitätenpolitik der Sowjetunion*. Frankfurt.
Kossiakof, M. (1886): Notes of a Journey in Karateghin and Darwas in 1882, in *Proceedings of the Royal Geograpical Society* N.S. VIII(1), 32–47.
Kouropatkine, M. (1885): *Les confins anglo-russes dans l'Asie centrale* (translation by G. le Marchand). Paris.
Krader, Lawrence (1962): *Peoples of Central Asia*. The Hague.
Krafft, Hugues (1902): *A travers le Turkestan russe*. Paris.
Kraudzun, Tobias (2004): *Mission Report on the Impact of Different Activities of the Pamir High Mountains Integrated Project* (PHIP). Hamburg (for ACTED).
Krausse, A. (1899): *Russia in Asia*. London.
Kreutzmann, Hermann (1995): Mobile Viehwirtschaft der Kirgisen am Kara Köl: Wandlungsprozesse an der Höhengrenze der Ökumene im Ostpamir und im westlichen Kun Lun Shan, in *Petermanns Geographische Mitteilungen* 139(3), 159–178.
Kreutzmann, Hermann (1996): *Ethnizität im Entwicklungsprozess. Die Wakhi in Hochasien*. Berlin.
Kreutzmann, Hermann (1997): Vom 'Great Game' zum 'Clash of Civilizations'? Wahrnehmung und Wirkung von Imperialpolitik und Grenzziehungen in Zentralasien, in *Petermanns Geographische Mitteilungen* 141, 163–186.
Kreutzmann, Hermann (1999): Rückzugsgebiet und Migration: Überlegungen zur Mobilität als Existenzsicherungsstrategie in Hochasien, in Jörg Janzen (ed.) *Räumliche Mobilität und Existenzsicherung*. Fred Scholz zum 60. Geburtstag. Berlin, 83–104.
Kreutzmann, Hermann (2002): Gorno-Badakhshan: Experimente mit der Autonomie – Sowjetisches Erbe und Transformation im Pamir, in *Internationales Asienforum* 33(1–2), 31–46.

Krist, Gustav (1941): *Allein durchs verbotene Land. Fahrten in Zentralasien*. Wien.
Kullmann, E. (1968/9): Expedition in die Heimat der Marco-Polo-Schafe – ein Beitrag über die Tierwelt des afghanischen Pamir, in *Freunde des Kölner Zoo* 11, 107–122.
Kurbanov, Sobir (2002): *Republic of Tajikistan: PRSP Process and Fiscal Dimensions of Poverty*. Presentation, Dushanbe.
Kuschel, Walter (1978): Unbewohnte und verfallende Gebäude im Talbecken von Sarhad, in Roger Senarclens de Grancy and Robert Kostka (eds) *Grosser Pamir*. Graz, 249–272.
Kussmaul, Friedrich (1965a): Siedlung und Gehöft bei den Tajiken in den Bergländern Afghanistans, in *Anthropos* 60, 487–532.
Kussmaul, Friedrich (1965b): Badakhshan und seine Tajiken, in *Tribus* 14, 11–99.
Kussmaul, Friedrich (1967): Ein Ritt zwischen Pamir und Hindukusch, in *Kosmos* 63, 89–98.
Kussmaul, Friedrich (1969–73): Kulala – ein Töpferdorf im afghanischen Hindukusch, in *Mitteilungen der Berliner Gesellschaft für Ethnologie* 2, 41–50.
Kussmaul, Friedrich (1972): *Bergvölker im Hindukusch*. Stuttgart (Catalogue of the Linden-Museum).
Lansdell, H. (1885): *Russisch-Central Asien*, 3 vols. Leipzig. (Engl. edition: *Through Central Asia*. London, reprint Nendeln 1978.)
Le Coq, Albert von (1926): *Auf Hellas Spuren in Ost-Turkestan*. Leipzig.
Le Coq, Albert von (1928): *Von Land und Leuten in Ostturkestan*. Leipzig.
Leitner, G. W. (1893): A Secret Religion in the Hindukush [the Pamir Region] and in the Lebanon. *The Imperial and Asiatic Quarterly* N.S. 5. London, 417–434.
Lentz, Wolfgang (1929): Bericht über sprachwissenschaftliche und ethnographische Arbeiten der Expedition, in H. von Ficker (ed.) *Die Alai-(Pamir) Expedition 1928*. Berlin, 147–168.
Lentz, Wolfgang (1931): *Auf dem Dach der Welt (Pamir)*. Berlin.
Lentz, Wolfgang (1933a): *Pamir-Dialekte I. Materialien zur Kenntnis der Schugni-Gruppe*. Göttingen.
Lentz, Wolfgang (1933b): War Marco Polo auf dem Pamir?, in *Zeitschrift der Deutschen Morgenländischen Gesellschaft*, N.S. 11, 1–31.
Lentz, Wolfgang (1939): *Zeitrechnung in Nuristan und am Pamir*. Berlin (reprint Graz 1978).
Van Leeuwen, Carel *et al.* (1994): *Nomads in Central Asia*. Amsterdam.
Levin, Isidor ([1986] 1997): *Märchen vom Dach der Welt. Überlieferungen der Pamirvölker*. Köln.
Lewis, Bernard (1940): *The Origins of the Ismâ'îlism*. Cambridge.
Lewis, Bernard (1967): *The Assassins*. London.
Linn, Johannes (2002): Central Asia: Ten Years of Transition. Talking Points for Central Asia Donors' Consultation Meeting, Berlin, Germany, 1 March.
Littledale, St George R. (1892): A Journey across the Pamir from North to South, in *Proceedings of the Royal Geographical Society* 14(1), 1–35.
Littledale, St George R. (1894): A Journey Across Central Asia, in *Geographical Journal* 3(6), 445–475.
Litvinsky, Boris A. (1984): *Eisenzeitliche Kurgane zwischen Pamir und Aral-See*. München.
Lorimer, D. L. R. (1958): *The Wakhi Language*. London.
Lüders, Michael (2003): *Tee im Garten Timurs. Die Krisengebiete nach dem Irak-Krieg*. Zürich and Hamburg.
Luknizki, Pawel (1954): *Sowjet-Tadshikistan*. Moskau.

Luknizki, Pawel (1957): *Gletscher, Räuber, blaue Steine. Gefährliche Reisen auf dem Pamir*. Leipzig.

Lullies, Hans (1887): Die Kenntnis der Griechen und Römer vom Pamir-Hochland und den benachbarten Gebieten Asiens. *Wissenschaftliche Beilage zum XII. Jahresbericht 1886/87 des Königlichen Wilhelms-Gymnasiums zu Königsberg i.P.* Königsberg.

Lyons, Gervais (1910): *Afghanistan, the Buffer State*. London.

Maahs, Rita and Bronowski, Heinz (1979): *Zentralasien*. Leipzig.

Machatschek, Fritz (1921): *Landeskunde von Russisch Turkestan*. Stuttgart.

Mark, Rudolf A. (1992): *Die Völker der ehemaligen Sowjetunion. Ein Lexikon* (2nd edn). Köln.

Markov, G. E. (1978): Problems of Social Change Among the Asiatic Nomads, in Wolfgang Weissleder (ed.) *The Nomadic Alternative. Modes and Models of Interaction in the African-Asian Deserts and Steppes*. The Hague, 305–311.

Maspero, G. (1876): *Histoire ancienne des peuples de l'Orient* (2nd edn). Paris.

Mayendorff, G. de (1826): *Voyage à Boukhara*. Paris.

Michaud, Sabrina and Michaud, Roland (1972): Winter Caravan to the Roof of the World, in *National Geographic* 4, 435–465.

Michaud, Sabrina and Michaud, Roland (1977): Die letzte Karawane, in *Geo-Magazin* 8, 68–80.

Michell, Robert (1884): The Regions of the Upper Oxus, in *Proceedings of the Royal Geographical Society* VI(9), 489–512.

Mirwald, Peter and Roemer, Hans (1967): Beobachtungen im Wakhan (NE-Afghanistan), in *Erdkunde* 21(1), 48–57.

Monogarova, L. F. (1972): *Preobrazovaniya v bytu i kul'ture pripamirskikh narodnostey* (Changes in the way of life and culture of the Iranian-speaking people of the Pamir). Moskwa.

Monogarova, L. F. (1978): Changes in the Family Structure of the Pamir Nationalities in the Years of Socialist Construction, in Wolfgang Weissleder (ed.) *The Nomadic Alternative. Modes and Models of Interaction in the African-Asian Deserts and Steppes*. The Hague, 297–304.

Montgomery, T. G. (1871): Report of 'the Mirza's' Exploration from Cabul to Kashgar, in *Journal of the Royal Geographical Society* 41, 132–193.

Moorcroft, William and Trebeck, George (1841): *Travels in the Himalayan Provinces of Hindustan and the Panjab, in Ladakh and Kashmir, in Peshawar, Kabul, Kunduz and Bokhara*. London.

Morden, William J. (1927): *Across Asia's Snows and Deserts*. New York.

Morgan, E. Delmar (1892): The Pamir: A Geographical and Political Sketch, in *Scottish Geographical Magazine* 8, 15–23.

Morgan, Gerald (1981): *Anglo-Russian Rivalry in Central Asia*. London.

Morgenstierne, Georg (1973): *Indo-Iranian Frontier Languages*. Vol. II, *Iranian Pamir Languages* (2nd edn). Instituttet for Sammenlignende Kulturforskning, Serie B: 35. Oslo.

Moser, Henri (1885): *A travers l'Asie Centrale*. Paris.

Moser, Henri (1894): *L'Irrigation en Asie Centrale*. Paris.

Mountain Societies Development Support Programme (MSDSP) (2004): 2002 *Baseline Survey of Gorno-Badakhshan Autonomous Oblast, Tajikistan*. Dushanbe.

Müller, Claudius and Raunig, Walter (1982): *Der Weg zum Dach der Welt*. Innsbruck.

Mukhammad-Zoda, K. and Shokh-Zoda, M. (1973): *Tarikh-e Badakhshan* (Russian: Istoriya Badakhshana [History of Badakhshan]). Moskwa.

Mukhiddinov, I. (1975): *Zemledelie pamirskikh tadzhikov Vakhana i Ishkashima v XIX – nachale XX v* (Agriculture of the Pamir Tajiks von Wakhân and Ishkashim from the nineteenth to the beginning of the twentieth century). Moskwa.

Mursajew, E. M. (1956): *Auf unbetretenen Pfaden. Durch Asiens Wüsten und Hochgebirge*. Leipzig.

Myrdal, Jan (1980): *The Silk Road: A Journey from the High Pamirs and Ili through Sinkiang and Kansu*. London.

Naumann, Clas M. (1974): Pamir und Wakhan, in *Afghanistan Journal* 1(4), 91–103.

Oluffsen [*sic*], Ole (1897a): Über die dänische Pamir-Expedition im Jahr 1896, in *Verhandlungen der Gesellschaft für Erdkunde zu Berlin* 24(6), 328–339.

Oluffsen [*sic*], Ole (1897b): Die dänische Pamir-Expedition, in *Gaea. Natur und Leben* 33, 707–714.

Olufsen, Ole (1900): Die zweite Dänische Pamir-Expedition, in *Verhandlungen der Gesellschaft für Erdkunde zu* Berlin 27(1), 134–150.

Olufsen, Ole (1904): *Through the Unknown Pamirs*. London.

Olufsen, Ole (1911): *The Emir of Bukhara and his Country*. Gyldendal.

D'Orléans et Bragance, Louis (1906): *A Travers l'Hindo-Kush*. Paris.

Olzscha, Reiner and Cleinow, Georg (1942): *Turkestan. Die politisch-historischen und wirtschaftlichen Probleme Zentralasiens*. Leipzig.

Orr, Michael (1997): The Russian Army and the War in Tajikistan, in Mohammad Reza Djalili *et al.* (eds) *Tajikistan: The Trials of Independence*. New York, 151–160.

Oschanin, L. V. (1882): Oschanin's Erforschung von Karategin, 1878, in *A. Petermann's Mittheilungen aus Justus Perthes' Geographischer Anstalt* 28, 210–216.

Oshanin, L. V. (1937): *Iranskie plemena zapadnogo Pamira* (Iranian folk dance of the Western Pamir). Tashkent.

Pander, Klaus (1982): *Sowjetischer Orient. Kunst und Kultur, Geschichte und Gegenwart der Völker Mittelasiens*. Köln.

Pandit Manphil (1872): see Yule (1872a).

Paquier, J.-B. (1876): *Le Pamir. Etude de géographie physique et historique sur l'Asie Centrale*. Paris.

Patzelt, Gernot and de Grancy, Roger Senarclens (1978): Die Ortschaft Ptukh im östlichen Wakhan, in Roger Senarclens de Grancy and Kostka, Robert (eds) *Grosser Pamir*. Graz, 215–247.

Pauly. Lexikon der Antike (1979): *Der Kleine Pauly in fünf Bänden*. München.

Peshchereva, E. (1927): Molochnoye khozyaystvo gornykh tadzhikov i nekotorye cvyazannye s nim obychai (The milking industry of the mountain Tajiks and some customs connected with it), in M. S. Andreev (ed.) *On Tajikistan*. Tashkent.

Petermann's Mittheilungen (1878): Das von Russland beanspruchte Gebiet in Vorder-Asien (note of the editor), in *A. Petermann's Mittheilungen aus Justus Perthes' Geographischer Anstalt* 24, 285–292.

Pierce, Richard A. (1960): *Russian Central Asia*. Berkeley.

Poggenpohl, Nicolas de (1909): Aux sources du Mouksou par la région montagneuse du Pamir occidental, in *La Montagne* 5(8), 461–486.

Poliakov, Sergei P. (1992): *Everyday Islam. Religion and Tradition in Rural Central Asia*. New York.

Polo, Marco (1997): *The Travels*. Ware (Hertfordshire).

De Poncins, Edmond (1897): *Chasses et explorations dans la région des Pamirs*. Paris.

De Ponfilly, Christophe (1988): *Massoud l'Afghan*. Paris.

Potagos, Paparotis (1885): *Dix années de voyage dans l'Asie Centrale*. Paris.
Poujol, Catherine (1998): Some Reflections on Russian Involvement in the Tajik Conflict, 1992–1993, in Mohammad Reza Djalili *et al.* (eds): *Tajikistan. The Trials of Independence*. Richmond, 99–110.
Proceedings of the Royal Geographical Society VI (1884): The Russian Pamir Expedition of 1883, paper translated from the *Isvestia Imp. Rusk. Geogr. Obshchestva Vuipusk* 4 (note of the editor).
Rakhimov, M. (1963): Articles on recent ethnographical research, in *Izvestiya AN Tadzhikstoy SSR. Otdelenie obshchestvennykh nauk* nr. 1(32). Dushanbe.
Rakowska-Harmstone, Teresa (1970): *Russia and Nationalism in Central Asia*. London.
Rashid, Ahmed (2002): *Heiliger Krieg am Hindukusch. der Kampf um Macht und Glauben in Zentralasien*. München. (Engl. edition: *Jihad. The Rise of Militant Islam in Central Asia*, New Haven and London.)
Raunig, Water (1975): Vorläufiger Kurzbericht über die ethnographischen Arbeiten im Rahmen von EXPLORATION PAMIR 75, in *Ethnologische Zeitschrift* (Zürich), 105–111.
Raunig, Walter (1978): Zur materiellen Kultur des Bewohner des Wakhan, in Roger S. de Grancy and Robert Kostka (eds) *Großer Pamir*. Graz, 275–285.
Raunig, Walter (1982): Pamir und Wakhân – ein kaum bekannter Kreuzweg der Kulturen in Zentralasien, in Alfred Wendehorst (ed.) *Begegnungsraum von Kulturen*. Neustadt, 125–134.
Rawlinson, Henry C. (1872): Monograph on the Oxus, in *Journal of the Royal Geographical Society* 42, 482–513.
Rawlinson, Henry C. (1873): Observations on Badakhshân and Wakhân, in *Proceedings of the Royal Geographical Society* N.S. XVII (2), 108–116.
Rawlinson, Henry C. (1875): *England and Russia in the East*. London.
Rayfield, Donal (1977): *Lhasa war sein Traum. Die Entdeckungsreisen von Nikolai Prschewalskij in Zentralasien*. Wiesbaden. (Engl. edition: *The Dream of Lhasa*. London 1976.)
Razumovsky, Dorothea (1996): Inszenierte Kämpfe?, in *Frankfurter Allgemeine Zeitung* (of 27 March).
Reclus, Elisée (1881): *Nouvelle Géographie universelle. L'Asie Russe*. Paris.
Regel, Albert (1884a): Übersicht über A. Regels Reisen am obern Amu-Darja, 1881–83, in *A. Petermann's Mittheilungen aus Justus Perthes' Geographischer Anstalt* 30, 86–89.
Regel, Albert (1884b): Voyage de A. Regel au Choughnan et au Badakchan, in *Comptes rendu des séances de la Société de Géographie* 1884(15), 446–452.
Regel, Albert (1885): Einige Bemerkungen über das Gesundheitsverhältnis der Länder des obern Amu-Darja, in *A. Petermann's Mittheilungen aus Justus Perthes' Geographischer Anstalt* 31, 171–175.
Renner, Georg (1975): *Biwak auf dem Dach der Welt*. Leipzig.
Rickenbach, Judith (1989): *Oxus: 2000 Jahre Kunst am Oxus-Fluss in Mittelasien*. Zürich.
Rickmers, Willi Rickmer (1914): Vorläufiger Bericht über die Pamirexpedition des Deutschen und Österreichischen Alpenvereins 1913, in *Zeitschrift des Deutschen und Österreichischen Alpenvereins* 45, 1–51.
Rickmers, Willi Rickmer (1929a): Die Alai-Pamir-Expedition 1928, in *Zeitschrift des Deutschen und Österreichischen Alpenvereins* 60, 59–63.
Rickmers, Willi Rickmer (1929b): On the Fringe of the Pamirs, in *The Alpine Journal* 41, 156–160.

Rickmers, Willi Rickmer (1930): *Alai! Alai! Arbeiten und Erlebnisse der Deutsch-Russischen Alai-Pamir-Expedition*. Leipzig.
Rickmers, Willi Rickmer *et al.* (1929): *Die Alai-(Pamir) Expedition 1928*. Berlin.
Ritter, Carl (1832): *Die Erdkunde, 2. Theil Band I. Die Erdkunde von Asien*. Berlin.
Roberts of Kandahar, Lord (1900): *Forty-One Years in India*. London.
Robertson, G. S. (1894): Kafiristan, in *Geographical Journal* 4(3), 193–218.
Rocca, Félix de (1896): *De l'Alai à l'Amou-Daria*. Paris.
Ro'i, Yaacov (1991): The Soviet and Russian Context of the Development of Nationalism in Soviet Central Asia, in *Cahiers du Monde Russe et Soviétique* 32, 123–142.
Rosenbaum, Monika (1991): *Frauenarbeit und Frauenalltag in der Sowjetunion*. Münster.
Roskoschny, Hermann (about 1890): *Das asiatische Russland*, 2 vols. Leipzig.
Rubin, Barnett R. (1993–4): The Fragmentation of Tajikistan, in *Survival* 35(4), 71–91.
Rudy, Zvi (1962): *Ethnosoziologie sowjetischer Völker*. Bern and München.
Saparbaev, A. and Temirkulov, K. (2003): *Pamir Kirgizdare* (Tales and poems from the Murghâb Kyrgyz). Osh.
Saray, Mehmet (1982): The Russian Conquest of Central Asia, in *Central Asian Survey* 1(2/3), 1–30.
Sarianidi, Viktor (1986): *Die Kunst des Alten Afghanistan*. Leipzig.
Satulowski, D. M. (1953): *Auf den Gletschern und Gipfeln Mittelasiens*. Leipzig.
Satulowski, D. M. (1964): *In Firn und Fels der Siebentausender*. Leipzig.
Schlaginweit-Sakünlünski, Hermann von (1880): *Reisen in Indien und Hochasien*. Vierter Band. *Hochasien: III. Ost-Turkistan und Umgebungen*. Jena.
Scholl-Latour, Peter (1991): *Den Gottlosen die Hölle. Der Islam in der Sowjetunion*. München.
Scholl-Latour, Peter (1996): *Das Schlachtfeld der Zukunft. Zwischen Kaukasus und Pamir*. Berlin.
Schultz, Arved von (1910a): Vorläufiger Bericht über meine Pamirexpedition 1909, in *A. Petermann's Mittheilungen aus Justus Perthes' Geographischer Anstalt* 56, 140–141.
Schultz, Arved von (1910b): Volks- und wirtschaftliche Studien im Pamir, in *A. Petermann's Mittheilungen aus Justus Perthes' Geographischer Anstalt* 56, 250–254.
Schultz, Arved von (1911/12): Zur Kenntnis der arischen Bevölkerung des Pamir, in *Orientalisches Archiv* II, 23–29.
Schultz, Arved von (1912): Bericht über den bisherigen Verlauf meiner Pamirexpedition 1911/12, in *A. Petermann's Mittheilungen aus Justus Perthes' Geographischer Anstalt* 58, 190–193, 261–265.
Schultz, Arved von (1914): *Der materielle Kulturbesitz der Pamirtadschik*. Gießen.
Schultz, Arved von (1916): *Landeskundliche Forschungen im Pamir*. Hamburg (Abhandlungen des Hamburger Kolonialinstituts 33).
Schurmann, H. F. (1962): *The Mongols of Afghanistan*. Gravenhage.
Schwarz, Franz von (1900): *Turkestan, die Wiege der indogermanischen Völker*. Freiburg.
Schweinitz, Hans-Hermann von (1910): *Orientalische Wanderungen*. Berlin.
Sehring, Jennifer (2000): Laboratorium der Völkerfreundschaft. Zentralasien: Nach der Staats- nun die Nationenbildung, in *Blätter des Informationszentrums 3. Welt*, No. 249, 28–30.
Semenov, A. A. (1916): *Istorya Shugnana* (History of Shugnan). Tashkent.
Severtzov, Nicolas (1890): Etudes de géographie historique sur les anciens itinéraires à travers le Pamir, in *Bulletin de la Société de Géographie* 11, 417–467, 553–610.

Shahrani, M. Nafiz Mohib (1979a): *The Kirgiz and Wakhi of Afghanistan: Adaption to Closed Frontiers*. Seattle and London. (Paperback-edition with new epilogue, Washington 2002.)

Shahrani, M. Nafiz Mohib (1979b): Ethnic Relations Under Closed Frontier Conditions: Northeast Badakhshan, in William O. McCagg and Brian D. Silver (eds) *Soviet Asian Ethnic Frontiers*. New York, 174–192.

Shaw, Robert (1872): *Reise nach der Hohen Tartarei, Yarkand und Kashgar und Rückreise über den Karakoram-Pass*. Jena. (Engl. edition: *Visit to the High Tartary, Yarkand and Kashgar*, London 1871.)

Shaw, Robert (1876): On the Ghalchah languages (Wakhí and Sarikolí), in *Journal of the Royal Society of Bengal* 45(1), 139–278.

Shaw, Robert (1877): On the Shighni (Ghalchah) Dialect, in *Journal of the Asiatic Society of Bengal* II, 97–126.

Shibaeva, Yu. A. (1973): *Zhivotnovodstvo u kirgizov Vostochnogo Pamira* (Kyrgyz livestock breeding in the Eastern Pamir). Trudy Instituta etnografii AN SSSR. Novaya seriya Vol. 98. Leningrad.

Sievers, Eric W. (2003): *The Post-Soviet Decline of Central Asia. Sustainable Development and Comprehensive Capital*. London and New York.

Simon, Gerhard (1982): Nationalismus und Nationalitätenpolitik in der Sowjetunion seit Stalin, in Georg Brunner and Boris Meissner (eds): *Nationalitäten-Probleme in der Sowjetunion und Osteuropa*. Köln, 45–66.

Singer, André (1987): Problems of Pastoralism in the Afghan Pamirs, in *Asian Affairs* 63, 156–160.

Snoy, Peter (1975): *Bagrot. Eine dardische Talschaft im Karakorum*. Graz.

Snoy, Peter (1992): Ethnographie Ost-Turkestans und Kaschmirs, in Claudius C. Müller and Walter Raunig (eds) *Der Weg zum Dach der Welt*. Innsbruck, 49–50.

Sommer, Johann Gottfried (ed.) (1842): Die Kirgisen, in *Taschenbuchzur Verbreitung geographischer Kenntnisse* 20. Prag, 26–76.

Soucek, Svat (2000): *A History of Inner Asia*. Cambridge.

Spear, Percival (1965): *A History of India. Vol. II, From the Sixteenth Century to the Twentieth Century* (reprint Delhi 1990).

St. George, George (1975): *Russland: Wüsten und Berge* (2nd edn) Amsterdam.

Stanjukowitsch, K. (1961): *Markansu – Tal des Todes. Forschungsfahrten in Pamir und Tienschan*. Leipzig.

Stein, Sir Aurel (1916): A Third Journey of Exploration in Central Asia, in *Geographical Journal* 47(5), 358–364; 48(2), 97–130; 48(3), 193–229.

Stein, Sir Aurel (1922): A Chinese Expedition across the Pamirs and Hindukush, AD 747, in *Geographical Journal* 59(2), 112–131.

Stein, Sir Aurel (1928): *Innermost Asia. Detailed Report of Explorations in Central Asia, Kan-su and Eastern Irân*, 4 vols. Oxford.

Stein, Sir Aurel (1929): *On Alexander's Track to the Indus. Personal Narrative of Exploration on the North-West-Frontier of India*. London.

Stein, Sir Aurel (1932): On Ancient Tracks Past the Pâmîrs, in *Himalayan Journal* IV, 1–26.

Stein, Sir Aurel (1933): *On Ancient Central-Asian Tracks* (reprint Chicago 1964).

Steiner, Walter (1982): *Auf den Gletschern des Pamir*. Leipzig.

Stellrecht, Irmtraut (ed.) (1998a): *Bibliography – Northern Pakistan. Pakistan–German Research Project*. Scientific Studies 1. Köln.

Stellrecht, Irmtraut (ed.) (1998b): *Karakorum – Hindukush – Himalaya: Dynamics of Change. Pakistan–German Research Project*. Scientific Studies 4 (I, II). Köln.

Stern, Bernhard (1893): Pamir, 'das Dach der Welt', in *Das Ausland* 66(13), 193–197, 246–250.

Steveni, W. Barnes (1891): Colonel Grambcheffsky's Pamir Explorations and the Indian Government, in *The Asiatic Quarterly Review* N.S. 2, 255–260.

Stiglitz, Joseph (2002) *Die Schatten der Globalisierung*. Berlin. (Engl. edition: *Globalization and its Discontents*. New York.)

Stone, Peter B. (ed.) (1992): *The State of the World's Mountains. A Global Report*. London and New Jersey.

Stringer, Alex (2003): Soviet Development in Central Asia. The Classic Colonial Syndrome?, in Tom Everett-Heath (ed.) *Central Asia. Aspects of Transition*. London and New York, 146–166.

Strong, Anna Louise (1930): *The Road to the Grey Pamir*. New York.

Tagaev, Borys (1898): Pamirskij pochod (The Pamir Campaign), in *Istoriceskij vestnik* 73, 111–138, 489–519, 859–888.

Tajikistan, Government of the Republic of (2002): *Poverty Reduction Strategy Paper*. Dushanbe.

Thackston, Wheeler M. (2002): *The Baburnama. Memoirs of Babur, Prince and Emperor*. New York.

Tilman. H. W. (1953): *Deux montagnes et une rivière*. Paris.

Tomaschek, Wilhelm (1877): *Centralasiatische Studien I. Sogdiana*. Wien.

Tomaschek, Wilhelm (1880): *Centralasiatische Studien II. Die Pamir-Dialekte*. Wien.

Toynbee, Arnold J. (1961): *Between Oxus and Jumna*. London.

Trotter, H. (1878): On the Geographical Results of the Mission to Kashgar, under Sir T. Douglas Forsyth in 1873–74, in *Journal of the Royal Geographical Society* 48, 173–234.

Trutanow, Igor (1994): *Zwischen Koran und Coca-Cola (Zentralasien)*. Berlin.

Ujfalvy, Charles E. de (1878): *Le Kohistan, le Ferghana et Kouldja*. Paris.

Ujfalvy, Charles E. de (1879): *Le Syr-Daria*. Paris.

Ujfalvy-Bourdon, de (1880): *De Paris à Samarkand. Le Ferghana, le Kouldja et la Sibérie Occidentale*. Paris.

Ujfalvy, Charles E. de (1884): *Aus dem westlichen Himalaya*. Leipzig.

Ujfalvy, Charles E. de (1887): Quelques observations sur les Tadjiks des montagnes, appelés aussi Galtchas, in *Bulletins de la Société d'Anthropologie de Paris*, 15–43.

Ujfalvy, Charles E. de (1896): *Les aryens au nord et au sud de l'Hindou-Kouch*. Paris.

United Nations Development Programme (UNDP) (2003): *Tapping the Potential. Improving Water Management in Tajikistan. National Human Development Report 2003*. Dushanbe.

United Nations Development Programme (UNDP) (2004): *Human Development Report 2004*. New York.

Vámbéry, Arminius (1865a): *Voyage d'un faux derviche dans l'Asie Centrale*. Paris.

Vámbéry, Arminius (1865b): *Reise in Mittelasien von Teheran durch die Turkmenische Wüste an der Ostküste des Kaspischen Meeres nach Chiwa, Bochara und Samarkand ausgeführt im Jahr 1863*. Leipzig.

Vámbéry, Hermann (= Arminius) (1868): *Skizzen aus Mittelasien*. Leipzig.

Vámbéry, Hermann (= Arminius) (1871): *Russlands Machtstellung in Asien*. Leipzig.

Vámbéry, Hermann (= Arminius) (1872): *Geschichte Bocharas*. Stuttgart.

Vámbéry, Hermann (= Arminius) (1876): *Sittenbilder aus dem Morgenlande*. Berlin.

Van den Berg, Gabrielle (1998): Religious Poetry in Tajik Badakhshan, in *ISIM Newsletter* 1, 21.

Vénukoff (Wenjukow), Michel (1884): La région du Haut-Oxus et les derniers voyages russes. Note de M. Michel Vénukoff, in *Comptes rendu des séances de la Société de Géographie* 1: 14–17.

Verrier, Anthony (1991): *Francis Younghusband and the Great Game*. London.

Voigt, G. (1933): *Kafiristan*. Breslau.

Wartenburg, Maximilian Yorck von (1900): *Das Vordringen des russischen Macht in Asien*. Berlin.

Weber, Max (1922): *Grundriss der Sozialökonomik*. III. *Abteilung: Wirtschaft und Gesellschaft*. Tübingen.

Wellhausen, J. (1902): *Das Arabische Reich und sein Sturz*. Berlin.

Wenjukow, M. (1874): *Die russisch-asiatischen Grenzlande*. Leipzig.

Wessels, C. S. J. (1924): *Early Jesuit Travellers in Central Asia 1603–1721*. The Hague.

Westermarck, Edward (1926): *Ritual and Belief in Morocco*, 2 vols. London.

Wheeler, Geoffrey (1964): *The Modern History of Central Asia*. London.

Wixman, Ronald (1984): *The Peoples of the USSR*. London.

Wood, J. (1872): *A Journey to the Source of the River Oxus* (2nd edn). London.

World Bank (1998/9): *World Development Report. Knowledge for Development*. Washington.

World Bank (2000a): *Republic of Tajikistan Poverty Assessment*. Washington.

World Bank (2000b): *Information on the Activity of Tajikistan Social Investment Fund (TASIF) as of June 20, 2000*. Dushanbe.

World Bank (2003) *Fighting Poverty in Tajikistan. The World Bank Group Activities 1994–2003*. Dushanbe.

World Bank (2004): *Tajikistan Poverty Assessment Update. Main Report*. Dushanbe.

Wriggins, Sally Hovey (1999): *Reisende auf der Seidenstraße*. Hamburg. (Engl. edition: *Xuanzang. A Buddhist Pilgrim on the Silk Road*. Boulder 1996.)

Younghusband, Frank E. (1892): Journeys in the Pamirs and Adjacent Countries, in *Proceedings of the Royal Geographical Society* 14(4), 205–234.

Younghusband, Frank E. (1896): *The Heart of a Continent*. New York.

Yule, Henry (1871, 1875): *The Book of Sir Marco Polo the Venetian*, 2 vols. London.

Yule, Henry (1872a): Papers Connected with the Upper Oxus Regions, in *Journal of the Royal Geographical Society* 42: 438–481.

Yule, Henry (1872b): An Essay on the Geography and History of the Regions on the Upper Waters of the Oxus, in J. Wood, *A Journey to the Sources of the River Oxus*. London, xix–xc.

Zarubin, I. I. (1918): Materialy i zametki po etnografii gornych tadzikov (Documents and remarks with regard to the ethnography of the Mountain Tajiks), in *Sbornik Muzeja Antropologii i Etnografii* 7(1), 97–148 (Petrograd).

Zarubin, I. I. (1936): *Trudy Pamirskoj Ekspeditsii* (Reports of the Pamir Expedition). Leningrad.

Zarubin, I. I. (1937): *Bartangskie i Rushanskie Teksty i Slovar* (Texts and Dictionary of the Bartang and Rushan [People]). Moskwa and Leningrad.

Zelinsky, A. N. (1965): Ancient Routes Through the Pamirs, in *Central Asian Review* 13(1), 44–54.

Zviagelskaya, Irina (1998): The Tajik Conflict: Problems of Regulation, in Mohammad Reza Djalili *et al*. (eds) *Tajikistan. The Trials of Independence*. Richmond, 161–179.